JOHN WESLEY'S TEACHINGS

Also by Thomas C. Oden

VOLUME 4

ETHICS AND SOCIETY

JOHN WESLEY'S TEACHINGS

THOMAS C. ODEN

Z ZONDERVAN®

ZONDERVAN

John Wesley's Teachings, Volume 4
Copyright © 2014 by Thomas C. Oden

This title is also available as a Zondervan ebook. Visit www.zondervan.com/ebooks.

Requests for information should be addressed to:

Zondervan, *Grand Rapids, Michigan* 49530

Library of Congress Cataloging-in-Publication Data

Oden, Thomas C.
    John Wesley's teachings / Thomas C. Oden.
        v. cm.
    Rev. ed. of: John Wesley's scriptural Christianity. c1994.
    Includes bibliographical references and indexes.
    Contents: v. 1. God and providence— v. 2. Christ and salvation— v. 3. Pastoral theology—
v. 4. Ethics and society.
    ISBN 978-0-310-58718-7 (softcover)
    1. Wesley, John, 1703-1791. 2. Theology, Doctrinal. 3. Methodist Church—Doctrines.
4. Theology, Doctrinal—History—18th century. 5. Methodist Church—Doctrines—History—
18th century. I. Oden, Thomas C. John Wesley's scriptural Christianity. II. Title.
    BX8331.3.O35 2012
    230'.7092—dc23   2012001655

Cover design: John Hamilton Design
Cover image: Corbis® Images
Interior design: Beth Shagene
Edited by Katya Covrett and Laura Dodge Weller

Printed in the United States of America

HB 09.10.2024

To Judy Cincotta

Contents

VOLUME FOUR
Ethics and Society

PART ONE: Social Ethics

Introduction: Molding the Practice of Faith Active in Love

A. The Rules of the Band-Societies (1738)

1. Giving Birth to Faith in Practice

2. Rules for Gathering a Band of Believers Seeking the Holy Life

3. Before Admission to the Band Societies

4. Questions of Self-Examination for Every Session

B. The Character of a Methodist

The Character of Those Who Live the Blessed Life

1. The Distinguishing Marks of a Blessed Soul

2. The Leading Features of the Happy Life

C. The Principles of a Methodist

1. The Ethical Import of Justification by Grace through Faith

2. God's Grace, Christ's Atoning Work on the Cross, and the Spirit's Work in Us

3. The Ethical Import of the Biblical Teaching of God's Perfecting Love

D. The Nature, Design, and General Rules of the United Societies (1743)

1. The Early Evangelical Societies for Spiritual Formation

2. Showing Evidence of Sincere Repentance

3. A Concise Summary of "Directions Given to the Band-Societies" (1744)

4. The Focus on Character

2. What Is Meant by Awakening from the Sleeping State?

3. Awake! Arise from the Dead!

PART THREE: **Political Ethics**

Introduction to Evangelical Political Ethics

A. *The Reformation of Manners (1763)*

1. Wesley as Moral Reformer

2. A Design for Those Seeking a Reformation of Morals

3. The Plan for Decency Reform

4. Seek Out Those Few Who Are Called to This Service

5. Reshaping Civil Discourse

B. *Public Diversions Denounced (1732)*

1. On Betting Games and Sports That Bring Out the Worst in People

2. No Matter How Foolish We Are, God Still Reigns

3. Harming Others through Seemingly Harmless Acts

A. *National Sins and Miseries (1775)*

1. When the Shepherd Does Wrong, the Sheep Suffer

2. The Economic and Political Calamity in the British-American Conflict

3. Sin and Suffering in the Revolutionary Environment

4. The Sins of Colonialism

5. The Remedy

B. *A Calm Address to Our American Colonies (1775)*

1. Peacemaking Based on Contemporary Legal Reasoning

2. The Misleading Analogy between Taxation and Slavery

3. Whether the Legislatures Have the Right to Tax under Existing Law

4. Appeals to Protection Are Forgotten amid Appeals to Private Consent

5. Whether the Free Citizen Is Governed Only by Laws to Which He Personally Has Consented

6. The Presumed Entitlement to Individual Consent as Self-Assertive Personal Will

PART FOUR: Theological Ethics

Preface

Volume 4 of this reader's guide to John Wesley's teaching focuses on the basic tenets of evangelical teaching on ethics and society. It is logically divided into four complementary parts: social ethics, economic ethics, political ethics, and theological ethics. Under these headings, Wesley has written extensively on the nurturing of responsible communities; accountability for the use of talents, time, and money; the politics of war and slavery; and the relation of gospel and law.

This volume seeks to deliver to the nonprofessional reader the gist of Wesley's teaching on basic questions of the daily practice of the Christian life. From Wesley's large corpus of writing, we will glean his teaching on faith active in love.

This last volume on ethics and society builds on crucial arguments set forth in volume 1 on God and providence, volume 2 on Christ and salvation, and volume 3 on pastoral theology. I recommend that readers who wish to begin with volume 4 keep the other three volumes handy for reference to key definitions and ideas previously discussed.

These expositions present a plain account of Wesley's teaching on the moral life, with constant citation from Wesley's own texts. For a guide to tracking references, see Tracking References to the Major Editions below. My goal is to convey concisely the core argument of major texts of John Wesley on such basic ethical themes as character, intention, action, purpose, obligation, and the happy life.

In Wesley's address to readers of his collected works of 1771, he made a preliminary attempt at a sequential organization of his instructional homilies: "I wanted to methodize these tracts, *to [ar]range them under proper heads*, placing those together which were on similar subjects, and in such order that one might illustrate another.... There is *scarce any subject of importance, either in practical or controversial divinity, which is not treated* of more or less, either professedly or occasionally."[1]

Wesley's own daily practice of prayer, Scripture study, and preaching were done with the Greek New Testament in hand. Since my purpose is to convey Wesley's teaching in ordinary modern English, I will use the New International Version of the

---

[1]"Preface to the Third Edition," J I:3, in a brief address "To the Reader" in the thirty-two duodecima volumes of 1774 (italics added).

Bible (NIV)[2] in cases where it significantly improves on the Authorized King James Version (KVJ), and the Book of Common Prayer, which Wesley followed day by day.

Wesley's moral guidance came mainly through teaching homilies and occasional essays. The issues most exhaustively treated on ethics are his thirteen discourses on the Sermon on the Mount as a summary of Christian ethics; the relation of gospel to law; and to a lesser extent, war, revolution, slavery, and what he called "the reformation of morals." Virtually no major issue common to philosophical ethics and Christian moral reflection is neglected in Wesley's corpus of teaching.

Wesley's intent was never to write a comprehensive systematic ethic such as one would find in Thomas Aquinas, Luis de Molina, Francisco Suárez, Alphonsus Liguori, Philipp Melanchthon, Johann Gerhard, or Richard Baxter. With the exception of a few addresses, his messages were primarily for not the university audience but small communities of those seeking to live a holy life grounded in grace.

Studying Wesley

The method I have used in examining Wesley's writings is argument analysis. This method holds closely to specific arguments in his published texts. I do not attempt to provide an account of the development of Wesley's thought nor a commentary on his works, but rather an analytical elucidation of his arguments. This means that I work textually with Wesley's key writings on ethical themes to provide a text-based analysis of his reasoning and argumentation. I ask, "What reasons does Wesley give for drawing his conclusions?" I show the precise location of his teaching by citations in the most frequently used editions of his Works. And I organize these texts in a commonsense arrangement so they present a coherent picture of the logic of Wesley's teaching on the right ordering of moral life.

Previous useful studies have set forth Wesley's theology, but none of them to my knowledge has attempted to do so as a systematic argument exegetically grounded on the whole range of his theological, pastoral, and ethical teaching corpus. Four volumes have been required to do justice to the content and magnitude of his reasoning and argumentation on the Christian faith and life.

Since Wesley reasoned out of Scripture and constantly in reference to Scripture texts, these texts are frequently referenced. Since Wesley also reasoned out of the classic Christian consensus, especially from patristic sources, those who wish to compare Wesley's reasoning with these patristic sources can do so by checking out the particular texts under consideration in the *Ancient Christian Commentary on Scripture* (*ACCS*).

---

[2]Other modern translations will be noted by using standard abbreviations such as NEB (New English Bible), and NRSV (New Revised Standard Version). To avoid anachronisms, I am following Wesley in the common eighteenth-century practice of allowing the word *mankind* to refer generically to all humankind.

Tracking References to the Major Editions

The preferred scholarly edition of *The Works of John Wesley* is the Oxford/Abingdon Bicentennial edition (Oxford: 1975 – 83; Nashville: 1984 –), signified by B.[3]

The most frequently reproduced edition, often still the only one appearing on library and pastoral bookshelves, is the Thomas Jackson edition, first published in 1829 – 31, signified by J for Jackson. Thus, whenever B or J appears in the footnotes, the reader is being directed to either the Bicentennial edition (B) or the Jackson edition (J). This is necessary because the reader may have access to one but not both editions. Many more copies of the Jackson edition have been distributed than the Bicentennial edition.

Here are the key guidelines for the scholarly apparatus:

• Volume references in Arabic numerals refer to the Bicentennial edition. Volume references in uppercase Roman numerals refer to the Jackson edition.

• Both the Bicentennial edition (B) and the Jackson edition (J) are available in searchable CD ROMs or online. In the case of B, the current disk is still incomplete, awaiting print publication of many volumes.

• Distinguishing a B reference from a J reference is easy: If the first digit is an Arabic numeral, the reference is to B. If the first digit is an uppercase Roman numeral, the reference is to J. A reference to B 4:133 indicates the Bicentennial edition, volume 4, page 133. But a reference to J IV:133 indicates the Jackson edition, volume 4 (IV), page 133.

• In cases where a new homily is being introduced in order to be discussed more fully, I have referenced in parentheses the Bicentennial edition (B) in this conventional order: the homily number, the date of the homily, and the volume and page references in the Bicentennial edition. Where the Jackson edition (J) is referenced, I have listed the homily number and the volume and page references in Jackson.

• At times the homily numbers appear in a different order and number in the Bicentennial than in the Jackson edition.[4]

My purpose is to assist those who wish to handily access the proper text in the available edition. Readers will more frequently be working out of either J or B but ordinarily not both. For convenience, I cite both editions. An appendix titled "Alphabetical Correlation of the Sermons in the Jackson and Bicentennial Editions" can be found at the back of all volumes. Those who are doing scholarly research work are advised to work with the Bicentennial edition whenever possible.

---

[3]In rare cases where Sugden's edition of the Standard Sermons (see Abbreviations: *SS*) is quoted, the reader's attention is directed especially to his annotations.

[4]For example, "The Trouble and Rest of Good Men" appears as Sermon 109 in the Bicentennial edition (B 109), and as Sermon 127 in the Jackson edition (J 127). The numbering is often the same but in some instances is different.

On Biblical References

Though Wesley expressed abiding gratitude for the King James Version, especially in its value for common worship, his study text was normally in the original language. In citing the lead text for his homilies, I ordinarily cite the King James Authorized text (KJV) from which Wesley was preaching or writing, unless specified otherwise.

When he published his own translation of the New Testament, many references in the Authorized Version of 1611 were altered to communicate with his plain-speaking audience of the 1700s. There is no reason to think that Wesley regarded his own English rendering of the Greek as definitive for future centuries of English readers for whom the language protocols and usages would have shifted as they normally do over decades.

Those who might assume that Wesley himself was constantly working out of the King James Version do well to recall that Wesley read the Greek New Testament fluently. He studied it daily in his early morning and evening meditation.

On Other Editions of Wesley's Works

The only collected edition published during Wesley's lifetime was the thirty-two-volume Bristol edition of *The Works of the Rev. John Wesley* (Bristol, UK: William Pine, 1771 – 74).

The second edition of *The Works of the Rev. John Wesley* was edited by Joseph Benson (17 vols., London: Conference Offices, 1809 – 13; repr. New York and Phila-delphia in 10 vols., 1826 – 27).

The most-used third edition of *The Works of the Rev. John Wesley*, edited by Thomas Jackson (14 vols., London, 1829 – 31), has been frequently reprinted in America and is employed here as one of two major available editions of Wesley's Works.[5]

Prior to the Bicentennial edition, the editions that presented an annotated editorial apparatus to the works of Wesley, with scholarly introductions according to modern standards, were Nehemiah Curnock's edition of the Journals (see *JJW* in Abbreviations) in 1916, Edward H. Sugden's edition of the Standard Sermons (see *SS*) in 1921, John Telford's edition of the Letters (see *LJW*) in 1931, and Albert C. Outler's selection of Wesley's key writings (see JWO) in 1964. These are all commended here. The Oxford/Abingdon Bicentennial edition (see B in Abbreviations)[6] will stand for generations to come as the definitive edition.

---

[5]That Telford, Sugden, Curnock, and Jackson (see Abbreviations) are hardly mentioned in the Bicentennial edition of the Sermons remains a puzzle. They all contain useful notes pertinent to this study. The American edition, edited by John Emory, was published in New York in 1831, based on the Jackson edition. In many libraries, the Jackson edition is the only one available.

[6]When "Articles of Religion" (Art.) are indicated, I am referring to Wesley's own recension of the Twenty-Four Articles (to which the 1784 American Methodist Church added a twenty-fifth), derived

Wesley's Patrimony

Wesley left behind an enormous corpus of literature. This vast body includes 151 teaching homilies, six decades of journals (1735 – 91), manuscript diaries (now published), eight volumes of letters, essays, doctrinal tracts, occasional writings, and prefaces. The untold numbers of hymns were mostly written by John's brother Charles but were often edited by John. These were the fruits of their editing and publishing over a very long time span. It is difficult to think of a single figure in the eighteenth century who left behind such a massive body of work as did John Wesley.

This series seeks to deliver the gist of the whole of Wesley's patrimony in systematic order. It provides a window into the basic wisdom of his Christian teaching. While it cannot claim to be comprehensive, it seeks to include core insights from all of these varied genres of literature.

This is why we need multiple volumes to examine this massive range of Wesley's works. A shorter series would threaten to cut off essential parts. For readers who want to investigate only one doctrine or idea, the Further Reading on each section will make these searches more accessible.

On This Edition

Zondervan has a distinguished reputation as a publisher of reference works and classics, many of them bound in multivolume editions. My hope is that this series will become a sufficiently useful resource for lay and professional readers that will in due time be made available digitally for international readers for decades to come. Nothing like this text-by-text review of the content of Wesley's teaching exists in Wesley studies.

In 1994 Zondervan published my earlier study of Wesley's doctrine under the title *John Wesley's Scriptural Christianity: A Plain Exposition of His Teaching on Christian Doctrine (JWSC)*. In this present edition, much of the content of that single volume is now expanded and extensively revised, quadrupling the information presented in the earlier single volume.

---

and edited down from the Anglican Thirty-Nine Articles. The Articles have played a central role in the American Wesleyan doctrinal traditions. They are included in the constitutions of many church bodies of the Wesleyan tradition. When Confession (Confes.) is referenced, I am indicating the summary of Wesleyan faith set forth in the 1962 Confession of the Evangelical United Brethren, which by a constitutionally restrictive rule has become a doctrinal standard of the United Methodist Church. A reference to the first article of the Confession appears as Confes. 1.

Abbreviations

ACCS	*The Ancient Christian Commentary on Scripture*. 29 vols. Edited by Thomas C. Oden. Downers Grove, IL: InterVarsity, 1997–2010.
AHR	*American Historical Review.*
AS	*Asbury Seminarian.*
B	Bicentennial edition of *The Works of John Wesley*. Edited by Frank Baker and Richard Heitzenrater. Oxford: Clarendon, and New York: Oxford University Press, 1975–83; Nashville: Abingdon, 1984–; in print: volumes 1, 2, 3, 4, 7, 18, 19, 20, 21, 22, 23, 24. Vols. 14–16 of the Bicentennial edition, on pastoral, ethical, and instructional writings, and on medicine and many other topics are as yet in preparation.
BCP	Book of Common Prayer.
CC	Thomas C. Oden. *Classic Christianity*. San Francisco: HarperOne, 2003.
CCJW	*The Cambridge Companion to John Wesley*. Edited by Randy L. Maddox and Jason E. Vickers. Cambridge: Cambridge University Press, 2009.
CH	*A Collection of Hymns for the Use of the People Called Methodists*. Volume 7 of the Bicentennial edition.
CL	Christian Library.
Confes.	1962 Confession of the Evangelical United Brethren.
diss.	dissertation.
DS	"Doctrine of Salvation."
DSWT	Thomas C. Oden. *Doctrinal Standards in the Wesleyan Tradition*. Grand Rapids: Zondervan, 1988.
EA	"An Earnest Appeal to Men of Reason and Religion."
ENNT	*Explanatory Notes upon the New Testament.*
ENOT	*Explanatory Notes upon the Old Testament.*

EQ	*Evangelical Quarterly.*
ESV	English Standard Version.
FA	"A Farther Appeal to Men of Reason and Religion."
FAP	Francis Asbury Press, Zondervan.
FW	Kenneth Collins. *A Faithful Witness: John Wesley's Homiletical Theology.* Wilmore, KY: Wesleyan Heritage, 1993.
HLQ	*Huntington Library Quarterly.*
HSP	*Hymns and Sacred Poems.*
Interpretation	*Interpretation: A Journal of Bible and Theology.*
J	Jackson edition of Wesley's Works. Edited by Thomas Jackson, 1829 – 32. 1872 edition reprinted in many 14-volume American editions (Eerdmans, Zondervan, Christian Book Distributors, et al.); digitally available at Wesley.nnu.edu.
JBT	*Journal of Bible and Theology.*
JJW	*The Journal of John Wesley.* Edited by Nehemiah Curnock. 8 vols. London: Epworth, 1916.
JWO	*John Wesley.* Edited by Albert C. Outler. Library of Protestant Theology. New York: Oxford University Press, 1964.
JWSC	Thomas C. Oden. *John Wesley's Scriptural Christianity: A Plain Exposition of His Teaching on Christian Doctrine.* Grand Rapids: Zondervan, 1994.
JWT	Thomas Oden. *John Wesley's Teachings.* 4 vols. Grand Rapids: Zondervan, 2012 – 13.
JWTT	Colin Williams. *John Wesley's Theology Today.* Nashville: Abingdon, 1960.
KJV	King James Version.
LCL	Loeb Classical Library.
LJW	*Letters of John Wesley.* Edited by John Telford. 8 vols. London: Epworth, 1931.
LQHR	*London Quarterly and Holborn Review.*
MH	*Methodist History.*
Minutes	"Minutes of Some Late Conversations between the Rev. Mr. Wesley and Others."
MM	*Methodist Magazine.*
MPL	*Patrologia Latina (Patrologiae cursus completus: Series latina).* Edited by J.-P. Migne. 217 vols. Paris: 1844 – 64. *Series graeca*, 1857 – 66.
MQR	*Methodist Quarterly Review.*

MR	*Methodist Review.*
MSG	*The Message.*
NIV	New International Version.
NKJV	New King James Version.
NLT	New Living Translation.
NRSV	New Revised Standard Version.
NT	New Testament.
OT	Old Testament.
pref.	preface.
PW	*Poetical Works of Charles Wesley and John Wesley.* Edited by George Osborn. 13 vols. London: Wesleyan Methodist Conference, 1868–72.
PWHS	*Proceedings of the Wesleyan Historical Society.*
QR	*Quarterly Review.*
RE	Henry D. Rack. *Reasonable Enthusiast.* Philadelphia: Trinity Press International, 1985.
RJW	George Croft Cell. *The Rediscovery of John Wesley.* New York: Henry Holt, 1935.
RL	*Religion in Life.*
SS	*The Standard Sermons of John Wesley.* Edited by Edward H. Sugden. 2 vols. London: Epworth, 1921; 3rd ed., 1951.
TCNT	*Twentieth Century New Testament.*
TJW	William R. Cannon. *Theology of John Wesley: With Special Reference to the Doctrine of Justification.* New York: Abingdon, 1946.
UMC	United Methodist Church.
unpubl.	unpublished.
WMM	*Wesleyan Methodist Magazine.*
WQR	*Wesleyan Quarterly Review.*
WS	Harald G. A. Lindström. *Wesley and Sanctification.* Nashville, Abingdon, 1946.
WTH	Albert C. Outler. *The Wesleyan Theological Heritage: Essays of Albert C. Outler.* Edited by Thomas C. Oden and Leicester R. Longden. Grand Rapids: Zondervan, 1991.
WTJ	*Wesleyan Theological Journal.*
XXV	Twenty-Five Articles. Adapted from the Sunday Service of 1784.
XXXIX	Anglican Thirty-Nine Articles of Religion.

PART 1

SOCIAL
ETHICS

CHAPTER 1

Nurturing the Community of Faith

Introduction: Molding the Practice of Faith Active in Love

Wesley sought to mold the actual practice of the life of faith active in love in small face-to-face communities. The dynamics of these communities are best revealed in five key early documents: "The Rules of the Band-Societies" (1738), "The Character of a Methodist" (1742), "The Principles of a Methodist" (1742), "The Nature, Design, and General Rules of the United Societies" (1743), and "Directions Given to the Band-Societies" (1744). We will take these documents in chronological order to show the development of faith and life in the early evangelical revival. Wesley was not primarily an ethical theorist but was an astute enabler of the practice of ethical behavior.

A. The Rules of the Band-Societies (1738)

1. Giving Birth to Faith in Practice

Wesley's contributions to Christian ethical teaching have been significant and long-lasting. Wesley had clear and well-developed ideas on perennial ethical issues such as character, virtue, justice, right, obligation, intention, action, purpose, duty, and consequence. But his contributions to the practice of these teachings were far more significant. Wesley's moral discourses had palpable historical influence not only on religion but on society. Wesley's era was a time of significant reflection on ethical theory and practice, and he was an active participant in the ongoing discussions.

There were many major theorists of ethics in the eighteenth century who still deserve serious critical reading. Among them I name only a few, most of which Wesley had read: John Locke (1632–1704), Samuel Clarke (1675–1729), George Berkeley (1685–1753), Francis Hutcheson (1694–1746), Joseph Butler (1692–1752), David Hume (1711–76), David Hartley (1705–57), Montesquieu (1689–1755), Richard Price (1723–91), Denis Diderot (1713–84), Jean-Jacques Rousseau (1712–78), Adam Smith (1723–90), and Thomas Reid (1710–96).

Wesley is seldom listed among these major ethical thinkers of the eighteenth century, but I will show reasons why he should be. Wesley was familiar with the writings of most of the above, and he made explicit responses to many of them. His empiricism was significantly influenced by Locke, but with some serious reservations. Wesley's work was directly opposed by Bishop Joseph Butler, which occasioned a lengthy defense against Butler's assistant, Josiah Tucker. Wesley was entirely unimpressed with Montesquieu. He was horrified at the family and educational consequences of the ideas of Rousseau. He wrote a trenchant defense against the reductive naturalism of Hutcheson and Hume. He resisted Richard Price on anarchic revolution. And although Kant was twenty-one years younger than Wesley, Kant's categorical imperative (act according to that maxim whereby you can, at the same time, will that it should become a universal law) was anticipated by Wesley in his treatment of empathy in the Golden Rule (Do unto others as you would have them do unto you).

I often put the above list before my PhD students in ethics, inviting them to present an argument that any one of them cared more than Wesley about the practical implementation of their ethical theories in committed communities of mutual accountability. They always had a hard time making a case for any one of these.

All of the above ethicists were concerned to a certain extent with the practice of their ideas. But few undertook to nurture actual communities in which the ethical life could be systematically cultivated and practiced. Wesley's main contribution was as a coach or mentor for personal accountability.

a. Building Small-Scale Communities of Moral Accountability

Wesley was intent on actually cultivating communities of faith through which the holy life could be nurtured. He offered wise counsel for living the good life he taught.

In 1738 Wesley set out deliberately to build small bands of believers all across England, Scotland, and Ireland. They were committed seriously to calling each other to accountability in their actual practice of the spiritual and moral teachings of Christianity. He was mentor and chief teacher for this whole movement. Person by person he tutored the leaders of these societies.

Early in the great evangelical revival, he wrote "The Rules of the Band-Societies" (drawn up on December 25, 1738, in some editions "Rules of the Bands"), so that those who had responded to his preaching and moral teaching might benefit by his continual guidance in the life of faith active in love. This document formed the ground rules for entering into the Methodist societies.

"Bands" referred to those who covenanted together to be honest to God and with each other. A band was voluntary, and it was small, because it sought a level of intimacy not possible in a large group.

In this plain two-page document, Wesley placed in the hands of every individual in his connection of spiritual formation the premises for entering these small groups or "bands." One who entered agreed to proceed with a searching weekly examination of conscience in the presence of a small group of caring and confessing believers committed to living out of God's justifying grace.

This short document was divided into three sections: (1) what would be expected of any who join and continue with this small band of believers seeking the holy life, (2) questions to be asked of each person before admission to this intensive experience, and (3) rules for self-examination by each participant at every weekly meeting.[1]

b. The Design for Accountability in the Societies

The aim of Christian living is quite simply "to obey the command of God." It is not to feel good about oneself but to will what God wills. Any who do not sincerely seek that aim would not likely find the society meetings a companionable environment. The bands were not primarily for increasing life's pleasures or aesthetic refinement or intellectual acuteness, but quite simply for walking daily in the way of grace.[2]

It was clear to all participants what would happen in these meetings: "Confess your faults one to another, and pray one for another, that ye may be healed."[3] "Healed" does not refer primarily to bodily healing but to the healing of the soul. Through being in an empathic community of friends who shared the same goal (obeying the will of God), participants would open up their lives before one another that they might counsel and admonish one another on how to better obey the will of God.

2. Rules for Gathering a Band of Believers Seeking the Holy Life

A key maxim of Wesley's ethic is a simple equation: "To be happy is to be holy." The holy life is received by grace through faith. The happy life is the holy life.

a. Six Preconditions for Participation in a Community Seeking a Holy Life

Wesley offered six rules for defining the rigorous process of serious seekers of life in Christ. Those who did not wish to bind themselves to these six commitments would not be ready for this conversation. No one should enter without clearly understanding what this process was about.

They needed to understand that learning how to follow God's will requires time and a deep commitment of the heart. The first four rules involve stewardship of time:

1. They would first agree to "meet once a week, at the least."[4] Ruled out of this frame of reference were any obstacles that would detract from the regularity of the process. This was "set-aside time," time sanctified for the purpose of nurturing the holy life.

---

[1]"Rules of the Band-Societies," B 9:77, J VIII:272, sec. 1.1.
[2]Ibid.
[3]James 5:16; "Rules of the Band-Societies," B 9:77, J VIII:272, sec. 1.1.
[4]"Rules of the Band-Societies," B 9:77, J VIII:272, sec. 1.1.

2. In order for one member not to abuse the valuable time of others, these time commitments had to be understood from the outset. "To come punctually at the hour appointed, without some extraordinary reason."[5] Those who did not want to be under this discipline should not consider beginning.

3. The conversation was from the outset placed in the context of the praise of God. "To begin (those of us who are present) exactly at the hour, with singing or prayer."[6] Without the plea for God's hearing presence, the context would be wholly misunderstood. This was a place where people not only talked with one another but talked and listened to God in prayer. Prayer might take the form of the music of praise.

4. Participants agreed "to speak each of us in order, freely and plainly, the true state of our souls."[7] This process was not for the faint of heart or for those who wanted to sit back and observe. It was profoundly participatory from the outset.

Contemporary readers can easily see the analogies between this interactive process and modern intensive group processes. Some degree of analogy may be found in today's primal therapy; Gestalt therapy; Bethel Human Relations Laboratory Training; transactional analysis; and various forms of group psychotherapy, humanistic psychological treatment, and existential therapy. The difference is that those forms do not begin with prayer and do not require participants to stand before God and speak the true state of their souls. Otherwise the level of depth in communication, empathic listening, and candid self-disclosure is remarkably the same.

The band societies utilized a group process in which every participant was expected to listen and contribute from the heart to the hearts of the others. They did not function in a professional setting but as a voluntary group of laypersons guided by Scripture and pastoral care. The process was not concerned with learning the jargon of personal transformation or a technical vocabulary or analytical speech according to a theory. Rather, ordinary people spoke "freely and plainly."[8] They spoke of the true state of their souls, with special attention to "the faults we have committed in thought, word, or deed, and the temptations we have felt, since our last meeting."[9]

Those who were not interested in confession of their sins were asked to reconsider beginning, since that was at the heart of the purpose of the small voluntary bands. Since the subject matter was repentance that lead to faith in grace, the beginning point for each conversation was the candid disclosure of recent (during the previous week) temptation and confession within a caring community. This meant that participants freely and personally revealed the condition of their souls during the preceding week. They were not just to deal with feelings but to confess what they had been thinking, speaking, and doing in any way they perceived was incon-

---

[5]"Rules of the Band-Societies," B 9:78, J VIII:272, sec. 1.2.
[6]"Rules of the Band-Societies," B 9:78, J VIII:272, sec. 1.3.
[7]Ibid.
[8]"Rules of the Band-Societies," B 9:78, J VIII:272, sec. 1.4.
[9]Ibid.

sistent with God's will. By removing the obstacles, they learned together to listen to God's will for their lives.

Other rules included the following:

5. Describing participants' relationship with God in the present was the central concern of the conversation. The whole dialogue was to be infused with the key elements of prayer: confession, petition, intercession, and doxology. It began in praise and ended in a way suitable to what the participants had been confessing. Therefore they were to "end every meeting with prayer, suited to the state of each person present."[10] Each person was singularly lifted up in prayer by all.

6. The conversation was not nondirective. It had a specific question as the starting point. One person would begin by addressing a question such as this: "Describe the present state of your soul — your emotive life, the gains and losses you have experienced in the last week."

The final precondition for participation was to be willing to call upon "some person among us to speak his own state first, and then to ask the rest, in order, as any and as searching questions as may be, concerning their state, sins, and temptations."[11] The conversation began with an invitation for someone to speak voluntarily of their own condition of soul, openly confessing their sins and temptations. The expectation was that others would voluntarily follow. Each person had the privilege of coming before God in the presence of the believing community to come clean and enjoy a clearer conscience.

Then it was up to the Holy Spirit to awaken an honest heart. This process did not begin with a particular Scripture but with a particular experience — seeking wisdom from Scripture.

3. Before Admission to the Band Societies

a. Questions to Be Answered before Admission

Trenchant questions for self-examination were proposed to anyone wishing to be admitted into this small circle of weekly confession. They all have to do with readiness to participate:

1. "Have you the forgiveness of your sins?"[12] Personally experiencing the pardon of God through the atoning work of God on the cross was a premise of all that would follow in the interaction. If they did not know that God forgives all penitent sinners and that they had experienced that pardon, they would not be ready for the ensuing conversation about living out that pardon through examining their sins and temptations.

2. "Have you experienced the peace that passes understanding that comes into a life lived under saving grace? Have you peace with God through our Lord Jesus Christ?"[13]

---

[10]"Rules of the Band-Societies," B 9:77, J VIII:272, sec. 1.5.
[11]"Rules of the Band-Societies," B 9:77, J VIII:272, sec. 1.6.
[12]"Rules of the Band-Societies," B 9:77, J VIII:272, sec. 2.1.
[13]"Rules of the Band-Societies," B 9:77, J VIII:272, sec. 2.2.

3. "Have you the witness of God's Spirit with your spirit that you are a child of God?"[14] The Holy Spirit poured into the church at Pentecost has the mission of witnessing with a believer's own spirit of God's intention to make God's embrace known. Do you realize you have joined a new family as a child of God?

4. "Is the love of God shed abroad in your heart?"[15] Have you welcomed the Holy Spirit into your daily life? Have you received the gifts the Spirit is seeking to give you?

5. "Has no sin, inward or outward, dominion over you?"[16] Note that anyone who knew Wesley's preaching knew the distinction between sin reigning and sin remaining: believers have been saved from sin; sin remains in believers though it does not reign. The act of trusting in God's pardon ends the reign of sin, but the roots of sin may remain to be further plowed, raked, and rooted out in practice.[17] The meetings' conversations were designed to identify and root out any sin that held participants in its power, that had dominion over their will so they could not will God's will.

6. Potential participants were asked candidly before they entered the conversation, "Do you desire to be told of your faults?"[18] In order to proceed with this process of rooting out the dominion of sin in their lives, they should expect to listen to friendly fellow believers who wanted to help them see their faults clearly. They were not there to accuse, but to illumine for the participant's benefit.

7. "Do you desire to be told of all your faults, and that plain and home?"[19] In other words, do you want admonitions to be plainly spoken for the good of your soul?

8. "Do you desire that every one of us should tell you, from time to time, whatsoever is in his heart concerning you?"[20] "From time to time" means as the occasion arises. If a person wanted to go deep in rooting out his voluntary misdeeds, was he ready to listen deeply to how others saw what he was saying about himself? To put it another way, "If you want to open up your heart to God, do you want your neighbor to open up his heart to you?"

9. "Are you ready to take seriously what others are feeling about you? How deep do you want disclosure to go?" That was a determination a person needed to make before proceeding. Hence, "Consider! Do you desire we should tell you whatsoever we think, whatsoever we fear, whatsoever we hear, concerning you?"[21]

10. "Do you desire that, in doing this, we should come as close as possible, that we should cut to the quick, and search your heart to the bottom?"[22] To "search your heart to the bottom" means to go as deeply as possible to get to the bottom of

---

[14]"Rules of the Band-Societies," B 9:77, J VIII:272, sec. 2.3.
[15]"Rules of the Band-Societies," B 9:77, J VIII:272, sec. 2.4.
[16]"Rules of the Band-Societies," B 9:77, J VIII:272, sec. 2.5.
[17]See *JWT* 2:271–72.
[18]"Rules of the Band-Societies," B 9:78, J VIII:272, sec. 2.6.
[19]"Rules of the Band-Societies," B 9:78, J VIII:272, sec. 2.7.
[20]"Rules of the Band-Societies," B 9:78, J VIII:273, sec. 2.8.
[21]"Rules of the Band-Societies," B 9:78, J VIII:273, sec. 2.9.
[22]"Rules of the Band-Societies," B 9:78, J VIII:273, sec. 2.10.

things that may cause sin to have dominion over some aspect of your life. Participants needed to decide whether they were going to give permission for friends to go straight to the point, to speak heart to heart.

11. Participants needed to answer whether they were willing to be open to others if others were willing to be completely open with them. "Is it your desire and design to be on this, and all other occasions, entirely open, so as to speak everything that is in your heart without exception, without disguise, and without reserve?"[23] This set a very high value on candor that reached from heart to heart. Are you ready for that? If so, you would be ready for participation in a Methodist society. The question of the readiness for self-disclosure "may be asked as often as occasion offers."[24]

4. Questions of Self-Examination for Every Session

The "rules of the bands" end with four penetrating questions that are expected to be asked in every meeting. If avoided, the meeting objective will not be achieved. They are as follows:

1. "What known sins have you committed since our last meeting?"[25] Voluntary known sins are distinguished from involuntary failings due to infirmity or human finitude. Think primarily of the misdeeds you know you have done willfully and recently.

2. "What temptations have you met with?"[26] It is to your interest to disclose recent occasions when a door has been opened to you to do something you very well know you should not do. By disclosing such occurrences, you can learn to sense when temptation is drawing you away from your goal of living a holy life.

3. Can you describe exactly how you averted that wrong path? Do you see how the Holy Spirit is guiding you to hold fast to faith, hope, and love? State it descriptively: "How were you delivered?"[27]

4. There may be other occasions that are ambiguous, when you are not sure whether you have been tempted to sin or have deliberately sinned. These situations are worth opening up to find out what wisdom might come from examining them. "What have you thought, said, or done, of which you doubt whether it be sin or not?"[28] Let the community of faith help you discern for your own benefit.

These are the rules of the bands. Out of these small bands and societies came prodigious energies for the personal behavior change enabled by divine grace. Out of personal behavioral changes emerged energies that had social consequences. Arguably they affected the secular history of the British and American cultures and ultimately became diffused into the worldwide movement of evangelical revivalism.

---

[23]"Rules of the Band-Societies," B 9:78, J VIII:273, sec. 2.11.
[24]"Rules of the Band-Societies," B 9:78, J VIII:273, sec. 3.1.
[25]Ibid.
[26]"Rules of the Band-Societies," B 9:78, J VIII:273, sec. 3.2.
[27]"Rules of the Band-Societies," B 9:78, J VIII:273, sec. 3.3.
[28]"Rules of the Band-Societies," B 9:78, J VIII:273, sec. 3.4.

B. The Character of a Methodist

The Character of Those Who Live the Blessed Life

All we have done thus far is define a process for self-disclosure and confession. But what behavioral outcomes are expected from this process? To answer we move next to Wesley's description of the character of one who is seeking to follow "the plain old religion." "The Rules of the Band-Societies" was written in 1738 during the year of Wesley's Aldersgate experience when his "heart was strangely warmed" by the realization that "he, even he," was the recipient of God's pardoning and justifying grace, all as God's gift without any merit of his own.[29]

Out of this came hundreds of local bands and societies. By 1742 Wesley was ready to write on "The Character of a Methodist." In this pivotal essay, Wesley reported behavioral outcomes of this community life.

Character is a major theme of Wesley's Christian ethic. The "people called Methodist" are those who are deliberately seeking to respond fully to the grace that God is constantly offering. The character traits and behavior patterns Wesley described show how different "the plain old religion" of the apostolic teaching is from Christianity in name only, which he called "The Almost Christian."[30] We are here investigating Wesley's core writings in ethics that reveal his determination to teach and coach and counsel his spiritual formation connection toward the full embodiment of life in Christ.[31]

1. The Distinguishing Marks of a Blessed Soul

The distinguishing marks of a blessed soul have nothing to do with "opinions of any sort" — not to

- assenting to this or that scheme of religion
- embracing any particular set of notions
- espousing the judgment of one theorist or another

a. Character Traits of Those Who Are Happy in God

The *telos* (goal, purpose) of evangelical Christianity is the happy life lived toward God and out of God's grace. Wesley described one who emerges through this process: "One who has 'the love of God shed abroad in his heart by the Holy Ghost given unto him,' one who 'loves the Lord his God with all his heart, and with all his soul, and with all his mind, and with all his strength.' God is the joy of his heart and the desire of his soul."[32]

Look at the behavior of those who are "happy in God."[33] This is not a happiness

---

[29]*JJW*, May 24, 1738.

[30]See the teaching homily on "The Almost Christian," *JWT*, 2:203 – 5.

[31]Some of the underlying theological premises of "The Character of a Methodist" have already been discussed in *JWT*, vol. 2. But since we are dealing here with the actual embodiment of the life of holy love, it is fitting that we revisit the behavior-change aspects of that essay.

[32]"The Character of a Methodist," B 9:35, J VIII:341, sec. 1.5; cf. Ps. 73:25 – 26; Mark 12:30.

[33]"The Character of a Methodist," B 9:35 – 36, J VIII:342, sec. 1.6.

that can be measured by the world's metric of happiness, which is forever passing away. Rather, the believer is "always happy, as having in him 'a well of water springing up into everlasting life,' and overflowing his soul with peace and joy."[34]

b. Clement of Alexandria Provided Wesley with the Model of the Christian Life

In setting forth this description of character, Wesley turned to one of his favorites among the ancient church fathers — a brilliant teacher writing on the continent of Africa about a hundred years after the last writers of the New Testament: Clement of Alexandria (AD 150 – 215).

Among Clement's body of work three major volumes have survived: The *Protrepticus* (exhortation) is an invitation to choose a new life beyond the idolatries of this world. It addresses a largely pagan audience with a better way of life under the instruction of Christ, the Word of God. The *Paedagogus* (the tutor) is a tutorial in truthful teaching. The best tutor for human behavior is God himself, who became incarnate to teach us the way of life. The truth is not limited to intellectual knowing but includes that knowledge that lives deeply out of the love of God. Christ himself is the only teacher worthy of following wholeheartedly. The life of the Son is a mirror to the life of God the Father. We are invited to participate in his life by faith. Christ himself coaches us in how to live simply. *Stromata* (miscellaneous sentences on the life of perfect love) was the book by Clement that most captured the mind of Wesley. This work ends with a simple description of the life lived in Christ. It is composed largely of New Testament texts that give us a clear picture of this life. True Christian knowledge shows the way to knowing God from the heart out of faith in the received apostolic witness. The Holy Spirit is working to bring this life of participation in Christ to complete fulfillment in the perfecting of love in human hearts.

To a remarkable degree, Wesley followed Clement's description of the character of the true Christian in the seventh part of *Stromata*. This is what he called "plain old Christianity."[35] Plain old Christianity is the oldest expression of the behavioral outcomes of Christianity, as old as the apostles and their immediate successors. It is plainly described by the apostles Peter, James, John, and Paul. Wesley valued the earliest Christian teachers of the generations following the apostles because they were the closest to the events reported in the New Testament, hence the most reliable. As distinguished from the heretical writings of the same period, they were received by the ecumenical church and recalled as trusted by Christian believers of all times and places, fit for reading in the churches all over the Christian world.

---

[34]Ibid.; cf. John 4:14; Rom. 15:13.
[35]See Neil D. Anderson's excellent monograph *A Definitive Study of Evidence Concerning John Wesley's Appropriation of the Thought of Clement of Alexandria*, Texts and Studies in Religion (Lewiston, NY: Edwin Mellen, 2004), 5:102. Cf. John Ferguson, *Clement of Alexandria* (New York: Ardent Media, 1974); Albert C. Outler, "The 'Platonism' of Clement of Alexandria," *Journal of Religion* 20, no. 3 (July 1940): 217 – 40; Eric Osborn, *Clement of Alexandria* (Cambridge: Cambridge Univ. Press, 2008).

The scriptural center of Clement's description is found in Philippians 2:5: "Let this mind be in you, which was also in Christ Jesus."[36] "Therefore if you have any encouragement from being united with Christ, if any comfort from his love, if any common sharing in the Spirit, if any tenderness and compassion, then make my joy complete by being like-minded, having the same love, being one in spirit and of one mind. Do nothing out of selfish ambition or vain conceit. Rather, in humility value others above yourselves, not looking to your own interests but each of you to the interests of the others."[37] The Christian life is lived "in Christ," sharing in and embodying the life of Christ.

Wesley took Clement's description and amplified it with further apostolic accounts. In "The Character of a Methodist," Wesley followed Clement's description of life in Christ. Out of Clement's teaching came the first theological school in the history of Christianity, the Catechetical School of Alexandria. The Christian school in Alexandria provided the earliest model of Christian education. Wesley's appropriation of the first major African theologian became the inspiration for the ethics of the evangelical revival in the eighteenth century. Here is Wesley's description of the character that emerges in the community that lives in Christ.

2. The Leading Features of the Happy Life

a. Fear Has Been Cast Out by Love

What makes people happy — eternally happy, happy in this life and the next?

They are living a life empowered by God's own Spirit. Their lives are happy because "'Perfect love casts out fear.'"[38] They are anxious for nothing because they have cast all care on the one who cares for them.[39]

They have peace with God. They enjoy the witness of assurance of salvation, since the Holy Spirit testifies with their spirits that they are children of God.[40]

Each one rejoices "whenever he looks forward, 'in hope of the glory that shall be revealed'; yea, this his joy is full, and all his bones cry out, 'Blessed be the God and Father of our Lord Jesus Christ, who, according to his abundant mercy, hath begotten me again to a living hope.'"[41]

b. In Everything They Give Thanks

Those who are happy in God give thanks in all things. They "rejoice always, pray continually, give thanks in all circumstances; for this is God's will for you in Christ Jesus."[42]

They receive all contingencies as standing under the permissive will of the Lord.

[36]Phil. 2:5.
[37]Phil. 2:1–4 NIV.
[38]"The Character of a Methodist," B 9:35–36, J VIII:342, sec. 1.6.
[39]"The Character of a Methodist," B 9:36–37, J VIII:342, sec. 1.7; cf. 1 Peter 5:7 NIV.
[40]"The Character of a Methodist," B 9:35–36, J VIII:342, sec. 1.6; cf. Rom. 8:16; 1 John 5:10.
[41]"The Character of a Methodist," B 9:35–36, J VIII:342, sec. 1.6; cf. 1 Peter 1:3–4.
[42]"The Character of a Methodist," B 9:36–37, J VIII:342, sec. 1.7; cf. 1 Thess. 5:16–18.

With Job they are freed to say honestly, "Naked I came from my mother's womb, and naked I will depart. The LORD gave and the LORD has taken away; may the name of the LORD be praised."[43] They have learned "to be content whatever the circumstances."[44]

c. They Pray without Ceasing

Those whose lives are blessed by God, hence are happy in God, "pray without ceasing."[45] Grace enables them "always to pray, and not to faint."[46] When they do not know how they ought to pray, "the Spirit himself intercedes ... through wordless groans."[47] "In retirement or company, in leisure, business, or conversation, [their hearts are] ever with the Lord."[48]

d. Their Hearts Are Full of Love

One who lives out of the love of God has his heart ever being refilled with the love of others. If it is not in his power to "'do good to them that hate him,' yet he ceases not to pray for them, though they continue to spurn his love, and still 'despitefully use him and persecute him.'"[49]

"The love of God has purified his heart from all revengeful passions, from envy, malice, and wrath, from every unkind temper or malign affection ... cleansed him from pride and haughtiness of spirit" from which come contentions.[50]

The ground of contention is cut off. "For none can take from him what he desires; seeing he 'loves not the world,' nor any of 'the things of the world'; being now 'crucified to the world, and the world crucified to him'; being dead to all that is in the world, both to 'the lust of the flesh, the lust of the eyes, and the pride of life.'"[51]

The one whose life is blessed by God has "one desire ... the one design of his life, namely, 'not to do his own will, but the will of Him that sent him.' His one intention at all times and in all things is, not to please himself, but Him whom his soul loveth. He has a single eye. And because 'his eye is single, his whole body is full of light.'"[52]

"God then reigns alone. All that is in the soul is holiness to the Lord. There is not a motion in his heart but is according to his will."[53]

e. They Are Known by Their Fruits

You will recognize them by their fruits if their lives are being blessed by God.

---

[43]Job 1:21 NIV.
[44]Phil. 4:11 NIV.
[45]1 Thess. 5:17.
[46]Luke 18:1.
[47]Rom. 8:26 NIV; "The Character of a Methodist," B 9:37, J VIII:343, sec. 1.8.
[48]"The Character of a Methodist," B 9:37, J VIII:343, sec. 1.8.
[49]"The Character of a Methodist," B 9:37 – 38, J VIII:343, sec. 1.9; cf. Matt. 5:44.
[50]"The Character of a Methodist," B 9:38, J VIII:343 – 44, sec. 1.10.
[51]Ibid.
[52]"The Character of a Methodist," B 9:38, J VIII:344, sec. 1.11; cf. Luke 11:34 – 36.
[53]"The Character of a Methodist," B 9:38, J VIII:344, sec. 1.11; cf. JWT 4:248 – 50.

They seek "a conscience void of offense toward God and toward man."[54] It is their glory to "do the will of God on earth, as it is done in heaven."[55]

The happy person "continually presents his soul and body as a living sacrifice, holy, acceptable to God; entirely and without reserve devoting himself, all he has, and all he is, to his glory. All the talents he has received, he constantly employs according to his Master's will; every power and faculty of his soul, every member of his body."[56]

f. They Do All to the Glory of God

Whatever these blessed people do, "it is all to the glory of God." In all employments of every kind, the happy person's "business and refreshments, as well as his prayers, all serve this great end.... The one business of his life; whether he put on his apparel, or labor, or eat and drink, or divert himself from too wasting labor, it all tends to advance the glory of God."[57]

He is on the outlook against temptation to "the least tendency to vice of any kind."[58]

He does not lay up treasures on earth or "make provision for the flesh to fulfill the lusts thereof."[59]

Purity of intent constrains his mouth. "He cannot utter an unkind word of anyone, for love keeps the door of his lips."[60] He follows the apostolic rule: "Do not let any unwholesome talk come out of your mouths, but only what is helpful for building others up according to their needs, that it may benefit those who listen."[61]

"Whatever is true, whatever is noble, whatever is right, whatever is pure, whatever is lovely, whatever is admirable — if anything is excellent or praiseworthy" — they think on such things.[62]

g. They Do Good to All They Meet

They do good to others whenever the opportunity arises, whether they are strangers, friends, or enemies. They do good of every possible kind, "not only to their bodies, by 'feeding the hungry, clothing the naked, visiting those that are sick or in prison,' but much more [do they] labor to do good to their souls."[63]

The best good believers can do for their souls is to communicate the love of God made known on the cross so all can know that "being justified by faith, they may have peace with God," and may "all come unto the measure of the stature of the fulness of Christ."[64]

---

[54]"The Character of a Methodist," B 9:39, J VIII:344, sec. 1.12.
[55]Ibid.; cf. Matt. 6:10.
[56]"The Character of a Methodist," B 9:39, J VIII:344 – 45, sec. 1.13; cf. Rom. 12:1.
[57]"The Character of a Methodist," B 9:39 – 40, J VIII:345, sec. 1.14.
[58]"The Character of a Methodist," B 9:40, J VIII:345, sec. 1.15.
[59]Ibid.; cf. Rom. 13:14.
[60]"The Character of a Methodist," B 9:40, J VIII:345, sec. 1.15; cf. Ps. 141:3.
[61]Eph. 4:29 NIV; "The Character of a Methodist," B 9:40, J VIII:345, sec. 1.15.
[62]Phil. 4:8 NIV; "The Character of a Methodist," B 9:40, J VIII:345, sec. 1.15.
[63]"The Character of a Methodist," B 9:41, J VIII:346, sec. 1.16; cf. Matt. 25:35 – 36.
[64]Rom. 5:1; Eph 4:13; "The Character of a Methodist," B 9:41, J VIII:346, sec. 1.16.

"These are the principles and practices" that show forth the character formed in the life that is lived in Christ.

But suppose you say, "Why, these are only the common fundamental principles of Christianity!" If so, you got it. These are the most familiar descriptions of life in Christ.

Such a person "is a Christian, not in name only, but in heart and in life. He is inwardly and outwardly conformed to the will of God" as known by the community of faith. He thinks, speaks, and lives according to the wisdom revealed in Jesus Christ. "His soul is renewed after the image of God, in righteousness and in all true holiness. And having the mind that was in Christ, he so walks as Christ also walked."[65]

The character of a Christian is describable. Since the times of the apostles and saints, it has been accurately described.

C. The Principles of a Methodist

Wesley wrote "The Principles of a Methodist"[66] in answer to three charges: that his view of justification by faith was deficient, that he believed in sinless perfection, and that he held views that were inconsistent.[67] In answering these questions, he laid the groundwork for Christian ethics.

1. The Ethical Import of Justification by Grace through Faith

Justification by grace through faith is not an ancillary teaching unrelated to the practice of the good life. Rather, it is at the heart of the Christian life and the Christian ethic.

To make this clear, Wesley confirmed the Scripture doctrine of justification as understood by the patristic writers and the continental Reformation and the English Reformation. His argument moves systematically through the key phases of the order of salvation.[68]

a. God's Pardon Is the Basis for True Human Freedom

The moral requirement of God is not secret knowledge. It is accessible by reason,

---

[65]"The Character of a Methodist," B 9:41, J VIII:346, sec. 1.17.

[66]A previous lengthy pamphlet had appeared in 1742 by Josiah Tucker titled "A Brief History of the Principles of Methodism, wherein the Rise and Progress, Together with the Causes of the Several Variations, Divisions, and Present Inconsistencies of This Sect Are Attempted to Be Traced Out, and Accounted For" (Bristol, UK: Farley, 1742). Tucker was chaplain to Bishop Joseph Butler in Bristol. In 1749 Tucker had preached a sermon in All Saints Church of Bristol, which "seemed to Wesley to proclaim justification 'on account of our own righteousness.'" Here Wesley, for the record, was seeking to correct some of its "mistakes."

[67]"The Principles of a Methodist," B 9:48, J VIII:361, sec. 1.1. Although in *JWT*, vol. 2, we have previously discussed Wesley's far more explicit teachings on two of these points (justification and sanctification), it is fitting to ask in this volume how they pertain centrally to Wesley's ethics and particularly to the focus of this chapter on practically nurturing and enabling communities of the life of faith active in love.

[68]See the previous discussion of the Order of Salvation in *JWT*, vol. 2, chaps. 2–9.

embedded in conscience, commanded in the history of Moses and the prophets, and fulfilled in Jesus.[69]

Eighteenth-century evangelicals were learning, as the "old plain [true, patristic] religion" taught, that "every one of the offspring of Adam is very far gone from original righteousness, and is of his own nature inclined to evil; that this corruption of our nature, in every person born into the world," is deserving of judgment by the incomparable justice of God. Only the remission of sins allows sinners to be "accounted righteous before God."[70]

No serious view of the blessing of God is possible without recognizing the radical fallenness of humanity. Only the merit of Christ is sufficient to remove the guilt of the tangled history of personal and social sin.

The favor of God shown on the cross is received only by faith, by trusting in God's promises of redemption. It is not earned due to "our own works or deservings of any kind. Nay, I am persuaded, that all works done before justification, have in them the nature of sin; and that, consequently, till he is justified, a man has no power to do any work which is pleasing and acceptable to God."[71]

2. God's Grace, Christ's Atoning Work on the Cross, and the Spirit's Work in Us

For the sinner to be justified, that is, "accounted righteous before God ... three things must go together": God's part, Christ's part, and our part. "Upon God's part, his great mercy and grace; upon Christ's part, the satisfaction of God's justice by the offering of his body and shedding of his blood; and upon our part, true and living faith in the merits of Jesus Christ."[72] The divine energy created by this confluence is able to change a miserable life to a happy life.

a. How God's Gift Enables Our Response

If all these come together, we have in our justification "not only God's mercy and grace, but his justice also. And so the grace of God does not shut out the righteousness of God in our justification, but only shuts out the righteousness of man, that is, the righteousness of our works."[73] God offers mercy and grace, Christ satisfies God's justice by offering his own body and blood on the cross, and believers receive by faith. What do we offer? Only a complete trust in the promises of God through merits of Christ.

This is why the apostolic teaching "requires nothing on the part of man, but only a true and living faith."[74] No works of ours justify us to stand before God, only our trust in God's mercy.

---

[69]"The Principles of a Methodist," B 9:48 – 49, J VIII:361, sec. 1.2.
[70]Cf. Gal. 3:6.
[71]"The Principles of a Methodist," B 9:48 – 49, J VIII:361, sec. 1.2.
[72]"The Principles of a Methodist," B 9:49, J VIII:361 – 62, sec. 1.3.
[73]Ibid.
[74]"The Principles of a Methodist," B 9:49 – 50, J VIII:362, sec. 1.4.

How could you make operable an ethic that begins by ruling out human action as the basis of righteousness? Does this leave human action out of any part in our justification? Yes. That is something God does for us. But does this mean we do nothing? No. We receive God's mercy in faith.

Here is the surprising beginning point for evangelical ethics, distinguishing it from all other ethical systems: "This faith does not shut out repentance, hope, and love, which are joined with faith in every man that is justified. But it shuts them out from the office of justifying."[75] Repentance, hope, and love are present in the one who is justified as fruits of faith, but none of these prevail as a condition of receiving God's mercy, but only faith. All classic Protestant confessions agree: faith alone. The one who is receiving God's grace needs only faith. But repentance, hope, and love spring out of faith.[76]

b. How Unmerited Reception of God's Righteousness Engenders Good Works

Faith does not "shut out good works." Good works spring out of the gratitude of faith. We are harmed in our ability to do good works if we have the intent of being justified by them. "Our justification comes freely, of the mere mercy of God; for whereas all the world was not able to pay any part toward their ransom, it pleased him, without any of our deserving, to prepare for us Christ's body and blood, whereby our ransom might be paid, and his justice satisfied. Christ, therefore, is now the righteousness of all them that truly believe in him."[77]

To say we are "justified by faith in Christ only," does not mean we are justified by faith as if it were our own act without God's grace and Christ's work for us and the Holy Spirit in us. Justified by faith does not mean that "our faith which is within us, justifies us," for that would imply that we were "to account ourselves to be justified by some act or virtue that is within us."[78] "We must renounce the merit of all, of faith, hope, love, and all other virtues and good works, which we either have done, shall do, or can do, as far too weak to deserve our justification."[79] God's pardon frees us to "trust only in God's mercy and the merits of Christ,"[80] since it is God alone who takes away our sins. So it is more precise to say that "God himself justifies us, of his own mercy, through the merits of his Son only."[81]

Wesley appeals not to the magisterial Reformation only but more directly to the

---

[75] Ibid.

[76] Ibid. Wesley's explicit texts on justification were discussed in *JWT*, vol. 2.

[77] "The Principles of a Methodist," B 9:51, J VIII:362, sec. 1.5. In much of the discussion that follows, Wesley is quoting from the Elizabethan Homilies of 1547, which confess the classic points of the magisterial reformation on justification by grace alone through faith alone grounded in Scripture alone. See *Certain Sermons or Homilies Appointed to Be Read in the Time of the Late Queen Elizabeth*, 1603; repr., Oxford, 1840. Wesley published a portion of these homilies under the title "Doctrine of Salvation." Correlated references to "Doctrine of Salvation" are found in the footnotes of the Bicentennial edition.

[78] "The Principles of a Methodist," B 9:52, J VIII:362, sec. 1.6.

[79] Ibid.

[80] Ibid.

[81] "The Principles of a Methodist," B 9:52, J VIII:362–63, sec. 1.7.

church fathers who taught, "'Faith without works,' and 'Faith alone,' justifies us."[82] So while we affirm all the virtues that grow out of faith in God's righteousness, we renounce faith if considered as if it were our own virtue. The reverberations of the whole history of sin in us are so deafening in us "that all our faith, charity, words, and works, cannot merit or deserve any part of our justification for us. And therefore we thus speak, humbling ourselves before God, and giving Christ all the glory of our justification."[83]

While we are justified by living faith, we are not justified by a dead faith that does not bear fruit in good works. "Faith which brings not forth good works is not a living faith" but a dead faith.[84] Even the demonic powers can believe that the Messiah has come and yet not have living faith that elicits hope and love.[85]

True Christian faith implies not only believing that the Holy Scriptures and the articles of our faith are true, but also having "a sure trust and confidence" in their truth "for me" personally.

"A loving heart, to obey his commandments"[86] follows out of gratitude for our salvation from sin.

God's pardon therefore forms the fundamental premise of Christian ethics. Moral and behavioral responses rest on a "sure trust and confidence in God, that by the merits of Christ his sins are forgiven, and he reconciled to the favor of God."[87]

3. The Ethical Import of the Biblical Teaching of God's Perfecting Love

All grace is God's grace. Though grace is one, its forms are many. Classic Christian teaching recognizes the flow from preparing grace to justifying grace to sanctifying grace. This flow reveals the unity of God's singular work of grace. Since humans are beings in time, it is useful to discern grace moving through time.

Justifying grace pardons the penitent sinner, while sanctifying grace works to draw the sinner toward full responsiveness to justifying grace through the work of the Holy Spirit. The Holy Spirit works to enable full responsiveness to God's saving act.[88] In Wesley's language, this distinguishes God's act for us from God's act in us, as we experience that singular grace within time. Wesley constantly preached that the Holy Spirit is working to bring faith into the fullest possible expression in God's perfecting love.

---

[82]Ibid.

[83]Ibid.

[84]"The Principles of a Methodist," B 9:52 – 53, J VIII:363, sec. 1.8.

[85]Ibid. In the following paragraphs, Wesley is quoting intermittently from his preface to *Hymns and Sacred Poems*, 1740, J XIV:323 – 25. In the Bicentennial edition, these quotes are easily identified by a small font. Since Wesley is quoting himself, I do not here distinguish the font sizes, but for those who wish to see these clearly distinguished, I recommend the Bicentennial edition, 9:53ff.

[86]"The Principles of a Methodist," B 9:53, J VIII:363, sec. 1.9.

[87]Ibid.; cf. "Doctrine of Salvation," J I:14 – 15.

[88]This point is set forth more fully in *JWT* 2, chap. 4.

a. Against Sinless Perfection Implying Freedom from Ignorance, Mistake, or Temptation

Wesley repeatedly insisted that "there is no such perfection in [a person's] life as implies an entire deliverance, either from ignorance or mistake, in things not essential to salvation, or from manifold temptations, or from numberless infirmities wherewith the corruptible body more or less presses down the soul. We cannot find any ground in Scripture to suppose that any inhabitant of a house of clay is wholly exempt, either from bodily infirmities, or from ignorance of many things; or to imagine any is incapable of mistake, or falling into divers temptations."[89]

Mistaking the unity of grace led to the erroneous charge from Josiah Tucker that Wesley taught "sinless perfection." This section of "Principles of a Methodist" sets forth Wesley's objections to the idea of sinless perfection when understood as transcending the common conditions of human finitude.[90]

Wesley had sought to make clear the dangers of an exaggerated teaching of Christian perfection: "We willingly allow, and continually declare, there is no such perfection in this life, as implies either a dispensation from doing good and attending all the ordinances of God; or a freedom from ignorance, mistake, temptation, and a thousand infirmities necessarily connected with flesh and blood."[91] It is useful to break down this condensed disclaimer into these parts:

There is no perfection in this life that implies the following:

- freedom from ignorance
- freedom from making mistakes
- freedom from temptation
- freedom from finite infirmities that are necessarily connected with flesh and blood, the very conditions of human existence
- license to abandon the worshiping community
- license to cease doing good

Those who imagine that any of the above misinterpretations are what is meant by God's perfecting love have misread the Scriptures. Wesley was alerting any who might say that he taught any of these disclaimers not to attribute any of them to him or his connection of spiritual formation.

The center of biblical teaching of the fullness of sanctifying grace is found in Ephesians: "To each one of us grace has been given as Christ apportioned it."[92] This is why Christ ascended: "to equip his people for works of service, so that the body of Christ may be built up until we all reach unity in the faith and in the knowledge of the Son of God and become mature, attaining to the whole measure of the fullness of Christ."[93] "Then we will no longer be infants, tossed back and forth by the

---

[89]"The Principles of a Methodist," B 9:53–55, J VIII:363–65, sec. 2.2.
[90]"The Principles of a Methodist," B 9:53, J VIII:363, sec. 2.1.
[91]"The Principles of a Methodist," B 9:53–55, J VIII:363–65, sec. 2.2.
[92]Eph. 4:7 NIV.
[93]Eph. 4:12–13 NIV.

waves, and blown here and there by every wind of teaching.... Instead, speaking the truth in love, we will grow to become in every respect the mature body of him who is the head, that is, Christ."[94] Emphatically this "attaining to the whole measure of the fullness of Christ" has never meant that we as finite humans have all knowledge even as God knows all.

b. The Goal of the Fulfilled Christian Life

In whom is God's perfecting love growing and bearing fruit? "One in whom 'is the mind which was in Christ.'"[95] "If anyone obeys his word, love for God is truly made complete in them. This is how we know we are in him: Whoever claims to live in him must live as Jesus did."[96] Does "truly made complete" mean almost complete? Or could it mean complete only in principle but not in reality? That would be tampering with the text. "Therefore, since we have these promises, dear friends, let us purify ourselves from everything that contaminates body and spirit, perfecting holiness out of reverence for God."[97] Does perfecting holiness mean approximating holiness? "If we walk in the light, as he is in the light, we have fellowship with one another, and the blood of Jesus, his Son, purifies us from all sin."[98] Is "all sin" just a euphemism for "most sin"? "Just as he who called you is holy, so be holy in all you do; for it is written: 'Be holy, because I am holy.'"[99] "Holy in all you do" cannot be reduced to "holy in *most* you do."

"The reason the Son of God appeared was to destroy the devil's work. No one who is born of God will continue to sin, because God's seed remains in them; they cannot go on sinning, because they have been born of God."[100] "Cannot go on sinning" means cannot within the frame of the intent of baptism continue to sin.[101] "Our fellowship is with the Father and with his Son, Jesus Christ. We write this to make our joy complete."[102] We see perfect love in action when one "can now testify to all mankind, 'I am crucified with Christ: Nevertheless I live; yet not I, but Christ liveth in me.'"[103] These words were not invented by Wesley. They are central to the New Testament. They reveal the goal of the Christian life, hence of Christian ethics: complete responsiveness to the will of God. That is not a fantasy promise. It is the promise of Scripture.

In none of these texts do we find the suggestion that those who are walking in perfect love are without some forms of ignorance or have transcended all finite limits or can never be sick. As noted above, Wesley strongly rejects the unscriptural

---

[94]Eph. 4:14–15 NIV.

[95]"The Principles of a Methodist," B 9:53–55, J VIII:363–65, sec. 2.4; cf. Phil. 2.

[96]1 John 2:5–6 NIV.

[97]2 Cor. 7:1 NIV.

[98]1 John 1:7 NIV; "The Principles of a Methodist," B 9:53–55, J VIII:363–65, sec. 2.4.

[99]1 Peter 1:15–16 NIV, in reference to Lev. 11:44, 45; 19:2.

[100]1 John 3:8–9 NIV.

[101]See the discussion of "sin remains but does not reign" in *JWT*, vol. 2, chap. 10, on "Sin Remaining after Justification," for a further clarification of Wesley's intent.

[102]1 John 1:3–4 NIV.

[103]"The Principles of a Methodist," B 9:53–55, J VIII:363–65, sec. 2.5; cf. Gal. 2:20.

notion of "sinless perfection" in that transfinite sense that is not attested in Scripture, involving freedom from finitude, illness, temptation, and all possible forms of ignorance.

God's perfecting grace calls for the faithful to "'continually … offer up every thought, word, and work as a spiritual sacrifice, acceptable to God through Christ.' In every thought of our hearts, in every word of our tongues, in every work of our hands, to 'show forth his praise, who hath called us out of darkness into his marvellous light.'"[104]

If there is anything unscriptural in these texts, "anything wild or extravagant, anything contrary to the analogy of faith, or the experience of adult Christians, let them 'smite me friendly and reprove me,'" and show others "the clearer light God has given them."[105] The remaining sections of "The Principles of a Methodist" are largely a point-by-point refutation of the essay on the same subject by his detractor, Josiah Tucker. These points have all been previously addressed in this series. Those who wish to see a systematic analysis of Wesley's views of the work of the Holy Spirit, grace, predestination, sanctification, and remaining sin after justification will find these subjects more thoroughly spelled out in volume 2 of this series, chapters 4, 5, 6, 9, and 10.

D. The Nature, Design, and General Rules of the United Societies (1743)

Let us return to the beginning point of this volume: Wesley's ethics. Wesley's major contribution to the history of Christian ethics was his persistent work of building small-scale communities of moral accountability through which the good life could be nurtured. He was firmly focused on encouraging small groups to call each other to the practice of the Christian life to the fullest extent. He was not a theorist of ethics or a professional counselor but a mentor of the leaders of these lay societies seeking the holy life. How are persons and societies to be changed? Through engendering face-to-face communities of behavioral change.

1. The Early Evangelical Societies for Spiritual Formation

The key writings of Wesley on nurturing communities of faith unfolded chronologically: "The Rules of the Band-Societies" (1738), "The Character of a Methodist" (1742), and "The Principles of a Methodist" (1742). By 1743 the behavioral outcomes of these intensive group processes had matured, and a more deliberate effort was focused on what Wesley called in a sermon of the same name, "The Nature, Design, and General Rules of the United Societies."

---

[104]"The Principles of a Methodist," B 9:53 – 55, J VIII:363 – 65, sec. 2.13. Although Wesley quotes this as from Archbishop James Ussher (1581 – 1656), it has not been clearly identified in Ussher's writings, but it may be Wesley's paraphrase of a passage in Ussher's *A Body of Divinity*, 5th ed. (London: Owsley and Lillicrap, 1658), 176.

[105]"The Principles of a Methodist," B 9:55, J VIII:365, sec. 2.3.

This document has become very important to the whole Wesleyan tradition. It has become integrated into the very constitutional documents of many Wesleyan heritage churches. Beyond its constitutional form, it has been implicitly incorporated into the practices of the holiness and sanctification traditions.

a. Their Nature, Design, and General Rules

Late in 1739, "eight or ten persons came to me in London, who appeared to be deeply convinced of sin, and earnestly groaning for redemption. They desired (as did two or three more the next day) that I would spend some time with them in prayer, and advise them how to flee from the wrath to come."[106]

The societies were not initiated by Wesley but began with a request for pastoral care. Wesley was responding to felt needs for prayer and spiritual counsel. "That we might have more time for this great work, I appointed a day when they might all come together, which from thenceforward they did every week, namely, on Thursday, in the evening. To these, and as many more as desired to join with them (for their number increased daily), I gave those advices, from time to time, which I judged most needful for them; and we always concluded our meeting with prayer suited to their several necessities."[107]

The great evangelical revival in Britain began in this small-scale way — with the convicted consciences, the felt needs, and the hunger for spiritual direction of ordinary people, mostly the poor. "This was the rise of the United Society, first in London, and then in other places."[108] By 1743 these societies under Mr. Wesley's care had spread from London to Bristol, Kingswood, and far north to Newcastle-upon-Tyne. Hence the title of Wesley's brief description of "The Nature, Design, and General Rules of the United Societies, in London, Bristol, Kingswood, Newcastle-upon-Tyne, Etc."

b. The Design of the Classes

The "class meeting" was described simply. It was a company of persons[109] "having the form and seeking the power of godliness, united in order to pray together, to receive the word of exhortation, and to watch over one another in love, that they may help each other to work out their salvation."[110] They were a close-knit community of prayer, seeking to embody the life of grace. They helped each other work out their salvation by hearing the Scripture opened up to them, praying, and receiving mutual counsel on their temptations and challenges.

In my book *The Intensive Group Experience*, I sought to trace the beginnings of modern group therapy and experimental group processes. I came to the conclu-

---

[106]"The Nature, Design, and General Rules of the United Societies," B 9:69, J VIII:269, sec. 1.
[107]Ibid.
[108]"The Nature, Design, and General Rules of the United Societies," B 9:69, J VIII:269, sec. 2.
[109]The texts says "men" but assumes women and men by generic implication. A large number of women were active in the classes and societies. This is evident from Wesley's huge correspondence with women seeking his counsel. See *LJW*.
[110]"The Nature, Design, and General Rules of the United Societies," B 9:69, J VIII:269, sec. 2.

sion that its beginning was at least as early as London in late 1739. All of the key elements of the intensive group processes that flourished in the last half of the twentieth century reflect the crucial elements present in these societies of spiritual formation under Mr. Wesley's guidance. Later their key features would be defined as empathy, authentic self-disclosure, and unconditional acceptance.[111] These secular groups were not intentionally seeking repentance and saving grace and faith, hope, and love, but in some sense they were seeking an analogous secular life-reversal, self-understanding, self-disclosure, and the recovery of meaning in their lives. So in language and worldview they were quite different but in reality and process they were quite similar. The modern forms of intensive group experience are secularized forms of the early evangelical societies. I will use the modern term "group process" to describe the conceptions, means, techniques, methods, and practices going on in these societies for spiritual formation. I concede that the Methodist societies had far broader goals than the modern intensive group experience. But the interactive processes were stunningly similar.

The classes were small groups that were joined into a larger local society under the care of Wesley himself. They were helping each other work out their own salvation. Classes were formed in neighborhoods and were related to societies in towns.[112] In 1743 the Methodists had almost no property. The chapels would come later. They met wherever they could find space, whether in a religious setting, a foundry, or a residence.

"There are about twelve persons in every class; one of whom is styled the Leader. It is his business ... to see each person in his class once a week at least, in order to inquire how their souls prosper."[113] This was an intensive group interaction that required serious commitment of time. The leader asked each one to honestly disclose how their souls were growing in grace. The focus was on care of souls.

Wesley took great care to see, insofar as possible, that the leader of the small class was prepared to study Scripture and pray with each participant. They had his teaching homilies available to them for guidance. That is what they were for. On this basis, each person present would have opportunity to give and receive advice and counsel heart to heart.

c. The Sick and the Poor

In these class meetings, the sick and the poor were not forgotten. Each member was expected to "give toward the relief of the poor" weekly as a discipline that was integral to their growth in grace.[114]

The participants met with the minister and stewards once a week "in order to inform the Minister of any that are sick."[115]

---

[111]Thomas C. Oden, *The Intensive Group Experience* (Philadelphia: Westminster, 1969); cf. "The Nature, Design, and General Rules of the United Societies," B 9:69, J VIII:269, sec. 2.

[112]"The Nature, Design, and General Rules of the United Societies," B 9:70, J VIII:269–70, sec. 3.

[113]"The Nature, Design, and General Rules of the United Societies," B 9:70, J VIII:269–70, sec. 3.1.

[114]Ibid.

[115]"The Nature, Design, and General Rules of the United Societies," B 9:70, J VIII:269–70, sec. 3.2.

To seek fitting repentance for continuing sins, the participants had agreed to be open, self-disclosing, and willing to receive admonition. One of the key duties of each participant was to warn another of their "bosom sins" and to help others avoid temptations. Any who "walk disorderly, and will not be reproved," were put under the care of the leader of the class or removed.[116]

Since the early Methodists were firm in their duty to give to the poor, they kept careful records of contributions to avoid any misuse of funds and to transmit them faithfully to those in need. Often these contributions were only schillings, since the financial resources of most participants were limited.[117]

d. Only One Condition for Admission

"There is one only condition previously required in those who desire admission into these societies — a desire 'to flee from the wrath to come, to be saved from their sins.' "[118] The door was open to any and all who had this desire to reshape their behavior toward living a life in Christ.

The first step in receiving the gospel is repentance. The order of salvation begins with repentance and faith.[119] Wherever sincere repentance "is really fixed in the soul, it will be shown by its fruits. It is therefore expected of all who continue therein that they should continue to evidence their desire of salvation."[120] Entry into the societies was wholly voluntary.

2. Showing Evidence of Sincere Repentance

a. Doing No Harm

Having set out on the road to sincere repentance, the next steps were to show fruits of repentance: "First, by doing no harm." The first rule of care of souls is similar to the physician's care of the body: relent from any action that might cause injury to each other.

What kind of harm was to be avoided? "Evil in every kind; especially that which is most generally practiced."[121] People who attended to conscience probably did not need to be told specifics. But "babes in Christ" may have needed elementary instruction and counsel, just as children need to know the boundaries for their own safety and benefit.

The following vices were obviously unacceptable:

- taking the name of God in vain
- profaning the day of the Lord, including working, buying, and selling
- drunkenness, buying or selling spirituous liquors, or drinking them, unless in cases of extreme necessity[122]

---

[116]Ibid.
[117]Ibid.
[118]Ibid.; cf. Matt. 1:21.
[119]"The Nature, Design, and General Rules of the United Societies," B 9:70–71, J VIII:270, sec. 4.
[120]Ibid.
[121]Ibid.
[122]"The Nature, Design, and General Rules of the United Societies," B 9:70, J VIII:269–70, sec. 3.2.

The following dysfunctional behaviors were to be avoided:

- fighting, quarreling, brawling
- brother going to law with brother
- returning evil for evil
- buying or selling illegally
- giving or taking things on excessive interest rate
- speaking uncharitably or unbeneficially
- doing to others what we would not wish to be done to ourselves[123]

Things such as the following, that were not for the glory of God, were to be avoided:

- laying up treasures on earth
- borrowing without a probability of paying
- engaging in needless self-indulgence
- wearing unseemly apparel[124]
- seeking diversions that could not be sought in the name of the Lord[125]

b. Positive Acts of Doing Good

Those who desired to continue in these societies were expected to engage in good works as fruit of their repentance and faith.[126] They were to be merciful and do good to all persons as they had opportunity and to do every good of every kind to all humanity, caring for both body and soul.[127]

They were to help with the physical necessities of the needy by doing the following:

- giving food to the hungry
- clothing the naked
- visiting or helping those who were sick or in prison[128]

And they were to care for their souls by the following actions:

- instructing
- admonishing
- encouraging[129]

Wesley warned against doing good only when a person felt like it and not when he didn't feel like it. That practice makes good works subservient to the fleeting patterns of subjective feelings. It leads to subjective evasions and rationalizations for doing nothing.[130]

---

[123]"The Nature, Design, and General Rules of the United Societies," B 9:70, J VIII:269–70, sec. 3.3–4.

[124]Especially if it detracted from giving sacrificially to the poor.

[125]"The Nature, Design, and General Rules of the United Societies," B 9:70, J VIII:269–70, sec. 3.2.

[126]"The Nature, Design, and General Rules of the United Societies," B 9:72, J VIII:270–71, sec. 5.

[127]Ibid.

[128]Ibid.

[129]Ibid.

[130]Ibid.

c. Especially Do Good for the Household of Faith

Those who expected to continue in the societies were alerted to obey the Scripture that says, "Therefore, as we have opportunity, let us do good to all people, especially to those who belong to the family of believers."[131] Believers are to pay special attention to honest people searching for a new life in Christ.

Doing good for the household of faith included down-to-earth help: employment, "helping each other in business,"[132] and caring for mutual interests. The family of God is to be viewed as an extension of a believer's family.

Believers were to do good for the household of faith in these ways:

- seeing to it that nothing they did brought ill repute to the family of God
- denying themselves and taking up their cross daily
- running with patience daily the race set before them
- being willing to bear the reproach of Christ
- engaging in all the ordinances of God: common prayer, hearing the Word, and the Lord's Table
- setting an example for one's own family by engaging in private prayer and searching of the Scriptures
- not letting the community of faith be diminished because of their individual actions[133]

d. Voluntary Conditions of Continuing

Since entry into the societies was voluntary and framed within a stated purpose, they could end voluntarily if the terms of entry were abused or not followed.

"These are the General Rules of our societies, all of which we are taught of God to observe, even in his written word, the only rule, and the sufficient rule, both of our faith and practice. And all these, we know, his Spirit writes on every truly awakened heart."[134]

Those "who habitually break any of them, let it be made known unto them who watch over that soul as they that must give an account. We will admonish him of the error of his ways; we will bear with him for a season: but then if he repent not, he hath no more place among us. We have delivered our own souls."[135]

This was the short but powerful document placed in the hands of any who sought entry into the class meetings and the societies.

3. A Concise Summary of "Directions Given to the Band-Societies" (1744)

One more founding document condenses the rules of the band societies. On Christmas Day 1744, Wesley offered a summary of counsel to the class meetings.

---

[131]Gal. 6:10 NIV.
[132]"The Nature, Design, and General Rules of the United Societies," B 9:72, J VIII:270–71, sec. 5.
[133]"The Nature, Design, and General Rules of the United Societies," B 9:73, J VIII:271, sec. 6.
[134]"The Nature, Design, and General Rules of the United Societies," B:9:73, J VIII:271, sec. 7.
[135]Ibid.

These were not a replacement of the previous directions, but a condensation of them. In plain language, he compressed the previous General Rules into only eighteen lines in three concise categories. This is best seen in outline form:

I. Abstain from doing evil.
   A. Not buying or selling on the Lord's day.
   B. Not having "spirituous liquor, no dram of any kind, unless prescribed by a Physician."
   C. Not haggling in business.
   D. Not pawning goods.[136]
   E. Not mentioning the fault of any behind his back and stopping short those who do.[137]
   F. Not wearing needless ornaments.
   G. Not engaging in acts of needless self-indulgence.[138]
II. Zealously maintain good works.
   A. To give to "the uttermost of your power."
   B. To reprove "all that sin in your sight, and that in love and meekness of wisdom."
   C. "To be patterns of diligence and frugality, of self-denial, and taking up the cross daily."[139]
III. Constantly attend to all the ordinances of God.
   A. To be "at church and at the Lord's Table every week, and at every public meeting of the Bands."[140]
   B. "To attend the ministry of the Word every morning, unless distance, business, or sickness prevent."
   C. "To use private prayer every day; and family prayer, if you are at the head of a family."
   D. "To read the Scriptures, and meditate therein, at every vacant hour."
   E. "To observe as days of fasting or abstinence all Fridays in the year."[141]

In this plain summary, Wesley showed how deeply he was committed to teaching Christian ethics. None of these teachings are difficult to understand. No one can miss their meaning.

4. The Focus on Character

John Wesley was a teacher of an ethic formally classifiable as an ethic of character. It combines other types of ethical reflection (on intent, on duty, on virtue, and on consequences) into the frame of reference of the gospel. It brings all of these approaches into a single focus on the building of character of the sort described in "The Character of a Methodist."

Since that essay was essentially a summary of part 7 of Clement of Alexandria's

---

[136]"Directions Given to the Band-Societies," J VIII:273, sec. 1.1–2.
[137]"Directions Given to the Band-Societies," J VIII:273, sec. 1.2–5.
[138]"Directions Given to the Band-Societies," J VIII:274, sec. 1.6–7.
[139]"Directions Given to the Band-Societies," J VIII:274, sec. 2.1–3.
[140]"Directions Given to the Band-Societies," J VIII:274, sec. 3.1.
[141]"Directions Given to the Band-Societies," J VIII:274, sec. 3.2–5.

Stromata, it is evident that Wesley was grounding his ethic in the earliest ethical teaching of classic ecumenical Christianity. Further, it is worth noting that Clement was living on the African continent. Thus the heart of Wesley's ethic derives from early African Christianity, not only in the case of Clement but also of Cyprian, Augustine, and Macarius. All of these were intent on character formation.

Further Reading on Social Ethics

Armistead, M. Kathryn. *Wesleyan Theology and Social Science: The Dance of Practical Divinity and Discovery.* Newcastle, UK: Cambridge Scholars, 2010.

Baker, Frank. *John Wesley and the Church of England.* Nashville: Abingdon, 1970.

Berg, Daniel. "The Marks of the Church in the Theology of John Wesley." In *The Church.* Edited by Melvin Dieter and Daniel Berg, 319–31. Anderson, IN: Warner, 1984.

Brantley, Richard E. *Locke, Wesley and the Method of English Romanticism.* Gainsville: Univ. of Florida Press, 1984.

Brown, Robert. *John Wesley's Theology: The Principle of Its Vitality and Its Progressive Stages of Development.* London: E. Stock, 1965.

Burwash, Nathaniel. *Manual of Christian Theology.* 2 vols. London: Horace Marshall, 1900.

Byrne, Herbert W. *John Wesley and Learning.* Salem, OH: Schmul, 1997.

Cahn, Ernst. "John Wesley als Vorkämpfer einer christlichen Sozialethik." *Die Christliche Welt* 46 (1932): 208–12.

Cannon, William R. "Methodism in a Philosophy of History." *MH* 12, no. 4 (1974): 27–43.

Cheek, H. Lee. *Confronting Modernity: Towards a Theology of Ministry in the Wesleyan Tradition.* Lake Junaluska, NC: Wesley Studies Society, 2010.

Clapper, Gregory S. *As If the Heart Mattered: A Wesleyan Spirituality.* Nashville: Upper Room, 1997.

———. *John Wesley on Religious Affections: His Views on Experience and Emotion and Their Role in the Christian Life and Theology.* Metuchen, NJ: Scarecrow, 1989.

Coleman, Robert E. *Nothing to Do but Save Souls. John Wesley: John Wesley's Charge to His Preachers.* Grand Rapids: Zondervan, 1990.

Coleson, Joseph E. *Be Holy: God's Invitation to Understand, Declare, and Experience Holiness.* Indianapolis: Wesleyan Publishing House, 2008.

Collins, Kenneth J. "The Conversion of John Wesley: A Transformation to Power." In *Conversion.* Edited by John S. Hong. Bucheon City, Kyungki-Do, South Korea: Seoul Theological Univ., 1993. Published in Korean.

———. *John Wesley: A Theological Journey.* Nashville: Abingdon, 2003.

Cushman, Robert E. *John Wesley's Experimental Divinity: Studies in Methodist Doctrinal Standards.* Nashville: Kingswood, Abingdon, 1989.

Davies, Rupert E. "The People of God." *LQHR* 184 (1959): 223–30. On Methodist doctrines.

Dieter, Melvin. "John Wesley and Creative Synthesis." *AS* 39, no. 3 (1984): 3–7.

Dreyer, Frederick. "Faith and Experience in the Thought of John Wesley." *AHR* 88, no. 1 (1983): 12 – 30.

Dunnam, Maxie D. *Going On to Salvation: A Study of Wesleyan Beliefs.* Nashville: Abingdon, 2008.

Eckhart, Ruth Alma. "Wesley and the Philosophers." *MR* 112 (1929): 330 – 45.

Edwards, Maldwyn. *John Wesley and the Eighteenth Century: A Study of His Social and Political Influence.* New York: Abingdon, 1933.

Ferguson, Duncan S. "John Wesley on Scripture: The Hermeneutics of Pietism." *MH* 22, no. 4 (1984): 234 – 45.

Flew, R. Newton. *The Idea of Perfection in Christian Theology*, 313 – 34. Oxford: Oxford Univ. Press, 1934.

Glasson, T. Francis. "Jeremy Taylor's Place in John Wesley's Life." *PWHS* 36 (1968): 105 – 7.

Glick, Dan. "The Pastoral Counseling of John Wesley through Written Correspondence: The Years 1777 – 1782." Dan Glick Wordpress. http://danglick.wordpress.com.

Green, John Brazier. *John Wesley and William Law.* London, Epworth, 1945.

Gunter, W. Stephen. *Considering the Great Commission: Evangelism and Mission in the Wesleyan Spirit.* Nashville: Abingdon, 2005.

Hagen, Odd. *Litt om Wesleys Laere om Kristleig Fullkommenheit* (Light on Wesley's Teaching on Christian Perfection). Oslo: Methodismen, 1938.

Harding, F. A. J. *The Social Impact of the Evangelical Revival.* London: Epworth, 1947.

Harper, Steve. *John Wesley's Theology Today.* Grand Rapids: Zondervan, 1983. Chap. 4 on converting grace.

Headley, Anthony J. *Family Crucible: The Influence of Family Dynamics in the Life and Ministry of John Wesley.* Eugene: Wipf & Stock, 2010.

Heitzenrater, Richard P. *The Elusive Mr. Wesley.* 2 vols. Abingdon, 1984.

Herbert, T. W. *John Wesley as Editor and Author.* Princeton: Princeton Univ. Press, 1940.

Hong, John Sungschul. *John Wesley the Evangelist.* Lexington, KY: Emeth, 2006.

Howard, Ivan. "The Doctrine of Assurance." In *Further Insights into Holiness.* Edited by K. Geiger. Kansas City: Beacon Hill, 1963.

Hughes, H. Trevor. "Jeremy Taylor and John Wesley." *LQHR* 174 (1949): 296 – 404.

Hulley, Leonard D. *Wesley: A Plain Man for Plain People.* Westville, South Africa: Methodist Church of South Africa, 1987.

Hurst, John Fletcher. *John Wesley the Methodist: A Plain Account of His Life and Work.* New York: Eaton & Mains, 1903. Authorship credited as "By a Methodist Preacher."

Hutchinson, F. E. "John Wesley and George Herbert." *LQHR* 161 (1936): 439 – 55.

Johnson, Susanne. *Christian Spiritual Formation in the Church and Classroom.* Nashville: Abingdon, 1989.

Jones, Charles E. *A Guide to the Study of the Holiness Movement.* Metuchen, NJ: Scarecrow, 1974.

Jones, Scott J. *Staying at the Table: The Gift of Unity for United Methodists.* Nashville: Abingdon, 2008.

Joy, James R. "Wesley: A Man of a Thousand Books and a Book." *RL* 8 (1939): 71 – 84.

Källstad, Thorvald. *John Wesley and the Bible: A Psychological Study.* Stockholm: Bokförlaget Nya Doxa, 1974.

Kissack, Reginald. *Church or No Church? A Study of the Development of the Concept of Church in British Methodism.* London: Epworth, 1964.

Knight, Henry H., and F. Powe. *Transforming Evangelism: The Wesleyan Way of Sharing Faith.* Nashville: Discipleship Resources, 2006.

Knight, Henry H., and Don E. Saliers. *The Conversation Matters: Why United Methodists Should Talk with One Another.* Nashville: Abingdon, 1999.

Koerber, Carolo. *The Theology of Conversion according to John Wesley.* Rome: Neo-Eboraci, 1967.

Langford, Thomas. *Practical Divinity: Theology in the Wesleyan Tradition.* Nashville: Abingdon, 1982. Chap. 6, "Holiness Theology."

Leach, Elsie A. "Wesley's Use of Geo. Herbert." *HLQ* 16 (1953): 183–202.

Lindström, Harald G. A. *Wesley and Sanctification.* Nashville: Abingdon, 1946.

Lloyd, A. K. "Doddridge and Wesley." *PWHS* 28 (1951): 50–52.

Luby, Daniel Joseph. *The Perceptibility of Grace in the Theology of John Wesley. A Roman Catholic Consideration.* Rome: Pontificia Studiorum Universitas A. S. Thomas Aquinas in Urbe, 1994.

Mathews, Horace F. *Methodism and the Education of the People, 1791–1851.* London: Epworth, 1949.

McIntosh, Lawrence. "The Nature and Design of Christianity in John Wesley's Early Theology." PhD diss., Drew Univ., 1966.

Moore, Sydney H. "Wesley and Fenelon." *LQHR* 169 (1944): 155–57.

Oden, Thomas C. *Doctrinal Standards in the Wesleyan Tradition.* Grand Rapids: Zondervan, 1988. Rev. ed., Nashville: Abingdon, 2008.

Outler, Albert C. "Pastoral Care in the Wesleyan Spirit." In *The Wesleyan Theological Heritage: Essays of Albert C. Outler.* Edited by Thomas C. Oden and Leicester R. Longden, 175–88. Grand Rapids: Zondervan, 1991.

———. *Theology in the Wesleyan Spirit.* Nashville: Discipleship Resources, 1975. Chap. 2, " 'Offering Christ,' The Gist of the Gospel."

Pope, William Burt. *A Compendium of Christian Theology.* 3 vols. London: Wesleyan Methodist Book-Room, 1880.

Rack, Henry. "Aldersgate and Revival." In *RE*, 137–81.

Rogal, Samuel J. "A Journal and Diary Checklist of John Wesley's Reading." *Serif* 11, no. 1 (1974): 11–33.

———. "Pills for the Poor: Wesley's Primitive Physick." *Yale Journal of Biology and Medicine* 51 (1978): 81–90.

Rowe, Kenneth, ed. *The Place of Wesley in the Christian Tradition.* Metuchen, NJ: Scarecrow, 1976.

Rupp, E. Gordon. "Son to Samuel: John Wesley, Church of England Man." In *The Place of Wesley in the Christian Tradition.* Edited by Kenneth E. Rowe, 39–66. Metuchen, NJ: Scarecrow, 1976.

Schmidt, Martin. *John Wesley: A Theological Biography.* Translated by Norman Goldhawk. 2 vols. Nashville: Abingdon, 1963.

Sermons and Homilies Appointed to Be Read in Church in the Time of Queen Elizabeth of Famous Memory (1547–71). Oxford: Clarendon, 1802.

Sherwin, Oscar. *John Wesley: Friend of the People*. Farmington Hills, MI: Twayne, 1961.

Shipley, David C. "The Ministry in Methodism in the Eighteenth Century." In *The Ministry in the Methodist Heritage*. Edited by Gerald McCulloh, 11–31. Nashville: Department of Ministerial Education, 1960.

Simon, John S. *John Wesley and the Methodist Societies*. London: Epworth. 1923.

———. *Wesley or Voltaire*. London: C. H. Kelly, 1904.

Smith, Timothy L. "John Wesley and the Wholeness of Scripture." *Interpretation* 39 (1985): 246–62.

———. *Whitefield and Wesley on the New Birth*. Grand Rapids: Zondervan, 1986.

Stoeffler, Fred Earnest. *The Rise of Evangelical Pietism*. Leiden: E. J. Brill, 1965.

———. "Tradition and Renewal in the Ecclesiology of John Wesley." In *Traditio-Krisis-Renovatio aus theologische Sicht*. Edited by B. Jaspert and R. Mohr, 298–316. Marburg, Germany: Elwert, 1976.

Sturm, Roy. *Sociological Reflections on John Wesley and Methodism*. Indianapolis: Central Publishing, 1982.

Sugden, Edward H. *The Standard Sermons of John Wesley*. Edited by Edward H. Sugden. 2 vols. London: Epworth, 1921, 3rd. ed., 1951.

Summers, Thomas O. *Systematic Theology*. 2 vols. Edited by J. J. Tigert. Nashville: Methodist Publishing House South, 1888.

Telford, John, ed. *Letters of John Wesley*. 8 vols. London: Epworth, 1931.

Thomas, Gilbert. "George Fox and John Wesley." *Methodist Recorder* (1924): 11.

Tyerman, Luke. *The Life and Times of the Rev. John Wesley, M.A., Founder of the Methodists*. 3 vols. New York: Harper and Brothers, 1872.

Tyson, John R. "John Wesley and William Law: A Reappraisal." *WTJ* 17 no. 2 (1982): 58–78.

Verhalen, Philippo A. *The Proclamation of the Word in the Writings of John Wesley*. Rome: Pontificia Universitas Gregoriana, 1969.

Vogel, John Richard. "Faith and the Image of God." Master's thesis, DePauw Univ., 1967.

Watson, Richard. *Theological Institutes*. 2 vols. New York: Mason and Lane, 1836, 1840; ed. John M'Clintock, New York: Carlton & Porter, 1850.

Wedgwood, Julia. *John Wesley and the Evangelical Reaction of the Eighteenth Century*. London: Macmillan, 1870.

Wesley, John. "A Scheme of Self-Examination Used by the First Methodists in Oxford." http://imarc.cc/one_meth/vol-01-no-12.html.

Yates, Arthur S. *The Doctrine of Assurance, with Special Reference to John Wesley*. London: Epworth, 1952.

Young, Frances. "The Significance of John Wesley's Conversion Experience." In *John Wesley: Contemporary Perspectives*. Edited by John Stacy, 37–46. London: Epworth, 1988.

PART 2

ECONOMIC
ETHICS

CHAPTER 2

Basic Evangelical Economic Ethics

Having discussed character building through communities of accountability as Wesley's major contribution to ethics, we now ask how that might impact accountability in the economic order.

Introduction to Evangelical Economic Ethics

The place where economic responsibility becomes most personal is in finances—how we gain and spend. Evangelical ethics is less interested in speculative theories of the economic order than in wisely using the resources we have been given and earned. We are given these resources by the Creator and are called to improve them through our imagination, reason, and effort. It is not a side issue on evangelical ethics to deliberate personally how we gain and spend temporal resources.

The focus on the person gaining and spending money is analogous to the practical spirit of part 1 on nurturing the community of faith. Wesley was less interested in theories of how the economy works than in nurturing the habits of the practice of stewardship of God's gifts of time and possessions. Wesley's gift as an ethics teacher of economic accountability was fixed on coaching good works out of inveterate sinners.

The Right Ordering of the Economic Life

As spiritual guide of the societies of the very ordinary people who were called Methodist, Wesley was called to deal with them where they were. Most were poor but were industrious and willing to learn the habits of responsible work and reasonable gaining and spending. His people were not in a university studying economic ethics. They were supporting their families by means of ordinary labor and according to commonsense rules of fairness.

Wesley had been asked to give them spiritual instruction for all aspects of their spiritual formation. This included guidance on down-to-earth economic responsibility, as revealed in reason, conscience, and Scripture. Each person in the small groups who met to order their lives according to Scripture had to decide how to supply their families with necessities and to use their limited resources wisely.

Among the most important of his economic teachings were his homilies on gaining, saving, and spending money. The three most important homilies were "The Use of Money," "The Danger of Riches," and "The Danger of Increasing Riches." They show that one who is faithful in little will be faithful in much, that riches tempt foolish desires, and that those who set their hearts on increasing riches will be driven by them. Add to these three his teaching homilies on self-denial and stewardship, and you have the heart of his economic ethic. The most celebrated of these sermons is on "The Use of Money."

A. The Use of Money

In the parable of the unjust steward, Jesus said, "The children of this world are in their generation wiser than the children of light. And I say unto you, Make to yourselves friends of the mammon of unrighteousness; that, when ye fail, they may receive you into everlasting habitations. He that is faithful in that which is least is faithful also in much: and he that is unjust in the least is unjust also in much" [Luke 16:8 – 10; Homily #50, "The Use of Money," B 2:266 – 80, J VI:124 – 35 (1760)]. The everlasting habitations are where genuine value lies. All that one can learn about being faithful in small things will contribute to being faithful in larger things.

1. Worldly and Godly Uses of Money

The poets of all ages have railed against money "as the grand corrupter of the world, the bane of virtue, the pest of human society."[1] Wesley did not rail against money; he viewed it as a training ground for eternity. Horace exhorted his countrymen to "throw all their money into the sea,"[2] without thinking of its providential purpose in human affairs. Wesley never would have said that. He was aware of Paul's caveat to Timothy that "'the love of money is the root of all evil,' but not the thing itself. The fault does not lie in the money, but in them that use it."[3] The training of the moral imagination and reasoning will develop character that uses money for sharing God's love through mercy and charitable acts for the needy. Evangelical ethics views money as an opportunity of grace to do good, to respond to God's gifts in a way fitting to their temporal and limited value.

Money is an economic feature of all societies that do not depend strictly on barter. Barter works without the convenience of money, hence under a burden of finding fitting conditions for the trade necessary to human sustenance and convenience. A money economy provides a rational means of exchanging goods and services. Jesus noted that the children of this world are considered wise in the ways of this world. They seek to use money shrewdly to advance their worldly values.[4] Christians have another value system that includes money but transcends it.

The children of light are those who see "the light of the glory of God in the face

---

[1] "The Use of Money," B 2:267 – 68, J VI:125 – 26, proem, sec. 2.
[2] Horace, *Odes* 3.24.49, LCL 33:257; "The Use of Money," B 2:267 – 68, J VI:125 – 26, proem, sec. 2.
[3] 1 Tim. 6:10; "The Use of Money," B 2:267 – 68, J VI:125 – 26, proem, sec. 2.
[4] See Luke 16:8 – 9.

of Jesus Christ."[5] Jesus calls his disciples to learn even from the ways of the world, so as to "use worldly wealth" for good. They are to use money fairly and wisely "so that when it is gone, you will be welcomed into eternal dwellings."[6]

When money is used only for self-gratification within the temporary values of this world alone, it is rightly called " 'the mammon of unrighteousness,' "[7] Those who "seek no other portion than this world," said Wesley, are in a sense " 'wiser' (not absolutely; for they are one and all the veriest fools, the most egregious madmen under heaven); but, 'in their generation,' in their own way; they are more consistent with themselves," truer to their acknowledged principles, and they "more steadily pursue their end than the children of light."[8] "In their generation" they are wise, but in relation to eternity they are foolish.

2. The Final Account

Jesus exhorted the people of God to be as wise as this worldly generation in the use of money, but for the purpose of the increase of faith, hope, and love. Make friends of wealth "by doing all possible good, particularly to the children of God; 'that, when ye fail,' — when ye return to dust, when ye have no more place under the sun — those of them who are gone before 'may receive you,' may welcome you, into the 'everlasting habitations.' "[9] The value of money is seen in relation to eternity.

Everyone must ultimately give an account not only of a monthly fiscal balance, but of a lifelong balance of accountability before the one who gives life.[10] Isn't it reasonable that the one who originally gives us all we have — our world, ourselves, our talents — has a right to call us to accountability for our use of those gifts? So each one is called to " 'give an account of your stewardship,' when ye 'can be no longer stewards.' "[11] In eternity money loses its value.

The right use of money is often discussed by men of the world but "not sufficiently considered by those whom God hath chosen out of the world." For Wesley, the use of money provided an opportunity to learn "an excellent branch of Christian wisdom" — namely, stewardship, care for others in need, and above all about God's providing believers with all things needful,[12] assuming they use their brains and brawn.

There is high moral importance in the right use of money and in the fitting practice "of this excellent talent" of prudence. Many have not learned how to employ prudence "to the greatest advantage"[13] — for the love of the neighbor. Wesley's purpose was to teach the people of faith how to use money wisely and fairly in a way that would find favor eternally.

---

[5] 2 Cor. 4:6; "The Use of Money," B 2:266, J VI:124, proem, sec. 1.
[6] Luke 16:9 NIV.
[7] The devouring god of acquisitive pride. "The Use of Money," B 2:266, J VI:124, proem, sec. 1.
[8] "The Use of Money," B 2:266, J VI:124, proem, sec. 1.
[9] Ibid.
[10] Ibid.
[11] Ibid.; cf. Luke 16:2.
[12] "The Use of Money," B 2:267 – 68, J VI:125 – 26, proem, sec. 2.
[13] Ibid.

3. The Prudent Use of Talents in a Fallen World

Money can be applied either to the best or worst uses. "It is of unspeakable service to all civilized nations, in all the common affairs of life: It is a most compendious instrument of transacting all manner of business, and (if we use it according to Christian wisdom) of doing all manner of good."[14] In the present fallen state of humanity, money is an excellent gift of God, which offers the opportunity of "answering the noblest ends."[15]

The church at Pentecost did not disavow money or throw it away, but used it in accord with God's will. If the community of faith today were like the church at Pentecost, it would be very different from its present state. In the earliest church in Jerusalem when all believers were "filled with the Holy Ghost ... 'no man counted anything he had his own.'"[16] This is not a demeaning of the value of property or honest labor or individual initiative or hard work. It is rather an act of proportional reasoning about using the resources God has given. The Spirit moved them to "bring the money to the apostles to give to those in need."[17] My winnings are not for me, but for the needy. At Pentecost the church was experiencing a new birth of Spirit, recognizing the new creation that springs from Jesus' death and resurrection and the coming of the Spirit.

Money in the hands of the children of light is a reasonable instrument for providing "food for the hungry, drink for the thirsty, [and] raiment for the naked," and for offering the stranger a place to lay his head. By right use of money, "we may supply the place of a husband to the widow, and of a father to the fatherless. We may be a defense for the oppressed, a means of health to the sick."[18]

Wesley summarized three simple guidelines on the right use of money. Anyone can easily understand them: "All the instructions which are necessary" for learning how to employ our talents "may be reduced to three plain rules":[19] gain all you can, save all you can, and give all you can.

4. Gain All You Can

There are moral limits on gain.

a. Observe the Limits to Gaining without Harm

Why is it our bounden duty to use our imagination and reason to gain what is necessary for life? "Here we may speak like the children of the world: We meet them on their own ground."[20] We have to be as good at using our talents as the shrewdest manager is in this world — only for the love of God and humanity. But there are limits to the right gaining of money.

---

[14]Ibid.
[15]Ibid.
[16]Ibid.
[17]Acts 4:35 NLT.
[18]"The Use of Money," B 2:267 – 68, J VI:125 – 26, proem, sec. 2.
[19]"The Use of Money," B 2:268, J VI:126, proem, sec. 3.
[20]"The Use of Money," B 2:268 – 69, J VI:126 – 27, sec. 1.1.

"We ought to gain all we can gain, without buying gold too dear, without paying more for it than it is worth." Do not waste. Do not overspend. Do not go into debt. Is it a duty to provide the necessities for your family and to pay your debts? Of course. Any levelheaded person can see that. But be reasonable. Do not make money foolishly at the risk of health: "We ought not to gain money at the expense of life [or] health,"[21] or bodily harm so "as to impair our constitution," such as working with arsenic or streams of melting lead. That only leads to poisoning the body God gives for your good, and for the neighbor's good. Nor should we continue in any business which "necessarily deprives us of proper seasons for food and sleep, in such a proportion as our nature requires."[22] Jesus taught, "Life is more valuable than meat and the body than raiment."[23]

We are also called to gain rightly all we can without hurting the spirit of a healthful mind.[24] Do not spend your valuable time in a way that risks depression or resentment. That makes no sense. These are simple limits based on good reasoning and moral prudence.

Do not gain illegally. Respect the laws of markets and fair trade. "We may not engage or continue in any sinful trade, any that is contrary to the law of God, or of our country."[25] Some employments virtually require cheating or lying or theft. Some require "conformity to some custom which is not consistent with a good conscience." So do not gain money at the cost of losing your soul.[26] Do not entangle yourself in any agreement or "company which would destroy your soul."[27] "Every man must judge for himself, and abstain from whatever he in particular finds to be hurtful to his soul."[28] The prudent person is not reasonably allowed to "do evil, that good may come."[29]

b. Gain without Hurting Our Neighbor Bodily or Spiritually

We are called to gain all we can "without hurting our neighbor." We cannot, if we love everyone as ourselves. We cannot hurt the next person we meet by not paying bills or requiring excess interest or engaging in illegal transactions or unfairly taking his land or house. For example, in fair trade "we cannot, consistent with brotherly love, sell our goods below the market price; we cannot study to ruin our neighbor's trade in order to advance our own."[30]

First, we are not to gain "by hurting our neighbor in his body. Therefore we may not sell anything which tends to impair health."[31] Spirituous liquors "may have

---

[21] Ibid.
[22] Ibid.
[23] Ibid.; cf. Luke 12:23.
[24] "The Use of Money," B 2:269–70, J VI:127–28, sec. 1.2.
[25] Ibid.
[26] Ibid.
[27] Ibid.
[28] Ibid.
[29] Rom. 3:8; "The Use of Money," B 2:270–71, J VI:128, sec. 1.3.
[30] "The Use of Money," B 2:270–71, J VI:128, sec. 1.3.
[31] "The Use of Money," B 2:271–72, J VI:128–29, sec. 1.4.

a place in medicine." But they can cause harm. Therefore only those who prepare and sell them for medical purposes may keep their conscience clear.[32] "But all who sell them in the common way, to any that will buy, are poisoners"[33] because of the likely harm done to the body. Wesley was convinced that alcoholic addictions had consequences to the third generation.

The body is God's gift. So equally corrupt are certain "surgeons, apothecaries, or physicians who play with the lives or health of men to enlarge their own gain," sometimes lengthening the pain, protracting "the cure of their patient's body in order to plunder his substance.... This is dear-bought gain."[34]

Second, and more profoundly, we are not to gain in any way that might hurt the neighbor's soul, for example, by drawing another into temptation, unchastity, or deceit. Wesley questions the moral ambiguity of those who gain from "taverns, victualling-houses, opera-houses, play-houses, or any other places of public, fashionable diversion. If these profit the souls of men, you are clear; your employment is good, and your gain innocent; but if they are either sinful in themselves or natural inlets to sin of various kinds, then, it is to be feared, you have a sad account to make."[35]

c. In Gaining Use Commonsense Business Practices

Wesley strongly commended hard work, good business practices, on-time discipline, and rigorous responsibility in handling money. "Gain all you can by honest industry. Use all possible diligence in your calling. Lose no time. If you understand yourself and your relation to God and man, you know you have none to spare. If you understand your particular calling as you ought, you will have no time that hangs upon your hands."[36]

So "whatsoever thy hand findeth to do, do it with thy might.... Do it as soon as possible: No delay! No putting off from day to day, or from hour to hour! Never leave anything till tomorrow which you can do today. And do it as well as possible. Do not sleep or yawn over it: Put your whole strength to the work. Spare no pains. Let nothing be done by halves, or in a slight and careless manner. Let nothing in your business be left undone if it can be done by labor or patience."[37]

Using diligent and fair business practices, believers should expect to compete well with those who do neglect these practices. Apply "in your business all the understanding which God has given you."[38] "You should be continually learning, from the experience of others or from your own experience, reading, and reflection, to do everything you have to do better today than you did yesterday.... Make the best of all that is in your hands."[39]

---

[32]Ibid.
[33]Ibid.
[34]"The Use of Money," B 2:272, J VI:129, sec. 1.5.
[35]"The Use of Money," B 2:272, J VI:129–30, sec. 1.6.
[36]"The Use of Money," B 2:272–73, J VI:130, sec. 1.7; cf. Eccl. 9:10.
[37]Ibid.
[38]"The Use of Money," B 2:273, J VI:130, sec. 1.8.
[39]Ibid.

It is proper to fear being unjust to your creditors. But that fear may become exaggerated into an excuse for lack of charity.[40] So systematically reduce your debts and pay your bills on time. Keep accurate and fair records. "Every man, whether engaged in trade or not, ought to know whether his substance lessens or increases."[41] If you have lost track of your borrowings or do not know whether you can pay your bills, you have not been a faithful steward of what God has enabled you to earn.

5. Save All You Can

The second simple maxim on the use of money: Having fairly gained all you can "by honest wisdom and unwearied diligence, save all you can.... Do not throw the precious talent into the sea."[42] Ordinarily providence endows us with sufficient resources of intelligence and imagination to take care of the necessities of a family. But you should "expend no part of it merely to gratify the desire of the flesh, the desire of the eye, or the pride of life."[43] To save well, avoid these three forms of idolatry.[44]

First, avoid temptations to satisfy the desires of the flesh. "Do not waste any part of so precious a talent merely in gratifying the desires of the flesh; in procuring the pleasures of sense." Do not become trapped in an "elegant epicurism." Rather, "be content with what plain nature requires."[45]

Second, "do not waste any part of so precious a talent merely in gratifying the desire of the eye."[46] "Do you really need opulent apparel, needless ornaments, and expensive furniture, costly pictures, painting, and gilding?"[47]

Third, "lay out nothing to gratify the pride of life, to gain the admiration or praise of men."[48] Stay away from vain imaginations that seek esteem or approval.[49] "Do not buy their applause so dear. Rather, be content with the honor that cometh from God."[50] Wesley commended the wise instructions of Psalm 49:16 – 19 (NIV):

> Do not be overawed when others grow rich,
> when the splendor of their houses increases;
> for they will take nothing with them when they die,
> their splendor will not descend with them.
> Though while they live they count themselves blessed —
> and people praise you when you prosper —
> they will join those who have gone before them,
> who will never again see the light of life.[51]

---

[40]"The Danger of Increasing Riches," B 4:179, J III:356, sec. 1.2.
[41]"The Danger of Increasing Riches," B 4:180, J III:357, sec. 1.4.
[42]"The Use of Money," B 2:273 – 74, J VI:130 – 31, sec. 2.1.
[43]Ibid.
[44]In all three homilies on "The Use of Money," "The Danger of Riches," and "The Danger of Increasing Riches," Wesley worked out of the three forms of unhappy affections found in 1 John 2:16.
[45]"The Use of Money," B 2:274, J VI:131, sec. 2.2.
[46]"The Use of Money," B 2:274, J VI:131, sec. 2.3.
[47]Ibid.
[48]"The Use of Money," B 2:274 – 75, J VI:131, sec. 2.4.
[49]Ibid.
[50]Ibid.
[51]Ibid.

Insofar as you avoid gratification of the desire of the flesh, the desire of the eye, and the pride of life, sufficient grace will supply your needs and comfort. "Daily experience shows, the more they are indulged, they increase the more. Whenever, therefore, you expend anything to please your taste or other senses," it is like paying a fee for sensuality. "When you lay out money to please your eye, you give so much for an increase of curiosity — for a stronger attachment to these pleasures which perish in the using."[52] When you are purchasing anything to win the applause of people, you are purchasing more vanity. Haven't you had enough of "vanity, sensuality, curiosity"? You do not need to pay those added taxes.[53] Spare yourself the trouble they cause.

a. Caveats on Leaving an Estate for Children

Wesley's rule on making a will: "Give each what would keep him above want, and ... bestow all the rest in such a manner as ... would be most for the glory of God."[54]

Suppose "all your children were equally ignorant of the true use of money?"[55] "Why should you throw away money upon your children, any more than upon yourself, in delicate food, in gay or costly apparel, in superfluities of any kind? Why should you purchase for them more pride or lust, more vanity, or foolish and hurtful desires?"[56] Enough already! "Nature has made ample provision for them" by giving them reason and conscience and imagination.[57] "Do not leave it to them to throw away. If you have good reason to believe that they would waste what is now in your possession in gratifying and thereby increasing the desire of the flesh, the desire of the eyes, or the pride of life at the peril of theirs and your own soul, do not set these traps in their way."[58]

"How amazing then is the infatuation of those parents who think they can never leave their children enough! What! Cannot you leave them enough of arrows ... [and of] foolish and hurtful desires? Not enough of pride, lust, ambition, and vanity?"[59] Better on your last day to have a zero balance with an eye to those in need.

On the other hand, some individual discernment is required. Wesley said, "If I had one child, elder or younger, who knew the value of money; one who I believed, would put it to the true use, I should think it my absolute, indispensable duty to leave that child the bulk of my fortune, and to the rest just so much as would enable them to live in the manner they had been accustomed to."[60] In giving away money to irresponsible people, you share in their irresponsibility.

---

[52]"The Use of Money," B 2:275, J VI:131 – 32, sec. 2.5.
[53]Ibid.
[54]"The Use of Money," B 2:276, J VI:132 – 33, sec. 2.8.
[55]"The Use of Money," B 2:275 – 76, J VI:132, sec. 2.7.
[56]Ibid.
[57]"The Use of Money," B 2:275, J VI:132, sec. 2.6.
[58]"The Use of Money," B 2:275 – 76, J VI:132, sec. 2.7.
[59]Ibid.
[60]Ibid.

6. Give All You Can

a. Gaining and Saving to Good Purpose

The last simple rule of the use of money: If you have done well in fairly making and saving money, it is imperative that you add this third rule to the two preceding: "Having, first, gained all you can, and, secondly, [having] saved all you can, then 'give all you can.'"[61] If you are a good steward of what has been given to you, give back unselfishly.

Do not imagine that you have done well with your talents if you merely gain all you can and save all you can. That is what misers do. They will have a hard time entering the narrow gate that leads toward eternal life. It will be as small as the eye of a needle.

To gain and to save are not ends in themselves but are for a good purpose — that you may give all the more for God's glory and human need.[62] You have not properly saved anything if you are only laying it up.[63]

Consider your resources in relation to your human purpose. Put the purpose of money in its proper context: "When the Possessor of heaven and earth brought you into being, and placed you in this world, he placed you here not as a proprietor, but as a steward. As such, he entrusted you, for a season, with goods of various kinds; but the sole property of these still rests in him, nor can it be alienated from him."[64] You yourself are not your own, but his. If so, all you imagine you own is actually God's gift. "Such is your soul and your body, not your own, but God's. And so is your substance in particular."[65]

b. Giving the Surplus after Necessities and Basic Conveniences

Jesus "has told you, in the most clear and express terms, how you are to employ it for him."[66] Here is the scriptural rule of giving in plain terms: If you are to be a good steward, provide first for your family and yourself sufficiently to preserve the body in health and strength. If you have a surplus, "do good to them that are of the household of faith," and if more, "as you have opportunity, do good unto all men."[67] Galatians 6:10 provides the rule for the order of giving: "Therefore, as we have opportunity, let us do good to all people, especially to those who belong to the family of believers" (NIV).

Provide for your household. All you do for the benefit of others is "really given to God. You 'render unto God the things that are God's,' not only by what you give to the poor, but also by that which you expend in providing things needful for yourself and your household."[68]

---

[61]"The Use of Money," B 2:276–77, J VI:133, sec. 3.1.
[62]Ibid.
[63]Ibid.
[64]"The Use of Money," B 2:277, J VI:133, sec. 3.2.
[65]Ibid.
[66]Ibid.
[67]"The Use of Money," B 2:277, J VI:133–34, sec. 3.3; cf. Gal. 6:10.
[68]"The Use of Money," B 2:277, J VI:133–34, sec. 3.3; cf. Matt. 22:21.

In giving, ask in prayer, "In expending this, am I acting according to my character? Am I acting herein, not as a proprietor, but as a steward of my Lord's goods? Am I doing this in obedience to his Word? In what Scripture does he require me so to do? Can I offer up this action, this expense, as a sacrifice to God through Jesus Christ? Have I reason to believe that for this very work I shall have a reward at the resurrection of the just?"[69] This is the divine economy: in giving temporally you are benefiting eternally.

With these guidelines you will seldom need anything more to remove any doubt. In this way you will receive clear light as to what to do.[70] "If your conscience bears you witness in the Holy Ghost that this prayer is well-pleasing to God, then have you no reason to doubt but that expense is right and good, and such as will never make you ashamed."[71]

c. Summing Up

This is how to "put to use that great talent, money." In sum: "Gain all you can, without hurting either yourself or your neighbor, in soul or body.... Save all you can, by cutting off every expense which serves only to indulge foolish desire; to gratify either the desire of flesh, the desire of the eye, or the pride of life.... Then, give all you can, or, in other words, give all you have to God."[72]

This is how to "use worldly wealth to gain friends for yourselves, so that when it is gone, you will be welcomed into eternal dwellings."[73] "Give all you have, as well as all you are as a spiritual sacrifice to him who withheld not from you his Son," and so you are "laying up in store for yourselves a good foundation against the time to come, that ye may attain eternal life!"[74]

7. Giving an Account to God of Money Management

a. Let the People of God Use Money according to God's Purpose

Some may be puzzled by the text for the homily on the use of money. It is found in Jesus' remarks after his telling of the parable of the shrewd manager, in which he taught about managing money in a way accountable to God and of eternal value. Wesley did not focus on the parable itself, but on the teaching that followed the parable:

> "The master commended the dishonest manager because he had acted shrewdly. For the people of this world are more shrewd in dealing with their own kind than are the people of the light. I tell you, use worldly wealth to gain friends for yourselves, so that when it is gone, you will be welcomed into eternal dwell-

---

[69]"The Use of Money," B 2:278, J VI:134, sec. 3.4.
[70]Ibid.
[71]"The Use of Money," B 2:278, J VI:134, sec. 3.5.
[72]"The Use of Money," B 2:278–79, J VI:135, sec. 3.6.
[73]Luke 16:9 NIV; "The Use of Money," B 2:278–79, J VI:135, sec. 3.6.
[74]"The Use of Money," B 2:279–80, J VI:135–36, sec. 3.7; cf. 1 Tim. 6:19.

ings. Whoever can be trusted with very little can also be trusted with much, and whoever is dishonest with very little will also be dishonest with much. So if you have not been trustworthy in handling worldly wealth, who will trust you with true riches? And if you have not been trustworthy with someone else's property, who will give you property of your own?"[75]

Why did the master commend the shrewd manager? Because he had acted cleverly and in a sense wisely in relation to the master's purpose. The people of the light must learn to use their resources wisely according to the Master's plan. Wisely means in relation to eternity. That plan does not focus on financial wealth in time but spiritual wealth in eternity.

The steward had used ironic and clever judgment to prepare for a future time. The future in mind is eternity. The master is the Lord. The money is symbolic of all human talents. The story is about a relation between a master and a servant entrusted with resources. All humans are entrusted with gifts to be used according to the master's plan. The imperative is this: Use the resources you have been given not only for present times shaped by the conditions of the world, but in a way fitting for eternity.

b. Be as Smart as the Smartest in the Fallen World

Jesus added this ironic comment: "The children of this world are in their generation wiser than the children of light."[76] They are wise in the ways of the world but often not in the ways of God. This assumes a basic difference between those who live in a covenant community oriented toward eternal light and those who are oriented toward this world alone, which is clouded by corruption and disappearing in time. The generation that is living toward this world is shrewdly fixed on worldly values. The generation living toward eternity is a new and highly creative community that is called to be astute in service to the neighbor in preparation for the real eternal future.

What is so "wise" about the shrewd worldly money manager? He was shrewd in dealing with "his own generation," the fallen order of the worldly economy. Jesus calls us to be just as clever within the new generation of the coming kingdom as the shrewd money manager, but for good ends. In this fallen world, quick-witted people know how to use resources for their own purposes. Jesus calls us to be equally quick-witted in using resources for the emerging reign of God. He wants us to be just as smart as the smartest in the fallen world, but on behalf of faith, hope, and love. That means using every setback to stimulate creative management of the resources of the kingdom, focusing on the essentials. So when this worldly economic order fails, we will then be ready for our eternal dwelling.

---

[75]Luke 16:8–12 NIV.
[76]Luke 16:8.

B. The Danger of Riches

We are pursuing Wesley's key writings on human economies in relation to the divine economy. The previous homily on "The Use of Money" (1760) was followed some years later by two more homilies that warn further of dangers in acquisition: "The Danger of Riches" (1781) and "The Danger of Increasing Riches" (1790).

1. Riches Tempt Foolish Desires

a. The Snare

Paul warned Timothy, "They that will be rich fall into temptation and a snare, and into many foolish and hurtful lusts, which drown men in destruction and perdition" [1 Tim. 6:9; Homily #87, "The Danger of Riches," B 3:227–46, J III:1–15 (January–February 1781)]. Wesley thought that ignoring this advice had resulted in the consequences of great suffering in human history. When people resist the temptation to riches that elicit foolish and destructive desires, the human condition is much happier. "How innumerable are the ill consequences which have followed from men's not knowing, or not considering, this great truth!"[77]

Riches are a trap that many fall into and by which many are destroyed. Riches appear so attractive, dazzling the eyes. Yet they elicit hurtful inward desires that lead to destroyed lives both in this world and in eternity. Regrettably very few resist these temptations. Even fewer take seriously Paul's warning so as to "lay it to heart."[78] Some who have been so solemnly warned may quickly forget. And others who study this text may put a spin on it to make it seem of little consequence.[79] But its consequences last from generation to generation. Wesley warned his hearers that hearing this warning may be the last opportunity. At any time we may be called to account.

b. The Deadly Neglect of the Warning

The instruction cannot be reduced to a mild warning about "gaining riches unjustly." It is far more about temptation to idolatry, to making a god out of money and what money can buy. This idolatry tends to lead toward unhappy desires, voluntarily chosen, that can dominate a life and ultimately lead to destruction of body and soul.[80]

When Wesley warned against the love of the world, he did not intend to demean what is good and beautiful in the world. Rather, he pleaded that we not set our affections on passing things in God's world to the neglect of the good of the soul. He called each person to "deal faithfully with his own soul."[81]

This is an "unfashionable truth" seldom preached from our pulpits: "I do not remember that in threescore years I have heard one sermon preached upon this subject," Wesley said.[82] Writing in 1791, he could find no author or book that "treats

---

[77]"The Danger of Riches," B 3:228, J III:1, proem, sec. 1.
[78]Ibid.
[79]Ibid.
[80]"The Danger of Riches," B 3:228–29, J III:1, proem, sec. 2.
[81]"The Danger of Increasing Riches," B 4:182–83, J III:359, sec. 1.10; cf. 1 John 2:16.
[82]"The Danger of Riches," B 3:229, J III:2, proem, sec. 3.

of it professionally." He recalled in his ninth discourse on the Sermon on the Mount (1748),[83] that he had dealt briefly with "the 'Mammon of unrighteousness,' but I have never yet either published or preached any sermon expressly upon the subject."[84] So, he said, "It is high time I should — that I should at length speak as strongly and explicitly as I can, in order to leave a full and clear testimony behind me, whenever it pleases God to call me hence."[85]

Wesley was under strong conviction on this matter: "O that God would give me to speak right and forcible words."[86] He felt the power of divine judgment reflected in Ezekiel 33:31 – 32: "My people come to you, as they usually do, and sit before you to hear your words, but they do not put them into practice. Their mouths speak of love, but their hearts are greedy for unjust gain. Indeed, to them you are nothing more than one who sings love songs with a beautiful voice and plays an instrument well, for they hear your words but do not put them into practice" (NIV).

In this homily, Wesley longed to bring hearers toward actually changing their behavior, not simply listening passively. He reminded his hearers of the promise of the apostle James: "Whoever looks intently into the perfect law that gives freedom, and continues in it — not forgetting what they have heard, but doing it — they will be blessed in what they do."[87]

2. The Desire to Be Rich

a. Provisions beyond Food and Covering

Wesley defines rich as " 'having food and raiment' (literally 'coverings,' for the word includes lodging as well as clothes),"[88] If we only have basic food, lodging, and clothing, we have sufficient reason to be content. Many in the world would rejoice with tears of gratitude to have only the basics. But we are not content. Those who have all these things want more. And more of more. They want it all. Their imagination goes wild about how they might have all that their eyes see. This longing to be rich is a matter of willing, and willing is voluntary, a free act for which the doer is responsible.

b. Beyond Life's Necessities and Conveniences

By "desiring riches," Wesley said the apostle meant "whatever is above the plain necessaries, or at most conveniences, of life. Whoever has sufficient food to eat, and raiment to put on, with a place where to lay his head, and something over, is rich."[89] Those who long to be rich desire more food, housing, and clothing "than the plain necessaries and conveniences of life."[90]

---

[83]Cf. Matt. 6:19 – 23.
[84]"The Danger of Riches," B 3:229, J III:2, proem, sec. 3.
[85]Ibid.
[86]"The Danger of Riches," B 3:230, J III:2, proem, sec. 4.
[87]James 1:25 NIV; "The Danger of Riches," B 3:230, J III:2, proem, sec. 4.
[88]"The Danger of Riches," B 3:230, J III:3, sec. 1.1.
[89]Ibid.
[90]Ibid.

This desire is a willed behavior that becomes habituated into a driving passion. All who "allow in themselves this desire, who see no harm in it, desire to be rich."[91] They are responsible for what they choose. They set their minds on procuring more and more and ever more than the simple necessities and conveniences of life. "All those that calmly, deliberately, and of set purpose endeavor after more than food and coverings" than is just and reasonable prove their desire to be rich by their intentional behaviors.[92] The definition of richness may vary from culture to culture, but in any culture it comes down to a distinction between necessity and superfluity.

c. The Legitimacy of Just Gain for Life's Necessities and Conveniences

Parents of children have a duty to provide basic provisions of food and covering for themselves and their little ones. This is not what is meant by "laying up treasures on earth." Earning and saving are not culpable but required. What is culpable is not to use the God-given resources of intellect and imagination to earn and save.

Scripture makes the following four allowances for justly accumulating necessary resources:

- for the protection of the household
- for carrying out plans, means, and efforts to provide for the family
- for modest bequests after death for their children that will "supply them with necessaries and conveniences after we have left the world"[93]
- for paying our debts so that we "owe no man anything"[94]

But to lay up more than the "plain necessities and conveniences of life" is to draw the soul into temptation to love too much the things of this world. When "deliberately done, it is a clear proof of our desiring to be rich. And thus to lay up money is no more consistent with good conscience than to throw it into the sea."[95]

Everything we can potentially own is the work of God's hands. God is originally, properly, and finally "the possessor of heaven and earth."[96] Think of it as God's "unalienable right" to reclaim what divine providence has lodged in our hands. The giver of life is analogous to the rightful proprietor of all. The recipients are temporary stewards of creation's wealth. Those who lay up more than necessary are like unfaithful stewards who reserve to themselves redundant resources.[97] "Over and above" these necessities and reasonable conveniences, "we are guilty of burying our Lord's talent in the earth, and on that account are liable" as unprofitable servants.[98]

---

[91]"The Danger of Riches," B 3:230–31, J III:3, sec. 1.2.
[92]"The Danger of Riches," B 3:231, J III:3, sec. 1.3.
[93]"The Danger of Riches," B 3:231, J III:3, sec. 1.4.
[94]Ibid.
[95]Ibid. This does not rule out savings for old age that fall within the "plain necessities and conveniences of life" premise.
[96]"The Danger of Riches," B 3:231–32, J III:4, sec. 1.5.
[97]Ibid.
[98]Ibid.; cf. Matt. 25:24–30.

d. The Foolish Lovers of Money

The "lovers of money"[99] in the biblical sense are "those that delight in money; those that take pleasure in it; those that seek their happiness therein."[100] Money is useful for trade, but "money of itself" brings temptation. "Money of itself does not seem to gratify any natural desire or appetite of the human mind." "Money of itself" is "a vice not natural to man."[101] Love of money is a species of covetousness. It leads to idolatry, to hoarding for oneself the resources God gives to all.

There is a demonic dimension to taking pleasure in money so that we love money more than the resources it buys. It is true that "gaining necessities, under proper restrictions, is innocent; nay, commendable. But when it exceeds the bounds (and how difficult is it not to exceed them!), then it comes under the present censure."[102] "Under proper restrictions" refers to the four points noted above.

Jesus plainly taught on the Mount: "Do not store up for yourselves treasures on earth, where moths and vermin destroy, and where thieves break in and steal."[103] Anyone can test by experience whether he is storing up treasures on earth. Here the maxim of the Lord in John 7:17 applies: "Anyone who chooses to do the will of God will find out whether my teaching comes from God."[104] Those "taught of God" will understand this temptation. Those who are already bound to money's endless temptations will not understand the trap toward which they are moving. "So utterly blind is our natural understanding touching the truth of God!"[105]

"The richest of men are, in general, the most discontented, the most miserable. Had not the far greater part of them more content when they had less? ... In seeking happiness from riches, you are only striving to drink out of empty cups."[106] "There is no necessity for this: it is your own voluntary act and deed." You have decided to hunger for riches, which have "wounded you in the tenderest part, by slackening, if not utterly destroying, your 'hunger and thirst after righteousness.'"[107]

3. The Desires of the Flesh and Eyes and the Pride of Life

a. Falling into Foolish and Hurtful Desires

When it comes to money, falling into temptation is subtle and deep. People "fall plumb down into it. The waves of it compass them about, and cover them all over." They "enter into" a dazzling new space. As in drowning, few escape.[108]

Foolish desire is a form of human fallenness. Money becomes itself a snare to the happiness it promises. The Greek word for "snare" "properly means a gin, a steel

[99]2 Tim. 3:2 NIV.
[100]2 Tim. 3:2; "The Danger of Riches," B 3:232, J III:4, sec. 1.6.
[101]"The Danger of Riches," B 3:232, J III:4, sec. 1.6.
[102]"The Danger of Riches," B 3:232 – 33, J III:4 – 5, sec. 1.7.
[103]Matt. 6:19 NIV.
[104]"The Danger of Riches," B 3:233, J III:5, sec. 1.8; cf. John 7:17 NIV.
[105]"The Danger of Riches," B 3:233, J III:5, sec. 1.8.
[106]"The Danger of Riches," B 3:240, J III:10 – 11, sec. 2.10.
[107]"The Danger of Riches," B 3:241, J III:11, sec. 2.11.
[108]"The Danger of Riches," B 3:233, J III:5, sec. 1.9.

trap, which shows no appearance of danger. But as soon as any creature touches the spring, it suddenly closes."[109] The trapper is the ancient demonic tempter of our best human aspirations.

Into what trap do those who seek after riches fall? "Into many foolish and hurtful desires," which are as contrary to reason as they are to religion.[110] They are hurtful because they drain the energies of the soul. These desires are destructive of faith, hope, and love.[111] Their root cause is "the desiring happiness out of God,"[112] as if a happiness without God could be true happiness. They love the creature more than the Creator. "The desire of riches naturally tends both to beget and to increase."[113]

b. Naming the Three Chief Types of Foolish and Hurtful Desires

How do we name the categories or branches of those desires that are so vicious that they end in destruction? The apostle John has clearly named them for us. Both in this homily and the succeeding one on "The Danger of Increasing Riches," Wesley turned to the instruction of 1 John 2:15 – 17: "Do not love the world or anything in the world. If anyone loves the world, love for the Father is not in them. For everything in the world — the lust of the flesh, the lust of the eyes, and the pride of life — comes not from the Father but from the world. The world and its desires pass away, but whoever does the will of God lives forever" (NIV).

All unholy desires are included under that general name "the world." To seek happiness in the things of the world is to inordinately love the worldly above God. Excessive love of the world's things "divides into three branches, 'the desire of the flesh, the desire of the eyes, and the pride of life.'"[114]

c. The Desire of the Flesh

The first branch of the inordinate love of the world is "the desire of the flesh," which means "the seeking of happiness in the things that gratify the senses" in a way that ignores the neighbor's suffering.[115] The "desire of the flesh" does not refer to one of the senses only "but takes in all the pleasures of sense, the gratification of any of the outward senses."[116] The inordinate desire of any creaturely object can become an idolatry that increases unhappiness.

The phrase refers not just to intemperance and gluttony, but more profoundly it refers to living "in a genteel, regular sensuality; in an elegant epicurism, which does not hurt the body but only destroys the soul."[117]

---

[109]"The Danger of Riches," B 3:233 – 34, J III:5, sec. 1.10.
[110]"The Danger of Riches," B 3:234, J III:6, sec. 1.11.
[111]Ibid.
[112]"The Danger of Riches," B 3:234, J III:6, sec. 1.12.
[113]Ibid.
[114]"The Danger of Increasing Riches," B 4:182 – 83, J III:359, sec. 1.10; cf. 1 John 2:16. Since section 1.12 of "The Danger of Riches" and section 1.10 of "The Danger of Increasing Riches" deal with the interpretation of this passage, I have conflated these two discussions to decrease repetition.
[115]"The Danger of Increasing Riches," B 4:182 – 83, J III:359, sec. 1.10.
[116]"The Danger of Riches," B 3:234 – 35, J III:6, sec. 1.13.
[117]Ibid.

d. The Desire of the Eyes

The second branch of the inordinate love of the world is "the desire of the eyes." " 'The desire of the eyes,' in its natural sense, is the desiring and seeking happiness in gratifying the imagination."[118] "Experience shows that the imagination is gratified chiefly by means of the eye."[119]

The three common ways[120] imagination is gratified by the desire of the eyes are grandeur, beauty, and novelty. Chief among these temptations is novelty, the worship of the new, since it intensifies the desire for grandeur and beauty. It is especially viral to the human imagination and can strike at any moment. The demonic desire for novelty can attach itself to anything, especially things that are either grand or beautiful. The desire for novelty can even be attached to that which is petty or ugly. Unattractive things can supply the ravenous hunger for novelty.[121]

However magnificent or attractive, those things once desired tend to grow old. They offend the hunger for novelty. They become boring. This is a numbing form of unhappiness.[122]

The desire of the eyes for novelty expresses itself in academia in the form of seeking happiness in learning, especially when learning is focused on the latest thing.[123] The intellectual search for novelty is found abundantly in "history, languages, poetry, or any branch of natural or experimental philosophy."[124] Fashionable clothing provides examples of that kind of boredom that follows the desire for novelty wherein the smallest trifles are pleasing as long as they are new.[125]

e. The Pride of Life

Third, "the pride of life" is the desire for "honor, of the esteem, admiration, and applause of men." Since riches attract much admiration, they stimulate the pride of life.[126] "Riches first beget and then increase" the "desire of ease,"[127] moving the arena of desire toward avoiding every discomfort or inconvenience. The pride of life consumes people with a desire to sleep away God-given life. They dream of going to heaven "on a feather-bed." It makes people "more and more soft and delicate; more unwilling, and indeed more unable, to 'take up their cross daily.' "[128]

---

[118] "The Danger of Riches," B 3:235, J III:6, sec. 1.14.
[119] Ibid.
[120] "The Danger of Increasing Riches," B 4:183, J III:359–60, sec. 10. Note that the remaining section references are variously numbered in different editions, some using the section numeral only, others using the part number in Roman numerals plus the section number. I am here following section numbering of the Bicentennial edition.
[121] "The Danger of Riches," B 3:235, J III:6, sec. 1.14.
[122] Ibid.
[123] "The Danger of Riches," B 3:235, J III:6–7, sec. 1.15.
[124] Ibid. Cf. my analysis of boredom in Thomas C. Oden, *The Structure of Awareness* (Nashville: Abingdon, 1968).
[125] "The Danger of Increasing Riches," B 4:183, J III:359–60, sec. 11.
[126] "The Danger of Riches," B 3:235, J III:7, sec. 1.16.
[127] "The Danger of Riches," B 3:235, J III:7, sec. 1.17.
[128] Ibid.

f. Unholy Desires

Every ungodly passion or temper is a consequence of unholy desires. These desires easily flow into "pride, anger, bitterness, envy, malice, revengefulness; to a headstrong, unadvisable, unreprovable spirit."[129] Desires shape behavior whether the object is possessed or not. The desire for riches in its turn intensifies these "foolish and hurtful desires; and by affording the means of gratifying them all, naturally tend[s] to increase [them]."[130]

People with unholy desires, though seeking happiness, actually diminish their capacity for happiness. However attractive, unholy desires lead to sorrow, because the world's things cannot satisfy. "In the same proportion as they prevail, they 'pierce men through with many sorrows.'"[131] Desires becomes addictive.

The idolatry on which unholy desires are based causes conscience to revolt in guilt. Sorrows flow from all the evil tempers they inspire or increase.[132] They are willed behavior even when they have hardened into being compulsive. "Every unholy desire is an uneasy desire,"[133] since it intensifies the very conditions that cause misery.

When one unholy desire clashes with another, the soul is torn, eliciting ambivalence and guilt. There is a drowning metaphor in the text: these desires "drown men in destruction."[134] They may end in engulfing body and soul in pain, disease, and destruction.

Those who might retort that "they can afford the expense" do well to ask themselves: Who gave you these resources, both your own talents and the goods of nature? You do better to see them more as a loan than a possession.[135] Ask "Who lodged it for a time in your hands as his stewards; informing you at the same time for what purposes he entrusted you with it?... Can you afford to waste your Lord's goods?"[136] Don't you know that "God entrusted you with that money (all above what buys necessaries for your families) to feed the hungry, to clothe the naked, to help the stranger, the widow, the fatherless.... How dare you defraud your Lord by applying it to any other purpose?"[137]

g. Wesley's Fervent Appeal

At age seventy-eight Wesley was feeling responsible for not sufficiently teaching his spiritual connection about the destructive dangers to the soul of yearning for riches. He called those who had ears to hear to listen as if their lives depended on it: "They that will be rich fall into temptation and a snare, and into many foolish and hurtful desires, which drown men in destruction and perdition."[138] "O that God

---

[129]"The Danger of Riches," B 3:236, J III:7, sec. 1.18.
[130]Ibid.
[131]"The Danger of Riches," B 3:236, J III:7, sec. 1.19.
[132]Ibid.
[133]Ibid.
[134]1 Tim. 6:9.
[135]"The Danger of Increasing Riches," B 4:183 – 84, J III:360, sec. 12.
[136]Ibid.
[137]Ibid.
[138]1 Tim. 6:9 KJV; "The Danger of Riches," B 3:236, J III:8, sec. 2.1.

would give me the thing which I long for! that, before I go hence and am no more seen, I may see a people wholly devoted to God ... a people truly given up to God, in body, soul, and substance!"[139]

Wesley pleaded for sober self-examination. Each believer must ask: Do I desire to be rich, to have more food than necessary, to have excess in clothing and furnishings? "Who of you desires to have more than the plain necessaries and conveniences of life? Stop! Consider! What are you doing? Evil is before you! Will you rush upon the point of a sword? By the grace of God, turn and live!"[140] Why do you keep on adding "house to house, and field to field"?[141] Be warned that God may at any time say to you what he said to the rich man who tore down his barns after a great harvest and built bigger ones: "'You fool! This very night your life will be demanded from you. Then who will get what you have prepared for yourself?' This is how it will be with whoever stores up things for themselves but is not rich toward God."[142]

Using intelligence, it is possible to gain fairly the basic necessities and ordinary conveniences without putting oneself under the tyranny of "desiring to be rich."[143] "You may gain all you can without hurting either your soul or body; you may save all you can by carefully avoiding every needless expense, and yet never lay up treasures on earth, nor either desire or endeavor so to do."[144] "Having gained, in a right sense, all you can, and saved all you can; in spite of nature, and custom, and worldly prudence, give all you can."[145]

Wesley reminded his connection of spiritual formation of his own lifelong habit, which most who followed him already knew: "I save all I can, not willingly wasting anything, not a sheet of paper, not a cup of water. I do not lay out anything, not a shilling, unless as a sacrifice to God. Yet by giving all I can, I am effectually secured from 'laying up treasures upon earth.'"[146] Wesley went further to offer a personal account of his own choices: "Two-and-forty years ago, having a desire to furnish poor people with cheaper, shorter, and plainer books than any I had seen, I wrote many small tracts, generally a penny a-piece; and afterwards several larger. Some of these had such a sale as I never thought of; and, by this means, I unawares became rich. But I never desired or endeavored after it. And now that it is come upon me unawares, I lay up no treasures upon earth: I lay up nothing at all.... I cannot help leaving my books behind me whenever God calls me hence; but, in every other respect, my own hands will be my executors."[147] Wesley sought a zero balance at the end of every year and at the end of life.

---

[139]Ibid.

[140]"The Danger of Riches," B 3:236, J III:8, sec. 2.2.

[141]Cf. Isa. 5:8.

[142]Luke 12:20–21 NIV; "The Danger of Riches," B 3:237, J III:8, sec. 2.4.

[143]"The Danger of Riches," B 3:237, J III:8–9, sec. 2.5.

[144]Ibid.

[145]"The Danger of Riches," B 3:239, J III:9–10, sec. 2.8.

[146]"The Danger of Riches," B 3:237–38, J III:9, sec. 2.6.

[147]"The Danger of Riches," B 3:238–39, J III:9, sec. 2.7.

h. Provide for Your Household and Give to the Poor

Those who desire to be faithful and wise stewards will provide needed things for their families for whom they are directly responsible. The rule: "If, when this is done, there be an overplus left, then do good to 'them that are of the household of faith.' If there be an overplus still, 'as you have opportunity, do good unto all men.'... You render unto God the things that are God's, not only by what you give to the poor, but also by that which you expend in providing things needful for yourself and your household."[148]

By this time, Wesley was speaking with special pathos to the Methodist societies whose rigorous work ethic had made many of them rich: "O ye Methodists, hear the word of the Lord! I have a message from God to all men; but to you above all. For above forty years I have been a servant to you and to your fathers. And I have not been as a reed shaken with the wind: I have not varied in my testimony. I have testified to you the very same thing from the first day even until now. But 'who hath believed our report'? I fear, not many rich."[149]

He recalled the stern warning that James gave to the rich: "Now listen, you rich people, weep and wail because of the misery that is coming on you. Your wealth has rotted, and moths have eaten your clothes. Your gold and silver are corroded. Their corrosion will testify against you and eat your flesh like fire. You have hoarded wealth in the last days.... You have lived on earth in luxury and self-indulgence. You have fattened yourselves in the day of slaughter."[150]

Ask yourself if your soul has been hurt by a loss of humility and patience. "Formerly one might guide you with a thread; now one cannot turn you with a cart-rope."[151] If you are rich, your meekness has been hurt. "You can bear nothing; no injury, nor even affront! How quickly are you ruffled! How readily does that occur."[152] Riches diminish the capacity for patience. "Do you still 'in patience possess your soul'?"[153]

Sadly Wesley recalled, "You once pushed on through cold or rain, or whatever cross lay in your way, to see the poor, the sick, the distressed. You went about doing good, and found out those who were not able to find you. You cheerfully crept down into their cellars, and climbed up into their garrets."[154] Then they were tender and meek Christians rejoicing in the rich pardon of God. But worldly riches beguiled them.

C. The Danger of Increasing Riches

Homily 131, "The Danger of Increasing Riches," follows closely homily 87, "The Danger of Riches."

---

[148]"The Danger of Riches," B 3:239, J III:9 – 10, sec. 2.8.
[149]"The Danger of Riches," B 3:237, J III:8, sec. 2.9.
[150]James 5:1 – 5 NIV; "The Danger of Riches," B 3:2, J III:8, sec. 2.9.
[151]"The Danger of Riches," B 3:242, J III:12, sec. 2.14.
[152]"The Danger of Riches," B 3:242 – 43, J III:12, sec. 2.15.
[153]"The Danger of Riches," B 3:243, J III:13, sec. 2.16.
[154]"The Danger of Riches," B 3:244, J III:13 – 14, sec. 2.18.

1. Do Not Set Your Heart on Riches

The text of the homily "The Danger of Increasing Riches" is Psalm 62:10: "If riches increase, set not your heart upon them" [Homily #131, "The Danger of Increasing Riches," B 4:178–86, J VII:355–62 (September 21, 1790)].

Those who earn all they can and save all they can and give all they can may nevertheless find in their growing resources a growing spiritual challenge. Increasing riches may mean increasing anxieties. For them Wesley has a stern warning: "Though your riches increase, do not set your heart on them."

a. No One Can Have Riches without Being Greatly Endangered by Them

The rich can be turned back toward simple faith, but it is difficult: "Though 'it is easier for a camel to go through the eye of a needle, than for a rich man to enter into the kingdom of heaven,' yet the things impossible with men are possible with God."[155] "No one can have riches without being greatly endangered by them."[156]

Wesley's theme in this homily on increasing riches is another warning to his increasingly prosperous connection: "If the danger of barely having them is so great, how much greater is the danger of increasing them!"[157]

Seeking riches is a temptation to the soul. Having them in increasing proportion is a greater temptation. In the worst case there is the obsession to increase them without limit. "This danger is great even to those who receive what is transmitted to them by their forefathers; but it is abundantly greater to those who acquire them by their own skill and industry."[158] "Great care is to be taken, that what is intended for a blessing does not turn into a curse."[159]

Those who are lovers of money, who hoard what they ought to give to the poor, soon find their souls troubled. Misers remain poor even if they have millions. "A person may have more than necessaries and conveniences for his family, and yet not be rich"; for example, a man of business may be afraid that "his debts are more than he is worth."[160]

b. Adding Field to Field

No one can deceive God. Whatever people may earn or save in time, eternity will take away. Do not be unprepared for the day when God will come unexpectedly and say, "Thou fool."[161] If you are obsessive about "adding money to money, house to house, or field to field,"[162] without giving to the poor at least one tenth, you may be surprised to hear "Thou fool." By whatever means your riches increase, "whether

---

[155]"The Danger of Riches," B 3:245–46, J III:14–15, sec. 2.20.
[156]"The Danger of Increasing Riches," B 4:178, J III:355, sec. 1.
[157]"The Danger of Increasing Riches," B 4:178, J III:355, proem, sec. 1.
[158]Ibid.
[159]"The Danger of Increasing Riches," B 4:178, J III:355, proem, sec. 2.
[160]"The Danger of Increasing Riches," B 4:179, J III:356, sec. 1.2.
[161]Luke 12:20; "The Danger of Increasing Riches," B 4:181, J III:357–58, sec. 1.6.
[162]"The Danger of Increasing Riches," B 4:181, J III:358, sec. 1.7; cf. Isa. 5:8.

with or without labor; whether by trade, legacies, or any other way,"[163] unless your charities increase in the same proportion as your riches, you are setting your heart on a world that passes away.

Meanwhile, "beware of forming a hasty judgment concerning the fortune of others. There may be secrets in the situation of a person, which few but God are acquainted with."[164]

c. Sin's Fierce Resistance to the Moral Use of Money

Although Wesley had been speaking passionately for half a century about excessive yearning for riches "with all the plainness that was in [his] power," he was amazed at how little effect it had. "I doubt whether I have, in all that time, convinced fifty misers of covetousness.... O do not stop your ears! Rather say, with Zacchaeus, 'Behold, Lord, the half of my goods I give to the poor; and if I have done any wrong to any man, I restore fourfold.'"[165]

Wesley spoke directly to the hearts of the rich: "I have a message from God unto thee, O rich man! whether thou wilt hear, or whether thou wilt forbear. Riches have increased with thee; at the peril of thy soul, 'set not thine heart upon them!'"[166] Rather, be thankful that God has given you "so much power of doing good."

Whatever you have earned gives you opportunity to do good in proportional measure. "Everyone to whom much was given, of him much will be required, and from him to whom they entrusted much, they will demand the more."[167]

d. If Given More, Give More

If God's providence entrusts you with more, it is in order that "you might do so much the more good, as you had more ability.... O no! do not make so poor a return to your beneficent Lord!"[168] The Lord has entrusted his servants "with talents far more precious than gold and silver, that you may minister in your various offices to the heirs of salvation.... Let us render unto God the things that are God's; even all we are, and all we have!"[169]

Some people unwisely love wealth directly "for its own sake, not only for the sake of what it procures."[170] Others are prone to loving money for the goods it brings, unaware that this might tempt them to rationalize the idolatry as a good.

Wesley noted that this vice is "very rarely found in children." It is more often found in elders who "have the least need of money, and the least time to enjoy it," as in the case of the parable of the rich man and Lazarus.[171] This stands as evidence for the unnaturalness of loving money for itself. Those who do are tempted to become

---

[163]"The Danger of Increasing Riches," B 4:181, J III:358, sec. 1.7.
[164]"The Danger of Increasing Riches," B 4:179–80, J III:356–57, sec. 1.3.
[165]"The Danger of Increasing Riches," B 4:181–82, J III:358, sec. 1.8; cf. Luke 19:8.
[166]"The Danger of Increasing Riches," B 4:182, J III:358–59, sec. 1.9.
[167]Luke 12:48 ESV.
[168]"The Danger of Increasing Riches," B 4:183–84, J III:360, sec. 12.
[169]"The Danger of Increasing Riches," B 4:184, J III:360–61, sec. 13.
[170]"The Danger of Increasing Riches," B 4:184–85, J III:361, sec. 14; cf. ENNT, 1 Tim. 6:9.
[171]Luke 16:19–31.

slaves of "that execrable hunger after gold" that can never be satisfied.[172] Juvenal rightly observed in his *Satires*: "'As money, so the love of money, grows; it increases in the same proportion.' The more you drink, the more you thirst."[173]

The preventative for this disease is also its remedy: After you have gained all you can with proper provision for those for whom you are responsible, "and saved all you can, wanting for nothing; spend not one pound, one shilling, or one penny, to gratify either the desire of the flesh, the desire of the eyes, or the pride of life." Employ money for no "other end than to please and glorify God."[174] Hoard nothing. The only way of "extracting the poison from riches" is to "lay up no treasure on earth, but give all you can; that is, all you have."[175]

e. An Imperative Appeal

Wesley ended with this passionate personal appeal to decision: "After having served you between sixty and seventy years; with dim eyes, shaking hands, and tottering feet, I give you one more [piece of] advice before I sink into the dust."[176]

Once again he turned to the admonition found in 1 Timothy 6:9 – 10: "Those who want to get rich fall into temptation and a trap and into many foolish and harmful desires that plunge people into ruin and destruction. For the love of money is a root of all kinds of evil. Some people, eager for money, have wandered from the faith and pierced themselves with many griefs" (NIV).[177] They fall into temptation voluntarily through their unholy desires. Only grace can deliver them.

Setting your heart on increasing riches is a snare, "a steel trap, which instantly crushes" the happy life into pieces.[178] "You, above all men, who now prosper in the world, never forget these awful words! How unspeakably slippery is your path! How dangerous every step! [May] the Lord God enable you to see your danger."[179]

"Since I am in anguish over you," said Wesley, "I will come still a little closer." It is as if he was now whispering poignantly to his own connection of spiritual formation, "You that receive two hundred, and spend but one, do you give God the other hundred? If not, you rob him of just so much." Your mistake is that what you think you possess "is not your own. It cannot be, unless you are Lord of heaven and earth." So "Lord, speak to their hearts!... Leave them enough to live on, not in idleness and luxury, but by honest industry. And if you have not children, upon what scriptural or rational principle can you leave a groat behind you more than will bury you.... Haste, haste, my brethren, haste! lest you be called away.... When this is done, you may boldly say, 'Now I have nothing to do but to die! Father, into thy hands I commend my spirit!'"[180]

[172]"The Danger of Increasing Riches," B 4:184 – 85, J III:361, sec. 14.
[173]Juvenal, *Satires* 21.139; "The Danger of Increasing Riches," B 4:184 – 85, J III:361, sec. 14.
[174]"The Danger of Increasing Riches," B 4:185, J III:361, sec. 15.
[175]Ibid.
[176]"The Danger of Increasing Riches," B 4:185 – 86, J III:361 – 62, sec. 16.
[177]Ibid.
[178]Ibid.
[179]Ibid.
[180]"The Danger of Increasing Riches," B 4:186, J III:362, sec. 17.

D. On Dress

The question of clothing is not merely an issue of aesthetic style or competitive pride, but of accountability before God and to the needy neighbor. Wesley's text for homily 88 was about beauty: "Your beauty should not come from outward adornment, such as elaborate hairstyles and the wearing of gold jewelry or fine clothes. Rather, it should be that of your inner self, the unfading beauty of a gentle and quiet spirit, which is of great worth in God's sight" [1 Peter 3:3 – 4 NIV; Homily #88, "On Dress," B 3:248 – 61, J VII:15 – 25 (December 30, 1786)].

This homily is a direct sequel to the series on the use of money, the danger of riches, and the danger of increasing riches. It takes up a particular case in point for living a modest life of service without excessive pride or ornamentation.[181] The goal is purity of heart, practical functionality, serviceability, and a hygienic and spotless appearance. It may at first seem to modern consciousness that it is petty to speak of dress as a moral concern, but not for Wesley. This instruction is not legalism, but an expression of how the gospel fulfills the law in the daily ordering of economic life. Every day we put covering upon ourselves. Are there moral implications in how we do this?

1. How Inward Centeredness of Spirit Affects Outward Appearance

a. Transformed by the Renewing of Our Minds

How are believing disciples to rightly participate in the body of Christ regarding apparel? Not with "outward adorning," but from the center, the hidden person, from the heart. Let them be adorned by "that which is not corruptible."[182] Let others see in the faithful "the ornament of a meek and quiet spirit, which is in the sight of God of great price."[183]

The apostle Paul taught that the faithful are being transformed by the renewing of their minds. They are offering up their bodies "as a living sacrifice, holy and pleasing to God — this is your true and proper worship. Do not conform to the pattern of this world, but be transformed by the renewing of your mind. Then you will be able to test and approve what God's will is — his good, pleasing and perfect will."[184] Is there a visible way of manifesting this inner transformation?

The nonconformity of the new life is the opposite of conformity with the world. Do not be conformed to the wisdom of the world, which is foolishness with God.

Wesley taught that it is "not beneath the wisdom of God to give us" pertinent directions about functional clothing. The almighty God does not hesitate to "condescend to take notice of such trifles."[185]

---

[181]On issues of modesty, Wesley relied in part on writers like Richard Baxter (1615 – 91). See *The Practical Works of the Rev. Richard Baxter*, 23 vols., ed. William Orme (1830).

[182]"On Dress," B 3:248, J VII:15, sec. 1.

[183]Ibid.

[184]Rom. 12:1 – 2 NIV.

[185]"On Dress," B 3:248, J VII:15, secs. 1 – 2.

b. Everything God Creates Is Good

When conflicts arose about food and sexuality, Paul went to the core problem in his instruction to Timothy: "For everything God created is good, and nothing is to be rejected if it is received with thanksgiving." It is fitting to attend to outward appearance if it is "consecrated by the word of God and prayer."[186]

Many who sincerely worship God have embraced the idea that clothing is adiaphora — among matters unrelated to salvation. They view such choices as a "branch of Christian liberty."[187] Some go further in resistance even to raising the question, saying: "I do not desire that any who 'dress plain' should be in our [religious] society."[188] Both antinomians and elitists were present in Wesley's societies.

Wesley rejected slovenliness. He turned to poet and pastor George Herbert on the range of God's intention for purity of heart as extending to all outward behaviors:

> Let thy mind's sweetness have its operation
> Upon thy person, clothes, and habitation.[189]

"The mind's sweetness" is the inner peace that comes from grace. Peace of mind and purity of intention may be reflected in your house and your personal appearance.

Should there be no difference between the apparel of Christians and of the worldly? "There may undoubtedly be a moderate difference of apparel between persons of different stations. And where the eye is single, this will easily be adjusted by the rules of Christian prudence."[190] An officer of the law has good reason to look different from ordinary citizens, because he is there to protect them.

2. Temptation to Pride, Vanity, Yearning Desire, and the Subversion of Good Works

The core of Wesley's argument on ornamental apparel is that it increases the temptation to much deeper vices: pride, vanity, and carelessness of consequences. The ornament of faith is purity of heart. The apparel may fittingly reflect that ornament.

a. Temptation to Pride

If so, then what is forbidden by Scriptures in dress? Explicitly "to be adorned with gold, or pearls, or costly apparel. But why? What harm is there therein?"[191]

"The first harm it does is, it engenders pride."[192] Where pride exists, it seeks to increase pride. To discern pride rightly is difficult for the proud. "Nothing is more natural than to think ourselves better because we are dressed in better clothes. And it is scarce possible for a man to wear costly apparel without in some measure

---

[186]1 Tim. 4:4–5 NIV; "On Dress," B 3:248, J VII:15–16, sec. 3.

[187]"On Dress," B 3:249, J VII:16, sec. 4.

[188]Ibid.

[189]George Herbert, *The Temple, the Church Porch*, Day 32, stanza 18 (Oxford, 1633); http://www.winwisdom.com/quotes/topic/cleanliness.aspx; "On Dress," B 3:249, J VII:16, sec. 5.

[190]"On Dress," B 3:250, J VII:16–17, sec. 6.

[191]"On Dress," B 3:250, J VII:17, sec. 8.

[192]"On Dress," B 3:251, J VII:17–18, sec. 9.

valuing himself upon it."[193] Is your valuing of yourself dependent on what you are wearing? If so, your sense of proportional value is off.[194] Ironically, the reverse is also true: One clad in sackcloth may be "as proud as he that is clad in cloth of gold."[195]

"Clothe yourselves with humility toward one another, because 'God opposes the proud but shows favor to the humble.'"[196] The pride that passionately desires gaining favor from your appearances sets you up for a fall.

b. Temptation to Vanity

Wesley said that wearing costly apparel "naturally tends to breed and to increase vanity. By vanity I here mean the love and desire of being admired and praised."[197] To be inordinately fond of dress comes from deep within. "You know in your hearts, it is with a view to be admired that you thus adorn yourselves."[198] Ask yourself if you would take such pains for your appearance if no one but God were present. "The more you indulge this foolish desire, the more it grows upon you. You have vanity enough by nature, but by thus indulging it, you increase it a hundredfold."[199] A better way: "Aim at pleasing God alone,"[200] then dress accordingly.

c. Temptation to Unseemly and Inordinate Excitement

Wesley notes on the text of 1 Peter 3:3 – 4 the contrast between "outward adornment" and "your inner self." The apostle Peter is here talking about beauty, not just the idea of beauty but "your beauty," your personal beauty. What makes you beautiful? It is not from "outward adornment, such as elaborate hairstyles and the wearing of gold jewelry or fine clothes. Rather, it should be that of your inner self, the unfading beauty of a gentle and quiet spirit, which is of great worth in God's sight" (NIV).

What makes you personally beautiful? It is a light from within. If that light is not lit from within, no matter what you put on will seem a little tawdry. The outward adornment, if lacking a light from within, cannot make up for what is missing in the eyes, since the eyes reveal the soul.

"The wearing of gay and costly apparel naturally tends to beget ... turbulent and uneasy passion."[201] Why? Its purpose is to attract and stimulate excitement. When that passing stimulant passes, what is left? Only a more extreme effort to stimulate. This is why this sort of temporary passion is always "uneasy."[202] God values exceedingly the movements of the "inner self." The holy life being formed within will let the expression of that inner self take its own outward shape.

Just as you cannot worship both God and mammon, you cannot "thoroughly

---

[193]Ibid.
[194]Ibid.
[195]"On Dress," B 3:251 – 52, J VII:18, sec. 10.
[196]1 Peter 5:5 NIV.
[197]"On Dress," B 3:252, J VII:18, sec. 11.
[198]Ibid.
[199]Ibid.
[200]Ibid.
[201]"On Dress," B 3:252, J VII:19, sec. 12.
[202]Ibid.

enjoy" your outward appearance if you are distracted from within. "It is only while you sit loose to that 'outward adorning' that you can 'in patience possess your soul.'"[203]

d. The Temptation to Inflame Yearning Desire

When yearning desire is inflamed, the costs may be higher than expected. As the story is told of a certain dean at Whitehall, "If you do not repent, you will go to a place which I have too much manners to name before this good company."[204] At age eighty-three, Wesley had not lost the capacity for jest. But Peter spoke more plainly: "Your enemy the devil prowls around like a roaring lion looking for someone to devour. Resist him, standing firm in the faith."[205]

Self-adornment may become, as Abraham Cowley wrote, "a barb'rous skill" that absorbs huge time and effort: "'Tis like the pois'ning of a dart, too apt before to kill."[206] Wesley asked, "You poison the beholder with far more of this base appetite than otherwise he would feel. Did you not know this would be the natural consequence of your elegant adorning?"[207] The cost is the increase of pride and the loss of humility.

There is a self-destructive logic in the yearning that begs constantly to be admired visually. When you "set to public view a specious face of innocence and virtue,"[208] you may set fires that cannot easily be predicted or controlled nor their consequences assessed in advance. "Meanwhile you do not yourself escape the snare which you spread for others. The dart recoils, and you are infected with the same poison with which you infected them. You kindle a flame which at the same time consumes both yourself and your admirers."[209]

e. The Temptation to Ignore the Needs of the Poor

"Outward adornment" is directly opposed to "being 'adorned with good works.'"[210] This homily subtly connects with the three previous homilies on money, the danger of riches, and the danger of increasing riches. Money spent on self-adornment is money not spent on care for the poor. It is lavished on oneself rather than the needy who have deficient warmth or worn-out clothing. "The more you lay out on your own apparel, the less you have left to clothe the naked, to feed the hungry, to lodge the strangers, to relieve those that are sick and in prison."[211]

Wesley insisted on pressing this ethical correlation of clothing oneself and

---

[203]Ibid. "Sit loose" means to relax attention.
[204]"On Dress," B 3:252 – 53, J VII:19 – 20, sec. 13. An anecdote that recurred in eighteenth-century literature, found in Alexander Pope's *Moral Essays, Complete Poetical Works* (n.p., 1731), 4:49 – 50.
[205]1 Peter 5:8 – 9 NIV.
[206]Abraham Cowley, *The Mistress*, "The Waiting-Maid" (1647), v. 4.
[207]"On Dress," B 3:252 – 53, J VII:19 – 20, sec. 13.
[208]Quoting Nicholas Rowe, *The Fair Penitent* (1703; repr., Lincoln: Univ. of Nebraska Press, 1992), act 2, sc. 1.
[209]"On Dress," B 3:252 – 53, J VII:19 – 20, sec. 13.
[210]"On Dress," B 3:254, J VII:20, sec. 14.
[211]Ibid.

clothing the poor: "Therefore every shilling which you needlessly spend on your apparel is in effect stolen from God and the poor."[212] You deprive yourself of "many precious opportunities of doing good.... How often have you disabled yourself from doing good by purchasing what you did not want?... How much good might you have done with that money! When you are laying out that money in costly apparel that you could have otherwise spared for the poor, you thereby deprive them of what God, the Proprietor of all, had lodged in your hands for their use. If so, what you put upon yourself you are, in effect, tearing from the back of the naked; as the costly and delicate food which you eat you are snatching from the mouth of the hungry."[213]

Wesley related the following incident. "Many years ago, when I was at Oxford, in a cold winter's day, a young maid (one of those we kept at school) called upon me. I said: 'You seem half starved. Have you nothing to cover you but that thin linen gown?' She said, 'Sir, this is all I have!' I put my hand in my pocket but found I had scarce any money left, having just paid away what I had.' Wesley was then conscience stricken that in the final judgment he might have to give account of what he had just spent that day that deprived him of responding to an immediate need. This is what he learned: "Everything about thee which cost more than Christian duty required thee to lay out is the blood of the poor!"[214] Late in his life, in 1786 when this homily was written, Wesley regretted that so many under his own spiritual care had not gotten this simple point straight.

To those who missed the point by saying, "But I can afford it," Wesley replied: "No Christian can afford to waste any part of the substance which God has entrusted him with."[215] "All the time you are studying this 'outward adorning,' the whole inward work of the Spirit stands still."[216]

You do not need to go to the opera to see this irrationality. Rather, "Look into, I do not say, the theatres, but the churches, nay, and the meetings of every denomination (except a few old-fashioned Quakers, or the people called Moravians); look into the congregations in London or elsewhere of those that are styled 'gospel ministers'; look into Northampton Chapel, yea, into the Tabernacle, or the chapel in Tottenham Court Road; nay, look into the chapel in West Street or that in the City Road; look at the very people that sit under the pulpit."[217]

f. A Warning to Those under Wesley's Spiritual Care

To those who appealed to universal custom, Wesley taught the biblical principle, "Do not follow the crowd in doing wrong."[218] "If millions condemn you, it will be enough that you are acquitted by God and your own conscience."[219]

---

[212]Ibid.
[213]"On Dress," B 3:254, J VII:20, sec. 15.
[214]"On Dress," B 3:255, J VII:21, sec. 16.
[215]"On Dress," B 3:255 – 56, J VII:21 – 22, sec. 17.
[216]"On Dress," B 3:256 – 57, J VII:22, sec. 19.
[217]"On Dress," B 3:257 – 58, J VII:23, sec. 21.
[218]Ex. 23:2 NIV.
[219]"On Dress," B 3:258, J VII:23, sec. 23.

To those who said they did not have strength to face criticism by others, Wesley answered: "No, not [strength] of your own; certainly you have not. But 'there is strength laid up for you on one that is mighty'! His grace is sufficient for you."[220]

At one time you renounced conformity to the world. You dressed "in every point neat and plain, suitable to your profession." Why did you not persevere? "Now, today, before the heart is hardened by the deceitfulness of sin, cut off at one stroke that sinful friendship with the ungodly and that sinful conformity to the world! Determine this day! Do not delay till tomorrow, lest you delay forever. For God's sake, for your own soul's sake, fix your resolution now!"[221]

"No man living can 'afford' to waste any part of what God has committed to his trust. None can 'afford' to throw any part of that food and raiment into the sea which was lodged with him on purpose to feed the hungry and clothe the naked."[222]

Do not "poison both yourself and others, as far as your example spreads, with pride, vanity, anger, lust, love of the world, and a thousand 'foolish and hurtful desires,' which tend to 'pierce' them 'through with many sorrows.' "[223] "Yet a little while, and we shall not need these poor coverings; for this corruptible body shall put on incorruption.... In the meantime, let this be our only care, to 'put off the old man,' our old nature, 'which is corrupt,' which is altogether evil; and to 'put on the new man, which after God is created in righteousness and true holiness.' "[224]

E. Self-Denial

Jesus' call to self-denial is central to the gospel. Jesus "said to them all, If any man will come after me, let him deny himself, and take up his cross daily, and follow me" [Luke 9:23; Homily #48, "Self-Denial," B 2:236–50, J VI:103–14 (1760)].

1. The Importance, Extent, and Necessity of Self-Denial

After Jesus had fed the five thousand and Peter had declared that Jesus is the Messiah, Jesus foretold his death and resurrection to his disciples. He said to them all: "Whoever wants to be my disciple must deny themselves and take up their cross daily and follow me. For whoever wants to save their life will lose it, but whoever loses their life for me will save it. What good is it for someone to gain the whole world, and yet lose or forfeit their very self?"[225]

All persons are called to listen to this gospel mandate for their own good. Wesley said, "The duty which is here enjoined is pertinent to all men in all times.... It is of the most universal nature, respecting all times and all persons."[226] It is addressed to "'any man,' of whatever rank, station, circumstances, in any nation, in any age of

---

[220]"On Dress," B 3:258–59, J VII:23–24, sec. 24.
[221]"On Dress," B 3:259, J VII:24, sec. 25.
[222]"On Dress," B 3:260, J VII:25, sec. 27.
[223]Ibid.
[224]"On Dress," B 3:260–61, J VII:25–26, sec. 28.
[225]Luke 9:23–25 NIV.
[226]"Self-Denial," B 2:238, J VI:103, proem, sec. 1.

the world." Whoever "'will' effectually 'come after me, let him deny himself' in all things; let him 'take up his cross' of whatever kind; yea, and that 'daily; and follow me.'"[227] This is the primary condition of discipleship. All who hear him are called to participate in the mission of the Servant Messiah.

Those who cannot align their wills to follow Jesus' command cannot be his disciples. Wesley said, "If we do not continually deny ourselves, we do not learn of Him, but of other masters. If we do not take up our cross daily, we do not come after Him, but after the world, or the prince of the world, or our own fleshly mind."[228] Our human responses determine whether we have heard his call or ignored it: "If we are not walking in the way of the cross, we are not following Him," but walking away from him.[229] The mandate requires a choice.

So much has been said about this theme. What more remains to be said? Though self-denial is a familiar theme to all Christians, Wesley thought that many had not had the opportunity to hear it expounded deeply enough. Worse, many who have written at length about it have not themselves sufficiently understood it.[230] "They did not see how exceeding broad this command is; or they were not sensible of the absolute, the indispensable necessity of it."[231] Wesley observed that he did not know of any "writer in the English tongue who has described the nature of self-denial in plain and intelligible terms, such as lie level with common understandings, and applied it to those little particulars which daily occur in common life."[232]

a. The Plain Meaning of Self-Denial

Admittedly all of our natural sentiments rise up against the very idea of self-denial. Those who live their lives out of the naturally self-assertive fallen will, rather than grace, abhor the very sound of self-denial. The devil moves every stone to keep it from being taught.[233]

Many who call themselves Christian just ignore the whole notion of denying themselves, "even those who have in some measure shaken off the yoke of the devil, who have experienced, especially of late years, a real work of grace in their hearts, yet are no friends to this grand doctrine of Christianity, though it is so peculiarly insisted on by their Master."[234] They blithely live "as if there was not one word about it in the Bible."[235] Timothy warned of times when "people will be lovers of themselves, lovers of money... lovers of pleasure rather than lovers of God — having a form of godliness but denying its power."[236] The level of evasion is often total. We deny even the thought of self-denial.

---

[227]Ibid.

[228]"Self-Denial," B 2:238, J VI:104, proem, sec. 2.

[229]Ibid.

[230]"Self-Denial," B 2:238, J VI:104–5, proem, sec. 4.

[231]"Self-Denial," B 2:239–40, J VI:105, proem, sec. 4.

[232]"Self-Denial," B 2:239–40, J VI:104–5, proem, sec. 4.

[233]"Self-Denial," B 2:240–41, J VI:105, sec. 1.1.

[234]Ibid.

[235]Ibid.

[236]2 Tim. 3:1–5 NIV.

b. Apart from Grace, Self-Denial Is a Hard Word

Both the legalistic moralists and the licentious antinomians misunderstand the gracious form of self-denial that lives out of God's love. If you are not deeply grounded in grace, "you are in constant danger of being wheedled, hectored, or ridiculed out of this important gospel doctrine, either by false teachers or false brethren (more or less beguiled from the simplicity of the gospel)."[237] With so much opposition, the believer does well to let the call to self-denial "be written in your heart by the finger of God, so as never to be erased."[238]

Self-denial has a simple logical premise: If God's will is our will, we will not press our own naturally self-assertive will as if above God's will, but simply accede to God's will.[239] Faith in divine grace has a deep conviction that the will of God is the only rule of action to make us happy and to bless our lives. God's will is exactly right because "it is he that hath made us, and not we ourselves."[240] God made us with a rational will capable of following this counterintuitive command, but only by the sufficient grace he gives. We can do it, but not by our own natural strength; rather by God's strength, since with God all things are possible.

Self-denial seems to be an especially hard word when viewed apart from grace.[241] Gracious self-denial means precisely this: to allow sufficient grace to transform the will. This grace enables us to refuse to follow our own distorted will. That refusal comes from a steady conviction that the will of God is the only rule of action ultimately good for us.

c. The Drastic Fall of Original Freedom

But the original freedom God has built into us has fallen. The history of sin proves that we have all gone astray from God's original creation. The fallen will which we now have embedded in our common human history is "wholly bent to indulge our natural corruption."[242] The will of man in its original creation before the fall was attuned to the will of God. It is now on an opposite path of rebellion throughout the whole of history after Eden.

By our own choices, habit builds upon habit. We become habituated to gratifying the desires of taste, the eyes, and pride. But this habituation reinforces the fallenness. "It is undoubtedly pleasing, for the time, to follow our own will by indulging, in any instance that offers, the corruption of our nature. But by following it in anything, we so far strengthen the perverseness of our will; and by indulging it, we continually increase the corruption of our nature."[243] It gratifies the taste but inflames the disorder.[244]

So what we call "our will" has become inveterately rebellious against God. Any

---

[237]"Self-Denial," B 2:240 – 41, J VI:105, sec. 1.1.

[238]Ibid.

[239]"Self-Denial," B 2:241 – 42, J VI:107, sec. 1.2.

[240]Ps. 100:3; "Self-Denial," B 2:241 – 42, J VI:107, sec. 1.2.

[241]"Self-Denial," B 2:241 – 42, J VI:107, sec. 1.2.

[242]"Self-Denial," B 2:242, J VI:107, sec. 1.3; cf. Ps. 51:5 (BCP).

[243]"Self-Denial," B 2:242, J VI:107, sec. 1.4.

[244]"Self-Denial," B 2:242, J VI:107, sec. 1.5.

realistic look at history will confirm this.[245] What we need is a redeemed will, which is what the good news of the resurrection offers us. The history of salvation calls us to awaken and live in the light.

To walk in one path is to quit the other.[246] We cannot walk in two ways at the same time. A person must "choose the one or the other: denying God's will to follow his own, or denying himself to follow the will of God."[247] Self-denial is "to deny ourselves any pleasure which does not spring from, and lead to, God."[248]

d. Taking Up His Cross

"A cross is anything contrary to our will, anything displeasing to our nature."[249] In following the race set before us, there is often a cross lying directly in the way. It is not only inconvenient; it is grievous. It is contrary to our rebellious will and displeasing to our self-assertive nature.

At that point, "the choice is plain: Either we must take up our cross, or we must turn aside from the way of God."[250] When the believer resists this cross, "the Lord then sits upon the soul as a refiner's fire, to burn all the dross thereof."[251] "The means to heal a sin-sick soul, to cure a foolish desire, an inordinate affection, are often painful,"[252] due to the idolatrous passions that underlie our yearning desires.

Do not think that an unchosen burden is a rare event in the human condition. Bearing unexpected burdens is generically common to all humanity, but when it happens to someone personally, it always seems peculiar to oneself. But by providential grace that obstacle is particularly prepared of God for that person. Against all natural intuitions, the obstacle "is given by God to him as a token of his love."[253] It is the common human lot to meet obstacles on the way and deal with them as they come. Freedom offers the choice to invite these obstacles to work for our long-range good even when their purpose is not seen.

Grace provides the means of meeting the obstacle and following steadily in the way.[254] In providing this means, the Lord is acting "as the Physician of our souls, not merely 'for his own pleasure, but for our profit, that we may be partakers of his holiness.'. . . He cuts away what is putrified or unsound in order to preserve the sound part."[255] Each occasion of cross bearing gives the opportunity of "embracing the will of God, though contrary to our own" fallen natural will, so as to strengthen the soul through testing.[256] When we endure with meekness and resignation what-

---

[245]"Self-Denial," B 2:242, J VI:107, sec. 1.3.
[246]"Self-Denial," B 2:242, J VI:107, sec. 1.4.
[247]Ibid.
[248]"Self-Denial," B 2:243, J VI:108, sec. 1.6.
[249]"Self-Denial," B 2:243, J VI:108, sec. 1.7.
[250]"Self-Denial," B 2:243, J VI:108, sec. 1.8.
[251]"Self-Denial," B 2:243, J VI:108, sec. 1.9.
[252]"Self-Denial," B 2:244, J VI:109, sec. 1.10.
[253]Ibid.; cf. 1 Cor. 10:13.
[254]"Self-Denial," B 2:245, J VI:109, sec. 1.12.
[255]B 2:245, J VI:110, sec. 1.13.
[256]"Self-Denial," B 2:245, J VI:110, sec. 1.14.

ever is laid upon us without our choice, we are in the proper sense bearing our cross.[257]

The promise is clear: "No temptation has overtaken you except what is common to mankind. And God is faithful; he will not let you be tempted beyond what you can bear."[258] Sufficient grace is promised to supply strength for bearing the load.

It is not surprising that the young man to whom the Lord said, "Go, sell what you have and give it to the poor," went away sorrowful."[259] But that was the only way to heal his covetousness, which had its roots in his idolatry of worldly goods.[260] You cannot worship God and mammon. One negates the other.

e. Case Studies of Relapse: The Consequences of the Lack of Self-Denial

The lack of self-denial deprives one of participating fully in life in Christ. "The great hindrance of our receiving or growing in the grace of God is always the want of denying ourselves, or taking up our cross."[261] The power to lift the cross is not lacking where the Word of God is heard and received and when we pray for grace to receive it.

One may hear the call to self-denial and acknowledge its truth but still remain unaffected by it behaviorally. "He remains 'dead in trespasses and sins,' senseless and unawakened. Why?" The real answer: "He will not part with his bosom-sin." He remains emotively unaffected, "because he will not deny himself.... His foolish heart is still hardened."[262]

Wesley asked, "Suppose he begins to awake out of sleep, and his eyes are a little opened, why are they so quickly closed again? Why does he again sink into the sleep of death? Because he again yields to his bosom-sin; he drinks again of the pleasing poison. Therefore it is impossible that any lasting impression should be made upon his heart: that is, he relapses into his fatal insensibility because he will not deny himself."[263]

There are times when the call does not wear away. It is deep and lasting. One mourns but is not comforted. Why does that happen to so many? "It is because they do not 'bring forth fruits meet for repentance'; because they do not, according to the grace they have received, 'cease from evil, and do good.'"[264] They do not leave behind "their besetting sin." In short, they do not receive the gift of faith "because they will not 'deny themselves' or 'take up their cross.'"[265]

Consider a person who had at one time "tasted of the powers of the world to come."[266] He saw "the light of the knowledge of the glory of God in the face of Jesus

---

[257]"Self-Denial," B 2:244, J VI:109, sec. 1.11.
[258]1 Cor. 10:13 NIV.
[259]See Matt. 19:21–22.
[260]"Self-Denial," B 2:244, J VI:109, sec. 1.10.
[261]"Self-Denial," B 2:245–46, J VI:110, sec. 2.1.
[262]"Self-Denial," B 2:246, J VI:110, sec. 2.2.
[263]"Self-Denial," B 2:246, J VI:110–11, sec. 2.3.
[264]"Self-Denial," B 2:246, J VI:111, sec. 2.4.
[265]Ibid.
[266]Heb. 6:5.

Christ," and felt the "peace ... which passeth all understanding."[267] But when given a cross to bear, "he did not stir up the gift of God which was in him; he gave way to spiritual sloth."[268] He refused to pray for perseverance, and so made shipwreck of the faith due to his lack of self-denial, and taking up his cross daily.[269]

Suppose another has "still a measure of the Spirit of adoption, which continues to witness with his spirit that he is a child of God," yet he is not committed to full and durable responsiveness to the grace given him. He has no thought of being made perfect in love or of "going on to perfection."[270] He is not "as once, hungering and thirsting after righteousness, panting after the whole image and full enjoyment of God, as the hart after the water-brook."[271] He has forgotten that faith matures by producing the fruits of good works.[272] He does not continue constantly in private and public prayer or in hearing the Word and receiving the sacraments. He refuses the benefits of "religious conference."[273] He is not zealous of works of charity. Why? "Because in time of dryness it is pain and grief unto him. He cannot feed the hungry or clothe the naked unless he retrench the expense of his own apparel or use cheaper and less pleasing food. Beside which, visiting the sick or those that are in prison is attended with many disagreeable circumstances."[274] Why so many? "Because he will not deny himself and take up his daily cross."[275] Daily. Steadily. Cross bearing is a gift and task for every day.

f. What We Learn from Cross Bearing

"It is always owing to the want either of self-denial, or taking up his cross, that a man does not thoroughly follow his Lord."[276] His behavior shows that he is not fully a disciple of Christ. Those who refuse to bear the cross "know neither the Scripture nor the power of God.... They are entirely unacquainted ... with true, genuine, Christian experience." They have not learned "of the manner wherein the Holy Spirit ever did, and does at this day, work in the souls of men!"[277] This is the real reason why so many "who were once burning and shining lights have now lost both their light" and the energy for faith active in love. But God teaches self-denial to every soul who is willing to hear his voice![278]

Hence, "It is not enough for a minister of the gospel not to oppose the doctrine of self-denial, to say nothing concerning it.... He must inculcate the necessity of it in the clearest and strongest manner; he must press it with his might, on all persons,

---

[267]2 Cor. 4:6; Phil. 4:7; "Self-Denial," B 2:247, J VI:111, sec. 2.5.
[268]"Self-Denial," B 2:247, J VI:111, sec. 2.5.
[269]Ibid.
[270]Cf. Heb. 6:1; or going on to full maturity in grace.
[271]Cf. Ps. 42:1.
[272]"Self-Denial," B 2:248, J VI:111, sec. 2.1; cf. James 2:22.
[273]"Self-Denial," B 2:247–48, J VI:111–12, sec. 2.6.
[274]Ibid.
[275]Ibid.
[276]"Self-Denial," B 2:248, J VI:112, sec. 2.7.
[277]"Self-Denial," B 2:248, J VI:113, sec. 3.1.
[278]"Self-Denial," B 2:248, J VI:113, sec. 3.2.

at all times."[279] Wesley exhorted, "Apply this, every one of you, to your own soul. Meditate upon it when you are in secret: Ponder it in your heart! Take care not only to understand it thoroughly, but to remember it to your lives' end! Cry unto the Strong for strength, that you may no sooner understand than enter upon the practice of it."[280]

F. The Stewardship of Time

1. On Redeeming the Time

The economy of time is analogous to the economy of physical resources. Both are of such great value that Wesley provided specific coaching and instruction. The use of time is akin to the use of money.

The stewardship of time begins every day at one specific moment: getting up and rolling out of bed.

a. Temporal Redemption

The sheer output of Wesley's life gives the best evidence of how he shepherded his own time: arising early, preaching early, maintaining a rigorous daily order of prayer and Scripture study, traveling by horseback to hundreds of villages per year, preaching, writing, and carrying on a huge correspondence of pastoral care and counsel.

The text that pulls together his view of temporal accountability is "On Redeeming the Time" [Homily #93, B 3:323–32, J VII:67–75 (January 20, 1782)]. The text is a phrase from Ephesians 5:16: "Redeeming the time."

It is best understood in its specific context: the command to walk in light:

Have no fellowship with the unfruitful works of darkness, but rather expose them. For it is shameful even to speak of those things which are done by them in secret. But all things that are exposed are made manifest by the light, for whatever makes manifest is light. Therefore He says:

"Awake, you who sleep,
Arise from the dead,
And Christ will give you light."

See then that you walk circumspectly, not as fools but as wise, redeeming the time, because the days are evil. Therefore do not be unwise, but understand what the will of the Lord is.[281]

The context of redeeming our personal time is the redeeming activity of God that calls us out of darkness into light.

Paul's instruction is to "walk circumspectly." This means walking not as fools but as the wise who redeem their time.[282] Wesley said that it implies "saving all the time

---

[279]"Self-Denial," B 2:249, J VI:113, sec. 3.3.
[280]"Self-Denial," B 2:250, J VI:113–14, sec. 3.4.
[281]Eph. 5:11–17 NKJV.
[282]"On Redeeming the Time," B 3:323, J VII:67, proem, sec. 1.

you can for the best purposes; buying up every fleeting moment out of the hands of sin and Satan, out of the hands of sloth, ease, pleasure, worldly business; the more diligently because the present 'are evil days,' days of the grossest ignorance, immorality, and profaneness."[283] A full day of light is given every day for you to redeem in the light of God's redemption of humanity.

This is the overall import of the text, but Wesley had a more specific purpose: "I purpose at present to consider only one particular way of 'redeeming the time,' namely, from sleep."[284] This isn't its only meaning, but this focus is fully justified by the preceding sentences: "Awake, you who sleep, arise from the dead, and Christ will give you light."[285] It is in this context of living in the light and waking up to the light that Scripture says, "Redeem the time."

Elsewhere in Wesley's homilies on salvation and eschatology, he teaches amply on the cosmic redemption of time.[286] But here he is teaching of the personal redemption of time, beginning every day with the simple act of waking up with intentionality.

Many have assumed that it is a petty issue: "an indifferent thing whether they slept more or less." They have seldom been challenged to consider their stewardship of sleep as "an important branch of Christian temperance."[287] This homily shows the following three things:

1. What it means to redeem the time from the stupor of a sleeping state
2. The harm in not redeeming the limited time given us
3. Ways to redeem time[288]

2. What It Means to Redeem Time

Wesley had explicitly spoken earlier of the sleeping state in his homilies "The Spirit of Bondage and of Adoption,"[289] "The Almost Christian,"[290] and "Walking by Sight and Walking by Faith."[291] When we are asleep we are less aware of the light of grace. When the light of grace opens our eyes, we awaken to a new day.

a. Taking the Measure of the Sleep You Require

To redeem the time from sleep means quite simply "to take that measure of sleep every night which nature requires, and no more."[292] We are to get enough sleep but not too much.

---

[283]Ibid.
[284]"On Redeeming the Time," B 3:323, J VII:67, proem, sec. 2.
[285]Eph. 5:14 NKJV.
[286]See *JWT*, vol. 2, chap. 11, "History and Eschatology"; and vol. 2, chap. 12, "Future Judgment and New Creation."
[287]"On Redeeming the Time," B 3:323, J VII:67, proem, sec. 2.
[288]"On Redeeming the Time," B 3:323, J VII:67, proem, sec. 3.
[289]See *JWT*, vol. 2, chap. 7, A.1.
[290]See ibid.
[291]See *JWT*, vol. 2, chap. 7, C.7.
[292]"On Redeeming the Time," B 3:324, J VII:67, sec. 1.1.

Wesley lived in an era of empirical investigation of both space and time. The measurement of time was an issue consonant with the spirit of his age.

By what criterion would you reasonably measure your own sleep time? By "that measure which is the most conducive to the health and vigor both of the body and mind."[293] Who judges what is conducive to your health? You do. What "vigor of body and mind" is required for your full functioning? You must decide.

b. Why One Standard Does Not Fit All

Wesley looked favorably on the maxim "One measure will not suit all." No, you must through self-examination and experiment decide how much sleep is fitting for yourself. Some require more, others less. No one can do this for another. Some require more sleep at certain times and less at other times. During sickness or after being weakened by sickness or hard labor, a person may need more sleep than usual. In such times "more of this natural restorative" is required than "when in perfect health."[294]

No one can better assess the correct measure of sleep for you than you yourself. Wesley said, "Whoever therefore they are that have attempted to fix one measure of sleep for all persons did not understand the nature of the human body."[295] Persons are widely different. Women are different from men. "One would wonder therefore that so great a man as Bishop [Jeremy] Taylor should have formed this strange imagination; much more that the measure which he has assigned for the general standard should be only three hours in four and twenty."[296] Just as unwisely, Richard Baxter, that "good and sensible man," thought that "four hours in four and twenty will suffice for any."[297]

Each person is unique. Wesley told the story of "an extremely sensible man who was absolutely persuaded that no one living needed to sleep above five hours in twenty-four. But when he made the experiment himself, he quickly relinquished the opinion."[298]

Wesley thought that there was a limit to reducing sleep hours, although it differed from person to person. He stated his own experience, not as normative, but as an observation: "I am fully convinced, by an observation continued for more than fifty years, that ... a human body can scarce continue in health and vigor without at least six hours' sleep in four and twenty."[299] But by that he was not prescribing six as a norm for all, rather only as a minimum, excepting a few extraordinary persons.

Determining the optimal number of hours of sleep calls for an individual self-assessment, which anyone can do. Compared to Taylor and Baxter, Wesley was more moderate: "If therefore one might venture to name one standard (though

---

[293]Ibid.
[294]"On Redeeming the Time," B 3:324, J VII:68, sec. 1.2.
[295]"On Redeeming the Time," B 3:324–25, J VII:68, sec. 1.3.
[296]Ibid.
[297]Ibid.
[298]Ibid.
[299]Ibid.

liable to many exceptions and occasional alterations), I am inclined to think this would come near the mark: healthy men, in general, need a little above six hours' sleep, healthy women, a little above seven, in four and twenty. I myself want six hours and a half, and I cannot well subsist with less."[300] But this is not a rule for others. It is a self-description of such a measurement that anyone can explore from personal experience. Wesley relied on his own experimental efforts to determine this for himself.[301]

3. The Harm in Not Redeeming Our Personal Time

Wesley well understood what we today call the "psychosomatic interface." Like many serving in both rural and urban ministries today, Wesley ministered to many who did not have adequate access to medical care. He was often asked to suggest home remedies for illnesses as he prayed for the sick. His book *Primitive Physik: An Easy and Natural Method of Curing Most Diseases*, was a small compendium of these remedies.[302]

Out of this pastoral context, he was asked about allowing time for sleep: "But why should anyone be at so much pains? What need is there of being so scrupulous? Why should we make ourselves so particular? What harm is there in doing as our neighbors do? — suppose in lying from ten till six or seven in summer, and till eight or nine in winter?"[303]

Those who seriously ask about how time is redeemed from sleep "will need a good deal of candor and impartiality."[304] Each one is called quietly to "Lift up therefore your heart to the Spirit of truth" and let it shine.[305] Discern for yourself the temporal limits of sufficient natural sleep.

Wesley presented reasons why the harm done by out-of-control sleep has significant effects not only on productivity and on the body, but also on the soul.

a. Do Not Throw Away Resources for Doing Good

The first principle: Do not throw away physical and temporal resources for doing good. "It is throwing away six hours a week which might turn to some temporal account. If you can do any work, you might earn something in that time, were it ever so small. And you have no need to throw even this away. If you do not want it yourself, give it to them that do: you know some of them that are not far off."[306] Your time is valuable. Employ it for good either for yourself or others.[307] Do not waste it. Do not sleep more "than your constitution necessarily requires."[308]

---

[300]"On Redeeming the Time," B 3:325, J VII:68, sec. 1.4.

[301]"On Redeeming the Time," B 3:325, J VII:69, sec. 1.5.

[302]John Wesley, *Primitive Physik: An Easy and Natural Method of Curing Most Diseases* (London, William Pine, 1765).

[303]"On Redeeming the Time," B 3:326, J VII:69, sec. 2.1.

[304]"On Redeeming the Time," B 3:326, J VII:69, sec. 2.2.

[305]Ibid.

[306]"On Redeeming the Time," B 3:326, J VII:69 – 70, sec. 2.3.

[307]Ibid.

[308]"On Redeeming the Time," B 3:326 – 27, J VII:70, sec. 2.4.

Second, inordinate sleep may do harm to the health of the body. Do not neglect the bodily strength required for doing good. Wesley had a strong conviction, based on the medical evidence of his day that too much sleep can harm a person's health. "Nothing can be more certain than this, though it is not commonly observed."[309] Wesley was basing this conclusion on medical studies that showed that "nervous disorders are so much more common among us than among our ancestors. Other causes may frequently concur; but the chief is, we lie longer in bed. Instead of rising at four, most of us who are not obliged to work for our bread lie till seven, eight, or nine."[310]

The insidious nature of incremental habit formation is the culprit: "It is not commonly observed because the evil steals on you by slow and insensible degrees. In this gradual and almost imperceptible manner, it lays the foundation of many diseases. It is the chief, real (though unsuspected) cause of all nervous diseases in particular."[311]

Wesley was interested in the physiology of oversleeping. The problem is not sleeping too long as such, but "lying too long in bed. By soaking (as it is emphatically called) so long between warm sheets, the flesh is, as it were, parboiled, and becomes soft and flabby. The nerves in the meantime are quite unstrung, and all the train of melancholy symptoms — faintness, tremors, lowness of spirits (so called) — come on, till life itself is a burden."[312] He was convinced that acuity of sight is effected by this process of creating flabby tissue. He compared his own eyesight with what it had been forty years earlier. He thought it had been strengthened through decades of consistent early rising. "The outward means" by which God had been "pleased to bless was the rising early in the morning."[313]

Just as "we cannot waste or (which comes to the same thing) not improve any part of our worldly substance, neither can we impair our own health" without sinning against the giver of mind and body.[314] Throwing money away is comparable to throwing time away. It is a waste of human resources.

Third, in addition to the harm done to useful productivity and to the body by out-of-control sleep is the deeper harm done to the soul. It is an offense to the Creator for the creature to be given such gifts and to waste them. Do not throw away spiritual resources for doing good by sleeping them away.[315] "This fashionable intemperance does also hurt the soul in a more direct manner. It sows the seeds of foolish and hurtful desires; it dangerously inflames our natural appetites, which a person stretching and yawning in bed is just prepared to gratify. It breeds and continually increases sloth, so often objected to [in] the English nation. It opens

---

[309]Ibid.

[310]Ibid.

[311]Ibid.

[312]"On Redeeming the Time," B 3:327, J VII:70, sec. 2.5. Parboiling is cooking food slightly in boiling water.

[313]"On Redeeming the Time," B 3:327, J VII:70, sec. 2.6.

[314]"On Redeeming the Time," B 3:327, J VII:70, sec. 2.7.

[315]"On Redeeming the Time," B 3:327, J VII:70, sec. 2.6.

the way and prepares the soul for every other kind of intemperance. It breeds a universal softness and faintness of spirit, making us afraid of every little inconvenience, unwilling to deny ourselves any pleasure, or to take up or bear any cross.... It totally unfits us for 'enduring hardship as good soldiers of Jesus Christ.'"[316] Paul wrote to Timothy: "Join with me in suffering, like a good soldier of Christ Jesus. No one serving as a soldier gets entangled in civilian affairs, but rather tries to please his commanding officer. Similarly, anyone who competes as an athlete does not receive the victor's crown except by competing according to the rules."[317]

Though Wesley had many differences with his former mentor, William Law, he thought Law was right in expecting Christians to protect their health by early rising and not being slaves to stupor. One who is prepared for morning prayers or Scripture study and fasting must be awake in spirit.[318]

Those who indulge sleep are tempted to give in to a softness in temperament that makes them unwilling to relish anything that does not suit an idle state of mind.[319] The epicure must renounce languid sensuality before even beginning to learn to relish the happiness of life with God. One who becomes addicted to sleep is not unlike one who is addicted to sex or food or drink. Self-denial lies at the center of Christian discipline. One who cannot even imagine taking up his cross and following Christ is not fit for discipleship. He has cut off his right hand, which could have been used for battle.[320]

Those who treat their time cavalierly mistake the deeper signals of their own hearts. They have hardened their hearts. Do not encourage a state of sensuality that renders them incapable of relishing the most essential joys of the Christian life. This lethargic temperament is contrary to the lively, zealous, watchful, self-denying spirit found in the apostles, saints, and disciples.[321] Rising early as an intentional act of self-denial demonstrates a will to exercise power over yourself in the war over your soul.[322]

4. Simple Suggestions on How to Redeem the Time

How do the faithful learn "most effectually to practice this important branch of temperance?"[323] The instructions are simple:

Begin instantly. You may not have a more favorable opportunity. You may be under conviction now, upon hearing the Scripture speak of "redeeming the time." Wesley said, "I advise all of you who are thoroughly convinced of the unspeak-

---

[316]"On Redeeming the Time," B 3:327 – 28, J VII:71, sec. 2.8; cf. 2 Tim. 2:3.

[317]2 Tim. 2:3 – 5 NIV. Here Wesley quoted William Law on bodily discipline. See William Law, *A Serious Call to the Devout and Holy Life* (1729), chap. 14, www.ccel.org/ccel/law/serious.

[318]"On Redeeming the Time," B 3:328, J VII:71, sec. 2.9.

[319]"On Redeeming the Time," B 3:328, J VII:71 – 72, sec. 2.10.

[320]Law, *A Serious Call*, chap. 14. "Concerning that part of devotion which relates to times and hours of prayer. Of daily early prayer in the morning. How we are to improve our forms of prayer, and how to increase the spirit of devotion." Cf. "On Redeeming the Time," B 3:329, J VII:72 – 73, sec. 2.11 – 12.

[321]Law, *A Serious Call*; cf. "On Redeeming the Time," B 3:329, J VII:72 – 73, sec. 2.12.

[322]Law, *A Serious Call*; cf. "On Redeeming the Time," B 3:329, J VII:73, sec. 2.12 – 13.

[323]"On Redeeming the Time," B 3:330, J VII:73 – 74, sec. 3.1.

able importance" of redeeming your time, not to permit this conviction to dwindle. Instantly begin to act on it.[324]

Do not depend on your own strength. "If you do, you will be utterly baffled. Be deeply sensible that as you are not able to do anything good of yourselves, so here in particular all your strength, all your resolution, will avail nothing. Whoever trusts in himself will be confounded. I never found an exception. I never knew one who trusted in his own strength that could keep this resolution for a twelvemonth."[325]

Cry out to the Strong for strength. "Call upon him that hath all power in heaven and earth; and believe that he will answer the prayer."[326] You cannot have too much confidence in God. If you set out in faith, "his strength shall be made perfect in your weakness."[327]

Add prudence to faith. "Use the most rational means to attain your purpose."[328]

To rise early, sleep early. Do this "in spite of the most dear and agreeable companions, in spite of their most earnest solicitations, in spite of entreaties, railleries, or reproaches, rigorously keep your hour. Rise up precisely at your time, and retire without ceremony. Keep your hour, notwithstanding the most pressing business: lay all things by till the morning."[329]

Be steady. "Keep your hour of rising without intermission. Do not rise two mornings and lie in bed the third; but what you do once, do always."[330]

Do not parley. If you feel uncommonly drowsy, "you must not parley — otherwise it is a lost case — but start up at once. And if your drowsiness does not go off, lie down for a while an hour or two after. But let nothing make a breach upon this rule: rise and dress yourself at your hour."[331]

Do not make excuses for yourself. To those who complained, "I have many disorders, my spirits are low, my hands shake," Wesley said, "All these are nervous symptoms; and they all partly arise from your taking too much sleep; nor is it probable they will ever be removed unless you remove the cause. Therefore ... in order to recover your health and strength, resume your early rising."[332]

Set out anew. "Bear the difficulty which you have brought upon yourself, and it will not last long."[333]

a. Whether This Will Make You a Christian

The final maxim: "Do not imagine that this single point, rising early, will suffice to make you a Christian. No: although that single point, the not rising, may keep

[324]Ibid.
[325]Ibid.
[326]"On Redeeming the Time," B 3:330, J VII:74, sec. 3.2.
[327]Ibid.
[328]Ibid.
[329]"On Redeeming the Time," B 3:330, J VII:74, sec. 3.3.
[330]"On Redeeming the Time," B 3:331, J VII:74, sec. 3.4.
[331]"On Redeeming the Time," B 3:331, J VII:74–5, sec. 3.5.
[332]"On Redeeming the Time," B 3:331–32, J VII:75, sec. 3.6.
[333]Ibid.

you a heathen, void of the whole Christian spirit."[334] Neglect of this discipline alone may keep you "cold, formal, heartless, dead, and make it impossible for you to get one step forward in vital holiness."[335]

Nonetheless, "this alone will go but a little way to make you a real Christian. It is but one step out of many, but it is one. And having taken this, go forward. Go on to universal self-denial, to temperance in all things, to a firm resolution of taking up daily every cross whereto you are called. Go on, in a full pursuit of all the mind that was in Christ, of inward, and then outward holiness; so shall you be not almost, but altogether, a Christian."[336]

Wesley thus provided for his connection of spiritual formation a clear set of instructions for beginning to exercise stewardship over the limited time we have been given. Here we see Wesley's personal and evangelical way of speaking of the economy of time. Wesley's contribution to Christian economics offers this clear opening point of temporal accountability: get up early.

G. Waking Up to the Value of Grace

1. Awake, Thou That Sleepest

Having discussed wakefulness in relation to the economy of time, we now come to wakefulness in relation to economy of salvation. Created as finite beings, we do not have an infinite amount of time to decide to live toward God.

This homily was preached by Charles Wesley, younger brother of John, before the University of Oxford, gathered at Christ Church Cathedral on April 4, 1742. As former students of Christ Church, the brothers Wesley had begun to shift their loyalties from Oxford to their ministries.[337] The evangelical conversion of Charles came in early May of 1738, only days before John Wesley personally experienced the unmerited grace of God in that pivotal event on Aldersgate Street in May 24, 1738. On that day, having heard the reading from Luther's *Introduction to the Epistle to the Romans*, the gospel of grace that he had preached penetrated his own heart. That converting event was the beginning of the evangelical revival in England, Wales, Scotland, and Ireland.

In the high pulpit of Christ Church, Charles Wesley took his text from Ephesians 5:14: "Awake thou that sleepest, and arise from the dead, and Christ shall give thee light" [Homily #3, "Awake, Thou That Sleepest," B 1:142 – 58, J V:56 (Oxford, April 4, 1742)].

This is the only sermon by Charles Wesley in this series. But it is important to reinforce the theme of awakening from the sleep of the natural state of humanity. The fact that it was placed third in the order of the Standard Sermons makes it of special value in the teaching homilies. It is parallel to the previous homily by John

---

[334]"On Redeeming the Time," B 3:332, J VII:75, sec. 3.7.
[335]Ibid.
[336]Ibid.
[337]JWO, introduction; B 1:111.

Wesley, "On Redeeming the Time." Both show the same sense of urgency and perseverance in receiving God's saving grace. John was talking mainly of physical sleep, while Charles was talking mainly of spiritual sleep.

His threefold purpose was to describe the sleepers to whom Paul addressed his letter; to sharpen and intensify the exhortation to the spiritual sleepers to awake from sleep and arise from the dead; and to explain "the promise made to such as do awake and arise — 'Christ shall give thee light.' "[338]

2. What Is Meant by Awakening from the Sleeping State?

a. Spiritual Sleep Is the Natural State of Humanity

"By sleep is signified the natural state of man." It is "that deep sleep of the soul into which the sin of Adam hath cast all who spring from his loins; that supineness, indolence, and stupidity, that insensibility of his real condition, wherein every man comes into the world and continues till the voice of God awakes him."[339]

Those who sleep away their spiritual lives sleep in the night. But what sort of night? Symbolically, "the state of nature is a state of utter darkness, a state wherein 'darkness covers the earth, and gross darkness the people.' "[340]

b. Without Knowledge of Oneself

No matter how much knowledge he may have of earthly matters, fallen man has limited "knowledge of himself."[341] He is unaware of who he is in God's presence. In this sleep, he knows nothing of his purpose, nothing of his destiny, nothing of his identity, nothing of his calling.

He does not know his own freedom, that it is fallen into the history of sin. He has no idea that he is a fallen spirit, that he is sleeping in darkness, that light has shown in the world for him. While asleep he cannot grasp that his "only business in the present world is to recover from his fall, to regain that image of God wherein he was created."[342]

He sees no necessity of doing the one thing needful for him to do.[343] The "one thing needful" is "that inward universal change, that 'birth from above.' "[344] That new birth is prefigured by baptism. It is "figured out[345] by baptism,"[346] which is "the beginning of that total renovation, that sanctification of spirit, soul, and body, 'without which no man shall see the Lord.' "[347]

---

[338]Charles Wesley, "Awake, Thou That Sleepest," B 1:142, J V:25, sec. 1.1; Eph. 5:14.
[339]"Awake, Thou That Sleepest," B 1:142, J V:25, sec. 1.1.
[340]"Awake, Thou That Sleepest," B 1:142–43, J V:25–26, sec. 1.2.
[341]Ibid.
[342]Ibid.
[343]See the homily "The One Thing Needful," discussed in *JWT*, vol. 1, chap. 7, B.2.a.
[344]Cf. John 3:3.
[345]The figure of regeneration is baptism, by which one dies to the world and rises to God. "Figured out" means imaging or showing forth the analogy between Jesus' death and resurrection and ours. By baptism we participate in Christ's dying and rising.
[346]"Awake, Thou That Sleepest," B 1:142–43, J V:25–26, sec. 1.2.
[347]Heb. 12:14; "Awake, Thou That Sleepest," B 1:142–43, J V:25–26, sec. 1.2.

c. Who Is Dreaming?

In his sleep the natural man dreams. In his dreams, "he fancies himself in perfect health."[348] In reality, in the presence of the all-holy God, he is "full of all diseases" in his fallen condition.[349] "Fast bound in misery ... he dreams that he is happy and at liberty. He says, 'Peace, peace,' while the devil as 'a strong man armed'[350] is in full possession of his soul."[351]

He sleeps unaware of the pit of hell[352] into which he is hurling, "from whence there is no return."[353] That pit has already "opened its mouth to swallow him up. A fire is kindled around him, yet he knoweth it not; yea, it burns him, yet he lays it not to heart."[354] This eternal future is the horrible danger in which the sleeper sleeps unaware.

Who is this sleeper? "By one who sleeps we are therefore to understand (and would to God we might all understand it!) a sinner satisfied in his sins, contented to remain in his fallen state, to live and die without the image of God; one who is ignorant both of his disease and of the only remedy for it; one who never was warned, or never regarded the warning voice of God 'to flee from the wrath to come.'"[355] In his drowsiness, he has never thought to cry out "in the earnestness of his soul, 'What must I do to be saved?'"[356]

d. Dead to God

The sleeper may be "a quiet, rational, inoffensive, good-natured professor of the religion of his fathers," or he may be "zealous or orthodox" in religion, but that does not matter if he remains wholly unaware of his destiny with God, the joys of grace, and the value of his own life.[357] He dreams that he has never done any wrong to anyone. "Meanwhile the wretched self-deceiver thanks God that he 'is not as other men are, extortioners, unjust, adulterers.'"[358] The apostle describes this condition as that of a person "who, 'having a form of godliness, denies the power thereof.'"[359] He may be found fasting or attending "all the means of grace, [being] constant at church and sacrament," and giving regular tithes and doing "all the good that he can"; but lacking faith in saving grace, he is still unaware of who he is in the presence of God.[360] He may lack "nothing of Christianity but the truth and the life."[361]

---

[348]"Awake, Thou That Sleepest," B 1:143, J V:26, sec. 1.3.
[349]Ibid.
[350]Luke 11:21.
[351]"Awake, Thou That Sleepest," B 1:143, J V:26, sec. 1.3.
[352]Hell means life without God throughout eternity. For Wesley's teaching on hell, see "Of Hell" in *JWT*, chap. 12, C.
[353]"Awake, Thou That Sleepest," B 1:143, J V:26, sec. 1.3.
[354]Ibid.
[355]Ibid.; Matt. 3:7.
[356]Acts 16:30; "Awake, Thou That Sleepest," B 1:143, J V:26, sec. 1.4.
[357]"Awake, Thou That Sleepest," B 1:144, J V:26, sec. 1.5.
[358]Luke 18:22; "Awake, Thou That Sleepest," B 1:144, J V:26, sec. 1.6.
[359]2 Tim. 3:5; "Awake, Thou That Sleepest," B 1:144, J V:26 – 27, sec. 1.6.
[360]"Awake, Thou That Sleepest," B 1:144, J V:26 – 27, sec. 1.6.
[361]Ibid.

He may have cleaned the outside of his cup, but within "his inward parts" he is full of disorder and hopelessness.[362] "Our Lord fitly compares him to a 'painted sepulcher,' which 'appears beautiful without' but nevertheless is 'full of dead men's bones and of all uncleanness.'"[363]

There is in him "no Spirit of the living God,"[364] without which he dwells in darkness. "He abides in death, though he knows it not."[365] He may have a lively intellect and outward appearance, but he is dead to God in his sins. Those dead to God will "lose the life of thy soul; thou shalt die to God, shalt be separated from him, thy essential life and happiness."[366] In the midst of natural life, they are now in spiritual death.

In this stupor, the natural man will remain "till the Second Adam becomes a quickening spirit to us, till he raises the dead, the dead in sin, in pleasure, riches, or honors."[367] Only when he hears the voice of the Son of God is he "made sensible of his lost estate, and receives the sentence of death in himself."[368] Then he will see how dead he has been even when he is alive and sleeping, "dead to God and all the things of God; having no more power to perform the actions of a living Christian than a dead body to perform the functions of a living man."[369]

One who is dead in sin has no senses to discern spiritual good. "Having eyes, he sees not; he hath ears, and hears not."[370] He does not "taste and see that the Lord is gracious."[371] The soul asleep in death has no perceptions of the things of the Spirit. "His heart is 'past feeling,'" altogether lacking understanding of these things.[372] "Having no spiritual senses, no inlets of spiritual knowledge, the natural man receiveth not the things of the Spirit of God.... He is not content with being utterly ignorant of spiritual things, but he denies the very existence of them. And spiritual sensation itself is to him the foolishness of folly."[373]

If so, "How can any man know that he is alive to God? Even as you know that your body is now alive. Faith is the life of the soul: and if ye have this life abiding in you, ye want no marks to evidence it to yourself."[374]

The prayer for coming alive is from Ezekiel in the valley of dry bones: "Then 'come from the four winds, O breath, and breathe upon these slain, that they may live."[375] "Do not ye harden your hearts and resist the Holy Ghost, who even now is come to 'convince you of sin,'" because you have not trusted in God's mercy and love in his Son.[376]

[362]"Awake, Thou That Sleepest," B 1:144–45, J V:27, sec. 1.7; cf. Matt. 23:25.
[363]"Awake, Thou That Sleepest," B 1:144–45, J V:27, sec. 1.7; cf. Matt. 23:27.
[364]"Awake, Thou That Sleepest," B 1:144–45, J V:27, sec. 1.7; cf. Rom. 8:9.
[365]"Awake, Thou That Sleepest," B 1:145, J V:27, sec. 1.8; cf. Eph. 2:1.
[366]"Awake, Thou That Sleepest," B 1:145, J V:27, sec. 1.8.
[367]"Awake, Thou That Sleepest," B 1:145, J V:27–28, sec. 1.9.
[368]Ibid.
[369]Ibid.
[370]"Awake, Thou That Sleepest," B 1:145–46, J V:28, sec. 1.10; cf. Mark 8:18.
[371]Cf. Ps. 34:8.
[372]"Awake, Thou That Sleepest," B 1:145–46, J V:28, sec. 1.10.
[373]"Awake, Thou That Sleepest," B 1:146, J V:28, sec. 1.11.
[374]Ibid.
[375]Ezek. 37:9; "Awake, Thou That Sleepest," B 1:146–47, J V:28, sec. 1.12.
[376]"Awake, Thou That Sleepest," B 1:146–47, J V:28, sec. 1.12; cf. John 8:46.

3. Awake! Arise from the Dead!

Charles Wesley's hearers at the university did not consider themselves asleep, but they were if they lacked the repentance and faith that awakens life from its natural stupor. As the person asleep may need a trumpet to wake him up, so rhetorically the awakening preacher must sharpen his exhortation to get through the daze. If any in his Oxford audience had not grasped the bad news of sin and the good news of grace, Charles Wesley as a student in Christ College spoke boldly: " 'Awake, thou that sleepest, and arise from the dead.' God calleth thee now by my mouth; and bids thee know thyself."[377] "Wake up! Call upon God. If so, God will turn to you that you do not perish." Learning whose you are is your "only concern below."[378] "A mighty tempest is stirred up round about thee, and thou art sinking into the depths."[379] Be attentive to the apostle's plea: "For if we would judge ourselves, we should not be judged."[380]

Stand up. Stir yourself up " 'to lay hold on the Lord,' 'the Lord thy righteousness, mighty to save!' "[381] It is the Lord speaking to your heart: "Shake thyself from the dust,"[382] and cry out: "What must I do to be saved?"[383] And do not drift back into sleep until you "believe on the Lord Jesus, with a faith which is his gift, by the operation of his Spirit."[384]

Those who hear God's voice today, while it is called today, do not harden your hearts. There may not be a tomorrow. Now awake you who sleep in spiritual death, that you will not sleep in eternal death. Receive your lost estate.[385]

a. Summing Up an Evangelical Economic Ethic

John Wesley, assisted by his brother Charles, provided the rudiments of a basic evangelical economic ethic. It is personal, and it begins from the purity of heart that arises out of grace. His ideas have vastly impacted the great eighteenth-century evangelical awakening in Britain and the second great awakening in America.

His main concerns for economic accountability are less focused on theory than practice. Wesley was coaching the small face-to-face communities in his connection of spiritual formation on the right ordering of their whole lives, including their use of their economic resources.

His practical focus was on the use of money and more broadly on the prudent use of talents in the fallen world. His memorable instruction was summarized simply: Gain all you can, save all you can, and give all you can. Gain justly without doing harm or hurting your neighbor in body or spirit. Gaining resources to care for a family is not a sin but a duty.

---

[377]"Awake, Thou That Sleepest," B 1:147, J V:28 – 29, sec. 2.1.
[378]Ibid.
[379]Ibid.
[380]1 Cor. 11:31; "Awake, Thou That Sleepest," B 1:147, J V:28 – 29, sec. 2.1.
[381]Cf. Jer. 23:6.
[382]Isa. 52:2.
[383]Acts 16:30.
[384]"Awake, Thou That Sleepest," B 1:147, J V:29, sec. 2.2.
[385]"Awake, Thou That Sleepest," B 1:152, J V:31 – 32, sec. 2.13.

Save and plan for contingencies, using commonsense business practices, without excessive acquisition, leaving sufficient but not inordinate resources to your children, since wealth tends toward indolence.

Above all, give all you can to the needy. Give in the measure you have received of God. Take care of your family necessities and modest conveniences. Then give the rest out of love to those less able to take care of themselves, as if you were giving an account to God of your use of God's resources.

Since riches tempt foolish desires, beware of the immense danger of riches to the soul, and even more of the danger of increasing riches endlessly. No one can possess riches without great danger to the soul.

Avoid falling into temptation to foolish and hurtful desires: the desires of the flesh and eyes and the pride of life. Unholy desires are a snare to the soul. Do not desire to be rich beyond the basic provisions of food and covering. Avoid indebtedness. Do not exceed the legitimate limits of just gain. Provide for your household and give to the poor. Do not set your heart on riches, adding field to field.

Everything God creates is good. Human reason, imagination, and hard work are required to utilize these God-given resources for the common good. If you are given more in talent and resources, give more.

Those who are being transformed by the renewing of their minds have no need to conform to worldly values, for example, in clothing and housing. Dress modestly. Let the inward life be accurately expressed in outward appearance. Excessive ornamentation detracts from that unmistakable inward beauty of those who live toward God.

Learn the maturity of denying yourself that which is not necessary. Be willing to take up your cross daily as discipleship requires. Redeem the limited time you have. Do good to all as the occasion arises.

Take the measure of sleep you personally require, but not more. Do not throw away resources for doing good. Rigorous time management will not of itself make you a Christian — that only comes by repentance and faith — but it will manifest your faith active in love.

Do not waste away your time in a sleeping stupor. Wake up. Arise from the natural sleep state of humanity.

Further Reading on Economic Ethics

Ball-Kilbourne, Gary. "The Christian as Steward in John Wesley's Theological Ethics." *WQR* 4, no. 1 (1984): 43–54.

Cobb, John B., Jr. *Grace and Responsibility: A Wesleyan Theology for Today.* Nashville: Abingdon, 1995.

Couture, Pamela D. "Sexuality, Economics, and the Wesleyan Alternative." In *Blessed Are the Poor? Women's Poverty, Family Policy, and Practical Theology*, 119–34. Nashville: Abingdon, 1991.

Dieter, Melvin E. "The Wesleyan Perspective." In *Five Views of Sanctification*. Edited by Melvin E. Dieter, 11–46. Grand Rapids: Zondervan, 1987.

Duque, José. *La Tradición Protestante en la Teología Latinoamericana*. San Jose, Costa Rica: DEI, 1983.

Haywood, Clarence. "Was John Wesley a Political Economist?" *Church History* 33 (1964): 314–21.

Heitzenrater, R. P. "John Wesley's Early Sermons." *PWHS* 31 (1970): 110–28; also in *Mirror and Memory*, 150–62. Nashville: Kingswood, 1989.

———, ed. *The Wesleys and the Poor: The Legacy and Development of Methodist Attitudes to Poverty, 1729–1999*, 59–81. Nashville: Kingswood, 2002.

Hulley, Leonard D. *To Be and to Do: Exploring Wesley's Thought on Ethical Behavior*. Pretoria: Univ. of South Africa, 1988.

Jennings, Theodore W., Jr. *Good News to the Poor: John Wesley's Evangelical Economics*. Nashville: Abingdon, 1990.

Kent, John. *Wesley and the Wesleyans: Religion in Eighteenth-Century Britain*. Cambridge: Cambridge Univ. Press, 2002.

Kingdom, Robert. "Laissez-Faire or Government Control: A Problem for John Wesley." *Church History* 26 (1957): 342–54.

Kirkpatrick, Dow, ed. *Faith Born in the Struggle for Life*. Grand Rapids: Eerdmans, 1988.

Kishida, Yuki. "John Wesley's Ethics and Max Weber." *WQR* 4 (1967): 43–58.

MacArthur, Kathleen Walker. *The Economic Ethics of John Wesley*. New York: Abingdon-Cokesbury, 1936.

Macemon, Shirley. *Wesley's Evangelical Economics*. New York: General Board of Global Ministry, 2003. www.gbgm-umc.org/.

Marquardt, Manfred. *John Wesley's Social Ethics: Praxis and Principles*. Nashville: Abingdon, 1992.

Meeks, M. Douglas, ed. *The Portion of the Poor*. Nashville: Kingswood, 1994.

Rogal, Samuel J. *The Financial Aspects of John Wesley's British Methodism (1720–1791)*. Edwin Mellen, 2002.

Rowe, G. Stringer. "A Note on Wesley's Deed Poll." *PWHS* 1 (1897): 37–38.

Runyan, Theodore, ed. *Sanctification and Liberation*. Nashville: Abingdon, 1981.

Semmel, Bernard. *The Methodist Revolution*, 75ff. New York: Basic Books, 1972.

Sherwin, Oscar. *John Wesley: Friend of the People*. New York: Twayne, 1961.

Simon, John S. "John Wesley's Deed of Declaration." *PWHS* 12 (1919): 81–93.

Van Noppen, Jean-Pierre. "Beruf, Calling and the Methodist Work Ethic." In *Wahlverwandtschaften in Sprache, Malerei, Literatur, Geschichte*. Edited by Irène Heidelberger-Leonard and M. Tabash, 69–78. Stuttgart: Verlag Hans-Dieter Heinz, 2000.

Walsh, John. "John Wesley and the Community of Goods." In *Protestant Evangelicalism*. Edited by Keith Robbins, 25–50. Oxford: Blackwell, 1990.

Weber, Theodore R. *Politics in the Order of Salvation: Transforming Wesleyan Political Ethics*. Nashville, Kingswood, 2001.

Wiseman, Frederick Luke. "Herbert and Wesley." *Methodist Recorder* (1933): 14.

PART 3

POLITICAL
ETHICS

CHAPTER 3

Taking a Stand Together

Having discussed character building through communities of accountability and how they impact accountability in the economic order, we now turn to the political order. Evangelical ethics moves from the primary community of faith to the family economy and from there to the political order. What can we take away from the Wesley corpus on political issues such as war, slavery, and social reform?

Introduction to Evangelical Political Ethics

There is little evidence that Wesley was a "political activist" in the modern sense of being actively engaged in influencing legislation or administrative law. Rather, he was focused on the formation of character and habits that would benefit society wherever they were applied. People whose hearts have been redeemed have a capacity to make the realm of legislation, law, jurisprudence, and political administration healthier. Wesley's vocation as a minister of the gospel and pastoral caregiver called him to focus on the heart but also to show the relevance of the renewed heart to public policy questions.

Wesley set forth his principal thoughts on political ethics in five major writings: "The Reformation of Manners," "Public Diversions Denounced," "National Sins and Miseries," a group of essays on war and the search for peace during the American Revolution, and "Thoughts upon Slavery."

A. The Reformation of Manners (1763)

1. Wesley as Moral Reformer

The eighteenth-century forms of evangelical engagement in social change and direct community involvement were focused first on the extremely poor, demoralized, and dysfunctional neighborhoods. No one can read John Wesley's daily journal without noticing his constant concern for the poor, his heart for the marginalized, his reaching out to the underclass on the edges of society.

The leading example of direct social action in Wesley's ministry is illustrated in his active involvement with the Society for the Reformation of Manners, designed to provide relief for the destitute, the sick, and the unemployed. Today's counterparts would be the homeless, street people, prostitutes, and alcoholics in the public parks and streets.

Wesley did not use the term *manners* as it is commonly used today to refer to etiquette. For Wesley, manners involved direct community engagement with the most alienated places in the city to seek one by one to change habituated behaviors.[1]

Founded in London in 1677, the Society for the Reformation of Manners invited John Wesley's father, Samuel Wesley (1662 – 1735), to speak at its annual meeting in 1695 on the reformation of manners. When Samuel's son John was similarly invited in 1763, he spoke to the reconstituted society on the same theme. His father's address "should be compared with this present sermon, sixty-eight years later, for their notable similarity."[2]

a. The Biblical Grounding for Cooperative Evangelical Efforts at Social Change

In this message, Wesley was speaking to persons whose hearts had already been awakened to the need for strong actions to help indigent and marginalize men, and especially the women and children they had neglected. The text is from Psalm 94:16: "Who will rise up for me against the evildoers?" [Homily #52, "The Reformation of Manners," B 2:300 – 323, J II:149 – 67 (preached before the Society for Reformation of Manners at the chapel in West Street, Seven-Dials, London, January 30, 1763)]. This sermon is an appeal to people of conscience to stand together in the worst neighborhoods of London.

In Psalm 94 the faithful are singing of the Lord's faithfulness in coming to relieve Israel in its worst days of trouble:

> Blessed is the one you discipline, LORD,
>   the one you teach from your law;
> you grant them relief from days of trouble,
>   till a pit is dug for the wicked.
> For the LORD will not reject his people;
>   he will never forsake his inheritance.
> Judgment will again be founded on righteousness,
>   and all the upright in heart will follow it.
> Who will rise up for me against the wicked?
>   Who will take a stand for me against evildoers?
> Unless the LORD had given me help,
>   I would soon have dwelt in the silence of death.
> When I said, "My foot is slipping,"
>   your unfailing love, LORD, supported me.

---

[1] The eighteenth-century meaning of *manners* dealt more broadly with decent human conduct, charitable moral behavior, demeanor fitting to the situation, and in general the way, or manner, in which people behave with fairness toward others.

[2] Albert C. Outler, "An Introductory Comment," "The Reformation of Manners," B 2:300. John Wesley's sermonic essay was included in his *Collected Works* of 1771, the third edition of which was published in 1778, and apparently was preached only on that one special occasion.

When anxiety was great within me,
your consolation brought me joy.[3]

b. Taking a Stand Together

The psalm calls the faithful to "take a stand" and to do so in a coordinated way. It reminds the faithful that they are in the long run being blessed as God's children by being disciplined. The community of faith is grateful for the history of salvation, when time and again God has in due time shown his faithfulness to his promises.

Wesley exhorted his colleagues to take a stand against public indecency, especially in regard to persistent public expressions of sick, demeaning, and harmful behavior. When people act together to change their neighborhoods, they multiply their power.

Cooperative human activity can serve either for good or ill. Those who have no love for God or humanity have often "combined together and formed confederacies to carry out evil plans,"[4] by which they have promoted the basest purposes. Similarly, cooperative action can serve the human good. Those who "fear God and desire the happiness of their fellow creatures have, in every age, found it needful to join together in order to oppose the works of darkness."[5]

The Savior himself instructed his disciples to join together "to spread the knowledge of God their Savior, and to promote his kingdom upon earth," in order that they might be united "in one body by one Spirit."[6] Cooperative action is required to follow the biblical command to challenge the demonic powers raging in the world.

The community of faith is more than a voluntary society for social change. Hence it is not analogous to a political interest group. It is a community of faith living by grace within the orders of this world. But within that calling, there are clearly times when the faithful are called to stand together for just social improvements.

Viewed empirically as a social organization, "the original design of the church" can be described as "a body of men compacted together, in order, first, to save each his own soul; then to assist each other in working out their salvation; and, afterwards, as far as in them lies, to save all men from present and future misery."[7] Each member of the community of faith is called to engage actively in the works of love, "otherwise he is not worthy to be called a member thereof, as he is not a living member of Christ."[8] So part of the task of God's church can be described as persons "united together for this very end, to oppose the devil and all his works, and to wage war against the world and the flesh."[9]

---

[3]Ps. 94:12–19 NIV.
[4]"The Reformation of Manners," B 2:301, J II:149, proem, sec. 1.
[5]Ibid.
[6]Ibid.
[7]"The Reformation of Manners," B 2:302, J II:150, proem, sec. 2. The phrase "compacted together" seems to imply a definition of the church as a voluntary body of believers. But elsewhere it is clear that Wesley views the church as a community called by God to share in the body of Christ. See *JWT*, vol. 3, chap. 6, A, "The Church."
[8]Ibid.
[9]"The Reformation of Manners," B 2:302, J II:150, proem, sec. 3.

Faith has social effects. At times the faithful are called to take a stand together. The makeup of this standing together is not always on a congregational or parish level but on a neighborhood or township level, often joining hands with those who have different opinions to correct social corruptions.

Wesley and his colleagues were aware that this "standing together" within a local church was not sufficient to deal with the blatant challenges to decency in their neighborhoods and towns. Rather, "I fear the greater part" of people in churches "are themselves [of] the world, — the people that know not God to any saving purpose; are indulging, day by day, instead of 'mortifying the flesh, with its affections and desires,' and doing, themselves, those works of the devil, which they are peculiarly engaged to destroy."[10] Wesley thought that "there was never more need than there is at this day, for them 'that fear the Lord to speak often together'" that they may "'lift up a standard against the iniquity' which overflows the land."[11]

c. The Purpose of the Society for the Reformation of Manners

This is why "a few persons in London, toward the close of the last century, united together, and after a while, were termed the Society for Reformation of Manners; and incredible good was done by them for near forty years. But then, most of the original members being gone to their reward, those who succeeded them grew faint in their mind, and departed from the work: So that a few years ago the Society ceased."[12] Such is the vacillating history of social movements. They often begin with charismatic leadership that wanes and needs recovery by new leadership, in this case by renewing the Society for the Reformation of Manners.[13] Its purpose had not changed, but the corruptions it faced had grown more viral.

Wesley had four goals in this discourse: to review the original design and to reaffirm the excellence of the design of this society; to answer commonly held objections to this sort of initiative; to define "what manner of men they ought to be who engage in such a design"; and finally, to ask "in what spirit, and in what manner, they should proceed."[14]

2. A Design for Those Seeking a Reformation of Morals

a. Offenses to Public Order

After almost a century of service, the Society for the Reformation of Manners was reorganized on a small scale on a Sunday in August 1757, six years before this address in 1763. The focus was on praying and conversing together, with an immediate interest in redressing "the gross and open profanation of that sacred day, by persons buying and selling, keeping open shop, tippling in alehouses, and standing or sitting in the streets, roads, or fields, vending their wares."[15]

---

[10]Ibid.
[11]"The Reformation of Manners," B 2:302 – 3, J II:150, proem, sec. 4.
[12]"The Reformation of Manners," B 2:303, J II:150 – 51, proem, sec. 5.
[13]"The Reformation of Manners," B 2:303, J II:151, proem, sec. 6.
[14]Ibid.
[15]"The Reformation of Manners," B 2:303 – 4, J II:151, sec. 1.1.

They selected six of their number to begin working in Moorfields, a particularly troubled market area where Wesley chose to launch his first beachhead in London. Starting in Moorfields in London would be analogous to starting in the Bowery in New York.[16] The formative developments in early Methodism were at the Foundry amid the poorest of the poor. Moorfields was a tough area that attracted vendors, auctions, shows, and unsavory dealings of all kinds, including prostitution, theft, banditry, addictive behaviors, homosexuality, and riots.

This was the socially marginal context in which Methodism was born — not in established urban churches or suburban neighborhoods. From this context arose the beginnings of social movements and public initiatives that in the nineteenth century would later turn into more extensive political efforts on the abolition of slavery, the temperance movement, and relief work like that of the Salvation Army.

b. Orderly Steps to Reach Out for the Neediest

The strategy of the Society for the Reformation of Manners was deliberate. Their first approach was aimed at judges, mayors, and police officers responsible for public order: "They first delivered petitions to the Right Honorable the Lord Mayor, and the Court of Aldermen; to the Justices sitting at Hick's Hall; and those in Westminster; and they received from all these honorable benches much encouragement to proceed."[17]

Next they sought to build a base of support in the neighboring religious communities, setting forth "their design to many persons of eminent rank, and to the body of the Clergy, as well as the Ministers of other denominations, belonging to the several churches and meetings in and about the cities of London and Westminster," to which hearty consent was given.[18]

Then they utilized print media to increase public awareness. They "printed and dispersed, at their own expense, several thousand books of instruction to Constables and other Parish Officers." At length they "printed and dispersed in all parts of the town dissuasives from public disorder."[19]

c. Facing Conflict

The society first sought by gentle persuasion to clear "the streets and fields of those notorious offenders who, without any regard either to God or the king, were selling their wares from morning to night."[20] They sought by rational argument to curb "tippling on the Lord's day, spending the time in alehouses."[21] This brought

---

[16]Five Corners is where Phoebe Palmer, a century later, would choose to start her urban missions of social service to addicts and derelicts in the Bowery, which grew out of evangelical holiness prayer meetings. Similarly, the dangerous area of East London was where William and Elizabeth Booth of the Wesleyan-based Salvation Army chose to begin.

[17]"The Reformation of Manners," B 2:304, J II:151, sec. 1.2.

[18]"The Reformation of Manners," B 2:304, J II:151, sec. 1.3.

[19]"The Reformation of Manners," B 2:304–5, J II:151–52, sec. 1.4. A dissuasive is an attempt to dissuade by reason and conscience.

[20]"The Reformation of Manners," B 2:305, J II:152, sec. 1.5.

[21]Ibid.

conflict and reproach by "the tipplers and those who entertained them," including the alehouse keepers, the prostitutes, the landlords of the alehouses, the bartenders, and in short, "all who gained by their sins."[22]

Some resistance to change came from "not only men of substance, but men in authority," the judges and magistrates "before whom the delinquents were brought."[23] The crowds of delinquents threw mud and stones at the reformers and called them vile names. Wesley recalls that the crowds often sought to "beat them without mercy, and to drag them over the stones, or through the kennels" — that is, the open sewers. It is a wonder that they did not murder them.[24]

The miscreants even put pressure on legitimate leaders and officials "to act contrary to their own conscience." When the reformers defended those who refused to give in to pressure, "far from resenting this, or looking upon it as an affront ... they sincerely thanked them for their labor, and acknowledged it as a real kindness."[25]

d. The Reform of Gamblers and Sex Traffickers

The next level of opposition to reform came from "gamesters of various kinds ... and gamblers; who make a trade of seizing on young and inexperienced men, and tricking them out of all their money; and after they have beggared them, they frequently teach them the same."[26] By the early 1760s, "several nests of these" offenders had been rooted out. The reformers persuaded "not a few of them honestly to earn their bread by the sweat of their brow and the labor of their hands."[27]

Then came efforts to remove the sex traffickers and prostitutes or to persuade them to desist. Some were brought to the hospital for treatment. Many of them were stopped in the plying of their trade. "In order to go to the root of the disease, many of the houses that entertained them" were identified and in some cases "prosecuted according to law."[28] Some of these sex traffickers "acknowledged the gracious providence of God and broke off their sins by lasting repentance."[29] Many of these unfortunate women were "stopped in their course of sin," finding "a desire of leading a better life, as it were in answer to that sad question, 'But if I quit the way I now am in, what can I do to live? For I am not mistress of any trade; and I have no friends that will receive me.'"[30] In the wisdom of divine providence, "just at this time, God has prepared the Magdalen Hospital. Here those who have no trade, nor any friends to receive them, are received with all tenderness."[31]

The community reformers kept careful records of outcomes. "The number of persons brought to justice, from August 1757 to August 1762 was 9,596." On the

---

[22]Ibid.
[23]Ibid.
[24]Ibid.
[25]"The Reformation of Manners," B 2:306, J II:152, sec. 1.6.
[26]"The Reformation of Manners," B 2:306–7, J II:153, sec. 1.8.
[27]"The Reformation of Manners," B 2:306, J II:153, sec. 1.7.
[28]"The Reformation of Manners," B 2:306–7, J II:153, sec. 1.8.
[29]Ibid.
[30]"The Reformation of Manners," B 2:307, J II:153, sec. 1.9.
[31]Ibid.

record were numbers relating to cases of selling pornography, unlawful gambling, and profane swearing.[32]

The work of the society was from the outset a transdenominational social action effort that encompassed Christians of many opinions united in the desire to make a poverty-stricken part of London a safer and better place in which to raise families.

There were about 160 regularly active members of the Society for the Reformation of Manners in 1763, along with others who offered occasional assistance. About twenty active members were in connection with George Whitefield, fifty with Wesley, and twenty from the Established Church. Another seventy were Reformed Dissenters, according to Wesley's report.[33] Thus Wesley's societies comprised about one-fourth of the Society for the Reformation of Manners, working closely on social reform among members who had significant doctrinal differences. Those interested in the historic roots of holiness social action movements such as the Salvation Army and later peace movements and antiwar activism do well to read this discourse.

3. The Plan for Decency Reform

a. Taking an Open Stand Together against Social Corruptions That Destroy Healthy Families

These ecumenical efforts sought to manifest the unity of the one body of Christ amid diverse debilitating social sins. People were "standing together" to make families safer and reduce public indecency.

Even if only a few joined to stand together, that did not diminish their influence if they were persistent and courageous. Each one was doing what he could to encourage a more just social order and diminish the effects of evil. But those who entered this hazardous arena had to stand steadfastly together. They were pledged to "render to God the honor due unto his name ... by a stronger proof than words" — namely, willingness to suffer for the neighbor's benefit.[34]

The purpose of this movement for public decency in a civil society was first to address practically "the dishonor done to [God's] glorious name, the contempt which is poured on his authority, and the scandal brought upon our holy religion by the gross, flagrant wickedness of those who are still called by the name of Christ!"[35] It sought "to stem in any degree the torrent of vice," and "the floods of ungodliness" that by their behaviors blaspheme the name of God.[36]

b. Social Peacemaking

Intrinsically related with this purpose was the desire to work for conditions that "conduce to the establishing of 'peace upon earth.'"[37] As our social sins have tended

---

[32]"The Reformation of Manners," B 2:307, J II:154, sec. 1.10.
[33]"The Reformation of Manners," B 2:307–8, J II:154, sec. 1.11.
[34]"The Reformation of Manners," B 2:308, J II:154, sec. 2.1.
[35]"The Reformation of Manners," B 2:308–9, J II:154–55, sec. 2.2.
[36]Ibid.
[37]"The Reformation of Manners," B 2:309, J II:155, sec. 2.3.

to destroy our peace with God and set neighbor against neighbor, "so whatever prevents or removes sin does in the same degree promote peace — peace in our own soul, peace with God, and peace with one another."[38]

"Such are the genuine fruits of this design, even in the present world."[39] What we do in present time and space has reverberations in eternity. The love of God covers a multitude of sins. As the apostle James wrote, "My brothers and sisters, if one of you should wander from the truth and someone should bring that person back, remember this: Whoever turns a sinner from the error of their way will save them from death and cover over a multitude of sins."[40] These efforts redound to the benefit of all, both in church and society, since "righteousness exalts a nation, but sin condemns any people."[41]

The peace of the domestic, economic, political, and civil order is severely damaged by unchallenged evil. The national interest is advanced by the promotion of righteousness.[42] God will reward these efforts and accomplish his promise: "Those who honor me I will honor, but those who despise me will be disdained."[43]

c. Answering Objections to the Design

The Society for the Reformation of Manners faced a flood of objections. Whatever the good intentions of the reformers, some of the critics and authorities said to them: "It does not concern you." Wesley assumed that the proper work of civil authorities was to protect the public against many of these evils. He thought the authorized officials should be taking their assigned duties seriously, but they were not in fact performing them.[44] And when this void of responsibility took command, someone needed to step in. The citizenry had a duty to call public authorities to do their duty.

But all efforts at outward social reformation are unavailing without a change in the heart. "It is true the Word of God is the chief, ordinary means, whereby [God] changes both the hearts and lives of sinners; and he does this chiefly by the ministers of the gospel. But it is likewise true that the magistrate is 'the minister of God,'" whose task is to maintain a just public order. Even if outward reforms do not change the heart, they may effectively resist the illusion that sin holds sway and thus lay less temptation in the path of others.[45]

Others said, "You probably have some commercial interest in your supposed reforms." Wesley challenged them to come forth with any evidence they had, for he knew there was no such evidence. This charge came close to being either defensive evasion or "willful slander."[46]

---

[38]Ibid.
[39]Ibid.
[40]James 5:19 – 20 NIV.
[41]Prov. 14:34 NIV; "The Reformation of Manners," B 2:309, J II:155, sec. 2.4.
[42]"The Reformation of Manners," B 2:309, J II:155, sec. 2.4.
[43]1 Sam. 2:30 NIV; "The Reformation of Manners," B 2:309, J II:155, sec. 2.4.
[44]"The Reformation of Manners," B 2:310, J II:155 – 56, sec. 2.5.
[45]"The Reformation of Manners," B 2:310 – 11, J II:156 – 57, sec. 2.8.
[46]"The Reformation of Manners," B 2:310, J II:156, sec. 2.6.

Others considered the entire effort futile, claiming that "vice is risen to such a head that it is impossible to suppress it; especially by such means. For what can a handful of poor people do in opposition to all the world?"[47] Admittedly the challenge is great, but Wesley recalled to them the words of Jesus: "With men this is impossible, but not with God."[48]

The quantity of the active reformers was less important than their tenacity and inward determination. "It is the same thing with God 'to deliver by many or by few.' "[49] Small committed armies can have great victories.[50] "The small number, therefore, of those who are on the Lord's side is nothing; neither the great number of those that are against him."[51]

Others wanted to rule out human hands altogether by objecting that social reform is not the work of either ministers or magistrates but the work of God. Wesley thought that this argument could become an evasion that ducked human responsibility by a feckless appeal to God's omnipotence. He believed the Spirit inspires human minds and hands to go to work in response to the sufficient grace of God who gives us freedom.

Some claimed that these measures made hypocrites of both the reformers and the supposedly reformed, "pretending to be what they [were] not." Wesley asked for evidence of hypocrisy: "We know none who have pretended to be what they were not." The outcome: "Some of them, far from being worse, are substantially better, the whole tenor of their lives being changed," and some are truly changed inwardly from darkness to light.[52]

Others cautioned, "But mild methods ought to be tried first." This, says Wesley, is exactly what they were doing at first, with mild admonitions and appeals to reason before any other actions were taken. "In every case the mildest method is used which the nature of the case will bear; nor are severer means ever applied but when they are absolutely necessary to the end."[53]

Others questioned the outcomes: "Well, but after all this stir about reformation, what real good has been done?" Wesley asked objectors to look carefully at the outcomes: "Unspeakably good and abundantly more than anyone could have expected in so short a time, considering the small number of the instruments and the difficulties they had to encounter."[54] Further, much evil has been prevented, and many have been inwardly changed.[55]

---

[47]"The Reformation of Manners," B 2:310, J II:156, sec. 2.7.
[48]"The Reformation of Manners," B 2:310, J II:156, sec. 2.7; cf. Matt. 19:26.
[49]"The Reformation of Manners," B 2:310, J II:156, sec. 2.7; cf. 1 Sam. 14:6.
[50]See, e.g., Judg. 7:7 NIV: "The LORD said to Gideon, 'With the three hundred men that lapped [water] I will save you and give the Midianites into your hands. Let all the others go home.'"
[51]"The Reformation of Manners," B 2:310, J II:156, sec. 2.7.
[52]"The Reformation of Manners," B 2:311, J II:157, sec. 2.9.
[53]"The Reformation of Manners," B 2:311, J II:157, sec. 2.11.
[54]"The Reformation of Manners," B 2:312, J II:157–58, sec. 2.12.
[55]Ibid.

JOHN WESLEY'S TEACHINGS — VOLUME 4

4. Seek Out Those Few Who Are Called to This Service

a. Qualities Required for Useful Participation

Frankly, not everyone is suited for the hazardous work of social reform. But greater effectiveness will not come from increasing numbers or lowering standards. "Though neither many, rich, nor powerful" were participating in the earlier work of the society, they broke "through all opposition, and were eminently successful in every branch of their undertaking." They were carefully chosen and fully committed. "But when a number of men less carefully chosen were received into that Society, they grew less and less useful, till, by insensible degrees, they dwindled into nothing."[56]

God works more powerfully through the few who are wholly committed than the many who are wavering. "This is a work of God. It is undertaken in the name of God and for his sake. It follows that men who neither love nor fear God have no part or lot in this matter."[57] So do not take on the covenant of reform if you yourself hate to be reformed. "Let none who stands himself in need of this reformation presume to meddle with such an undertaking. First let him 'pull the beam out of his own eye.' "[58]

b. You Must Be More Than a Harmless Person

Everyone engaging in this work is called to be more than a "harmless man."[59] He should be "a man of faith, having at least such a degree of that 'evidence of things not seen,' as to 'aim not at the things that are seen, which are temporal, but at those that are not seen, which are eternal.' "[60]

Those to be sought out as colaborers must have "such a faith as produces a steady fear of God, with a lasting resolution, by his grace, to abstain from all that he has forbidden, and to do all that he has commanded." Their confidence in God "enables one to stand against and 'chase a thousand,' knowing in whom his strength lies."[61] Joshua's dying words to his best leaders picture the kind of person required for this struggle: "One of you routs a thousand, because the LORD your God fights for you, just as he promised."[62]

This work requires courage regarding the future and patience in the present.[63] Its leaders need steadiness to hold fast to their profession of faith. This is no place

---

[56]"The Reformation of Manners," B 2:312, J II:158, sec. 3.1.
[57]"The Reformation of Manners," B 2:312 – 13, J II:158, sec. 3.2.
[58]Ibid.
[59]In 1978 John Murray Cuddihy of the City University of New York wrote *No Offense: Civil Religion and Protestant Taste* (New York and Greenwich: Seabury). He provided a critique of American civil religion that has lost its distinctive religious memory in order to accommodate perceived majority opinions. Thus the religious leader in modern America has become a timid voice, a "harmless man." A similar critique was anticipated two centuries earlier by Wesley, who urged reformers to "cut off an occasion for offense" if it intends to increase hostility, but let Christ be the offense he truly is to human self-righteousness.
[60]"The Reformation of Manners," B 2:313, J II:158 – 59, sec. 3.3; cf. 2 Cor. 4:18.
[61]"The Reformation of Manners," B 2:313, J II:158 – 59, sec. 3.2 – 3.
[62]Josh. 23:10 NIV; "The Reformation of Manners," B 2:313, J II:158 – 59, sec. 3.3.
[63]"The Reformation of Manners," B 2:313 – 14, J II:158 – 59, sec. 3.4 – 5.

for the "double minded" who "is unstable in his ways."[64] "A reed shaken with the wind is not fit for this warfare, which demands a firm purpose of soul, a constant, determined resolution."[65]

Avoid choosing one who sets his hand to the plow but soon looks back.[66] "Indeed, it is hard for any to persevere in so unpleasing a work, unless love overpowers both pain and fear."[67] He must be ready to lay down his life for his brothers, and indeed for "every soul for which Christ died."[68] This love must not be puffed up, but must elicit courage, patience, and humility. God resists the proud but gives grace only to the humble.[69]

5. Reshaping Civil Discourse

The work of reform is not accomplished through anger. "Everyone should be quick to listen, slow to speak and slow to become angry, because human anger does not produce the righteousness that God desires."[70] Those who undertake this work must "learn of him who was meek, as well as lowly."[71]

a. The Gentle Character of Christian Social Reform

Walk with a single eye toward God's glory for the benefit of human good. "If ... thine eye be single, thy whole body shall be full of light."[72]

In every word and act, "nothing is to be spoke or done, either great or small, with a view to any temporal advantage; nothing with a view to the favor or esteem, the love or the praise, of men. But the intention, the eye of the mind, is always to be fixed on the glory of God" at work for the good of broken humanity.[73] The Lord on the Mount taught, "The eye is the lamp of the body. If your eyes are healthy, your whole body will be full of light. But if your eyes are unhealthy, your whole body will be full of darkness. If then the light within you is darkness, how great is that darkness!"[74]

The temperament of Christian social engagement will flow from the motive. With courage, patience, and steadiness, "let him 'take the shield of faith.' This will quench a thousand fiery darts. Let him exert all the faith which God has given him, in every trying hour."[75] Let "all his doings be done in love," clothed with humility, "filling his heart, and adorning his whole behavior."[76] Let that mind be in him which

---

[64]James 1:8; "The Reformation of Manners," B 2:314, J II:160, sec. 3.6.
[65]"The Reformation of Manners," B 2:314, J II:160, sec. 3.6; cf. Matt. 11:7.
[66]"The Reformation of Manners," B 2:314, J II:160, sec. 3.6; cf. Luke 9:62.
[67]"The Reformation of Manners," B 2:314, J II:160, sec. 3.7.
[68]"The Reformation of Manners," B 2:315, J II:160, sec. 3.8.
[69]Ibid.; cf. 1 Peter 5:5.
[70]James 1:19 – 20 NIV.
[71]"The Reformation of Manners," B 2:316, J II:160, sec. 3.10; cf. Matt. 11:29.
[72]Matt. 6:22.
[73]"The Reformation of Manners," B 2:316 – 17, J II:161 – 62, sec. 4.1.
[74]Matt. 6:22 – 23 NIV; "The Reformation of Manners," B 2:316 – 17, J II:161 – 62, sec. 4.1.
[75]"The Reformation of Manners," B 2:317, J II:162, sec. 4.2; cf. Eph. 6:16.
[76]"The Reformation of Manners," B 2:317, J II:162, sec. 4.2.

was in Jesus Christ.[77] "Clothe yourselves with compassion, kindness, humility, gentleness and patience. Bear with each other and forgive one another if any of you has a grievance against someone. Forgive as the Lord forgave you. And over all these virtues put on love, which binds them all together in perfect unity."[78] Do all things with "recollection of spirit, watching against all hurry or dissipation of thought."[79] Continue always in prayer, "offering all to God through the Son of his love."[80]

As to the manner or outward expression of efforts at social reform, let the outward behavior "be expressive of these inward tempers."[81] Do not foolishly employ evil means for good ends. Do not "do evil that good may come."[82] "Use no fraud or guile, either in order to detect or to punish any man, but 'by simplicity and godly sincerity' 'commend yourself to men's consciences in the sight of God.'"[83] "Suit your words and whole behavior to the persons with whom you have to do; to the time, place, and all other circumstances."[84] "Cut off occasions of offense, even from those who seek occasion, and to do things of the most offensive nature in the least offensive manner that is possible."[85]

b. Do Not Be in Haste to Increase Numbers

In the work of societal reform, do not be "in haste to increase your numbers."[86] Do not regard "wealth, rank, or any outward circumstance" as criteria. Better to work closely as a person of "faith, courage, patience, steadiness ... [and] a lover of God and man. If so, he will add to your strength, as well as number."[87]

Do not be afraid to remove any who do not have these qualities.[88] "By thus lessening your number, you will increase your strength."[89] Do not allow your intent to be "stained with any regard either to profit or praise."[90]

Take specific conditions into full account: "Know what you are about; be thoroughly acquainted with what you have in hand; consider the objections which are made to the whole of your undertaking; and before you proceed, be satisfied that those objections have no real weight: Then may every man act as he is fully persuaded in his own mind."[91]

---

[77]See Phil. 2:5.
[78]Col. 3:12–14 NIV.
[79]"The Reformation of Manners," B 2:317, J II:162, sec. 4.2.
[80]Ibid.
[81]"The Reformation of Manners," B 2:317–18, J II:162, sec. 4.3.
[82]Ibid.
[83]Ibid.; cf. 2 Cor. 4:2.
[84]"The Reformation of Manners," B 2:318, J II:163, sec. 4.4.
[85]Ibid.
[86]"The Reformation of Manners," B 2:319, J II:163–64, sec. 5.2.
[87]Ibid.
[88]Ibid.
[89]Ibid.
[90]Ibid.
[91]"The Reformation of Manners," B 2:318–19, J II:163, sec. 5.1.

c. Do Not Miss Any Opportunity

Do what is at hand to do. "Whatever you do, work at it with all your heart, as working for the Lord, not for human masters, since you know that you will receive an inheritance from the Lord as a reward. It is the Lord Christ you are serving."[92] "Do not aim at pleasing yourself in any point, but at pleasing him whose you are and whom you serve. Let your eye be single, from first to last; eye God alone in every word and work."[93] "As you have opportunity do good to all men."[94] Do not miss any opportunity.

If so, the Almighty under whom you stand with awe "has qualified you for promoting his work in a more excellent way."[95] "You can stand with boldness before them that despise you, and make no account of your labors."[96]

Do not say, "This is too heavy a cross; I have not strength or courage to bear it!" Your strength comes not from yourself but the Lord. Believe that you "can do all things through Christ strengthening you."[97] "All things are possible to him that believeth."[98] "No cross is too heavy for him to bear, knowing that they that 'suffer with him, shall reign with him.'"[99] "Take ... no thought for the morrow,"[100] but "cast all your care on him that careth for you!"[101]

B. Public Diversions Denounced (1732)

"The Reformation of Manners" discourse was given in 1763 when Wesley was sixty years old. Thirty-one years before when he was twenty-nine years old, he was serving as an assistant in his father's parish at Epworth. He entered into a public controversy on a hotly contested local issue of importance to the people of Lincoln County: the moral hazards of betting.

1. On Betting Games and Sports That Bring Out the Worst in People

When Wesley spoke of "public diversons," he was thinking of activities like horse racing, games of chance, bearbaiting, boxing, and cockfighting. He thought these events made little contribution to the public good. But more seriously, they tempted the soul toward the desires of the flesh, the desires of the eyes, and the pride of life.

There is a backstory here. A disastrous fire occurred in Epworth that caused extensive damage to the town on August 31, 1732. A horse race on Friday at

---

[92]Col. 3:23 – 24 NIV.
[93]"The Reformation of Manners," B 2:319, J II:164, sec. 5.3.
[94]Cf. Gal. 6:10.
[95]"The Reformation of Manners," B 2:321 – 23, J II:165 – 67, sec. 5.7.
[96]Cf. Wisd. Sol. 5:1.
[97]Phil. 4:13.
[98]Mark 9:23.
[99]Cf. 2 Tim. 2:12.
[100]Matt. 6:34.
[101]"The Reformation of Manners," B 2:321 – 23, J II:165 – 67, sec. 5.7; cf. 1 Peter 5:7.

Epworth was thought to be connected in the public mind with this terrifying fire that did horrible damage to the town. The fire had started in a malt liquor kiln owned by Wesley's ne'er-do-well brother-in-law, Richard Ellison, who had married Wesley's sister Susanna. Many in the community viewed the negligence as a sign of divine judgment.

Four days later, on September 3, John Wesley preached this sermon from the pulpit where his father was rector, and he likely preached it on only this one occasion. It remained in his papers and was later published as "On Public Diversions" [Homily #140, J #143, "Public Diversions Denounced," B 4:318 – 28, J 500 – 508 (September 3, 1732)]. The prophet Amos had warned of seemingly harmless occasions that may cause great harm both to the person and to the society. Wesley's text came from an urgent call to action from this fiery prophet:

> "Is a trumpet blown in a city,
>   and the people are not afraid?
> Does disaster come to a city,
>   unless the LORD has done it?
> For the Lord GOD does nothing
>   without revealing his secret
>   to his servants the prophets.
> The lion has roared;
>   who will not fear?
> The Lord GOD has spoken;
>   who can but prophesy?"[102]

a. The Question

The plain sense of this prophecy of Amos is paraphrased by Wesley: "Are there any men in the world so stupid and senseless, so utterly void of common reason, so careless of their own and their neighbors' safety or destruction, as when an alarm of approaching judgments is given, to show no signs of apprehension, to take no care in order to prevent them, but go on as securely as if no alarm had been given?"[103]

The Christian teaching of providence perceives the hand of God in all things, whether by permission or active judgment of human follies. In the previous volumes of this series, I have examined Wesley's teaching on providence and judgment.[104] This homily provides a case in point of negligence leading to disaster. There were two opinions in the town about this event: it was either business as usual or a disaster as a warning to repent.

b. Spurn High-Risk Voluntary Actions to Avoid Still Greater Evils

These forewarnings of disaster serve a purpose: "to warn men to avoid still

---

[102] Amos 3:6 – 8 ESV. Wesley focused primarily on the sixth verse: "Shall a trumpet be blown in the city, and the people not be afraid? shall there be evil in the city, and the LORD hath not done it?" (KJV).

[103] "Public Diversions Denounced," B 4:320 – 21, J VII:500 – 501, sec. 1.

[104] See JWT, vol. 1, chap. 6, C, "Providence"; and vol. 2, chap. 6, "Predestination."

greater evils."[105] They have a gracious purpose. They show that God permits "these lighter marks of his displeasure to awaken mankind, so that they may shun his everlasting vengeance." They call sinners "to change their ways that his whole displeasure may not arise."[106] That larger displeasure points not only to God's daily judgment of sin in this world, but final judgment on the last day. All who have their eyes open and know the omnipotence of God should be able to discern that whatever evil befalls humanity, it comes by the just permissive will of the divine Judge.

Wesley focused on three truths about high risk taking in voluntary events:

1. "There is no evil in any place but the hand of the Lord is in it."[107]
2. "Every uncommon evil is the trumpet of God blown in that place, so that the people may take warning."[108]
3. All are called to "consider whether, after God has blown his trumpet in this place," all the populous should have been put on notice.[109]

The trumpets that accompany disastrous events are a warning that seeks behavioral change not only in individuals but in communities.

2. No Matter How Foolish We Are, God Still Reigns

a. There Is No Evil in Which the Hand of the Omnipresent God Is Absent

The first gracious purpose of warning signals amid disasters is this: wherever evil appears in history, it is not beyond the reach of God's capacity to turn it to good.

"No evil, that is, no affliction or calamity, whether of a public or of a private nature, whether it concerns only one, or a few persons, or reaches to many, or to all" — nothing occurs without God's hand in it in some unseen way.[110] Such events "never happen but by the knowledge and permission of God."[111]

The omniscient and omnipotent Lord can express his will either directly through his judgment or indirectly through permission for these warnings to occur, allowing time for behavioral change. God is not unjust in sending these gracious forewarnings. In the disaster at hand, the Lord was either actively intervening with his direct and immediate power, by the strength of his own right hand, or by permitting disastrous consequences to happen through human hands exercising their freedom of the will.[112] In this indirect and permissive way, his will is being done even by forewarnings and constraints. However tragic, amid all this "the Lord God Omnipotent still reigns."[113]

---

[105]"Public Diversions Denounced," B 4:320, J VII:501, proem.
[106]Ibid.
[107]Ibid.
[108]Ibid.
[109]Ibid.
[110]"Public Diversions Denounced," B 4:320–21, J VII:500–501, sec. 1.1.
[111]Ibid.
[112]Ibid. This does not override human freedom but expresses God's attention to the consequences of freedom.
[113]"Public Diversions Denounced," B 4:320–21, J VII:500–501, sec. 1.1.

Through acts of forewarning, God may "permit a smaller evil that he may prevent greater." Hence God is no less gracious when he mercifully permits what humans call evil in order to bring them a greater good.[114] God's purpose can be expressed in human history by any means God chooses, even "the mistakes, carelessness, or malice of men."[115]

b. The Trumpet Is Blown in Order to Be Heard as a Dire Warning

"Every uncommon evil is the trumpet of God blown in that place where it comes, that the people may take warning."[116] The warning itself is a beneficial gift of God. "But if any extraordinary affliction occurs, especially when many persons are concerned in it, we may not only say that in this God speaks to us, but that the God of glory thunders," demanding "the deepest attention of all to whom it comes."[117] The thunder is addressed not only to a single person but all about him, in order that "all people ... should tremble at the presence of God!"[118] Gross public immorality and evil are like a trumpet of God to forewarn the faithful "not to continue in anything that displeases him."[119]

Had the Lord been blowing this trumpet in relation to Epworth's high-risk diversions? Wesley takes this event as a case in point of ignoring public duty and good judgment. When such a public event has already had disastrous consequences, what are the faithful to learn from it?[120]

c. The Warning Leaves Us without Excuse

The warning in this case was the fire that spread quickly through town. It called for general repentance from careless behavior. No one had an excuse for not listening to such a clear trumpet sound. Everyone beheld the flames and smoke of its devastation. Rather than ignoring it, Wesley was calling the whole town and nearby countryside to seek God with their whole hearts. Many in the towns surrounding Epworth had also heard the warning signs. They should have striven "to make [their] calling and election sure."[121]

No one can see into the hearts of others. But each one, without judging rashly, must ask inwardly what form of judgment and accountability is required in the disaster.[122]

d. Ignoring the Warning

The next day after the fire in which the "voice of God had so dreadfully commanded us to exchange our mirth for sadness," the horse racing blithely resumed! It

---

[114]Ibid.
[115]Ibid.
[116]"Public Diversions Denounced," B 4:321 – 22, J VII:501 – 2, sec. 2.1.
[117]Ibid.
[118]Ibid.
[119]Ibid.
[120]"Public Diversions Denounced," B 4:322 – 23, J VII:502 – 3, sec. 3.1.
[121]2 Peter 1:10; "Public Diversions Denounced," B 4:322 – 23, J VII:502 – 3, sec. 3.1.
[122]"Public Diversions Denounced," B 4:322 – 23, J VII:502 – 3, sec. 3.1.

was as if no trumpet had ever sounded. "Crowds of people flocked out of that very town where the destruction had been wrought the day before" to be the first to get to "the place of entertainment!"[123]

Picture the irony: on one side of the street "were the mourners bewailing the loss of their goods and the necessities of their families; on the other, the feasters delighting themselves with the sport they had gained. Surely, such a mixture of mirth and sadness, of feasting and mourning, of laughing and weeping, hath not been seen from the day in which our forefathers first came up into this land, until yesterday."[124] They seemed unwilling to examine their consciences so as to "avoid whatever is displeasing in [God's] sight."[125]

3. Harming Others through Seemingly Harmless Acts

a. When Harm Is Mixed with Seeming Good

The gracious purpose of warning signals arising from such a disaster is to call people to "consider whether, after God has blown his trumpet in this place," they have been responsive.[126] They make us aware of our finitude. They call us to stand in awe over the presence of God and to alert us to serious danger. Especially ruinous disasters give us every reason to reassess our own security.[127]

Spiritous liquors, for example, may seem harmless. Consider whether their use is mixed with harm to others. It is better to ask if they might have poisonous potential consequences.[128] "Might there be harm to others in a diversion that is supposed to be harmless in itself?"[129]

If a seemingly harmless activity is not damaging to you, have you asked how it may be damaging to others?[130] Why should your supposed strength against potentially addictive habituation be an excuse for bringing trouble to the weak brother for whom Christ died?[131] The one who warns against bad habits is not uncharitable.

The same analogy may be applied to other fixed habits accompanying seemingly harmless diversions such as lying, cheating, and unjust gain.[132] Everyone has seen small habituations become large, with even larger consequences for the eternal destiny of the soul.[133]

b. Temptation in High-Risk Behavior

This truth is illustrated by one of the most insidious of temptations — covetousness. For many people their very reason for betting and gaming is to win a large sum of

[123]"Public Diversions Denounced," B 4:323 – 24, J VII:503 – 4, sec. 3.2.
[124]Ibid.
[125]Ibid.
[126]"Public Diversions Denounced," B 4:320, J VII:501, proem.
[127]"Public Diversions Denounced," B 4:324 – 25, J VII:504 – 5, sec. 4.1.
[128]Ibid.
[129]Ibid.
[130]Ibid.
[131]Ibid.
[132]Ibid.
[133]Ibid.

money. The diversion gives an occasion "to all who please to lay wagers with one another, which commonly brings so strong a desire of possessing what is another's as will hardly cease when that one point is decided, but will be exceedingly likely to leave such a thirst in the mind as not all the winning in the world will satisfy."[134] "What amends can the trifling sport of a thousand people make for one soul thus corrupted and ruined?" Christian teaching "values one soul more than the whole world,"[135] since the soul is eternal and earthly things are temporal.

Some public diversions are "apt to inflame those passions which [God] so earnestly commands us to quench." The naive are prone to become "heated on such occasions."[136] Their passions may lead to brawling or even in this case the burning down of a city.[137]

Until these consequences are considered, "let no one say, 'What hurt is there in a horse race?'" Young persons are especially vulnerable to temptation when the risk seems small and the potential reward great. The desires of the eyes may be inflamed. The betting game may "nourish that friendship which is enmity with God."[138] The temptation may strengthen "affections which are already too strong — the desire of the eye and the pride of life."[139] The harm may be widely dispersed beyond all expectations. Even a horse race may elicit unhappy habituations. We pray that we not be "led into temptation." The tempted may gamble away "that seed which might have borne fruit to eternity!"[140]

Do not give a hazardous opportunity to those who are unaware of the hazard. If you had exercised protective care to your helpless brethren, "your blessed Redeemer would have esteemed it as done unto himself."[141] Do not throw away a talent that might have been "an everlasting gain" to you and to others.

The poor are "most hurt of all." Do not throw away "what your wife and family wanted at home. If so, you have denied the faith."[142] Had you not run after trifling diversions, you might have been "employed in honest labor," adding value to family and society.[143]

c. An Appeal to Christians Tempted to High-Risk Behavior

Wesley personally called the faithful to "an understanding heart, and a discerning spirit — who, if they have formerly erred, are now resolved by the grace of God to return no more…. The time has come, not only to avoid, but also earnestly to oppose, whatsoever is contrary to the will of God."[144]

[134]Ibid.
[135]"Public Diversions Denounced," B 4:325, J VII:505, sec. 4.2.
[136]Ibid.
[137]"Public Diversions Denounced," B 4:326, J VII:505, sec. 4.3.
[138]"Public Diversions Denounced," B 4:326–27, J VII:505–6, sec. 4.4; cf. James 4:4.
[139]"Public Diversions Denounced," B 4:326–27, J VII:505–6, sec. 4.4.
[140]Ibid.
[141]Ibid.
[142]Ibid.; cf. 1 Tim. 5:8.
[143]"Public Diversions Denounced," B 4:326–27, J VII:505–6, sec. 4.4.
[144]"Public Diversions Denounced," B 4:327–28, J VII:507–8, sec. 5.

If you are rich, "scorn all employments that are useless, but much more if they are sinful."[145]

If you are elderly "bestow all the time which you can spare from the necessary business of this life, in preparing yourself and those about you for their entrance into a better life."[146]

If you are rich, "labor that you may be rich in good works. For you are those to whom much is given, not to throw away, but to use well and wisely; and of you much shall be required."[147]

Each one is called to "provide for your own household."[148] Labor "that you may give to him that needs — not to him that needs diversions, but to him that needs the necessaries of nature ... clothes to cover him, food to support his life, or a house where to lay his head."[149] Show all the mercy you can to those afflicted by sins that seem innocent but have consequences.

To modern readers it may seem petty to take the unfortunate occasions of a fire associated with a sporting event as an example of careless irresponsibility with unexpected consequences. But to those in Epworth who lost their houses in the fire, it was not petty.

Having now discussed two cases of Wesley's political ethics, "The Reformation of Manners" (1763), and "Public Diversions Denounced" (1732), we turn to several of Wesley's essays on war and the search for peace during the early stages of the American Revolution (1775 – 78), concluding with his "Thoughts upon Slavery" (1774).

---

[145]Ibid.
[146]Ibid.
[147]Ibid.
[148]Ibid.
[149]Ibid.

CHAPTER 4

War and the Search for Peace

Before and during the early part of the American Revolution, John Wesley was seeking a way of peace between American aspirations and British law. As one who had lived in America and returned to England, he empathized with both sides. He sought solutions within established law to resolve conflict. In "National Sins and Miseries," we see him as a pastor and grief counselor caring for widows of soldiers who had fallen in the American conflict.

A. National Sins and Miseries (1775)

"National Sins and Miseries" is a compassionate speech on behalf of women and children who were suffering from violence and anarchy. The specter of anarchy in 1775, just before the American and French Revolutions, was unnerving, especially to those who valued just law and safe public order.

Wesley himself had been personally threatened or attacked several times by mobs.[1] At times the law stood between him and the mob. But at Wednesbury, Walsall, and Darleston in Staffordshire,[2] he was hounded by a roving mob of over two hundred. He had to wade into the agitated crowd to calm them. Wesley strongly believed in the rule of law. The opposite of the rule of law is anarchy. Anarchists seek the complete breakdown of law. Wesley thought that wild utopian dreams would become the root of immense suffering.

1. When the Shepherd Does Wrong, the Sheep Suffer

The earliest battles of the American Revolution caused an unexpectedly high number of casualties among British soldiers. Wesley was invited to address a solemn gathering, called together to support the widows and orphans of British war casualties. He spoke compassionately on the theme of the nations' miseries, making it one of the most poignant moments in which he defended the rule of law.

Wesley chose a moving moment from the story of David when he became aware

---

[1]See *JJW*: Various mob actions and riots were reported or suppressed in Birmingham, 5:48–49; Bolton, 3:442–43; Cork, 3:409–14, 3:471–72; London, 2:522–23; Penzance, 3:307–9; Wrangle, 3:533; Shepton Mallet, 3:249–50; Port Isaac, 3:308; Falmouth, 3:189–90, and about a dozen other places.
[2]*JJW*, 3:98–104; October 20–21, 1743.

that his own actions had caused many innocents to suffer: "When David saw the angel who was striking down the people, he said to the LORD, 'I have sinned; I, the shepherd, have done wrong. These are but sheep. What have they done? Let your hand fall on me and my family'" [2 Sam. 24:17 NIV, "National Sins and Miseries," Homily #130, B 3:546 – 76, J VII:400 – 408 (1775)].

The major theme of this homily is judgment on sin and mercy toward the innocent. But in it Wesley ties together many subthemes, including covenants between the government and its citizens, the social nature of sin, a theodicy of innocent social suffering, political partisanship, the morality of law and revolution, the sins of colonialism, and the critique of colonialism. The beginning point is mercy to the families of the fallen.

a. For the Benefit of Widows and Orphans of Those Fallen Near Boston

The situation to which Wesley had been invited to speak was filled with grief and pathos. The occasion was "for the benefit of the widows and orphans of the soldiers who lately fell, near Boston, in New England."[3] This was during the year before the Declaration of Independence was signed. The American Revolution was only barely beginning. Wesley warned, "Beware how you impute this [conflict] to the fountain of love and holiness!"[4] The merciful God had not directly caused this suffering, but he permits the conditions of freedom, which when misused, cause uncontrollable social consequences.

Speaking at St. Matthew's Church in Bethnal Green, London, on November 7, 1775, Wesley was called to comfort and support the families of those wounded or killed in the war. His words were an expression of compassion and empathy for the women and children left behind.

He asked, who is left amid this madness to care for "the wife of the soldier's youth" who is "now left a disconsolate widow," often with no one to care for her? She is "deprived of her only comfort and support, and not having where to lay her head."[5] Even worse, "Who considered his helpless children, now desolate orphans — it may be, crying for bread, while their mother has nothing left to give them but her sorrows and her tears?"[6] Wesley was not speaking here as a political theorist or public policy advocate, but as a pastor. He was engaged in a poignant act of personal pastoral consolation of grief.[7]

The theological premise of his message was this: Do not attribute evil to God. Attribute to the judgment of God the fair punishment of recalcitrant sin.

b. Social Sin in the Covenant Relation between Rulers and People

The biblical story finds King David at a despairing moment of his life, strug-

---

[3] "National Sins and Miseries," B 3:566, J VII:400, proem, sec. 1.
[4] Ibid.
[5] "National Sins and Miseries," B 3:572, J VII:405, sec. 1.6.
[6] Ibid.
[7] Ibid.

gling to understand his responsibility and praying for divine guidance. He had just realized after taking a census that he had done wrong. He prayed for mercy: "Now, LORD, I beg you, take away the guilt of your servant. I have done a very foolish thing."[8] But his error had already harmed innocent people.

Personal sin elicits social consequences. People share in the political sins of their country. "God frequently punishes a people for the sins of their rulers, because they are generally partakers of their sins, in one kind or other."[9] Regardless of whether the sin is due to the will of an individual or the will of a community, the judgment may fall on the whole community. The unseen justice of divine judgment is lodged finally in the mystery of the omniscient God. Like David, we can pray for moral discernment in such times.

When there is such a general wickedness spread abroad, all suffer, even when they did not directly participate in the decisions that eventually led to a calamity. Why? Because nations and families have entered jointly into covenant with God. Divine-human covenants may be corporately made with whole nations involved. As divine benefits accrue from just behavior, so does divine judgment accrue from unjust behavior, and it may affect everyone in the covenanting community — both the guilty and the innocent.[10] From this we learn that we do not live a solitary existence as if in an individualistic bubble, but in a community called to social accountability. The sin we knowingly do contributes to the burden of sin dispersed through the whole society.

c. The Cause of Social Misery

This reliable principle is clear from an examination of historical experience: "Vice is the parent of misery."[11] The conflict in the American colonies is a case in point. The anarchic threat of disruption of the rule of law had become an occasion for a social theodicy — a shared, corporate, interdependent occasion of suffering: "Are not our own vices sufficient to account for all our sufferings? Let us fairly and impartially consider this; let us examine our own hearts and lives."[12] We all suffer, and we have all sinned. Everyone's own sins bring "sufferings both on himself and others."[13]

The populace often suffers from the unwise decisions of its rulers. They assume or acquire general consent by the active or passive wills of many in interdependent relationships. "When we speak of sin as the cause of misery, we usually mean the sin of other people and suppose we suffer because they sin."[14] This can be illustrated in the economic order as it impacts the political order. The very conditions of colonialism provide a tragic case in point.

---

[8]2 Sam. 24:10 NIV.
[9]"National Sins and Miseries," B 3:567, J VII:401, proem, sec. 4.
[10]"National Sins and Miseries," B 3:567–68, J VII:401, proem, secs. 3–5.
[11]"National Sins and Miseries," B 3:568, J VII:402, proem, sec. 5.
[12]"National Sins and Miseries," B 3:568, J VII:401, sec. 1.1.
[13]Ibid.
[14]Ibid.

2. The Economic and Political Calamity in the British-American Conflict

Wesley was a keen observer of both economic and political processes and their consequences.

a. A Theodicy of the Colonial Crisis

Wesley began his social theodicy of the colonial crisis with a discussion of economic dislocation. This he knew personally. He traveled constantly from village to village and had a close look at the ground-level economy. He was keenly aware of the social effects of trade and economic activity on families and nations. His message begins with observations on the high unemployment in Britain that resulted in part from the ambiguous actions in New England.

The economic suffering of people all over the English countryside was evident: "Thousands and tens of thousands are at this day deeply afflicted through want of business.... Thousands of people in the west of England, throughout Cornwall in particular, in the north, and even in the midland counties, are totally unemployed ... deprived not only of the conveniences, but most of the necessaries of life."[15]

Wesley knew the rural poor well. He had traveled on horseback to provide spiritual formation for hundreds of villages all over England. He sat at their tables and slept under their roofs. He poignantly described the desperate economic condition of many villagers: "I have seen not a few of these wretched creatures, within little more than an hundred miles of London, standing in the streets with pale looks, hollow eyes, and meager limbs; or creeping up and down like walking shadows. I have known families, who a few years ago lived in an easy, genteel manner, reduced to just as much raiment as they had on, and as much food as they could gather in the field. To this one or other of them repaired once a day, to pick up the turnips which the cattle had left; which they boiled, if they could get a few sticks, or otherwise ate them raw. Such is the want of food to which many of our countrymen are at this day reduced by want of business!"[16]

When the economy is in gridlock, everybody suffers. But not in body only: "It is a great affliction to be deprived of bread, but it is still greater to be deprived of our senses."[17] Wesley thought that a dangerous form of social madness was widespread. He described the near frenzy of those who sought a quick, utopian solution to the calamity of widespread social sin. He was searching for the deeper cause of the social madness so rife in 1775 England.

b. The Consequences of Partisan Fervor

Wesley knew firsthand about colonial America because he had spent two years in Georgia. Wesley was a critic of instant political solutions based on egocentric passion without examining the resultant consequences.

---

[15] "National Sins and Miseries," B 3:568, J VII:402, sec. 1.1.
[16] Ibid.
[17] "National Sins and Miseries," B 3:569, J VII:403, sec. 1.2.

Both in the American colonies and in England, many were "screaming out for liberty." The irony is that, in Wesley's view, they already possessed more civil liberties than almost everyone else in the world. They had liberty "to so great an extent, that the like is not known in any other nation under heaven." This is so "whether we mean civil liberty, a liberty of enjoying all our legal property — or religious liberty, a liberty of worshiping God according to the dictates of our own conscience. Therefore all those who are either passionately or dolefully crying out, 'Bondage! Slavery!' while there is no more danger of any such thing, than there is of the sky falling upon their head, are utterly distracted; their reason is gone."[18] Irrational exuberance over inordinate political expectations had become obsessive.

How sad that people who already possessed a civil order that provided for a huge measure of civil liberty unknown in the rest of the world were throwing it to the winds on behalf of an ephemeral dream of immediate revolutionary change. Wesley had in mind the civil unrest and emerging violence that was leading up to the revolutions soon to come to America in 1776 and that would come even more virulently to France in 1789.

This madness was not a small calamity. In 1775, before the Declaration of Independence, an unreasonable partisan political fervor had swept the land. Wesley said, "If you saw, as I have seen, in every county, city, town, men who were once of a calm, mild, friendly temper, [now] mad with party zeal, foaming with rage against their quiet neighbors, ready to tear out one another's throats, and to plunge their swords into each other's bowels; if you had heard men who once feared God and honored the king, now breathing out the bitterest invectives against him, and just ripe, should any occasion offer, for treason and rebellion; you would not then judge this to be a little evil, a matter of small moment, but one of the heaviest judgments which God can permit to fall upon a guilty land."[19] Exaggerated political self-interests can create exasperating economic consequences for innocent people.

3. Sin and Suffering in the Revolutionary Environment

a. The Heady Wine of Revolution

"Such is the condition of Englishmen at home. And is it any better abroad? I fear not. From those who are now upon the spot, I learn that in our colonies also many are causing the people to drink largely of the same deadly wine."[20] What wine? The desire for immediate political solutions, mixed with lack of attention to the consequences of inordinate self-assertion. This heady potion has been known to result in clamor and war. Thousands are "inflamed more and more, till their heads are utterly turned, and they are mad to all intents and purposes. Reason is lost in rage; its small still voice is drowned by popular clamor. Wisdom is fallen in the streets. And where is the place of understanding? It is hardly to be found in these provinces."[21]

---

[18]Ibid.
[19]"National Sins and Miseries," B 3:573, J VII:401, sec. 1.3.
[20]"National Sins and Miseries," B 3:570–71, J VII:404, sec. 1.4.
[21]Ibid.

Wesley was describing both America and England in 1775. This captivity to visions of instant political solutions was like a form of slavery. "Real slavery indeed, most properly so called" — was turning into political madness. The colonies were just beginning to enter into a violent rebellion. He could sense it coming.

In such a heated environment, Wesley was concerned fundamentally with civil liberties, especially freedom of the press: "For the regular, legal, constitutional form of government is no more. Here is real, not imaginary, bondage: not the shadow of English liberty is left. Not only no liberty of the press is allowed — none dare print a page, or a line, unless it be exactly conformable to the sentiments of our lords, the people."[22] Wesley was not a populist revolutionary. His deepest political conviction was that we derive our civil rights from God, not from violent and anarchic mobs. He had faced mobs. "Their tongue is not their own. None must dare to utter one word, either in favor of King George, or in disfavor of the idol they have set up — the new, illegal, unconstitutional government, utterly unknown to us and to our forefathers."[23]

Wesley had earlier commented favorably on American demands for civil liberties: "An oppressed people asked for nothing more than their legal rights."[24] But when these pleas later turned to reckless bloodshed in surprise attacks on civilly constituted authorities, Wesley considered that violence unjust.[25]

b. The Costs and Consequences of Revolution

In such a volatile revolutionary situation, "a man has no security for his trade, his house, his property, unless he will swim with the stream." Amid the clamor, there is "no liberty of conscience" for those who dissent from the mob. "A sense of duty prompts them to defend from the vile calumnies" that are continually vented against the public order.[26] Arbitrary power and anarchy prevent families from "enjoying the fruit of their labor," and lawlessness reigns.[27]

c. The Madness of Unnecessary War

The horrible consequence of this spiritual madness is war: "Who can describe the complicated misery which is contained in this? Hark! the cannons roar! A pitchy cloud covers the face of the sky. Noise, confusion, terror, reign over all! Dying groans are on every side. The bodies of men are pierced, torn, hewed in pieces; their blood is poured on the earth like water! Their souls take their flight into the eternal world, perhaps into everlasting misery. The ministers of grace turn away from the horrid scene; the ministers of vengeance triumph. Such already has been the face of things in that once happy land where peace and plenty, even while banished from a great part of Europe, smiled for near a hundred years."[28]

---

[22]"National Sins and Miseries," B 3:573, J VII:401, sec. 1.3.
[23]Ibid.
[24]Letter to Lord North, June 13, 1775.
[25]See JWO note, B 3:570n.
[26]"National Sins and Miseries," B 3:573, J VII:401, sec. 1.3.
[27]"National Sins and Miseries," B 3:573, J VII:404, sec. 1.4.
[28]Ibid.

What force is it that "drags on these poor victims into the field of blood? It is a great phantom, which stalks before them, which they are taught to call, liberty!... Real liberty, meantime, is trampled underfoot and is lost in anarchy and confusion," with a thirst for vengeance and contempt of life.[29]

d. The Suffering of Innocents

David prayed for the innocent: "These are but sheep. What have they done?"[30] The good news of Jesus Christ calls all to repent and believe in God's grace. "It therefore behooves us to consider our own sins — the cause of all our sufferings.... It behooves each of us to say, 'Lo, I have sinned.'"[31]

Commenting on David, Wesley offered some guidance for conscience amid this growing violence. He called for an act of general repentance in his own society. Wesley asked a flood of questions for self-examination. "Where is mercy to be found?... Deceit and fraud go not out of our streets. Who is it that speaks the truth from his heart?"[32]

He regarded this societal illness as far deeper than a clash of political opinions. It came down to pride, idolatry, and a lack of truth telling both in America and England: "Whose words are the picture of his thoughts? Where is he that has 'put away all lying,' that never speaks what he does not mean?"[33] "O truth, whither art thou fled? How few have any acquaintance with thee! Do not we continually tell lies for the nonce [for the specific occasion], without gaining thereby either profit or pleasure? Is not even our common language replete with falsehood?... What would he [Shakespeare writing on 'lowly fawning'] have said had he lived a century later, when that art [of lying] was brought to perfection?"[34]

"Why does it create such anger to call another a liar?" Wesley sought a socio-psychological answer. He proposed a hypothesis, and a very shrewd one: "Because a man can bear to be blamed when he is conscious of his own innocence. But if you say he is a liar, you touch a sore spot: he is guilty, and therefore cannot bear it."[35]

4. The Sins of Colonialism

a. Elegant Vice

Political conflict is a matter of the heart. The heart of both the British and the Americans had been lately turned toward idolatrous hedonism. Wesley asked, "Is not our belly our god? Are not eating and drinking our chief delight, our highest happiness? Is it not the main study (I fear, the only study) of many honorable men to enlarge the pleasure of tasting? When was luxury (not in food only, but in dress,

---

[29]"National Sins and Miseries," B 3:574, J VII:404, secs. 1.4 – 5.
[30]2 Sam. 24:17 NIV; "National Sins and Miseries," B 3:572, J VII:405, sec. 2.1.
[31]"National Sins and Miseries," B 3:572, J VII:405, sec. 2.1.
[32]"National Sins and Miseries," B 3:572 – 73, J VII:405, sec. 2.2.
[33]Ibid.
[34]"National Sins and Miseries," B 3:573, J VII:406, sec. 2.3.
[35]"National Sins and Miseries," B 3:573, J VII:406, sec. 2.4.

furniture, equipage) carried to such a height in Great Britain ever since it was a nation?"[36]

The British had infected the world with their sins: "We have lately extended the British empire almost over the globe. We have carried our laurels into Africa, into Asia, into the burning and the frozen climes of America."[37] The influence of Britain had infested cultures around the world with these hedonic aspirations.

What had resulted from colonial imperialism? "All the elegance of vice."[38] Vice in its most elegant form had been transported and replanted into the cultures of India, southeast Asia, and the Americas.

b. A Postcolonial Critique

Already in 1775 Wesley was formulating a postcolonial critique. British desire to acquire "field after field" had overreached. What Britons had really been exporting to their colonies was largely gluttony for themselves and degeneracy to indigenous cultures.[39]

One evidence of this degeneracy was sloth. "Britons, from their temperate, active forefathers" had through colonial wealth drifted into indolence. Wesley pointed out that the Parliament a century before the American conflict had met at 5:00 a.m. If George Herbert had previously described England as "full of sin, but most of sloth!" what would he have said now?[40] Another evidence of moral indolence is blasphemous swearing in "utter contempt of God," more excessive than any other country with the possible exception of Ireland.[41]

5. The Remedy

a. Purify Your Hearts

The plague of excessive self-assertiveness had spread to both England and America, with devastating ravages everywhere. "What can we do, in order that it may be stayed?"

The remedy is a change of heart. The biblical corrective is clear: Is there any better way "to turn aside the anger of God, than that prescribed by St. James?"[42] "Come near to God and he will come near to you. Wash your hands, you sinners, and purify your hearts, you double-minded."[43]

Moral accountability for this corruption in England and abroad must be brought down to the personal level of each hearer: "Now let each of us lay his hand upon

---

[36]"National Sins and Miseries," B 3:574, J VII:406, sec. 2.5.

[37]"National Sins and Miseries," B 3:574, J VII:406–7, sec. 2.6.

[38]"National Sins and Miseries," B 3:574, J VII:406, sec. 2.5.

[39]"National Sins and Miseries," B 3:574, J VII:406–7, sec. 2.6.

[40]Ibid. George Herbert, *The Temple, the Church Porch* (Oxford, 1633), 16.1.1, http://www.winwisdom.com/quotes/topic/cleanliness.aspx.

[41]"National Sins and Miseries," B 3:574–75, J VII:407, sec. 2.7.

[42]"National Sins and Miseries," B 3:575–76, J VII:407–8, sec. 2.9.

[43]James 4:8 NIV.

his heart and say, 'Lord, is it I?' Have I added to this flood of unrighteousness and ungodliness, and thereby to the misery of my countrymen?"[44] Others suffer because of our sins. British sins are "one great cause of their sufferings,"[45] from the East Indies to the West Indies and to Africa by the slave trade.

Purify your hearts from pride, party zeal, anger, resentment, and bitterness, "from all prejudice, bigotry, narrowness of spirit; from impetuosity and impatience of contradiction; from love of dispute." Embrace all humanity, "without hypocrisy … putting away with all malice, all clamor."[46]

Wesley's political vision focused on changing the heart by grace. "Let 'the wisdom from above' sink deep into your hearts … 'full of mercy and good fruits; without partiality.'"[47] "The wisdom that comes from heaven is first of all pure; then peace-loving, considerate, submissive, full of mercy and good fruit, impartial and sincere. Peacemakers who sow in peace reap a harvest of righteousness."[48] This is the heart of evangelical political ethics.

b. Seeking Peace

"Do not let any unwholesome talk come out of your mouths, but only what is helpful for building others up according to their needs, that it may benefit those who listen. And do not grieve the Holy Spirit of God, with whom you were sealed for the day of redemption. Get rid of all bitterness, rage and anger, brawling and slander, along with every form of malice. Be kind and compassionate to one another, forgiving each other, just as in Christ God forgave you."[49]

"Speak to every man the truth from your heart. Renounce every way of acting, however gainful, which is contrary either to justice or mercy. Do to everyone as, in parallel circumstances, you would wish he should do unto you.… Labor to have a conscience void of offense toward God and toward man."[50] Then rely on the almighty grace of him that loved you, and gave himself for you, so as to enable you to "purify your hearts by faith."[51]

The times call for repentance and renewed faith: "Be no longer double-minded, halting between earth and heaven, striving to serve God and mammon."[52] "When you ask, you must believe and not doubt, because the one who doubts is like a wave of the sea, blown and tossed by the wind. That person should not expect to receive anything from the Lord. Such a person is double-minded and unstable in all they do."[53]

---

[44]"National Sins and Miseries," B 3:575, J VII:407, sec. 2.8.
[45]Ibid.
[46]"National Sins and Miseries," B 3:575–76, J VII:407–8, sec. 2.9.
[47]Ibid.
[48]James 3:17–18 NIV; "National Sins and Miseries," B 3:575–76, J VII:407–8, sec. 2.9.
[49]Eph. 4:29–32 NIV; "National Sins and Miseries," B 3:575–76, J VII:407–8, sec. 2.9.
[50]"National Sins and Miseries," B 3:575–76, J VII:407–8, sec. 2.9.
[51]Ibid.; cf. Acts 15:9.
[52]"National Sins and Miseries," B 3:575–76, J VII:407–8, sec. 2.9; cf. Matt. 6:24.
[53]James 1:6–8 NIV; "National Sins and Miseries," B 3:575–76, J VII:407–8, sec. 2.9.

c. Show Mercy to Widows and Orphans of the War

With compassionate concern for the widows and orphans of the conflict, he appealed to the hearts of his hearers: "Show mercy more especially to the poor widows, to the helpless orphans, of your countrymen who are now numbered among the dead, who fell among the slain in a distant land." Pray that the Lord will "calm the madness of the people, will quench the flames of contention, and breathe into all the spirit of love, unity, and concord. Then brother shall not lift up sword against brother, neither shall they know war any more. Then shall plenty and peace flourish in our land."[54]

Four days after this "charity sermon," Wesley sadly wrote in his journal, "England is in a flame — a flame of malice and rage against ... almost all that are in authority.... I labor to put out this flame."[55] The war machine was heating up on both continents.

B. A Calm Address to Our American Colonies (1775)

In 1775, a year before the Declaration of Independence was signed, the hottest public policy issue was taxation in the American colonies. The occasion: the four Coercive Acts enacted by the British Parliament in 1774 in response to the Boston Tea Party of December 1773.

The great literary figure of England, Dr. Samuel Johnson, had written an essay titled "Taxation No Tyranny," which prompted Wesley to write his "A Calm Address to Our American Colonies." In it Johnson wrote, "That the Americans are able to bear taxation is indubitable; that their refusal may be overruled is highly probable; but power is no sufficient evidence of truth. Let us examine our own claim, and the objections of the recusants, with caution proportioned to the event of the decision, which must convict one part of robbery, or the other of rebellion."[56]

Wesley undertook calmly to investigate the justice of the British claim to exact taxes from colonial profits in "A Calm Address to Our American Colonies" [J XI:80 – 88, secs. 1 – 14 (late September 1775)].

On first glance, American readers may find Wesley's responses resistant to many aspects of the familiar moral claims of Americans to independency. It was a time when, from the viewpoint of the American revolutionaries, the whole system of British law was pitted against the deepest American aspirations. On closer view, however, this essay is a plea for peace, a plea to avert the anarchy and tyranny that war would almost certainly bring. It is above all a plea for true liberty based on the rule of law.

---

[54]"National Sins and Miseries," B 3:576, J VII:408, sec. 2.10.

[55]*JJW*, entry of November 11, 1775.

[56]"The Works of Samuel Johnson," vol. 14 (Troy, NY: Pafraets & Co., 1913), 93 – 144. Wesley borrowed heavily from the arguments of Johnson and in some cases from his exact language or by paraphrase.

1. Peacemaking Based on Contemporary Legal Reasoning

Wesley's pleading was to avoid war before it was too late. This essay was an urgent appeal to avert eminent war. It was an urgent appeal to peace based on legal reasoning in the democratic tradition.

Wesley had been to both Boston and Georgia and knew the intensity of feeling in the colonies. He was well aware of the obsessions and myths present in the debate. It was occurring both in his own communities of faith in Britain and in the Methodist societies that had been established in America since 1769. Both were looking to him for guidance. He was making a plea for peace based on accepted law.

The motive of peacemaking was made entirely clear from the beginning of his essay, with a poignant quotation from the *Aeneid* of Virgil: "O check your wrath, my sons; the nations spare; and save your country from the woes of war."[57]

He was entering this unfamiliar arena as a clergyman and a mediator. Prompted by Johnson's essay, he wrote, "As soon as I received more light myself, I judged it my duty" to impart to others extracts from Johnson's essay with his reflections, with an added "application to those whom it most concerns," namely both British and American political societies inflamed by competing claims on taxation rights. He sought to lower the passion of partisans who were prone to be too quick to resort to oversimplifications and dismissive speech.[58]

In his recent essay "Revisiting the 'Calm Address,'" Glen O'Brien rightly warned against pigeonholing Wesley simply as a political Tory. Rather, he "supported a constitutional monarchy since its finely tuned balance of power between king, parliament, and people needed only to be preserved in order for genuine liberty to prevail."[59]

2. The Misleading Analogy between Taxation and Slavery

The revolutionary voices were asserting that one who is taxed without his own consent is a slave. Really? Slave? People who use that analogy have no idea how horrible slavery really is. Wesley had seen it in Georgia. These partisans who already "enjoy[ed] both civil and religious liberty to the utmost extent"[60] were nothing like actual slaves. The two conflicting parties, Americans and British, were among the freest human beings in the whole world.

Those who cavalierly compared slavery to taxation put themselves under investigation: "'Who then is a slave?' Look into America, and you may easily see. See that Negro, fainting under the load, bleeding under the lash! He is a slave. And is there

---

[57]Virgil: *"Ne, pueri, ne tanta animis assuescite bella, Neu patriÆ validas in viscera vertite vires,"* according to the translation of Christopher Pitt (Dodsley, 1740).

[58]"A Calm Address to Our American Colonies," J XI:80, proem. One of these partisans was Anglican minister Dr. William Smith of Philadelphia, quoted by Wesley in extracts at the end of this essay. They repeat the revolutionary arguments that Wesley thought would tend toward war, tyranny, and anarchy. Dismissive words such as "Contemptible sophistry! Fallacious to the last degree! Childish quirks! Pitiful sophisms!" had clouded rational argument.

[59]Glen O'Brien, "Revisiting the 'Calm Address,'" *MR* 4 (2012): 31 – 55.

[60]"A Calm Address to Our American Colonies," J XI:81, proem.

'no difference' between him and his master? Yes; the one is screaming, 'Murder! Slavery!' the other silently bleeds and dies!"[61]

The enormous difference between liberty and slavery is this: the person at liberty exercises his will freely. The slave does not. To diminish the moral heinousness of slavery by comparing it with taxation is to reduce argument to caricature.[62]

This essay is Wesley's calm rejoinder: "I now speak according to the light I have. But if anyone will give me more light, I will be thankful."[63]

3. Whether the Legislatures Have the Right to Tax under Existing Law

First, Wesley sought rationally to consider the merits of the discordant legal question of whether the British Parliament had a right under existing law to tax the American colonies.[64]

The very definition of a colony according to then-existing law was a number of persons to whom the government "grants a charter, permitting them to settle in some far country as a corporation, enjoying such powers as the charter grants, to be administered in such a manner as the charter prescribes."[65] The Americans cannot fairly proceed without recalling how they got there.

Can colonies make law for themselves? Yes and no according to Wesley: Yes, "as a corporation they make laws for themselves," but no "as a corporation subsisting by a grant from higher authority; to the control of that authority they still continue subject."[66] Does the American legislative process exist "by a grant from higher authority"? Under existing law before the revolution it did.

But the advocates of independence argue, "It is the privilege of a freeman and an Englishman to be taxed only by his own consent. And this consent is given for every man by his representatives in Parliament. But we have no representatives in Parliament. Therefore we ought not to be taxed thereby."[67] This is the heart of their argument, which Wesley wished to analyze. It asserts, "If the Parliament cannot tax you because you have no representation therein, for the same reason it can make no laws to bind you. If a freeman cannot be taxed without his own consent, neither can he be punished without it; for whatever holds with regard to taxation holds with regard to all other laws.... Therefore he who denies the English Parliament the power of taxation denies it the right of making any laws at all."[68]

---

[61] Ibid.
[62] Ibid.
[63] Ibid.
[64] "A Calm Address to Our American Colonies," J XI:82, sec. 1.
[65] Ibid.
[66] Ibid.
[67] Ibid.
[68] "A Calm Address to Our American Colonies," J XI:82, sec. 2.

4. Appeals to Protection Are Forgotten amid Appeals to Private Consent

Wesley was convinced that the taxation question had been recurrently debated in British law, but that in his day it had a settled interpretation: "From the Restoration, the colonies were considered as part of the realm of England, in point of taxation, as well as everything else."[69] Wesley established this point by quoting a long list of legislation to show the history of taxation of colonies. These laws were on commodities exported from plantations, post office revenue, imported rum, sugar and molasses, and many more products.[70] Within these existing laws, it is clear that by precedent "the English Parliament [had] an undoubted right to tax all the English colonies."[71] America would not even have existed without this safety net of British law in which it was born and raised.

American did like protection under British law when it was to their interest. For example, wrote Wesley, "A few years ago, you were assaulted by enemies, whom you were not well able to resist. You represented this to your mother country and desired her assistance. You were largely assisted, and by that means wholly delivered from all your enemies. After a time, your mother country, desiring to be reimbursed for some part of the large expense she had been at, laid a small tax (which she had always a right to do) on one of her colonies."[72]

This power of taxation had a history of not being disputed when it was to the advantage of the colony to seek protection from the founding government. Wesley reminded the colonists, "You have always admitted statutes for the punishment of offenses," which logically implies "the necessity of admitting taxation" under the constituted authority.[73] Stated plainly, if they were going to have the privileges of protection, it was reasonable that they pay taxes and not try to carve out a special interest in taxation as an exception. The umbrella of protection could not be divided.

5. Whether the Free Citizen Is Governed Only by Laws to Which He Personally Has Consented

Wesley objected to the very foundation of the plea "that 'every freeman is governed by laws to which he has consented.' As confidently as it has been asserted, it is absolutely false. In wide-extended dominions, a very small part of the people are concerned in making laws. This, as all public business [meaning government], must be done by delegation; the delegates are chosen by a select number. And those that are not electors, who are far the greater part, stand by, idle and helpless spectators."[74] Those who do not understand the principle of delegation do not have the

---

[69]"A Calm Address to Our American Colonies," J XI:85, sec. 9.
[70]Ibid.
[71]"A Calm Address to Our American Colonies," J XI:85 – 86, sec. 10.
[72]Ibid. The "enemies" were the French and their allies.
[73]"A Calm Address to Our American Colonies," J XI:82, sec. 2.
[74]"A Calm Address to Our American Colonies," J XI:82 – 83, sec. 3.

least understanding about what representative democracy is and how it actually works.

Even the elected legislators were often "near equally divided," which limited the claims of absolute consent. Hence "almost half of them must be governed, not only without, but even against, their own consent." Pure democracy has been often attempted but seldom sustained in its absolute form, since children must be represented by parents, and all citizens by some citizens.[75] That is what democracy realistically assumed. The alternative is disorder.

The law has durability from generation to generation. It is not just for children or grandparents or the grandchildren of present citizens. It is in effect until it is legally repealed under constitutional processes. Wesley asked, "How has any man consented to those laws which were made before he was born? Our consent to these, nay, and to the laws now made even in England, is purely passive. And in every place, as all men are born the subjects of some state or other, so they are born, passively, as it were, consenting to the laws of that state. Any other than this kind of consent, the condition of civil life does not allow."[76] So consent is not individualistic but through intergenerational communities. Consent is not just for now but through time. Children, upon being born, do not wait to benefit from the law. They receive the benefits of peace and public order before they can vote.

Few have noticed that Wesley was here laying out a political theory grounded in the Christian teaching of original sin. Voluntary sin has interpersonal consequences. Interpersonal sin has transgenerational consequences. Representative democracy is relatively just compared to all other existing systems, by allowing consent to law that has been established intergenerationally to protect against injustices that are committed through social processes and transmitted through time.

6. The Presumed Entitlement to Individual Consent as Self-Assertive Personal Will

If you reply that you "are entitled to life, liberty, and property by nature; and that you have never ceded to any sovereign power the right to dispose of these without your consent," that is a speculative idea that cannot be found tangibly in history. Strictly speaking, individual consent implies that every person is a law unto himself. We have enough experience in history to realize that this does not work.[77]

Excessive focus on individual consent without regard to the history preceding it pretends that its advocates "speak as the naked sons of nature."[78] This implies that they are abstracted out of a history of sin, as if history did not exist. Those who advocate absolute individual consent are all too quick to appeal to an argument from history and ancestry. Here is how it sounds: " 'Our ancestors, at the time they settled these colonies, were entitled to all the rights of natural-born subjects within

---

[75]Ibid.
[76]Ibid.
[77]Ibid.
[78]Ibid.

the realm of England.' This likewise is true; but when this is granted, the boast of original rights is at an end."[79] One cannot rationally appeal at the same time to ancestry and to arbitrary private consent.

Colonial trade did not by immigration to another continent forfeit any privileges derived from the existing law, nor to responsibilities under it. When the traders claim to "inherit all the right which their ancestors had of enjoying all the privileges of Englishmen," they immediately appeal to a history of struggle to achieve the proximate justice of representative democracy, however imperfect.[80]

7. The Actual Loss of the Hypothetical "State of Nature"

It is evident that Wesley is here punching holes in the fantasies of Rousseau about "the state of nature."[81] The fact is that we "are no longer in a state of nature." We exist in a history. We are members of a community of laws, and these laws have a history. In 1775 American law had virtually no history apart from British law.

These laws do not grant to every separate individual the "power of disposing, without their consent" their free use of liberty for whatever purpose they imagine or invent, but only according to law, which itself is an intergenerational product.[82]

Wesley is using the debate over taxation to recall a form of political reasoning that has deep roots in classic Christian teaching on covenants.[83]

8. Competing English Ideological Motives Embedded in the American Conflict

Why were some ready to set all America aflame? Wesley answered, "I will tell you my opinion freely.... I have nothing to hope or fear from either side. I gain nothing either by the government or by the Americans, and probably never shall. And I have no prejudice to any man in America: I love you as my brethren and countrymen."[84]

Wesley was offering a historical explanation of the impending revolution, which he was pleading to avert. It is rooted in English religious history. The deeper struggle against British law began in England. Only later did it spread to America.

Why the uproar? Because a minority in England who had for generations been "determined enemies to monarchy," had for some years "been undermining it with all diligence."[85] The revolutionary talk was motivated by a politics of envy and resentment based on a long history of dissent.

---

[79]"A Calm Address to Our American Colonies," J XI:83, sec. 4.

[80]"A Calm Address to Our American Colonies," J XI:84, sec. 6.

[81]J. J. Rousseau, *The Social Contract* (1762; repr., New York: Penguin, 2007); human nature not fallen.

[82]"A Calm Address to Our American Colonies," J XI:83, sec. 4.

[83]"A Calm Address to Our American Colonies," J XI:84, sec. 7. Wesley proposed this curious analogy: "The legislature of a colony may be compared to the vestry of a large parish, which may lay a cess [levy] on its inhabitants, but still regulated by the law, and which whatever be its internal expenses, is still liable to taxes laid by superior authority." This is a very Anglican way of looking at the parish, a way against which dissenting traditions both in Britain and America would dispute.

[84]"A Calm Address to Our American Colonies," J XI:85–86, sec. 10.

[85]"A Calm Address to Our American Colonies," J XI:86–87, sec. 11.

They had shifted their arena of resentment from England to America and had steadily enflamed this resentment "by inflammatory papers, which are industriously and continually dispersed throughout the town and country; by this method they have already wrought thousands of the people even to the pitch of madness.... They are still pouring oil into the flame, studiously incensing each against the other, and opposing, under a variety of pretences, all measures of accommodation."[86]

Based on his own experience in America, Wesley argued on the contrary that most of "the Americans in general love the English, and the English in general love the Americans."[87] He thought revolutionary talk was a minority voice in America as much as in Britain.

9. The Plea for True Liberty and the Specter of Tyranny

Wesley was pleading for liberty, true liberty, not ephemeral fantasies of liberty that would eventuate in violence. He was asking his American friends candidly, "What more liberty can you have? What more religious liberty can you desire, than that which you enjoy already? May not everyone among you worship God according to his own conscience? What civil liberty can you desire, which you are not already possessed of? Do not you sit, without restraint, 'every man under his own vine'? Do you not, everyone, high or low, enjoy the fruit of your labor? This is real, rational liberty," more fully enjoyed by our conjoint legal tradition than "by any other people in the habitable world."[88]

Wesley told the colonists that if America went to war, "it would hardly be possible for you to steer clear between anarchy and tyranny."[89] This is where most American comment on Wesley's view of the American Revolution has fallen short by failing to see his motive, which was the avoidance of three faces of evil: anarchy, tyranny, and war. These were the motives of his passion. They were not patriotic sentimentalism, nor were they a stubborn resistance to social change.

Wesley was convinced that any massive revolution would almost necessarily lead, as it later did in France, to a despotic and arbitrary government.[90] Insofar as it risked being built on the anarchy of a "state of nature," it would surely fall. The anarchy would turn to tyranny, as he pointed out in the real history of the perennial problems of revolution-prone governments such as those of Venice and Genoa.[91]

10. The Unpredictable Consequences of War

Wesley was writing before the beginning of full-scale war: "For O! what convulsions must poor America feel, before any other government was settled? Innumerable mischiefs must ensue before any general form could be established. And the

---

[86]Ibid.
[87]Ibid.
[88]"A Calm Address to Our American Colonies," J XI:87, sec. 12; cf. Mic. 4:4.
[89]"A Calm Address to Our American Colonies," J XI:87, sec. 12.
[90]Ibid.
[91]Ibid.

grand mischief would ensue when it was established; when you had received a yoke which you could not shake off."[92] Wesley was accurately predicting what would soon happen in revolutionary France with its hazardous swings between absolute anarchy and absolute tyranny. That it did not happen in America may be due to the very temperament of British law against which it was rebelling.

Wesley warned his American brothers not to become "dupes of designing men!... I do not mean any of your countrymen in America" but those partisans in England "who have laid their scheme so deep, and covered it so well, that thousands, who are ripening it, suspect nothing at all of the matter."[93]

With his high doctrine of original sin, Wesley could see trouble ahead for the excesses of pride and envy. "Do not ruin yourselves for them that owe you no good-will, that now employ you only for their own purposes and in the end will give you no thanks."[94] These deistic and ideological revolutionaries "love neither England nor America, but play one against the other, in subserviency to their grand design of overturning the English government."[95]

Wesley pleaded with the colonists, "Follow after peace!... Let us not bite and devour one another, lest we be consumed one of another!"[96] He thought that the time was short to consider these risks.

C. A Calm Address to the Inhabitants of England (1777)

1. The Setting

The accelerating American revolution presented a dilemma for Wesley, who was a citizen of Great Britain with members of his own societies in America. As a firm believer in the rule of law, he supported the right of Parliament to tax the colonies under British law. His legal premise was that the colonies had ceded to the British government their rights by their very presence in America under British consent.

Wesley had planned to send to American readers "A Calm Address to Our American Colonies" (1775; see above), but, he said, "The ports being just then shut up by the Americans, I could not send it abroad as I designed." However, a large number of copies (between fifty thousand and a hundred thousand) were nonetheless circulated in Britain with eye-opening effect. "[The British] found they had been led unawares into all the wilds of political enthusiasm, as far distant from truth and common sense as from the real love of their country."[97]

---

[92]"A Calm Address to Our American Colonies," J XI:87, sec. 13.

[93]"A Calm Address to Our American Colonies," J XI:88, sec. 14. The biblical metaphor Wesley applied to such an embittered conspirator was Ahithophel in the Bible. He had been overlooked in David's appointments of judges. In rabbinic literature and in Christian typology, Ahithophel cast longing eyes on things not belonging to him. In doing so, he also lost the things he possessed. When David sought his counsel during a time of peril, Ahithophel had withheld help and therefore was judged harshly.

[94]Ibid.

[95]Ibid.

[96]Ibid.

[97]"A Calm Address to the Inhabitants of England," J XI:129, sec. 1.

Two years later, in "A Calm Address to the Inhabitants of England,"[98] Wesley addressed his countrymen. In doing so, he disavowed having any private interest: "I attend no great man's table. I have nothing to ask, either of the king or any of his ministers.... But I have a view to contribute all that in me lies to the public welfare and tranquility."[99] The flame that once "threatened to involve the whole nation" had by this time of writing been "greatly checked" but was still smoldering.[100]

Wesley's aim was to lessen "the misunderstandings under which many honest, well-meaning men are laboring to this day; misunderstandings which have caused much animosity, nay, much bitterness and rancor in their minds against those who equally 'strive to have a conscience void of offense toward God and toward man.'"[101] He hoped to encourage gratitude for "the Giver of every blessing," that all "may love one another as He has loved us."[102]

2. The State of Affairs in 1777 That Occasioned Misunderstanding

In the intervening period between Wesley's "A Calm Address to the American Colonies" (1775) and "A Calm Address to the Inhabitants of England" (1777), much had transpired: the Boston Tea Party, the Declaration of Independence, and the beginning of the War of Independence. At this time of writing of the second Calm Address, the battles in the war had largely gone in favor of the British. At this time, Wesley could not see ahead to the surprising end of the Revolution with the surrender of Cornwallis to Washington. So his arguments at this stage must be read in the context of what then seemed to Wesley to be a futile effort bound to fail.

3. The Facts Calmly Reviewed

Wesley's first task was to plainly set down the "the real state of those affairs which have occasioned these misunderstandings; and then add two or three short reflections."[103]

Having lived in Georgia for two years, and having commissioned Methodist preachers to form Methodist societies in North America, Wesley had continued to receive an "abundance of letters from persons in America, on whose judgment, veracity, and impartiality I could safely depend, especially from the provinces of New York, Virginia, Maryland, and Pennsylvania. I have likewise had the opportunity of conversing freely and largely with many that came from those provinces, and of comparing together the accounts of those who were attached to one or the

---

[98]"A Calm Address to the Inhabitants of England" (London: J. Fry and Co., 1777), sold at the Foundry, near Upper Moorfields.

[99]"A Calm Address to the Inhabitants of England," J XI:129, sec. 2.

[100]Ibid.

[101]"A Calm Address to the Inhabitants of England," J XI:130, sec. 3; cf. Acts 24:16.

[102]"A Calm Address to the Inhabitants of England," J XI:130, sec. 3.

[103]"A Calm Address to the Inhabitants of England," J XI:130, sec. 4.

other party. And I shall endeavor to deliver the plain facts, without speculations concerning them."[104]

On his return trip from Georgia to England, John's brother Charles was blown off course to Boston, where talk of independency was already rife. This was forty years before "The Calm Address to the Inhabitants of England" was written in 1777. "In the year 1737, my brother [Charles] took ship, in order to return from Georgia to England. But a violent storm drove him up to New England; and he was for some time detained at Boston. Even then he was surprised to hear the most serious people, and men of consequence, almost continually crying out, 'We must be independent; we shall never be well till we shake off the English yoke.'" At that time they spoke "without any formed design, or having concerted any measures upon the head."[105]

4. The Economics of Independency

America grew robustly in its early stages. This occurred with "unparalleled lenity[106] of the government they were under, and the perfect liberty they enjoyed, civil as well as religious."[107] As their wealth increased, the spirit of independence was kindled. Then arose the question of taxes on this trade. Wesley remembered from his earlier days that there was much stealth in avoiding them. "Whole shiploads of uncustomed goods were imported, particularly at Boston," in which John Hancock was "one of the greatest dealers in this kind."[108] Any attempts to collect customs became the occasion of "huge indignation, and strong marks of resentment.... By this means the customs of North America, which ought to have brought in so considerable a sum as would have gone far toward defraying the expense of the government, were reduced to a very small pittance."[109]

The Tea Party story, so well known to Americans, was not understood in England in the same way it was in Boston. Wesley took on the task of calmly explaining it from his point of view to his fellow countrymen. When "the English government a few years ago thought it equitable to lay a small duty upon the stamps in America," the cry for revolution was heard, and "echoed across the Atlantic Ocean, from America to England." The storm spread "on both sides the ocean, and the Stamp Act was repealed."[110] Having nothing to fear from Canada, those in New England especially "judged their allies were growing stronger and stronger." They began "by diligently cultivating the republican notions which they had received from their

[104]"A Calm Address to the Inhabitants of England," J XI:130, sec. 5.
[105]"A Calm Address to the Inhabitants of England," J XI:130–31, sec. 6. Charles returned to England earlier than John.
[106]"Lenience."
[107]"A Calm Address to the Inhabitants of England," J XI:131, sec. 7.
[108]"A Calm Address to the Inhabitants of England," J XI:131, sec. 8.
[109]Ibid.
[110]"A Calm Address to the Inhabitants of England," J XI:131–32, sec. 9.

forefathers,"[111] and continued by carrying out reproachful propaganda against the established British government.

When the English Parliament laid a small duty on the tea imported into America, "a violent outcry arose" throughout all the American provinces and spread to England.[112] "Under the auspices of Mr. Hancock (whose interest was particularly at stake) ... [they] threw the English tea into the sea. This was the first plain overt act of rebellion.... The Parliament ordered Boston harbor to be shut up."[113] Though the Americans continued to profess their loyalty, "all this time they were using all possible art and diligence to blacken" the English government. The storm that arose in Boston spread to Pennsylvania and "on toward the southern colonies.... A new supreme power, called a Congress, appeared. It openly assumed the reins of government, exercised all the rights of sovereignty."[114]

When "the Americans talked of allegiance, and said they desired nothing but the liberty of Englishmen ... many in England cordially believed them; I myself for one."[115] Many prominent persons in England encouraged the Americans to "make no concessions; give up nothing. Stand your ground. Be resolute, and, you may depend upon it, in less than a year and an half, there will be such commotions in England, that the Government will be glad to be reconciled to you upon your own terms."[116]

As the civil disobedience actions increased, "privateers swarmed on every side." The Dutch and French, already antagonistic to the British, supplied them with "all sorts of arms and ammunition.... In the meanwhile, the few English troops that were in America were closely shut up in Boston, by a numerous army holding them in on every side, and gaping to swallow them up.... This they gloried in, as a manifest proof that God was on their side."[117]

5. The Outbreak of Serious Warfare

a. Viewed from the Early British Victories

By 1777 a tipping point had been reached. Self-assertiveness had turned to pride and contempt. The king had called his nation to repentance through "a Proclamation for a General Fast in England, that we might 'humble ourselves before God, and implore his blessing and assistance.'" This act of humility was perceived as weakness. This call was mocked and considered hypocrisy in the colonies. "From this very time, the tide turned," and the two armies were soon at war.[118] This evolved

---

[111]"A Calm Address to the Inhabitants of England," J XI:132, sec. 10.
[112]"A Calm Address to the Inhabitants of England," J XI:132–33, sec. 11.
[113]Ibid.
[114]"A Calm Address to the Inhabitants of England," J XI:133, sec. 13.
[115]Ibid., in reference to the Americans.
[116]"A Calm Address to the Inhabitants of England," J XI:133, sec. 14.
[117]"A Calm Address to the Inhabitants of England," J XI:134, sec. 15.
[118]"A Calm Address to the Inhabitants of England," J XI:134–35, sec. 16.

into robbery, plunder and destruction, turning "a well-peopled and fruitful land into a wilderness."[119]

The colonies, having "declared themselves independent states, openly renounced their allegiance" to the British. Wesley described the dilemma the revolutionaries had made for themselves. The Revolution in the period between the Minutemen of Lexington and Concord in April 19, 1775, and the publication of Wesley's "A Calm Address to the Inhabitants of England," was chiefly filled with British victories. After the Declaration of Independence was signed on July 4, 1776, the military situation appeared bleak for the revolution. After the battles of Long Island, New York City, and Harlem Heights, there followed Washington's capture of Trenton and Princeton. But there were still more British victories in early 1777 at Brandywine, Philadelphia, and Germantown. Then in midwinter Washington retreated to Valley Forge. By August of 1777, the British abandoned Philadelphia. The winter of late 1777 – early 1778 was the terrible winter of Washington's retreat to near Morristown.

Here is Wesley's description of the state of the conflict in 1777: "Their armies are scattered; their forts and strongholds lost; their provinces taken one after another. Meantime, are they humbled? No; they roar like a wild bull in a net.... O American virtue! Are these the men who are proposed as a pattern to all Europe?"[120] He then described the condition that he considered a loss of true liberty being sacrificed to the spirit of independency, much as he did earlier, and some of it quoted from "A Calm Address to the American Colonies," as lacking civil liberties and public order.[121] "No man hath any security, either for his goods or for his person, but is daily liable to have his goods spoiled or taken away, without either law or form of law, and to suffer the most cruel outrage as to his person, such as many would account worse than death. And there is no legal method wherein he can obtain redress for whatever loss or outrage he has sustained."[122]

b. The Duty of Christians to Civil Obedience

The faithful on both continents were called to "be cheerfully 'subject to the higher powers,'" in the light of the confession that there is no power but of God.[123] "Let everyone be subject to the governing authorities, for there is no authority except that which God has established. The authorities that exist have been established by God. Consequently, whoever rebels against the authority is rebelling against what God has instituted, and those who do so will bring judgment on themselves...."

---

[119]"A Calm Address to the Inhabitants of England," J XI:135, sec. 17.

[120]"A Calm Address to the Inhabitants of England," J XI:135, sec. 18.

[121]It is hard for Americans to read this without a bit of a smile, since our whole historical memory has taught us to see these events as defending civil liberties against injustice, instead of on the other side of the Atlantic where Wesley was living. My task is to be strictly faithful to articulating and analyzing Wesley's arguments as best I can.

[122]"A Calm Address to the Inhabitants of England," J XI:135 – 36, sec. 19.

[123]"A Calm Address to the Inhabitants of England," J XI:137 – 40, sec. 22; cf. Rom. 13:1.

Therefore, it is necessary to submit to the authorities, not only because of possible punishment but also as a matter of conscience."[124]

Wesley was puzzled as to how far many British had espoused "the cause of those that are in open rebellion." He called all partisans to "humble yourselves before God, and act more suitably to your character. Wherever you are, far from countenancing, repress the base clamors of the vulgar."[125] Better that you recall "the blessings you enjoy. Let common sense restrain you, if neither religion nor gratitude can." Otherwise, "then farewell to the liberty you now enjoy."[126]

Wesley then felt called upon to "add a few more words" to those in his connection of spiritual formation: "Do any of you blaspheme God or the king? None of you, I trust, who are in connection with me."[127] Rather than demeaning British law, Wesley was deeply grateful for the liberties it had insured. What more could this government have done for you than what has been done? "Have you not full liberty of conscience in every respect.... Have you not full liberty, with regard to your life, to your person, and to your goods? In what other country upon earth is such civil liberty to be found?... Is it prudence to speak in so bitter and contemptuous a manner of such governors as God has given you?"[128] To those who openly support the cause of rebellion, he quipped, "Nay, undoubtedly, when things of greater moment are settled," perhaps you will be more reasonable. But "your present behavior will then be remembered; perhaps not altogether to your advantage."[129]

D. The Work of God in Religious Revival in North America

1. The Late Work of God in North America (1778)

A year later, in 1778, and three years after his 1775 charity sermon on behalf of the war widows of London, Wesley was still brooding over the mystery of providence in political and economic affairs. The widows' soldier husbands had fallen in America. The sins of colonialism to which Wesley had pointed were yielding bitter fruit. They had been stirred into the heady wine of revolution. The consequences of fervent partisanship were increasingly complex. The need to interpret the theodicy of the colonial crisis was still unfolding.

In 1778 Wesley wrote his poignant essay "The Late Work of God in North America." It was time to ponder what had happened in the two years following the signing of the Declaration of Independence. His theme was the providence of God that works in unforeseen ways toward rough justice in a fallen world. This essay is not primarily about politics or war or revolution, but about the mystery of providence working amid human pride.

---

[124]Rom. 13:1 – 2, 5 NIV.
[125]"A Calm Address to the Inhabitants of England," J XI:137 – 40, sec. 22.
[126]Ibid.
[127]Ibid.
[128]"A Calm Address to the Inhabitants of England," J XI:137 – 40, sec. 23.
[129]Ibid.

The outcome of the revolution appeared still to favor the British by a large margin. All of the following essays on political ethics were written before the American Constitution was written. Critics of Wesley have sometimes overlooked this chronology. The Bill of Rights was not ratified until December 15, 1791, after Wesley's death on March 2. Wesley's reservations about the revolution had to do with the specter of anarchy, which has as its central objective the overturning of established law. That specter was haunting England as well as America and France.

Pondering the mystery of providence, Wesley turned to the Bible for consolation.

2. Ezekiel's Vision

The biblical text Wesley chose for "The Late Work of God in North America" is Ezekiel's intriguing metaphor of "a wheel within a wheel." "The appearance was, as it were, a wheel in the middle of a wheel" [Ezekiel 1:16; Homily #113, B 3:595 – 608, J VII:409 – 19 (1778)].

Wheels of hidden providence were actually turning within the wheels that were visible. God was obscurely at work amid these tragic human conflicts.

In his first vision in Babylonian captivity, Ezekiel had seen the heavens open during a windstorm. He saw an immense cloud with flashing lightning amid a brilliant light. "I saw a wheel on the ground beside each creature with its four faces. This was the appearance and structure of the wheels: They sparkled like topaz, and all four looked alike. Each appeared to be made like a wheel intersecting a wheel. As they moved, they would go in any one of the four directions the creatures faced; the wheels did not change direction as the creatures went. Their rims were high and awesome, and all four rims were full of eyes all around."[130]

The question raised by Ezekiel's vision is, how does God's providence work behind the scenes in the visible world? "Whatever may be the primary meaning of this mysterious passage of Scripture, many serious Christians in all ages have applied it in a secondary sense to the manner wherein the adorable providence of God usually works in governing the world."[131] Ezekiel's metaphor of wheels working in dynamic correlation was applied by Wesley to the providential work of God in revolutionary America.

3. The Wheels of Providence

In America Wesley saw the mysterious wheels of providence turning, "adapting one event to another, and working one thing by means of another."[132] The metaphor of wheels is a dynamic model of ironic historical change in which God's grace and human freedom are interacting in unexpected ways, but always with God in ultimate control, and without diminishing the reality of human freedom. Human freedom is placed in the context of divine judgment. Wesley knew that Ezekiel's

---

[130]Ezek. 1:15 – 18 NIV.
[131]"The Late Work of God in North America," B 3:595, J VII:409, proem, sec. 1.
[132]Ibid.

prophecy was one that could not be understood until it was explained by subsequent events in a developing history.

The first wheel of providence in America preceded the American Revolution. It was the work of God in the beginnings of the evangelical revival. Wesley reviewed the time between his mission in Georgia in 1736 and the Declaration of Independence in 1776. In those forty years, God was quietly planting seeds for the renewal of gospel preaching of faith and grace in a new world.

The second wheel of providence Wesley saw turning was composed of a combination of economic success and political resentment. What was God doing in history amid these changes? How had the consequences of human freedom worked to elicit both grace and judgment? How could God's justness be explained during these upheavals? What was happening in the interface between religious revival and the struggle for independence?

4. The Revival of Religion in America

Without pretending to grasp the full meaning of the events in North America, Wesley thought they were something like wheels within wheels that at length provided a glimpse into "the dispensations of divine providence."[133] In this essay, Wesley sought first to trace the meaning of "each wheel apart," and then "to consider both, as they relate to and answer each other."[134]

5. Early Indications of the First Great Awakening of Religion in America

a. The Complementary Missions of Wesley, Whitefield, and Edwards

Wesley reviewed the history of the Great Awakening in America by comparing the work of the Wesleys in 1736 to the American Methodist societies in 1769.[135] He did not propose "to give a particular detail of the late transactions in America, but barely to give a simple and naked deduction of a few well-known facts."[136] He was aware that it would be difficult to treat American issues fairly without offending one or another partisan, especially among those "warmly attached to either party." So he sought to use the "softest terms" he could find that would fairly portray the colonial conflict, seeking to avoid all "reproachful language ... without either betraying or disguising the truth."[137]

He began by describing the early evidences of the evangelical revival in America, including himself and the Moravians in Georgia, and then told of the revivals of Jonathan Edwards and George Whitefield in the North. Wesley downplayed his own role in the religious revival in America, but he was a participant before Whitefield, whom he had mentored, and contemporary with Jonathan Edwards, who had

---

[133]"The Late Work of God in North America," B 3:595, J VII:409, proem, sec. 2.
[134]Ibid.
[135]Wesley was writing in 1778 about the beginnings of the revival that began forty years earlier.
[136]"The Late Work of God in North America," B 3:596, J VII:410, sec. 1.1
[137]Ibid.

published his "Faithful Narrative of the Surprising Work of God" in Northampton in 1737. The Wesley brothers set sail for America in 1735. Whitefield came in 1738.

Wesley summarized: "In the year 1736 it pleased God to begin a work of grace in the newly planted colony of Georgia, then the southernmost of our settlements on the continent of America. To those English who had settled there the year before, were then added a body of Moravians, so called; and a larger body who had been expelled from Germany by the archbishop of Saltzburg. These were men truly fearing God and working righteousness. At the same time there began an awakening among the English, both at Savannah and Frederica; many inquiring what they must do to be saved, and 'bringing forth fruits meet for repentance.'"[138]

He then spoke of the next event: "In the same year there broke out a wonderful work of God in several parts of New England. It began in Northampton, and in a little time appeared in the adjoining towns. A particular and beautiful account of this was published by Mr. Edwards, minister of Northampton. Many sinners were deeply convinced of sin, and many truly converted to God. I suppose there had been no instance in America of so swift and deep a work of grace, for an hundred years before; nay, nor perhaps since the English settled there."[139] Then "the work of God spread by degrees from New England toward the south."[140]

In 1738, after Wesley began his work in Georgia, "Mr. Whitefield came over to Georgia, with a design to assist me in preaching, either to the English or the Indians. But as I was embarked for England before he arrived, he preached to the English altogether, first in Georgia, to which his chief service was due, then in South and North Carolina, and afterwards in the intermediate provinces, till he came to New England."[141] Whitefield's preaching stirred many hearts. A wave of revival spread "from Georgia to New England."[142] Thus, throughout the colonies in the last half of the 1730s, a significant revival of religion was sweeping across "all the provinces" of North America.[143]

By Whitefield's last journey to America, Wesley could see the major flaw in the revival in America: lack of intentional nurture of discipline in the Christian life. Few were bringing forth fruit in holy living.[144] Wesley was not surprised, since he knew preaching without follow-up discipling would be short-lived. His critique:

---

[138]Ibid.

[139]"The Late Work of God in North America," B 3:596, J VII:410, sec. 1.2.

[140]"The Late Work of God in North America," B 3:597, J VII:410, sec. 1.3. Wesley and Edwards were born in the same year, 1703. In many ways, their ministries were on similar paths: In July 1731 Wesley preached "The Wisdom of Winning Souls" and Jonathan Edwards preached "God Glorified — in Man's Dependence." In 1737 when Wesley was in Georgia, Edwards was preaching in Northampton. In 1738 when Wesley wrote "Salvation by Faith," Edwards wrote "A Faithful Narrative of the Surprising Work of God in the Conversion of Many Hundreds of Souls in Northampton." In 1741 when Wesley wrote "The Almost Christian," Edwards wrote "Sinners in the Hands of an Angry God." Both Wesley and Edwards wrote significant treatises on original sin, Wesley in 1756 and Edwards in 1758.

[141]"The Late Work of God in North America," B 3:598, J VII:411, sec. 1.7.

[142]"The Late Work of God in North America," B 3:597, J VII:410, sec. 1.4.

[143]"The Late Work of God in North America," B 3:597, J VII:410–11, sec. 1.5.

[144]"The Late Work of God in North America," B 3:597–98, J VII:411, sec. 1.6.

"They had no shadow of discipline; nothing of the kind. They were formed into no societies. They had no Christian connection with each other, nor were ever taught to watch over each other's souls."[145] Wesley heard from his associates in America that many of those previously converted had fallen "into lukewarmness" and had no supportive community to lift them up.[146] What the first American awakening lacked was exactly what the original band societies had provided.

b. The American Methodist Societies

At the "yearly Conference, at Bristol, in the year 1769," Wesley presented the case for nurturing supportive communities of mutual accountability in prerevolutionary America. A new start was made in American Methodist initiatives when Richard Boardman and Joseph Pillmoor offered themselves for service in America. Their labors bore abundant fruit in New York and Philadelphia. "What was wanting before was now supplied,"[147] namely, the discipline of small groups with rigorous accountability.

They "began to watch over each other in love. Societies were formed, and Christian discipline introduced in all its branches."[148] By "the beginning of the late troubles [the Revolution] there were three thousand souls connected together in religious societies."[149] So in the short time between 1769 and 1776, Methodist discipline had been firmly planted in America. But there were two major hindrances that emerged to slow down the progress of the revival, one economic and the other political.

6. Hindrances to the Progress of the Revival of Religion: Greed and Slavery

a. Economic Wealth

Due to the abundance of natural resources in America, there appeared "a grand hindrance to the progress of religion: the immense trade of America." Economically America "rose from indigence to opulent fortunes, quicker than any could do in Europe."[150] This was predictably accompanied by a temptation toward an increase of the desires of the flesh, the desires of the eyes, and the pride of life. The more riches, the more pride.

This pride expressed itself in political form in national self-assertiveness: "As they rose in the world, they rose in their opinion of themselves." This deterioration confirmed the saying, "A thousand pounds supplies the want of twenty thousand qualities."[151] This is the natural consequence of wealth: it is followed by luxury, which is followed by pride and indolence.

---

[145]"The Late Work of God in North America," B 3:598, J VII:411, sec. 1.7.
[146]Ibid.
[147]"The Late Work of God in North America," B 3:598–99, J VII:411–12, sec. 1.9.
[148]Ibid.
[149]"The Late Work of God in North America," B 3:599, J VII:412, sec. 1.10.
[150]"The Late Work of God in North America," B 3:600, J VII:412, sec. 1.11.
[151]"The Late Work of God in North America," B 3:600, J VII:412, sec. 1.12.

b. The Slave Trade

Add to this a second hindrance to religion, a horrible feature of American society: the slave trade. Much of the American wealth was due to a slave economy.

Wesley was among the first to argue that the slave trade was intrinsic to the corruption of American society. This hideous traffic in persons made in God's image was a major factor in supplying the wealthy with all their needs and wishes. Wesley described the slave owners in their luxuries: They could "hardly bear to put on their own clothes. The slave must be called to do this, and that, and everything."[152] Americans were caught up in a syndrome of moral failure that accompanied economic success. "This complication of pride, luxury, sloth, and wantonness, naturally arising from vast wealth and plenty, was the grand hindrance to the spreading of true religion through the cities of North America."[153] This was the economic wheel turning.

7. The Second Wheel of Divine Providence

a. The Spirit of Independency

The New England colonies, especially in the Boston area, from the outset had a strong "hankering after independency." The desire for political independence from Britain became a potent cauldron. Again Wesley was not surprised, based on what he had earlier witnessed in Boston: "It could not be expected to be otherwise, considering their families, their education, their relations, and the connections they had formed before they left their native country."[154] These were talented people who had let their economic success go to their heads.

Add to this picture severe and dubious treatment from England especially concerning taxation. This intensified their desire for revolution. They desired to shake off "that dependence, to which they were never thoroughly reconciled."[155] The resentments of the dissenters of the 1600s in England was passed on and intensified among their American descendants of the 1700s. No matter what benefits and resources they received from English culture and political order, nothing could efface that inveterate bitterness.

This was especially so in Boston. Once again Wesley related the 1737 experience of his brother. "My brother, being detained there some time, was greatly surprised to hear almost in every company, whether of ministers, gentlemen, merchants, or common people, where anything of the kind was mentioned, 'We must be independent!... We will be our own governors!'"[156] This was in 1737, almost forty years before the actual revolution. The politics of resentment were fuming.

What Wesley meant by "the spirit of independency" was not simply a political

---

[152]"The Late Work of God in North America," B 3:600–601, J VII:413, sec. 1.14.
[153]"The Late Work of God in North America," B 3:601, J VII:413, sec. 1.15.
[154]"The Late Work of God in North America," B 3:601, J VII:414, sec. 2.1.
[155]Ibid.
[156]"The Late Work of God in North America," B 3:602, J VII:414, sec. 2.2.

view but more so a deeply rooted politics of resentment and rebelliousness. This was not in his view a spirit of true liberty. The spirit of genuine liberty depended on the rule of law, in his view, not the destruction of the social compact. What he called "legal liberty" was the freedom that emerged only out of constituted governance under law.[157]

b. Revolutionary Overreach

Wesley recounted his perception of the events in America after the Stamp Act and the Boston Tea Party. These events gave the revolutionaries an opportunity for a public act of defiance. Taxation became the common cause for stirring up further resentment.

Wesley was well informed about the heated rhetoric that had been seething from Boston since 1737. He thought the motivations for rebellion were based on caricature and needless resentment. The British were "vilified, first, the English ministry, representing them, one and all, as the veriest wretches alive, void of all honesty, honor, and humanity."[158]

On August 3, 1776, "Dr. Witherspoon, president of the college in New Jersey, in his address to the Congress," said: "'Those who seemed to take the part of America in the British Parliament, never did it on American principles. They either did not understand, or were not willing to admit, the extent of our claim.'"[159] Without arguing whether this independency was defensible or not (which Wesley regarded as "another question"),Wesley described this spirit of independency as an "open and avowed defection" from the rule of law. It was an act for which the Americans in his view had already paid heavily in stable economic trade and political disruption.

8. How Providence Was Working within These Two Wheels

This recklessness made the way for the next phase of the interface between the two wheels: Scarcity took the place of wealth. Throughout this whole sequence, divine providence was working amid human affairs to judge sin and offer grace.

a. The Turning of Wheels within Wheels

How did the first wheel (the evangelical revival) relate to the second wheel (economic and political overreach)? Having spoken of the two wheels separately, Wesley then turned to show how providence had been working through the unfolding correlation of these two wheels. Both were still unfolding in 1778.

The conjoint turning of these wheels had two effects: economic and political. The economic dimension was "trade, wealth, pride, luxury, sloth, and wantonness." The political dimension was the resentful "spirit of independency."[160] These two were complementary and interrelated. Both wheels interrupted the progress of the

---

[157]"The Late Work of God in North America," B 3:602, J VII:414, sec. 2.3.
[158]"The Late Work of God in North America," B 3:602–3, J VII:415, sec. 2.4.
[159]"The Late Work of God in North America," B 3:603, J VII:415, sec. 2.5.
[160]"The Late Work of God in North America," B 3:604, J VII:416, sec. 2.8.

evangelical revival. Wesley thought that the revolution derailed the religious revival, but only for a time.

How did these wheels of economic successes and failures and political resentments combine to affect the work of God in North America?

b. A Social Theodicy

Wesley's central purpose in this essay is neither political nor economic but a theological reflection on providence and theodicy. These developments revealed how God works in history. They point to a social theodicy, an attempt to reconcile the judgment of God with the mercy of God in the context of sin and suffering.

In this crucial essay, he showed "how the wise and gracious providence of God uses one to check the course of the other, and even employs (if so strong an expression may be allowed) Satan to cast out Satan."[161] "If Satan drives out Satan, he is divided against himself. How then can his kingdom stand?"[162] In the interface between economic disruptions and political overreach, God's providence was allowing one wheel to cancel out the other, viewed from a wider historical perspective.

The hunger for religious freedom had brought the colonists to America in the first place, especially in New England. From 1736 to 1769 the religious revival was growing. But as the colonists grew in pride, they became entangled in their own successes. Both movements caused the religious revival to wane. The waning of the revivals was marked by the rise of the revolutionary spirit. Economic wealth and its attendant temptations took the revival off course temporarily.

Weakened religion turned into bad politics and disastrous economics. Excessive wealth turned into the injustices of slavery and political overreach.

The demonic powers were active in the temptations to pride and hedonic self-assertion. For a while it seemed that these two wheels were almost prepared to overturn the whole work of God in America.[163]

But the purposes of God are ultimately secured despite human folly. While the nations fought, God who sits on his heavenly throne was amused at the temporary pretenses of human pride and envy.[164] God acts to correct the follies of human freedom.

c. The Second Psalm

The theological core of Wesley's providential argument lies in Psalm 2, where the psalmist asks, what is God's purpose in these events?

> Why do the nations conspire
> and the peoples plot in vain?
> The kings of the earth rise up
> and the rulers band together
> against the LORD and against his anointed, saying,

---

[161]Ibid.
[162]Matt. 12:26 NIV.
[163]"The Late Work of God in North America," B 3:604, J VII:416, sec. 2.8.
[164]Ibid.

"Let us break their chains
  and throw off their shackles."
The One enthroned in heaven laughs;
  the Lord scoffs at them.
He rebukes them in his anger
  and terrifies them in his wrath.[165]

Psalm 2 contains all the elements of Wesley's social theodicy: plotting in vain, political discord, the desire for instant redress, and the divine judgment of sin. All these phases were providentially guided. God was allowing human freedom to test itself against God's redemptive purposes.

d. Amid Social Conflict, Divine Providence Is Gradually Overturning Every Hindrance

Wesley's central thesis was that "by means of this very spirit" — economic greed combined with political overreach — "there is reason to believe God will overturn every hindrance" to the work of God in America. This was not a dismal political analysis or a harsh expression of economic pique. Rather, it was a ringing affirmation of God's purpose in history: to redeem his fallen creatures made in his likeness.[166]

How did these interconnected political and economic motives work together to produce a deeper renewal of the work of God in America? Again Wesley turned not to political theory but to a profound theological argument about the economic consequences of pride. By the breaking out of this spirit of independency, "an effectual check was given to the trade of those colonies."[167] "They themselves, by a wonderful stroke of policy, threw up the whole trade of their mother country." The consequences were disastrous: their "trade too was brought almost to nothing.... When wealth fled away ... so did plenty."[168] This reset the whole premise of a thwarted revival. Now it could proceed without the economic and political hindrances.

"The wheel now began to move within the wheel. The trade and wealth of the Americans failing, the grand incentives of pride failed also."[169] All of the conflicted parties had "grievously miscalculated their own strength."[170]

This was written in 1778 when the outcome of the revolution was still in question. What was certain, in Wesley's view, was that the previous economic abundance could not be sustained on a wartime economy. At that time, the British armies had "swept away all before them; and ... what remained bore so high a price, that exceeding few were able to purchase them."[171]

---

[165]Ps. 2:1 – 5 NIV; "The Late Work of God in North America," B 3:604, J VII:416, sec. 2.8.
[166]"The Late Work of God in North America," B 3:604, J VII:416, sec. 2.8.
[167]"The Late Work of God in North America," B 3:605, J VII:416 – 17, sec. 2.9.
[168]Ibid.
[169]"The Late Work of God in North America," B 3:605, J VII:417, sec. 2.10.
[170]Ibid. Note the chronology here. When this was written in 1778, the Revolutionary War had not been concluded, Britain was winning the most crucial battles, and Wesley wrongly assumed the probable outcome.
[171]"The Late Work of God in North America," B 3:606, J VII:417, sec. 2.12.

Thus it was by divine providence that the main hindrances of the work of God in America were being removed. The First Great Awakening in America was battered by this testing. But with the Second Great Awakening in the nineteenth century came the exponential growth of the work of God in North America. The Methodist societies were in the forefront of those significant historical changes.

Wesley could not see into the future. In fact, things turned out quite differently than he had been expecting in 1778. But the same providential argument is more deeply confirmed by seeing what actually did happen. Methodist discipline would take deep root in America after the Revolution. It would have sufficient vitality to sweep into every crevice of the frontier, nurturing committed religious societies in every newly founded village of the frontier. Many were committed to the holy life of salvation by grace through faith alone. So strong was the Spirit at work over the nineteenth century that by the twentieth century every county in the United States would have a Methodist church. Methodists were spread more evenly in American counties than any other Protestant denomination. More so, out of the eighteenth-century evangelical awakening led by Wesley would emerge the second evangelical awakening in nineteenth-century America, with hundreds of thousands of converts who would become millions worldwide within a hundred years after this essay.

So seen from the times after this writing, it is fitting to celebrate how the providence of God has worked in "how wonderful a manner — such as it never could have entered into the heart of man to conceive!"[172] God foresaw and transcended what human pride could not envision. However mistaken Wesley was on the military outcome of the revolution, he was not wrong about the providence of God working through it.

Wesley summarized the wheels of providence: "What God foresaw would prove the remedy grew up with the disease, and when the disease was come to its height then only began to operate."[173] The disease was the pride that emerged out of sloth. The remedy was the work of God in North America. It had to come to a crisis level before the grace it embodied could become fulfilled. By the time of Wesley's death in 1791, this was already occurring.

e. The Providence of One Wheel Answering to Another

That human self-assertiveness "which so many call liberty, is overruled by the justice and mercy of God, first to punish those crying sins, and afterwards to heal them."[174] "He punishes that he may amend, that he may first make them sensible of their sins ... and then bring them back to ... the spirit of humility, temperance, industry, chastity; yea, and a general willingness to hear and receive the word which is able to save their souls. 'O the depth, both of the wisdom and knowledge of God!

---

[172]"The Late Work of God in North America," B 3:606, J VII:417–18, sec. 2.13.
[173]Ibid.
[174]"The Late Work of God in North America," B 3:606–7, J VII:418, sec. 2.14.

How unsearchable are his judgments, and his ways past finding out!' — unless so far as they are revealed in his Word and explained by his providence."[175]

Through pondering these perilous cycles of suffering, we may learn that "spiritual blessings are what God principally intends ... that they should all minister to the general spread of 'righteousness, and peace, and joy in the Holy Ghost.'"[176] From these spiritual blessings "God will add many temporal blessings." God will send not the spirit of self-assertive pride, but "liberty, real, legal liberty, which is an unspeakable blessing."[177]

In short, "God permitted this strange dread of imaginary evils to spread over all the people, that he might have mercy upon all, that he might do good to all, by saving them from the bondage of sin, and bringing them into 'the glorious liberty of the children of God!'"[178]

Wesley thought that God would "superadd to Christian liberty, liberty from sin, true civil liberty; a liberty from oppression of every kind — from illegal violence; a liberty to enjoy their lives, their persons, and their property."[179] The Americans would be freer by having had the steady witness of Christian freedom — the freedom to receive the unmerited grace of God.

After the American victory in the Revolutionary War, and finally the Peace of Paris in 1783, Wesley would make an adjustment to the new circumstance in America under the advice of Francis Asbury and others. By 1784 at the Baltimore Christmas General Conference, a new beginning would be made for the reconstruction of the Methodists in postwar America.

---

[175]Ibid.
[176]"The Late Work of God in North America," B 3:607 – 8, J VII:418 – 19, sec. 2.15.
[177]Ibid.
[178]Ibid.
[179]Ibid.

CHAPTER 5

The Execrable Villainy
of Slavery

A. Confronting the Moral Failures of Slavery

1. Wesley's Letter to Wilberforce

John Wesley was a lifelong opponent of slavery. I have seen in the United Methodist Archive at Drew University the last letter Wesley wrote, only six days before his death. It is displayed in the room where my PhD students were examined in defense of their dissertations. The letter was addressed to the great adversary against slavery, William Wilberforce, who had been converted under Wesley's ministry. He became a member of Parliament and its most outspoken opponent of slavery. In this one-page letter, Wesley expressed his outrage against slavery and urged Wilberforce to press his case against slavery in the public debate in England. Through moral advocates like Wesley and Wilberforce, Parliament finally outlawed England's participation in the slave trade in 1807. Wesley's letter to Wilberforce is worth quoting in full:

> Balam, February 24, 1791. Unless the divine power has raised you to be as *Athanasius contra mundum*, I see not how you can go through your glorious enterprise in opposing that execrable[1] villainy which is the scandal of religion, of England, and of human nature. Unless God has raised you up for this very thing, you will be worn out by the opposition of men and devils. But if God be for you, who can be against you? Are all of them together stronger than God? O be not weary of well doing! Go on, in the name of God and in the power of his might, till even American slavery (the vilest that ever saw the sun) shall vanish away before it. Your affectionate servant, John Wesley.[2]

Wesley preceded Wilberforce in the abolitionist cause. Wesley had lived in the American South during the early days of slavery in Georgia. In October 1735, John and Charles Wesley sailed for America, where General Oglethorpe had recently founded the colony of Georgia at Savannah. The Wesleys also served a mission to

---

[1] *Execrable* means "unequivocally detestable." The Latin *exsecrari* means to curse, or that which is worthy of a curse. This is the archaic adjective that Wesley chose to describe the moral claims of slavery. It famously appeared in the last letter of his life — to William Wilberforce.

[2] Online at ctlibrary.com.

Fort Frederica on St. Simons Island. It is likely that Wesley had seen slaves sold in Savannah and Charleston.

Some of Wesley's most passionate writing was against slavery. We will focus on the arguments of a single lengthy text, "Thoughts upon Slavery."

B. Thoughts upon Slavery (1774)

Writing in 1774, when slavery in America was rampant and crucial to the economic and social systems of the American South, and before the British Parliament began to debate this terrible practice in England seriously, Wesley offered his "Thoughts upon Slavery" [J XI:59–79 (1774)]. He set forth a careful moral argument against this dehumanizing practice at a time when it was rife.

1. Defining Slavery

Involuntary servitude is always unjust and always a denial of the image of God in humanity. Wesley thought it almost impossible to convey all the tragic consequences of involuntary servitude. It is wholly different from voluntary domestic service, which may or may not be just.[3]

"Slavery imports an obligation of perpetual service, an obligation which only the consent of the master can dissolve." This generally gives "the master an arbitrary power of any correction not affecting life or limb," and in some countries even life and limb of the slave are not protected. "Sometimes even these are exposed to his will: or protected only by a fine, or some slight punishment, too inconsiderable to restrain a master of a harsh temper."[4]

Those who are in chains have no capacity to acquire anything except for the benefit of the master. These unjust laws allow the master to treat the slave as chattel. Worse, slavery "descends in its full extent from parent to child, even to the latest generation."[5]

2. The Sad History of Human Slavery

The injustices of slavery date "from the remotest period of which we have an account in history."[6] Sadly, the earliest known societies had to fight frequently against becoming captive to competitors.[7] Between the eighth and fourteenth centuries, slavery gradually spread to most of the kingdoms of Europe. With the discovery of the Americas in the fifteenth century, it increased exponentially, especially in "the western and eastern coasts of Africa."[8]

In their effort to "cultivate their new possessions in America," the Spanish, with

---

[3]"Thoughts upon Slavery," J XI:59, sec. 1.1.
[4]"Thoughts upon Slavery," J XI:59, sec. 1.2.
[5]Ibid.
[6]"Thoughts upon Slavery," J XI:60, sec. 1.3.
[7]Ibid.
[8]Ibid.

the help of the Portuguese, "procured negroes from Africa, whom they sold for slaves to the American Spaniards. This began in the year 1508, when they imported the first negroes into Hispaniola."[9] After an attempt in 1540 by the king of Spain to end black slavery, the other nations "acquired possessions in America and followed the examples of the Spaniards, and slavery has now taken deep root in most of our American colonies."[10]

C. Reflections on the History of Slavery

Wesley actively protested the common stereotypes of "an African temperament." Wesley set out to break those stereotypes by seeking out contemporary eighteenth-century eyewitness accounts of the culture, abilities, and work habits of native West Africans in their native Africa before they were forcibly extracted from those lands.[11]

1. The Stable African Home of Displaced American Slaves

Wesley used contemporary eyewitness reports to show that the land from which the slaves came was "fertile, producing abundance of rice and roots. Indigo and cotton thrive without cultivation; fish is in great plenty; the flocks and herds are numerous, and the trees loaded with fruit." Most of the slaves were taken captive along the eastern coast of Africa between Senegal and Sierra Leone, and down into the Congo and Angola.[12] They were taken from a land that was fruitful and well improved.

Eyewitness accounts of Africa from the 1730s and 1740s give an entirely different picture than the stereotypes of Africans in America. Monsignor Adanson of the Royal Academy of Sciences of Paris reported of Senegal: "Which way soever I turned my eyes, I beheld a perfect image of pure nature: an agreeable solitude, bounded on every side by a charming landscape; the rural situation of cottages in the midst of trees; the ease and quietness of the negroes, reclined under the shade of the spreading foliage, with the simplicity of their dress and manners. The whole revived in my mind the idea of our first parents, and I seemed to contemplate the world in its primitive state. They are generally speaking, very good-natured, sociable, and obliging." So the stereotype of these Africans as savage needs "considerable abatement."[13] "All are constantly employed, the men in agriculture, the women in spinning and weaving cotton."[14] Wesley continued with a description of the economies, cultures, and temperament of the peoples of the Gold Coast and Benin.[15]

---

[9]Now the Dominican Republic and Haiti. "Thoughts upon Slavery," J XI:60, sec. 1.4. Wesley was relying on historical accounts available in his day.
[10]"Thoughts upon Slavery," J XI:60, sec. 1.4.
[11]"Thoughts upon Slavery," J XI:60–65, sec. 2.3–11.
[12]"Thoughts upon Slavery," J XI:60, sec. 2.1.
[13]"Thoughts upon Slavery," J XI:63, sec. 2.8.
[14]"Thoughts upon Slavery," J XI:63, sec. 2.9.
[15]"Thoughts upon Slavery," J XI:63–65, sec. 2.10–11.

Monsignor Brue similarly reported that the land in far west Africa was so well cultivated "scarce a spot lay unimproved. The low lands, divided by small canals, were all sowed with rice: The higher grounds were planted with Indian corn and peas of different sorts. Their beef is excellent; poultry plenty and very cheap, as are all the necessaries of life."[16] The west coast of Africa in general, "far from being a horrid, dreary, barren country, is one of the most fruitful, as well as the most pleasant countries in the known world."[17] "They are governed by their chief men, who rule with much moderation. Few of them will drink anything stronger than water, being strict Mahometans. The government is easy because the people are of a good and quiet disposition and so well instructed in what is right that a man who wrongs another is the abomination of all. They desire no more land than they use, which they cultivate with great care and industry."[18]

Wesley sharply rejected negative stereotypes of Africans: "Upon the whole, therefore, the negroes who inhabit the coast of Africa, from the river Senegal to the southern bounds of Angola, are so far from being the stupid, senseless, brutish, lazy barbarians, the fierce, cruel, perfidious savages they have been described, that on the contrary, they are represented by them who had no motive to flatter them, as remarkably sensible, considering the few advantages they have for improving their understanding. As very industrious, perhaps more so than any other natives of so warm a climate. As fair, just, and honest in their dealings, unless where white men have taught them to be otherwise. And as far more mild, friendly and kind to strangers, than any of our forefathers were. Our forefathers! Where shall we find at this day, among the fair-faced natives of Europe, a nation generally practicing the justice, mercy, and truth, which are related of these poor black Africans?"[19]

2. The Unconscionable Treatment of Africans in America

Wesley related the sad narrative of the history of American slavery. Deception and warfare played major roles in the capture of slaves. Wesley considered it necessary to document the procedures for procurement in order to make a strong case against slavery.

The slaves were procured by force and fraud. Some were invited to come on board ships and then put in chains and carried away. The so-called "Christians"

---

[16]"Thoughts upon Slavery," J XI:61, sec. 2.3.
[17]"Thoughts upon Slavery," J XI:61, sec. 2.5.
[18]"Thoughts upon Slavery," J XI:61–62, sec. 2.6; see eyewitness reports on eighteenth-century West African culture by Monsignor Adanson, correspondent of the Royal Academy of Sciences at Paris from 1749 to 1753. Michel Adanson, *A Voyage to Senegal, Goree, and the River Gambia* (London: J. Nourse, 1759). Chief among these sources were the reports of Francis Moore, appointed in 1730 by the Royal African Company of England to James Island on the Gambia River. After serving in Joar, he went five hundred miles inland, making careful observations and drawings. He was in Georgia as a shopkeeper during May 1735 to July 1736 at about the same time Wesley was there. See Moore's "Travels into the Inland Parts of Africa, Containing a Description of the Several Nations for the Space of Six Hundred Miles Up the River Gambia" (London, 1738), and his account of the settling of Frederica in "A Voyage to Georgia" (London, 1744).
[19]"Thoughts upon Slavery," J XI:63–65, sec. 2.10–11.

landing on African coasts "seized as many as they found, men, women and children, and transported them to America. It was about 1551 that the English began trading to Guinea: at first, for gold and elephants' teeth, but soon after for men. In 1566 Sir John Hawkins sailed with two ships to Cape Verde, where he sent eighty men on shore to catch negroes"[20] and sell them in Caribbean ports.

Wesley provided specific information on the cruelty of slave procurement. "It was some time before the Europeans found a more compendious way of procuring African slaves, by prevailing upon them to make war upon each other, and to sell their prisoners."[21] "The white men first taught them drunkenness and avarice, and then hired them to sell one another."[22] "So Mr. [Francis] Moore (officer of the African Company in 1730) informs us, 'When the king of Barsalli wants goods or brandy, he sends to the English governor at James' fort, who immediately sends a sloop. Against the time it arrives, he plunders some of his neighbors' towns, selling the people for the goods he wants. At other times he falls upon one of his own towns and makes bold to sell his own subjects."[23] "Some of the natives are always ready [when well paid] to surprise and carry off their own countrymen."[24] "Many of the slaves sold by the negroes are prisoners of war or are taken in the incursions they make into their enemy's territories."[25]

To amplify these descriptions, Wesley included extracts of two voyages to Guinea taken verbatim from the original manuscript of surgeon's journals,[26] one on the town of Sestro in Liberia where nearby villages were burned and tribal wars incited.[27]

To establish proximate numbers of deaths in transit, Wesley quoted "Mr. Anderson in his history of trade and commerce, [who] observes, 'England supplies her American colonies with Negro slaves, amounting in number to about an hundred thousand every year.' That is, so many are taken on board our ships; but at least ten thousand of them die in the voyage: About a fourth part more die at the different islands, in what is called the seasoning. So that at an average, in the passage and seasoning together, thirty thousand die: that is, properly are murdered. O earth, O sea, cover not thou their blood!"[28]

While boarding slave ships, the Africans were treated unmercifully. Wesley wrote, "When they are brought down to the shore in order to be sold, our surgeons

---

[20]"Thoughts upon Slavery," J XI:65, sec. 3.1.
[21]"Thoughts upon Slavery," J XI:66, sec. 3.2.
[22]Ibid.
[23]Ibid.
[24]Ibid.
[25]Ibid.
[26]"Thoughts upon Slavery," J XI:66, sec. 3.3–4.
[27]"Some Historical Account of Guinea," and "Accounts of the Cruel Methods Used in Carrying On of the Slave Trade." James Barbot, "A Supplement to the Description of the Coasts of North to South Guinea, in Awnsham and John Churchill, *Collection of Voyages* (London, 1732), http://www.ipoaa.com/slave_narratives2_barbot.htm.
[28]"Thoughts upon Slavery," J XI:67, sec. 3.5.

thoroughly examine them, and that quite naked, women and men, without any distinction: Those that are approved are set on one side. In the meantime a burning iron, with the arms or name of the company, lies in the fire, with which they are marked on the breast. Before they are put into the ships, their masters strip them of all they have on their backs so that they come on board stark naked, women as well as men. It is common for several hundreds of them to be put on board one vessel, where they are stowed together in as little room as it is possible for them to be crowded. It is easy to suppose what a condition they must soon be in, between heat, thirst, and stench of various kinds. So that it is no wonder so many should die in the passage, but rather, that any survive it."[29]

Why was Wesley so intent on getting accurate information about slave procurement? In order to contrast the high competencies of native Africans with the stereotypes of American slaves.

3. Empathy for Those in Bondage

The empathy of Wesley for the slaves is evident in these explicit descriptions. Upon arrival "they are separated to the plantations of their several masters, to see each other no more. Here you may see mothers hanging over their daughters, bedewing their naked breasts with tears, and daughters clinging to their parents, till the whipper soon obliges them to part. And what can be more wretched than the condition they then enter upon? Banished from their country, from their friends and relations for ever, from every comfort of life, they are reduced to a state scarce any way preferable to that of beasts of burden."[30] "Are these thy glorious works, Parent of Good?"[31]

The horrible torture of slaves reported by Wesley included chopping off half a foot, whipping until raw with pepper in wounds, dropping melted wax on skin, cutting ears off, and burning skin — all this torture simply for their "asserting their native liberty, which they have as much right to as the air they breathe."[32]

D. Slavery Cannot Be Reconciled with Moral Reason or Conscience

1. When the Law Reinforces Oppression: A Rational Critique of the "Laws of Slavery"

Wesley then exposed to view the ways in which the law had deteriorated to reinforce oppression. Parish churches entered into this collusion in some states. In the colony of Virginia, for example, the law provided that "where any slave shall be set free by his owner, otherwise than is herein directed, the church-wardens of the parish wherein such negro shall reside for the space of one month are hereby

---

[29]"Thoughts upon Slavery," J XI:67, sec. 3.6.
[30]"Thoughts upon Slavery," J XI:67 – 68, sec. 3.7.
[31]Ibid.
[32]"Thoughts upon Slavery," J XI:68, sec. 3.8.

authorized and required, to take up and sell the said negro, by public outcry."[33] Further, "After proclamation is issued against slaves that run away, it is lawful for any person whatsoever to kill and destroy such slaves, by such ways and means as he shall think fit."[34]

In Jamaica another law stated that "fifty pounds are allowed, to those who kill or bring in alive a rebellious slave."[35] The law of colonial Barbados provided that "'if any man of wantonness, or only of bloody-mindedness or cruel intention, wilfully kill a negro of his own' (Now observe the severe punishment!) 'He shall pay into the public treasury fifteen pounds sterling!'"[36]

Wesley was one who typically defended the rule of law, but in these cases of unjust law, he concluded: "If the most natural act of 'running away' from intolerable tyranny deserves such relentless severity, what punishment have these lawmakers to expect hereafter, on account of their own enormous offenses?"[37] In exposing these "legal" arrangements, Wesley had written the most poignant and heartrending essay of his whole authorship.

Wesley was arguing in the public square, not making reference to Scripture but to reason and conscience. He proceeded to "enquire, whether these things can be defended, on the principles of even heathen honesty? Whether they can be reconciled (setting the Bible out of the question) with any degree of either justice or mercy."[38]

2. Examining Dubious Justifications of Colonial Slavery

These terrible laws existed and were enforced. But by what moral right? Wesley pondered, "Can law, human law, change the nature of things?... By no means. Notwithstanding ten thousand laws, right is right, and wrong is wrong still. There must still remain an essential difference between justice and injustice, cruelty and mercy. So that I still ask, Who can reconcile this treatment of the negroes, first and last, with either mercy or justice. Where is the justice of inflicting the severest evils on those who have done us no wrong?"[39]

No slaveholding is consistent with natural justice. "An Angolan has the same natural right as an Englishman" — that very "natural right" on which the English set such a high value.[40]

Although Wesley typically formed arguments based on Scripture, in the case of slavery he was arguing from nature, reason, and conscience within a diverse public square. Wesley was willing to waive "for the present, all other considerations," such as appeals to divine revelation and mercy: "I strike at the root of this complicated

---

[33]"Thoughts upon Slavery," J XI:68–69, sec. 3.9.
[34]"Thoughts upon Slavery," J XI:69, sec. 3.11.
[35]"Thoughts upon Slavery," J XI:69, sec. 3.10.
[36]"Thoughts upon Slavery," J XI:69, sec. 3.11.
[37]Ibid.
[38]"Thoughts upon Slavery," J XI:70, sec. 4.1.
[39]"Thoughts upon Slavery," J XI:70, sec. 4.2.
[40]Ibid.

villainy. I absolutely deny all slaveholding to be consistent with any degree of even natural justice."

3. Natural Justice

In the fourth part of "Thoughts upon Slavery," Wesley rested his case on the legal reasoning of British common law as summarized by the great Justice Blackstone in "The History of the Right of Slavery." Wesley used Blackstone's exquisite legal reasoning to disprove the arguments of Justinian law, which says that since "slavery is said to arise from captivity in war," the conqueror has "a right to the life of his captive; if he spares that, he has then a right to deal with him as he pleases." If it is said that "a man has a right to kill his enemy," that law is morally limited, since "he has only a right to kill him in particular cases ... of absolute necessity for self-defense."[41] Slave traders cannot use a self-defense argument.

"If war is justified only on the basis of self-preservation," says Justice Blackstone, the law reasonably "gives us no right over prisoners but to hinder their hurting us by confining them. Much less can it give a right to torture, or kill, or even to enslave an enemy when the war is over. Since therefore the right of making our prisoners slaves depends on a supposed right of slaughter, that foundation failing, the consequence which is drawn from it must fail likewise."[42]

Voluntarily "a man may sell himself to work for another: But he cannot sell himself to be a slave.... Every sale implies an equivalent given to the seller in lieu of what he transfers to the buyer. But what equivalent can be given for life or liberty? ... Of what validity then can a sale be, which destroys the very principle upon which all sales are founded?"[43]

Again, is it reasonable that children may be born into slavery? "If neither captivity nor contract can by the plain law of nature and reason reduce the parent to a state of slavery, much less can they reduce the offspring."[44]

If slaveholding is inconsistent with reason, can it be reconciled with mercy? Wesley replied, "Slaveholding is utterly inconsistent with mercy."[45] Did the slavers "seize upon men, women and children, who were at peace in their own fields or houses, merely to save them from death? Was it to save them from death that they knocked out the brains of those they could not bring away? ... Was it not themselves? They know in their own conscience it was, if they have any conscience left."[46]

4. The Specious Colonial Argument That Slavery Is Necessary to the Economy

When slavery was argued as an economic necessity for agricultural production,

---

[41]"Thoughts upon Slavery," J XI:70–71, sec. 4.3.
[42]Ibid.
[43]Ibid. See William Blackstone, "The History of the Right of Slavery," *Commentaries* 1:411–13 (1765), http://www.teachingamericanhistory.org/.
[44]"Thoughts upon Slavery," J XI:70–71, sec. 4.3, cf. Blackstone, "History of the Right of Slavery."
[45]"Thoughts upon Slavery," J XI:71–72, sec. 4.4.
[46]Ibid.

Wesley answered, "You stumble at the threshold: I deny that villainy is ever necessary. It is impossible that it should ever be necessary for any reasonable creature to violate all the laws of justice, mercy, and truth. No circumstances can make it necessary for a man to burst in sunder all the ties of humanity. It can never be necessary for a rational being to sink himself below a brute."[47]

Even if slavery were considered a necessary means for a particular economic activity, "How is that end necessary?" To the evasive argument that "white men are not able to labor in hot climates," Wesley answered, "It were better that all those islands should remain uncultivated forever ... than that they should be cultivated at so high a price as the violation of justice, mercy, and truth."[48] Wesley knew from his own experience in Georgia that white men could actively work in hot climates. "The summer heat in Georgia" is frequently "hotter than Barbados ... yet I and my family ... did employ all our spare time there, in felling of trees and clearing of ground, along with a German family of forty in hard labor.... And this was so far from impairing our health that we all continued perfectly well.... It is not true therefore that white men are not able to labor, even in hot climates, full well as black. But if they were not, it would be better that none should labor there ... than that myriads of innocent men should be murdered and myriads more dragged into the basest slavery."[49]

Is slavery ever "necessary for the trade, and wealth, and glory of our nation?" Wesley answered: "Wealth is not necessary to the glory of any nation; but wisdom, virtue, justice, mercy, generosity, public spirit, love of our country. These are necessary to the real glory of a nation.... It is far better to have no wealth than to gain wealth at the expense of virtue. Better is honest poverty than all the riches brought by the tears, and sweat, and blood of our fellow creatures."[50]

Wesley rejected the argument that the slaves were stupid. Any limitations they may have had in being able to improve themselves lay "at the door of their inhuman masters: who give them no means, no opportunity of improving their understanding.... They were no way remarkable for stupidity, while they remained in their own country. The inhabitants of Africa, where they have equal motives and equal means of improvement, are not inferior to the inhabitants of Europe."[51]

To those who deprived the Africans of all means of improvement, Wesley wrote: "It is not their fault, but yours. You must answer for it, before God and man."[52] "Have you carefully taught them, that there is a God, a wise, powerful, merciful Being, the Creator and Governor of Heaven and Earth?... You first acted the villain in making them slaves (whether you stole them or bought them). You kept them stupid and

---

[47]"Thoughts upon Slavery," J XI:72, sec. 4.5.
[48]"Thoughts upon Slavery," J XI:72–73, sec. 4.6.
[49]Ibid.
[50]"Thoughts upon Slavery," J XI:73–74, sec. 4.7.
[51]"Thoughts upon Slavery," J XI:74, sec. 4.8.
[52]Ibid.

wicked by cutting them off from all opportunities of improving either in knowledge or virtue."[53]

E. The Appeal to Abolish Slavery

Wesley entered the arena of the antislavery movement very early: before the Clapham Sect, before Shaftsbury, long before the American antislavery movement of the abolitionists was formed in 1833. Wesley wrote this sermon in 1774, at a time when Methodist preaching had been following his leadership on the above points in most areas of the North. The Methodist Church was officially formed in 1784 and was undivided until 1844. The American Methodists were reading Wesley closely from the 1770s to the 1840s. Wesley's "Thoughts upon Slavery" would have significant impact on the forming of the abolition movement that belatedly ended slavery in America in 1863.

Wesley did not mince words. He spoke with pastoral concern for the souls of those who were engaged in slave trade. He prayed for the redemption of their souls, so their inner intention would be transformed into outward behavior. Wesley overtly sought to influence public policy, not on partisan political grounds, but on strictly moral grounds. He thought the hearts of the traders and planters had to be changed one at a time.[54] His words went directly to the heart to those most responsible.

1. A Personal Word to Ship Captains

Wesley's poignant words to transatlantic ship captains reveal how much he was reaching out to change the hearts of offenders:

> Most of you know the country of Guinea: several parts of it at least, between the river Senegal and the kingdom of Angola. Perhaps now, by your means, part of it is become a dreary uncultivated wilderness, the inhabitants being all murdered or carried away, so that there are none left to till the ground. But you well know how populous, how fruitful, how pleasant it was a few years ago. You know the people were not stupid, not wanting in sense, considering the few means of improvement they enjoyed. Neither did you find them savage, fierce, cruel, treacherous, or unkind to strangers. On the contrary, they were in most parts a sensible and ingenious people. They were kind and friendly, courteous and obliging, and remarkably fair and just in their dealings. Such are the men whom you hire their own countrymen to tear away from this lovely country — part by stealth, part by force, part made captives in those wars, which you raise or foment on purpose. You have seen them torn away, children from their parents, parents from their children, husbands from their wives, wives from their beloved husbands, brethren and sisters from each other. You have dragged them who had never done you any wrong, perhaps in chains, from their native shore. You have forced them into your ships like a herd of swine, them who had souls immortal

---

[53]"Thoughts upon Slavery," J XI:74–75, sec. 4.9.
[54]"Thoughts upon Slavery," J XI:75, sec. 5.1.

as your own. (Only some of them have leaped into the sea and resolutely stayed underwater till they could suffer no more from you.) You have stowed them together as close as ever they could lie, without any regard either to decency or convenience. And when many of them had been poisoned by foul air or had sunk under various hardships, you have seen their remains delivered to the deep, till the sea should give up his dead.[55]

To all who made money off the slave trade, Wesley spoke pointedly heart to heart: "May I speak plainly to you? I must. Love constrains me: love to you, as well as to those you are concerned with. Is there a God? You know there is. Is he a just God? Then there must be a state of retribution: A state wherein the just God will reward every man according to his works. Then what reward will he render to you? O think betimes [before it is too late]! Before you drop into eternity! Think now, he shall have judgment without mercy, that showed no mercy."[56]

In Wesley's voice you can hear this deep pastoral concern:

Are you a man? Then you should have a human heart. But have you indeed? What is your heart made of? Is there no such principle as compassion there? Do you never feel another's pain? Have you no sympathy? No sense of human woe? No pity for the miserable? When you saw the flowing eyes, the heaving breasts, the bleeding sides and tortured limbs of your fellow-creatures, [were] you a stone, or a brute? Did you look upon them with the eyes of a tiger? When you squeezed the agonizing creatures down in the ship, or when you threw their poor mangled remains into the sea, had you no relenting? Did not one tear drop from your eye, one sigh escape from your breast? Do you feel no relenting now?[57]

Wesley was reaching to awaken any forgotten degree of empathy that his hearers might have once had.

The address was to the heart of the perpetrator with concern for his soul: "If you do not, you must go on, till the measure of your iniquities is full. Then will the great God deal with you, as you have dealt with them, and require all their blood at your hands. And at that day it shall be more tolerable for Sodom and Gomorrah than for you! But if your heart does relent, though in a small degree, know it is a call from the God of love."[58]

He called for an immediate change of heart: "Today, if you hear his voice, harden not your heart. Today resolve, God being your helper, to escape for your life. Regard not money! All that a man hath will he give for his life? Whatever you lose, lose not your soul: nothing can countervail that loss. Immediately quit the horrid trade."[59]

This sort of pastoral admonition changed the heart of former slave trader John Newton, who wrote, "Amazing grace! How sweet the sound that saved a wretch like me." It became the most widely sung hymn from the evangelical revival. Newton

---

[55]"Thoughts upon Slavery," J XI:76, sec. 5.2.
[56]"Thoughts upon Slavery," J XI:76–77, sec. 5.3.
[57]Ibid.
[58]Ibid.
[59]Ibid.

was conscience stricken and completely turned around to become a leader in the first generation of the evangelical revival, especially through the ministry of Wesley and of George Whitefield, whom Wesley had mentored in the Christian life.[60]

2. A Word to Those Who Cooperate with the Practice of Slavery

As a mark of Wesley's understanding of the social sin, original sin, transgenerational influence, and the social complexity of evil, he viewed all merchants and consumers who in any way were benefiting from the slave trade as complicit in the slave trade. To them Wesley wrote, "It is you that induce the African villain to sell his countrymen; and in order thereto, to steal, rob, and murder men, women and children without number, by enabling the English villain to pay him for so doing, whom you overpay for his execrable labor. It is your money that is the spring of all, that empowers him to go on, so that whatever he or the African does in this matter, it is all your act and deed. And is your conscience quite reconciled to this? Does it never reproach you at all?"[61]

Wesley's admonition to "every gentleman that has an estate in our American plantations" was equally strong: "Men-buyers are exactly on a level with men-stealers. Indeed you say, 'I pay honestly for my goods,'" but "you know they are procured by a deliberate series of more complicated villainy, of fraud, robbery and murder than was ever practiced either by Mahometans or pagans.... You are the spring that puts all the rest in motion: they would not stir a step without you: therefore the blood of all these wretches, who die before their time, whether in their country or elsewhere, lies upon your head."[62]

All of these arguments are made on the basis of reason and conscience without any necessary assistance from Scripture or revelation.

3. A Word to the Inheritors of Slaves

Finally, Wesley spoke incisively to the inheritors of slaves. Are they innocent according to reason's sense of justice? Wesley's arguments here focus on indirect collusive responsibility, when one joins together with others to harm another without acknowledging indirect cooperative responsibility.

Wesley's last argument was against those who said they owned slaves but they were "left me by my father." Wesley said to them, "It cannot be that either war or contract can give any man such a property in another as he has in sheep and oxen.

---

[60]John Newton (1725–1807), the son of a ship merchant, served on a slave ship that took him to the coasts of Sierra Leone. He then became the servant of a slave trader and ultimately became captain of his own slave ship. He survived a violent storm, after which, in Liverpool he met George Whitefield, who had been an early member of the Methodist societies under Wesley's care. Whitefield was twenty-two years younger than Wesley and was closely associated with Wesley's efforts both in England and America. In time he became the major leader of the Calvinistic Methodist Church. Newton met John Wesley and later became a minister at Olney in Buckinghamshire.

[61]"Thoughts upon Slavery," J XI:77–78, sec. 5.4.

[62]"Thoughts upon Slavery," J XI:78, sec. 5.5.

Much less is it possible that any child of man should ever be born a slave. Liberty is the right of every human creature, as soon as he breathes the vital air. And no human law can deprive him of that right, which he derives from the law of nature."[63]

Rather, "Let none serve you but by his own act and deed, by his own voluntary choice.... Away with all whips, all chains, all compulsion! Be gentle toward men. And see that you invariably do unto every one, as you would he should do unto you."[64]

4. Prayer for Deliverance

Wesley ended his message with this moving prayer:

O thou God of love, thou who art loving to every man and whose mercy is over all thy works; thou who art the father of the spirits of all flesh and who art rich in mercy unto all; thou who hast mingled of one blood all the nations upon earth: have compassion upon these outcasts of men who are trodden down as dung upon the earth! Arise and help these that have no helper, whose blood is spilt upon the ground like water! Are not these also the work of thine own hands, the purchase of thy Son's blood? Stir them up to cry unto thee in the land of their captivity, and let their complaint come up before thee; let it enter into thy ears! Make even those that lead them away captive to pity them, and turn their captivity as the rivers in the South. O burst thou all their chains in sunder, more especially the chains of their sins. Thou, Savior of all, make them free, that they may be free indeed![65]

Further Reading on Political Ethics

Barker, Joseph. *A Review of Wesley's Notions Concerning the Primeval State of Man and the Universe*. London: n.p., ca. 1855.

Brigden, Thomas E. "The Wesleys and Islam." *PWHS* 8 (1911): 91–95.

Burdon, Adrian. *Authority and Order: John Wesley and His Preachers*. Farnham Surrey, UK: Ashgate, 2005.

Cho, John Chongnahm. "John Wesley's View of Fallen Man." In *Spectrum of Thought: Essays in Honor of Dennis Kinlaw*. Edited by Michael L. Peterson. Wilmore, KY: Francis Asbury Press, 1982.

Coppedge, Allan. "John Wesley and the Issue of Authority in Theological Pluralism." In *A Spectrum of Thought: Essays in Honor of Dennis Kinlaw*. Edited by Michael L. Peterson. Wilmore, KY: Francis Asbury Press, 1982.

Cragg, C. R. *Reason and Authority in the Eighteenth Century*. Cambridge: Cambridge Univ. Press, 1964.

Cubie, David Livingstone. "Eschatology from a Theological and Historical Perspective." In *The Spirit and the New Age*. Edited by R. L. Shelton and A. R. G. Deasley, 357–414. Anderson, IN: Warner, 1986.

---

[63]"Thoughts upon Slavery," J XI:79, sec. 5.6.
[64]Ibid.
[65]"Thoughts upon Slavery," J XI:79, sec. 5.7.

Dayton, Donald W. *Discovering an Evangelical Heritage.* Peabody, MA: Hendrickson, 1988. Reprint of the 1976 edition.

Dorr, Donald. "Total Corruption and the Wesleyan Tradition: Prevenient Grace." *Irish Theological Quarterly* 31 (1964): 303–21.

Edwards, Maldwyn. *John Wesley and the Eighteenth Century: A Study of His Social and Political Influence.* London: Allen & Unwin, 1933.

Fox, Harold G. "John Wesley and Natural Philosophy." *University of Dayton Review* 7, no. 1 (1970): 31–39.

Frost, Stanley B. *Authoritäteslehre in den Werken John Wesleys.* München: Ernst Reinhardt, 1938.

Gunter, W. Stephen. *The Limits of "Love Divine": John Wesley's Response to Antinomianism and Enthusiasm.* Nashville: Kingswood, 1989.

Hildebrandt, Franz. *From Luther to Wesley.* London: Lutterworth, 1951.

Kirkpatrick, Dow, ed. *The Finality of Christ.* Nashville: Abingdon, 1966.

Kisker, Scott. *Mainline or Methodist: Discovering Our Evangelistic Mission.* Nashville: Discipleship Resources, 2008.

Lacy, H. E. "Authority in John Wesley." *LQHR* 189 (1964): 114–19.

Lipscomb, Andrew A. "Providence of God in Methodism." In *Wesley Memorial Volume*, 383–403. Edited by J. O. A. Clark. New York: Phillips & Hunt, 1881.

Maddox, Graham, ed. *Political Writings of John Wesley: Primary Sources in Political Thought.* Durham, UK: Univ. of Durham, 1998.

Maddox, Randy L. "Responsible Grace: The Systematic Perspective of Wesleyan Theology." *WTJ* 19, no. 2 (1984): 7–22.

Marriott, Thomas. "John Wesley and William Wilberforce." *WMM* 68 (1945): 364–65.

Meeks, Douglas M., ed. *The Future of the Methodist Theological Traditions.* Nashville: Abingdon, 1985.

Moore, Robert L. *John Wesley and Authority: A Psychological Perspective.* Missoula, MT: Scholars, 1979.

Oswalt, John N. "Wesley's Use of the Old Testament." *WTJ* 12 (1977): 39–53.

Outler, Albert C. "How to Run a Conservative Revolution and Get No Thanks for It." In *Albert Outler: The Churchman.* Edited by Bob W. Parrott, 397–416. Anderson, IN: Bristol House, 1985.

———. *Theology in the Wesleyan Spirit.* Nashville: Tidings, 1975. Chap. 1, "Plundering the Egyptians."

Petry, Ray C. "The Critical Temper and the Practice of Tradition." *Duke Divinity School Review* 30 (Spring): 1965.

Piette, Maximin. *John Wesley in the Evolution of Protestantism.* Translated by J. B. Howard. New York: Sheed & Ward, 1938.

Rack, Henry. "Piety and Providence." In *Reasonable Enthusiast*, 420–71. Philadelphia: Trinity Press International, 1985.

Reist, Irwin W. "John Wesley and George Whitefield: The Integrity of Two Theories of Grace." *EQ* 47, no. 1 (1975): 26–40.

Rivers, Isabel. "Dissenting and Methodist Books of Practical Divinity." In *Books and Their Readers in Eighteenth Century England.* Edited by Isabel Rivers, 127–64. New York: St. Martins, 1982.

Runyan, Theodore, ed. *Sanctification and Liberation.* Nashville: Abingdon, 1981.

Stoeffler, F. Ernest. "The Wesleyan Concept of Religious Certainty — Its Prehistory and Significance." *LQHR* 33 (1964): 128–39.

Walls, Jerry L. "The Free Will Defense: Calvinism, Wesley, and the Goodness of God." *Christian Scholar's Review* 13 (1983): 19–33.

Weber, Theodore R. *Politics in the Order of Salvation: Transforming Wesleyan Political Ethics.* Nashville: Kingswood, 2001.

Wood, R. W. "God in History: Wesley a Child of Providence." *MQR* 78 (1929): 94–104.

PART 4

THEOLOGICAL
ETHICS

CHAPTER 6

The Believer's Guide to the Good Life

Having discussed character building through communities of accountability and how they impact behavior in the economic and political orders, we now turn to the core of Wesley's theological ethics. That core is found in his thirteen discourses on Jesus' Sermon on the Mount and his three discourses titled "The Law Established through Faith."

An Introduction to Evangelical Ethics

Of all the divisions of Wesley's ethical thought — community building, political, economic, and theological — the most demanding to master is his theological ethics. This is not because his thoughts are difficult to understand, but because the rigorous nature of the Christian life is so difficult to embrace without grace enabling it.

The Theological Foundation of Christian Ethical Teaching: The Sermon on the Mount

Introduction to Wesley's Thirteen Discourses on the Sermon on the Mount

Wesley's major work on ethics came in the form of thirteen teaching homilies on the Sermon on the Mount. More than one-third of the forty-four[1] Standard Sermons recognized as doctrinal standards in the Wesleyan tradition were on the Sermon on the Mount. Wesley preached more than a hundred times on the Sermon on the Mount between 1739 and 1746. He sought in all of these sermons to define the particular character of the Christian life. All were about ethics — evangelical ethics.

The Christian life is the fruit of justifying faith. It arises not as a result of an idea but in response to an event: God's grace made known in the cross and resurrection.

Since the times of the apostolic teachers, the Lord's Sermon on the Mount has been understood as the epitome of moral promise and moral fulfillment. It redefines the law in the light of the gospel. As stable doctrine, it is "a summary of the

---

[1]Variously numbered 44, 52, and 53. For clarification see *DSWT*.

Christian life, beginning with repentance and proceeding through justification to perfect love."[2]

In volume 2 of this series on Christ and salvation, I discuss in detail the scriptural ground of salvation in its logical order, from preparing grace through penitential grace, justifying grace, and full responsiveness to God's sanctifying grace. Here I seek to discern the ethical implications of divine grace.

The Harmony of All Parts of Jesus' Sermon

Each verse of Christianity's greatest sermon is a part of a tightly cohesive view of ethics. In short, it is the ethics of the coming reign of God. In few words, Jesus teaches every branch of gospel obedience necessary to the present and future Christian life of believers.

The structure of Jesus' teaching in Matthew 5–7 has three organizing themes: the sum of true religion, right intention that shapes all outward acts, and hindrances to the Christian life. The Sermon on the Mount "lays down at once the whole plan of his religion, to give us a full prospect of Christianity."[3] Everything essential to Christian ethics, according to John Wesley, is touched on by Jesus in the Sermon on the Mount.

The Sermon on the Mount is the ethical foundation of a happy life, a blessed life, a life lived in full enjoyment of and accountability to God.

A. The Good Life Blessed by God

In Wesley's thirteen homilies on Jesus' Sermon on the Mount, we see Jesus clearly setting out the way to the good life. He describes how the citizens of the coming kingdom will live a fulfilling life blessed by God. He shows what the good life looks like when people come under the gracious governance of God. How different these people are from their environing culture. No matter what culture Jesus' teaching enters, it transforms persons in that culture, and to some extent the culture itself. Jesus is calling his people to a new life in a new era that is completely different from ordinary life in the fallen world. It is a redeemed world. Its name is the kingdom of God.

1. The Beatitudes

A beatitude is a maxim of the blessed life, a way to maximize happiness from here to eternity.

After John the Baptist was imprisoned, Jesus began to teach in the synagogues of Galilee. He was "preaching the gospel of the kingdom, and healing all manner of sickness."[4]

The scene shifts to a mountain in Galilee, where Jesus is surrounded by a mul-

---

[2]SS 1:313.
[3]"Sermon on the Mount," 21, B 1:468, JWO, introduction.
[4]Matt. 4:12, 23; "Sermon on the Mount," 21, B 1:469, J V:247, proem, sec. 1.

titude. He has been performing miracles. Now he is ready to teach the people what these miracles are all about: the coming reign of God, already begun, welcoming their participation.

As a result of Jesus' early ministry of healing, "large crowds from Galilee, the Decapolis, Jerusalem, Judea and the region across the Jordan followed him."[5] So large were these crowds that no synagogue could contain them, so Jesus "went up on a mountainside and sat down. His disciples came to him, and he began to teach them."[6] Matthew reported what Jesus taught: "He ... taught them, saying, 'Blessed are the poor in spirit: for theirs is the kingdom of heaven. Blessed are they that mourn: for they shall be comforted.'"[7]

The text of Wesley's first discourse on the Sermon on the Mount consists of the first and second of the Beatitudes — those on poverty of spirit and on mourning penitentially for the sin that has prevented the blessed life [Matt. 5:1 – 4; Homily #21, "Upon Our Lord's Sermon on the Mount: Discourse 1," B 1:469 – 97, J V:247 – 61 (1748)].

2. The Sum of All True Religion

a. Who Is Speaking? What Right Does He Have to Speak, and What Responsibility Do We Have to Listen?

The speaker here is God's own Son, a man who is God in person. He does not cease to be God in becoming incarnate as man. The one speaking here is "the Lord of heaven and earth, the Creator of all; who, as such, has a right to dispose of all his creatures; the Lord our Governor, whose kingdom is from everlasting, and ruleth over all; the great Lawgiver, who can well enforce all his laws."[8]

So take heed to listen to "the eternal Wisdom of the Father, who understands our inmost frame." As truly God and truly man, he "knows how we stand related to God, to one another, to every creature."[9] He knows the divine-human relationship from both sides. He knows our human condition completely. He knows the Father's heart for fallen humanity.

Since the Son has lived a human life, he knows "how to adapt every law he prescribes to all the circumstances" in which human freedom and conscience live.[10] The classic apostolic consensus held that Jesus Christ was truly human and truly divine. This is the firm premise of the Sermon on the Mount. No one but the incarnate Lord is qualified to speak in this authoritative way to broken human beings.

So if you think you are hearing just another teacher, you do not know who you are listening to. Who is speaking on the Mount? Not just anybody. It is he "whose 'mercy is over all his works,' the God of love, who, having emptied himself of his

---

[5]Matt. 4:25 NIV.
[6]Matt. 5:1 – 2 NIV.
[7]Matt. 5:2 – 4.
[8]"Sermon on the Mount," 21, B 1:470, J V:247 – 48, proem, sec. 2.
[9]Ibid.
[10]Ibid.

eternal glory, is come forth from his Father to declare his will to the children of men," and then to return to the Father.[11]

The speaker is that unique one sent of God, according to the prophets, "to open the eyes of the blind, and to give light to them that sit in darkness."[12] He is completely human but "something more than human ... the Being of beings, JEHOVAH, the self-existent, the Supreme, the God who is over all."[13]

Bare assertions are not a sufficient proof to establish a point of such great importance. Jesus' humanity and deity are proved by the examination of the actual historical events subsequent to the Sermon on the Mount.[14] To hear the Sermon as if it would not lead to the cross is to misunderstand who is speaking.

b. The Audience

In this sermon, Jesus was not just teaching his closest disciples but "all who desired to learn of him," indeed "all the multitudes who went up with him into the mountain." He taught them as "one having authority, and not as the scribes."[15] In teaching about the happy life, the life blessed by God, Jesus was teaching once for all "the way of salvation" to "all the children of men; the whole race of mankind; the children [who] were yet unborn; all the generations to come, even to the end of the world."[16] What is said of humility and poverty of spirit pertains to all mankind, not just to Christians.[17] It was not for an audience in Galilee alone but for all humanity.[18]

c. The Unity and Coherence of Jesus' Teaching on the Mount

All sentences of the sermon are "joined as the stones in an arch, of which you cannot take one away without destroying the whole fabric."[19] In this inaugural teaching, Jesus spoke "as no man ever spoke."[20] He spoke "not as the holy men of old," although they also spoke "as they were moved by the Holy Ghost."[21] His words were not those of Peter, James, or John, but of the incarnate Lord. They were the leading apostles, "but still in this, in the degrees of heavenly wisdom, the servant is not as his Lord."[22] Each part of the Sermon on the Mount relates to the whole of it, each part and the whole being related to the whole of humanity of all times and places.

In no other sacred text does Jesus "lay down at once the whole plan of his religion; to give us a full prospect of Christianity; to describe at large the nature of that holiness without which no man shall see the Lord."[23] There are many fragments of

---

[11]Ibid.
[12]Ibid.; cf. Luke 1:79; John 10:21.
[13]"Sermon on the Mount," 21, B 1:474, J V:251, proem, sec. 9.
[14]"Sermon on the Mount," 21, B 1:472, J V:249–50, proem, sec. 5.
[15]"Sermon on the Mount," 21, B 1:471–72, J V:249, proem, sec. 4; Matt. 7:29.
[16]"Sermon on the Mount," 21, B 1:471–72, J V:249, proem, sec. 4.
[17]"Sermon on the Mount," 21, B 1:472, J V:249–50, proem, sec. 5.
[18]Ibid.
[19]"Sermon on the Mount," 21, B 1:473–74, J V:250, proem, sec. 6.
[20]Cf. John 7:46.
[21]Cf. 2 Peter 1:21.
[22]"Sermon on the Mount," 21, B 1:474, J V:250, proem, sec. 7.
[23]Ibid.

this whole teaching in sacred Scripture, but we have nothing comparable "in all the Bible" to Jesus' teaching on the Mount.[24]

Here he is showing us nothing less than "the way to heaven; to the place which he has prepared for us; the glory he had before the world began. He is teaching us the true way to life everlasting; the royal way which leads to the kingdom." Those who choose different paths will find them leading to destruction.[25]

He is teaching not one bit too much or too little for us to walk in the way. He teaches plainly and simply "the full and perfect will of God," with nothing contrary to the intent of his heavenly Father.[26]

In doing so, he was refuting the distortions of the scribes and Pharisees who had perverted the Mosaic and prophetic word of God. But more so, in Wesley's view, he was anticipating for all future times "all the practical mistakes that are inconsistent with salvation." These mistaken ways were all attempted in the future of the believing community after Jesus. Get his meaning straight in this one sermon and you will avoid future perversions of the word of God.[27]

d. The Sum of All True Religion in Three Chapters

Three parts of the Sermon on the Mount mark the way to the good life:

- the sum of all true religion laid down in eight particulars in the Beatitudes (Matt. 5)
- the priority of right intention to outward actions (Matt. 6)
- warnings "against the main hindrances of religion" (Matt. 7)[28]

This teaching is not set forth as several stages or steps of a journey but as a single unified teaching of the Lord. It reveals the way to happiness.

B. The Ethical Foundation of the Happy Life

1. What Makes People Happy?

The Beatitudes of Jesus teach about the blessed life. Wesley equates blessedness with happiness, so Jesus' sermon is about the happy life: "'Blessed,' or happy, 'are the poor in spirit'" — those whose lives are completely humbled in the presence of the glory of God.

In today's English, we use the words *happy* and *blessed* with different nuances. The Greek word *makarios* embraces both nuances. In modern parlance, to be happy seems to be less than to be truly blessed. To be happy is to feel good at the moment. To be blessed is to be touched by the grace of God. But Wesley used *happy* and *blessed* as synonyms. To be happy is to be blessed. To be eternally happy is to be eternally blessed.

---

[24]Ibid.
[25]"Sermon on the Mount," 21, B 1:470–71, J V:248, proem, sec. 3.
[26]Ibid.
[27]Ibid.
[28]"Sermon on the Mount," 21, B 1:474, J V:251, proem, sec. 10.

In speaking of the happy life, Jesus was showing us what our souls most deeply yearn for and have long sought in vain.[29]

What character patterns make way for a happy life? The beginning point in human happiness is an all-embracing sense of humility.

2. The Happy Life of the Humble

"Blessed [happy] are the poor in spirit."[30] The foundation of all in the Christian life is poverty of spirit. Jesus reached out to the poor of the world to help them "make a transition from temporal to spiritual things."[31] In his Sermon on the Mount, he is speaking about happiness — temporal and eternal. The word *blessed* embraces the best aspects of every form of happiness conceivable when rightly viewed. This happiness is seen in its most comprehensive frame of reference: from the viewpoint of eternity. Happy are the poor in spirit.[32]

But poor does not refer to outward circumstances, since the reference is to those who are "poor in spirit." This means "they who, whatever their outward circumstances are, have that disposition of heart which is the first step to all real, substantial happiness, either in this world or in that which is to come."[33] It is to be lowly of heart.

By "poor in spirit" the Lord did not mean, strictly speaking, those who love poverty or those who have wholly divested themselves of worldly goods. Those senses of the expression do not fit the larger design of the Lord's Sermon, which is "to lay a general foundation whereon the whole fabric of Christianity may be built."[34] Rather, "the poor in spirit" are "the humble; they who know themselves; who are convinced of sin; those to whom God hath given that first repentance, which is previous to faith in Christ."[35]

To know oneself rightly is to know one's own limitations. One who is poor in spirit is convinced that he is spiritually poor indeed, hence dependent on grace. He has a deep sense of the sin for which he is voluntarily responsible. He knows how deeply sin "overspreads his whole soul and totally corrupts every power and faculty."[36]

"Real Christianity always begins in poverty of spirit and goes on in the order here set down, till the 'man of God is made perfect.' We begin at the lowest of these gifts of God, yet so as not to relinquish this when we are called of God to come up higher," toward "the highest blessings of God."[37]

---

[29]"Sermon on the Mount," 21, B 1:474, J V:251, proem, sec. 8.
[30]Matt. 5:3.
[31]"Sermon on the Mount," 21, B 1:475, J V:252, sec. 1.2.
[32]"Sermon on the Mount," 21, B 1:475, J V:251 – 52, sec. 1.1.
[33]"Sermon on the Mount," 21, B 1:475, J V:252, sec. 1.2.
[34]"Sermon on the Mount," 21, B 1:476, J V:252 – 53, sec. 1.3.
[35]"Sermon on the Mount," 21, B 1:477 – 78, J V:253 – 54, sec. 1.4.
[36]Ibid.
[37]"Sermon on the Mount," 21, B 1:475, J V:251 – 52, sec. 1.1.

3. The Lowliest of God's Gifts

One who is poor in spirit is the opposite of one possessed with a constant bias to "think of himself more highly than he ought to think."[38]

Those poor in spirit have learned the vanity of thirsting for honor among men. That vanity appears in ten thousand shapes: "The love of the world, the self-will, the foolish and hurtful desires, which cleave to his inmost soul."[39]

The thirst for vanity may take the form of speech. Those who are poor in spirit are conscious of how deeply they have offended by their tongues, "if not by profane, immodest, untrue, or unkind words, yet by discourse which was not 'good to the use of edifying,' not 'meet to minister grace to the hearers.'"[40] They know themselves well and know that counting their sins would be like trying to "number the drops of rain, the sands of the sea, or the days of eternity."[41]

Those who are poor in spirit know their guilt as if it were immediately present to them — directly in their faces.[42] They are able to ask how they could possibly come into the presence of the Lord as such. How could they pay the moral debt they owe? Wesley said of one who is poor in spirit, "Were he from this moment to perform the most perfect obedience to every command of God," this would make insufficient amends. At the deepest level he is aware that "he owes God all the service he is able to perform, from this moment to all eternity," since he is "utterly helpless with regard to atoning for his past sins, utterly unable to make any amends to God, to pay any ransom for his own soul."[43] This is what it means to be poor in spirit.

Wesley continued, "[Even] if God would forgive him all that is past, on this one condition, that he should sin no more, that for the time to come he should entirely and constantly obey all his commands, he well knows that this would profit him nothing, being a condition he could never perform. He knows and feels that he is not able to obey even the outward commands of God; seeing these cannot be obeyed while his heart remains in its natural sinfulness and corruption; inasmuch as an evil tree cannot bring forth good fruit. But he cannot cleanse a sinful heart: with men this is impossible: so that he is utterly at a loss even how to begin walking in the path of God's commandments.... He knows not how to get one step forward in the way. Encompassed with sin, and sorrow, and fear, and finding no way to escape, he can only cry out, 'Lord, save, or I perish!'"[44] Awareness of sin brings him closer to poverty of spirit.

Paul spoke of that condition where "every mouth might be stopped, and all the world become guilty before God,"[45] and where people feel entirely "helpless as well

---

[38]Rom. 12:3; "Sermon on the Mount," 21, B 1:475, J V:251–52, sec. 1.1.

[39]"Sermon on the Mount," 21, B 1:475, J V:251–52, sec. 1.1.

[40]"Sermon on the Mount," 21, B 1:477–78, J V:253–54, sec. 1.4; cf. Eph. 4:29.

[41]"Sermon on the Mount," 21, B 1:477–78, J V:253–54, sec. 1.4.

[42]"Sermon on the Mount," 21, B 1:478, J V:254, sec. 1.5.

[43]"Sermon on the Mount," 21, B 1:478–79, J V:254–55, sec. 1.6.

[44]Ibid.

[45]"Sermon on the Mount," 21, B 1:479–80, J V:255, sec. 1.8; cf. Rom. 3:19.

as guilty."[46] This is exactly what Paul meant when he said that no flesh shall be justified by the deeds of the law.[47]

4. Christian Ethics Begins Where Natural Morality Ends

Repentance is the door to faith. The humility necessary to true repentance is the tender point where the sermon begins. Poverty of spirit is the only starting point for hearing the good news of pardon.

For who is ready to ask for pardon who does not recognize he needs it? Only then is he in mind to grasp the meaning of Romans 3:21 – 22: "But now the righteousness of God without the law is manifested, being witnessed by the law and the prophets; even the righteousness of God which is by faith of Jesus Christ unto all and upon all them that believe." Therefore "we conclude that a man is justified by faith without the deeds of the law."[48] These expressions show why poverty of spirit is the first step toward redemption. This conviction "casts the sinner, stripped of all, lost and undone, on his strong Helper, Jesus Christ the Righteous."[49]

Christianity begins just where natural, rational morality often ends. The best reasoning of the natural man in the history of ethics seldom begins with radical repentance. Christianity does begin in "poverty of spirit, conviction of sin, the renouncing ourselves, the not having our own righteousness (the very first point in the religion of Jesus Christ), leaving all pagan religion behind."[50] Neither a classic Greek nor a classic Roman ethic is prone to take this first step. But the poor in spirit feel palpably what classic Greco-Roman ethics could never quite express as the first step: "Sinner, awake! Know thyself!" Know and feel that you were shaped by the long history of sin and have yourself voluntarily contributed to that corruption.[51]

Only the poor in spirit will be in proper frame of mind to hear the Good News. Therefore, "Happy are the poor in spirit: for theirs is the kingdom of heaven."[52] What is this reign of God? It is within us, awaiting to be recognized. It is that " 'righteousness, and peace, and joy in the Holy Ghost.' And what is 'righteousness,' but the life of God in the soul; the mind which was in Christ Jesus; the image of God stamped upon the heart, now renewed after the likeness of him that created it? What is it but the love of God, because he first loved us, and the love of all mankind for his sake?"[53] The evangelical ethic begins by taking this first step toward peace in God. This step is not a human achievement but a joyful response to the grace of God preparing the heart for faith.

---

[46]"Sermon on the Mount," 21, B 1:479 – 80, J V:255, sec. 1.8.
[47]See Rom. 3:20.
[48]Rom. 3:28.
[49]"Sermon on the Mount," 21, B 1:479 – 80, J V:255, sec. 1.8.
[50]"Sermon on the Mount," 21, B 1:480, J V:256, sec. 1.9.
[51]"Sermon on the Mount," 21, B 1:480 – 81, J V:256, sec. 1.10; cf. Ps. 51:5 (BCP).
[52]"Sermon on the Mount," 21, B 1:480 – 81, J V:256, sec. 1.10.
[53]"Sermon on the Mount," 21, B 1:481, J V:256 – 57, sec. 1.11.

5. The Inheritance of the Poor in Spirit: Theirs Is the Kingdom of Heaven

Whoever you are to whom God is giving the gift of becoming poor in spirit, "his peace is already purchased for you by the blood of the crucified Lord. This peace is very near at hand. You are standing on the brink of heaven! Another step and you will enter into the kingdom of righteousness, and peace, and joy! Those who are poor in spirit are prepared to 'Behold the Lamb of God, who takes away the sin of the world!' "[54]

Are you unable to atone for the least of your sins? Then you are prepared to hear that "he is the propitiation" for all of them. "Now believe on the Lord Jesus Christ, and all thy sins are blotted out!" Here is the "fountain for sin and uncleanness!... 'Arise, and wash away thy sins!' Stagger no more at the promise through unbelief! Give glory to God! Dare to believe!"[55] This is genuine Christian humility that flows from a sense of the love of God. It springs out of God's reconciling work for us through his Son. It teaches us to be lowly of heart.[56]

"Poverty of spirit, in this meaning of the word, begins where a sense of guilt and of the wrath of God ends; and is a continual sense of our total dependence on him, for every good thought, or word, or work."[57] The humble heart is a first step, but not in the sense that poverty of spirit is left behind and progresses beyond humility. Rather, "the more we grow in grace, the more do we see of the desperate wickedness of our heart. The more we advance in the knowledge and love of God, through our Lord Jesus Christ, the more do we discern "the necessity of our being entirely renewed in righteousness and true holiness."[58] God's love draws us toward lowliness of heart that we may have the peace of God. Repentance is the beginning point for evangelical ethics.

6. Toward a Right Inward Intention for All Outward Actions

a. The Blessed Life of Those Who Mourn

The text of our Lord's sermon then continues in the second beatitude: "Blessed are those who mourn, for they will be comforted."[59] The Lord has taken his hearer into the first step of true religion, poverty of spirit. This is the first beatitude — the first step into human happiness. From here on the other beatitudes seek to guide the penitent toward that right intention by which we may "preserve in all our outward actions, unmixed with worldly desires, or anxious cares for even the necessaries of life."[60]

But the tone of the second beatitude at first sounds demoralizing. It is about

---

[54]"Sermon on the Mount," 21, B 1:482, J V:257, sec. 1.12; John 1:29.
[55]"Sermon on the Mount," 21, B 1:482, J V:257, sec. 1.12.
[56]Cf. Matt. 11:29.
[57]"Sermon on the Mount," 21, B 1:482, J V:257, sec. 1.13.
[58]"Sermon on the Mount," 21, B 1:482–83, J V:257–58, sec. 1.13.
[59]Matt. 5:4 NIV.
[60]"Sermon on the Mount," 21, B 1:483, J V:258, sec. 2.1.

mourning. Are we going to begin talking about mourning just after we have spoken of beginning to know "the inward kingdom of heaven"?

The Lord faced directly the issue of our mourning over idolatrous losses by saying, "Blessed are they that mourn: for they shall be comforted."[61] Do not imagine that the way from the humble heart to peace with God will be untroubled. Do not expect to be "borne aloft in the chariots of joy and love," soaring "as upon the wings of an eagle."[62] Humility brings the gracious capacity to mourn over our sins and the sins of the world.

We may imagine that "this promise belongs to those who mourn only on some worldly account," sorrowing over disappointments: loss of reputation, friends, or fortune, or temporal evil.[63] But the mourners of whom our Lord was here speaking are those who mourn for quite another reason. They mourn after God, over the loss of God, and over the dominions of idolatry that they leave behind. Toward what end is this mourning heading? Toward the one in whom they will "'rejoice with joy unspeakable,' when he [gives] them to 'taste the good,' the pardoning 'word and the powers of the world to come.' But he now 'hides his face, and they are troubled.'"[64]

b. The Harvest of Discipline: The Comfort of God

When Paul wrote to the Corinthians, he promised "grace and peace,"[65] praising the God of all comfort:

> Praise be to the God and Father of our Lord Jesus Christ, the Father of compassion and the God of all comfort, who comforts us in all our troubles, so that we can comfort those in any trouble with the comfort we ourselves receive from God. For just as we share abundantly in the sufferings of Christ, so also our comfort abounds through Christ. If we are distressed, it is for your comfort and salvation; if we are comforted, it is for your comfort, which produces in you patient endurance of the same sufferings we suffer. And our hope for you is firm, because we know that just as you share in our sufferings, so also you share in our comfort.[66]

Jesus had promised, "They will be comforted."[67] Comforted with worldly comforts? No, comforted by the comfort of God. Those who are mourning often "cannot see him through the dark cloud." All they can see is "temptation and sin, which they fondly supposed were gone never to return, arising again, following after them amain [with full force], and holding them in on every side. It is not strange if their soul is now disquieted within them and trouble and heaviness take hold upon them."[68]

---

[61] Ibid.; Matt. 5:4.
[62] "Sermon on the Mount," 21, B 1:483, J V:258, sec. 2.1.
[63] "Sermon on the Mount," 21, B 1:483, J V:258, sec. 2.2.
[64] "Sermon on the Mount," 21, B 1:483 – 84, J V:258 – 59, sec. 2.3.
[65] 2 Cor. 1:2 NIV.
[66] 2 Cor. 1:3 – 7 NIV.
[67] Matt. 5:4 NIV.
[68] "Sermon on the Mount," 21, B 1:483 – 84, J V:258 – 59, sec. 2.3.

THE BELIEVER'S GUIDE TO THE GOOD LIFE

When we face the loss of our gods, the ancient enemy is there to pester us: "Where is now thy God? Where is now the blessedness" you hoped for? Maybe God's promise was "only a dream, a mere delusion, a creature of thy own imagination."[69] So speaks the tempter, and so increases the heaviness of heart. But the loss prepares for the larger gift. In despair the mourner cries out, "Maybe I have made a shipwreck of the faith, 'and my last state be worse than the first.' "[70] At this point we are wisely instructed by the letter to the Hebrews: "No discipline seems pleasant at the time, but painful. Later on, however, it produces a harvest of righteousness and peace for those who have been trained by it."[71]

The faithful will not be turned away "by the miserable comforters of the world."[72] Mourning over lost gods offers the opportunity to learn patience in God's own time. "Blessed are they who 'follow on to know the Lord,' and steadily refuse all other comfort. They shall be comforted by the consolations of his Spirit."[73] The blessed are those who move in God's own time, not their own.

c. Full Assurance

With the discipline of patience, Scripture promises that they will in due time experience "a fresh manifestation of his love ... as shall never more be taken away from them."[74] "This 'full assurance of faith' swallows up all doubt, as well as all tormenting fear; God now giving them a sure hope of an enduring substance, and 'strong consolation through grace.' "[75]

By this gracious assurance, we glimpse the power resting on us to enable us to exclaim:

> Who shall separate us from the love of Christ? Shall trouble or hardship or persecution or famine or nakedness or danger or sword? ... No, in all these things we are more than conquerors through him who loved us. For I am convinced that neither death nor life, neither angels nor demons, neither the present nor the future, nor any powers, neither height nor depth, nor anything else in all creation, will be able to separate us from the love of God that is in Christ Jesus our Lord.[76]

d. Full Assurance Turns Mourning into Joy

The movement from repentance to faith is a process "both of mourning for an absent God, and recovering the joy of his countenance."[77] This is made clear in the way the Lord spoke to his apostles the night before his passion: "Jesus saw that

---

[69]Ibid.
[70]Ibid.
[71]Heb. 12:11 NIV; "Sermon on the Mount," 21, B 1:485, J V:259 – 60, sec. 2.4.
[72]"Sermon on the Mount," 21, B 1:485, J V:259 – 60, sec. 2.4.
[73]Ibid.
[74]Ibid.
[75]Ibid.
[76]Rom. 8:35, 37 – 39 NIV.
[77]"Sermon on the Mount," 21, B 1:485 – 86, J V:260, sec. 2.5.

they wanted to ask him about this [his death], so he said to them, 'Are you asking one another what I meant when I said, "In a little while you will see me no more, and then after a little while you will see me"?' "[78] This question became a teaching moment for Jesus with the disciples on how the disciples' grief would turn to joy. They wanted to know what he meant by "a little while."[79]

Jesus answered, "Very truly I tell you, you will weep and mourn while the world rejoices."[80] The disciples experienced the cycle of grief turning into joy in the resurrection. The cycle would recur on many future occasions. You will think your joy will not be comforted by any consolation. At that point, when you can no longer see the Lord, "your grief will turn to joy"[81] by the return of the crucified Lord.[82] This is a promise of the Servant Messiah to all in this world who mourn: your mourning will turn to joy when you see your situation in an eternal frame of reference. By analogy, "a woman giving birth to a child has pain because her time has come; but when her baby is born she forgets the anguish because of her joy that a child is born into the world."[83] "So with you: Now is your time of grief."[84] In this temporal world, you will grieve not only over your worldly losses, but over the false imagination of an eternal loss. Jesus said you will be so down that "in that day you will no longer ask me anything."[85] At that moment, you will not even have the courage to ask for an end to your mourning. As it will occur in the crucifixion, you will not even think of asking for a resurrection.

At that moment, Jesus gives the faithful an eternal promise: "Very truly I tell you, my Father will give you whatever you ask in my name. Until now you have not asked for anything in my name. Ask and you will receive, and your joy will be complete."[86]

"So with you: Now is your time of grief"; you mourn and cannot be comforted, "but I will see you again and you will rejoice" with calm, inward joy, "and no one will take away your joy."[87] This mourning is "lost in holy joy." The despair is not absolute. Death is the signal of real life. Mourning is a training ground for hope.

e. Mourning over the Sins of Mankind

Beyond this mourning ending in joy, there is another mourning, "and a blessed mourning it is, which abides in the children of God. They still mourn for the sins and miseries of mankind."[88] They "weep with them that weep."[89] They weep for them that do not weep for themselves. They weep for those who sin against their

---

[78]Ibid.; cf. John 16:19 NIV.
[79]John 16:18 NIV.
[80]John 16:20 NIV.
[81]Cf. John 16:21.
[82]"Sermon on the Mount," 21, B 1:485 – 86, J V:260, sec. 2.5.
[83]John 16:21 NIV; "Sermon on the Mount," 21, B 1:485 – 86, J V:260, sec. 2.5.
[84]John 16:22 NIV.
[85]John 16:23 NIV.
[86]John 16:23 – 24 NIV; "Sermon on the Mount," 21, B 1:485 – 86, J V:260, sec. 2.5.
[87]John 16:22 NIV; "Sermon on the Mount," 21, B 1:485 – 86, J V:260, sec. 2.5.
[88]"Sermon on the Mount," 21, B 1:486, J V:260 – 61, sec. 2.6.
[89]Rom. 12:15; "Sermon on the Mount," 21, B 1:486, J V:260 – 61, sec. 2.6.

own souls.[90] This is a grief over "the dishonor continually done to the Majesty of heaven and earth." Meanwhile the eyes of the faithful are wide open to eternity. They see "the vast ocean of eternity, without a bottom or a shore, which has already swallowed up millions of millions of men and is gaping to devour them that yet remain."[91] They see the house of God eternal in the heavens and the destruction of all sin. They therefore "feel the importance of every moment, which just appears and is gone forever!"[92] But of course "all this wisdom of God is foolishness with the world." It is interpreted as either melancholy or moping or dullness. "The whole affair of mourning and poverty of spirit is with them stupidity and dullness." These are judgments "passed by those who know not God."[93]

Wesley offered an analogy for these two opposite responses to eternity: "Suppose, as two persons were walking together, one should suddenly stop, and with the strongest signs of fear and amazement, cry out, 'On what a precipice do we stand! See, we are on the point of being dashed in pieces!' ... The other looked forward and saw nothing of all this."[94] Eternity seems to him foolishness. The faithful mourn over his faithlessness.[95]

Wesley called the faithful who walk in the light not to be inordinately diverted by those who persist in walking in darkness.[96] Faith knows that "God and eternity are real things. Heaven and hell are in very deed open before you; and ye are on the edge of the great gulf. It has already swallowed up more than words can express, nations, and kindreds, and peoples, and tongues; and still yawns to devour, whether they see it or not."[97]

So, said Wesley, "lift up your voice to him who grasps both time and eternity, both for yourselves and your brethren, that ye may be counted worthy to escape the destruction that cometh as a whirlwind!"[98] Pray that you may be brought safe through all the waves and storms into the eternal haven promised. There the Lord will wipe away the tears from your faces and "put a period to misery and sin." There "the knowledge of the Lord shall cover the earth, as the waters cover the sea."[99]

C. The Blessed Life of the Meek

The text of Wesley's second discourse on the Sermon on the Mount consists of the third, fourth, and fifth beatitudes: "Blessed are the meek: for they shall inherit the earth. Blessed are they which do hunger and thirst after righteousness: for they shall be filled. Blessed are the merciful: for they shall obtain mercy" [Matt. 5:5 – 7;

[90]"Sermon on the Mount," 21, B 1:486, J V:260–61, sec. 2.6.
[91]Ibid.
[92]Ibid.
[93]"Sermon on the Mount," 21, B 1:486–87, J V:261, sec. 2.7.
[94]Ibid.
[95]Ibid.
[96]"Sermon on the Mount," 21, B 1:487, J V:261, sec. 2.8.
[97]Ibid.
[98]Ibid.
[99]Ibid.

Homily #22, "Upon Our Lord's Sermon on the Mount: Discourse 2," B 1:488–509, J V:262–77 (1748)].

1. Blessed Are the Meek Who Are Balanced in Their Affections

The time frame of the meek is after they have passed through poverty of spirit and mourning: "When 'the winter is past,' when 'the time of singing is come, and the voice of the turtle[dove] is heard in the land'; when he that comforts the mourners is now returned, 'that he may abide with them for ever'; when, at the brightness of his presence, the clouds disperse, the dark clouds of doubt and uncertainty, the storms of fear flee away, the waves of sorrow subside, and their spirit again rejoiceth in God their Saviour," this is the time for meekness. Those whom God has comforted attest the blessedness of the meek. They are happy. For they shall inherit the earth.[100]

Who are "the meek"? Meekness is sometimes mistaken for apathy. The meek do not lack feeling. They are not characterized by either ignorance or insensibility.[101] They are not those who are sheltered from the shocks of life. Meekness does not imply being without zeal for God. It is unthinkable that the church fathers would confuse meekness with any of these descriptions.[102]

Rather, meekness "keeps clear of every extreme, whether in excess or defect. It does not destroy but balances the affections." God's design for humanity is not that the affections be rooted out, but rather brought in balance under rational control. Meekness "poises the mind aright. It holds an even scale, with regard to anger, and sorrow, and fear; preserving the mean [the middle way between excess or defect] in every circumstance of life, and not declining either to the right hand or the left."[103]

When we consider meekness as an internal balance within ourselves, "we style it patience or contentedness. When it is exerted toward other men, then it is mildness to the good and gentleness to the evil."[104] It is neither an extreme excess or an extreme deficit. When this due composure of mind has reference to God, "it is usually termed resignation; a calm acquiescence in whatsoever is his will concerning us, even though it may not be pleasing to nature." Eli is the biblical model of meekness. "Samuel told him everything, hiding nothing from him. Then Eli said, 'He is the LORD; let him do what is good in his eyes.'"[105]

2. Rightly Expressing and Restraining Anger

The meek can be "zealous for the Lord of hosts; but their zeal is always guided by knowledge, and tempered, in every thought, and word, and work, with the love of man, as well as the love of God. They do not desire to extinguish any of the passions which God has for wise ends implanted in their nature; but they have the mastery

---

[100]"Sermon on the Mount," 22, B 1:488, J V:262, sec. 1.1.
[101]"Sermon on the Mount," 22, B 1:489, J V:263, sec. 1.3.
[102]"Sermon on the Mount," 22, B 1:488–89, J V:262, sec. 1.2.
[103]"Sermon on the Mount," 22, B 1:489, J V:263, sec. 1.3.
[104]"Sermon on the Mount," 22, B 1:489, J V:263, sec. 1.4.
[105]1 Sam. 3:18 NIV; "Sermon on the Mount," 22, B 1:489, J V:263, sec. 1.4.

of all. They hold them all in subjection and employ them only in subservience to those ends."[106]

In the meek "even the harsher and more unpleasing passions are applicable to the noblest purposes; even hatred, and anger, and fear, when engaged against sin and regulated by faith and love, are as walls and bulwarks to the soul, so that the wicked one cannot approach to hurt it."[107] Meekness does not only restrain outward actions, as the scribes and Pharisees taught, but acts as a ballast amid inward passions like anger.[108] The meek can "clearly discern what is evil; and they can also suffer it ... but still meekness holds the reins."[109]

This divine temper in the faithful seeks "not only to abide but to increase in us day by day. Occasions of exercising, and thereby increasing it, will never be wanting while we remain upon earth." We need patience so that after we have suffered we may receive the promise. We need resignation in order that we may in all circumstances say, "Not as I will, but as thou wilt."[110] "We need gentleness toward all, especially toward the evil and unthankful."[111] Patience, resignation, and gentleness are all virtues made easier through meekness.

Even inward anger that goes no further than the heart is viewed by our Lord as ranked under the heading of an intimation of murder. Meekness "does not show itself by an outward unkindness, no, not so much as a passionate word."[112] Whoever, lacking meekness, "feels any unkindness in his heart, any temper contrary to love," or "is angry ... without a cause shall be in danger of the judgment."[113]

We may be legitimately angry or grieved at another's hardness of heart, as was the Lord in Mark 3:5. But anger accompanied by contempt is foolish. Anyone who says, "Thou fool," with an attitude of reproach or reviling, "shall, in that instant, be liable to the highest condemnation."[114] Jesus "warns us that the performing of our duty to God will not excuse us from our duty to our neighbor; that works of piety, as they are called, will be so far from commending us to God, if we are wanting in charity, that, on the contrary, that want of charity will make all those works an abomination to the Lord."[115]

The spirit of meekness prevails at the altar: "Therefore, if you are offering your gift at the altar and there remember that your brother or sister has something against you, leave your gift there in front of the altar. First go and be reconciled to them; then come and offer your gift."[116] "Settle matters quickly with your adversary

---

[106]"Sermon on the Mount," 22, B 1:491, J V:264, sec. 1.7.
[107]"Sermon on the Mount," 22, B 1:490, J V:263, sec. 1.5.
[108]"Sermon on the Mount," 22, B 1:491, J V:264, sec. 1.7.
[109]"Sermon on the Mount," 22, B 1:490, J V:263, sec. 1.5.
[110]Matt. 26:39.
[111]"Sermon on the Mount," 22, B 1:490 – 91, J V:263 – 64, sec. 1.6.
[112]"Sermon on the Mount," 22, B 1:491 – 92, J V:264, sec. 1.8.
[113]Ibid.; Matt. 5:21 – 22.
[114]"Sermon on the Mount," 22, B 1:492, J V:264 – 65, sec. 1.9.
[115]"Sermon on the Mount," 22, B 1:493, J V:265, sec. 1.10.
[116]Matt. 5:23 – 24 NIV.

who is taking you to court. Do it while you are still together on the way, or your adversary may hand you over to the judge."[117]

3. The Consolation They Will Be Given: The Meek Shall Inherit the Earth

The meek shall inherit the earth. God "takes a peculiar care to provide them [the meek] with all things needful for life and godliness; he secures to them the provision he hath made, in spite of the force, fraud, or malice of men; and what he secures he gives them richly to enjoy. It is sweet to them, be it little or much."[118]

In their meekness, they will find all that is on the earth their inheritance. "As in patience they possess their souls, so they truly possess whatever God hath given them. They are always content, always pleased with what they have. It pleases them because it pleases God, so that while their heart, their desire, their joy is in heaven, they may truly be said to 'inherit the earth.'"[119]

Wesley saw an end-time meaning in the meek inheriting the earth: the meek "shall have a more eminent part in 'the new earth where righteousness dwells.' ... In keeping with his promise, we are looking forward to a new heaven and a new earth, where righteousness dwells."[120] This is the earth the meek will inherit.

Wesley saw in Revelation 20:4–6 a picture of the meek in the resurrection. Those who in their meekness had been beheaded because of their testimony "came to life and reigned with Christ a thousand years.... Blessed and holy are those who share in the first resurrection. The second death has no power over them, but they will be priests of God and of Christ and will reign with him for a thousand years" (NIV).[121]

D. Hungering for Righteousness

To this point our Lord's Sermon on the Mount has been focused on "removing the hindrances of true religion."[122] The first of these is pride, which is taken away by poverty of spirit; the second is thoughtlessness, which is removed by holy mourning; and the others are "anger, impatience, discontent, which are all healed by Christian meekness."[123] Once these cravings are removed, "the native appetite of a heaven-born spirit returns; it hungers and thirsts after righteousness."[124] This clears the way for the fourth of eight beatitudes: "Blessed are those who hunger and thirst for righteousness, for they will be filled."[125]

---

[117]Matt. 5:25 NIV; "Sermon on the Mount," 22, B 1:493, J V:265–66, sec. 1.11.
[118]"Sermon on the Mount," 22, B 1:494, J V:266, sec. 1.12.
[119]Ibid.
[120]"Sermon on the Mount," 22, B 1:494–95, J V:266, sec. 1.13; cf. 2 Peter 3:13.
[121]"Sermon on the Mount," 22, B 1:494–95, J V:266, sec. 1.13.
[122]"Sermon on the Mount," 22, B 1:495, J V:267, sec. 2.1.
[123]Ibid.
[124]Ibid.
[125]Matt. 5:6 NIV.

1. Righteousness

What is righteousness? It is "the image of God, the mind which was in Christ Jesus. It is every holy and heavenly temper in one; springing from, as well as terminating in, the love of God, as our Father and Redeemer, and the love of all men for his sake."[126] They are happy who hunger for righteousness above all other cravings.

As hunger and thirst are the strongest of all our bodily appetites, so the strongest of all our spiritual appetites are hunger and thirst after the image of God already implanted in us. Once tasted and awakened in the heart, "it swallows up all the rest in that one great desire — to be renewed after the likeness of Him that created us."[127]

From the time we begin to physically hunger and thirst, those appetites do not cease. They grow. Similarly, "from the time that we begin to hunger and thirst after the whole mind which was in Christ, these spiritual appetites do not cease, but cry after their food with more and more importunity; nor can they possibly cease, before they are satisfied, while there is any spiritual life remaining."[128]

Suppose you give to someone who is hungry "all the world beside, all the elegance of apparel, all the trappings of state, all the treasure upon earth, yea thousands of gold and silver; if you would pay him ever so much honor — he regards it not. All these things are then of no account with him."[129] So it is with every soul who "truly hungers and thirsts after righteousness. He can find no comfort in anything but this.... Whatever you offer besides, it is lightly esteemed."[130] What the redeemed soul longs for is "having that mind which was in Jesus Christ."[131]

a. How They Shall Be Filled with Righteousness

The hunger for true religion looks toward filling the soul with righteousness. Outward and conventional religion does not necessarily fill the soul.

What the world calls religion may seek to satisfy the hungering soul, but often without avail, lacking the mind which was in Christ. Worldly religion "implies three things: (1) The doing no harm, the abstaining from outward sin; at least from such as is scandalous, as robbery, theft, common swearing, drunkenness. (2) The doing good, the relieving the poor; the being charitable, as it is called. (3) The using the means of grace; at least the going to church and to the Lord's Supper. He in whom these three marks are found is termed by the world a religious man."[132]

But if I do all these things and have not the mind of Christ, is my hunger satisfied? The hungering soul "wants a religion of a nobler kind, a religion higher and deeper than this. He can no more feed on this poor, shallow, formal thing than he can 'fill his belly with the east wind.' "[133] What he thirsts for is being joined to the

---

[126]"Sermon on the Mount," 22, B 1:495, J V:267, sec. 2.2.
[127]"Sermon on the Mount," 22, B 1:495 – 96, J V:267 – 68, sec. 2.3.
[128]Ibid.
[129]Ibid.
[130]Ibid.
[131]"Sermon on the Mount," 22, B 1:496 – 97, J V:268, sec. 2.4.
[132]Ibid.
[133]Ibid.

Lord in one Spirit, having fellowship with the Father and the Son, walking in the light as God is in the light.[134]

The promise is that those who hunger and thirst after righteousness shall be filled. How filled? With the things for which they longed — righteousness and true holiness. "God shall satisfy them with the blessings of his goodness."[135] Here biblical metaphors abound: filled with the bread of heaven, the manna of his love. God "shall give them to drink of his pleasures as out of the river, which he that drinks of shall never thirst."[136]

You cannot "dig happiness out of the earth." Quit spending your money on that which is not truly nourishing. Do not labor for that which does not satisfy.[137] Instead, invest all you have in "the entire renewal of thy soul in that image of God wherein it was originally created."[138]

2. Blessed Are the Merciful

a. How the Merciful Are Blessed by Showing Mercy

The fifth beatitude through which we are made happy is this: "Blessed are the merciful, for they will be shown mercy."[139] "The more they are filled with the life of God, the more tenderly will they be concerned for those who are still without God in the world."[140] Those who hunger after righteousness will feel a special compassion for those who do not know the blessings of God. Their hearts are softened to love the next person they meet as they do themselves. The works of mercy flow from life with God.[141]

Yet we learn from Paul that even though we might give "all our goods to feed the poor, and our very bodies to be burned, it would profit us nothing," without love, without loving others as God loved us.[142]

b. What Does Mercy Look Like in Action?

Wesley finds in Paul's beautiful language of 1 Corinthians 13 the key to the description of mercy as love. Verse by verse, Wesley shows what it means to be merciful: "Love is patient, love is kind. It does not envy, it does not boast, it is not proud. It does not dishonor others, it is not self-seeking, it is not easily angered, it keeps no record of wrongs."[143]

Merciful love is not rash or hasty in judging. "It first weighs all the evidence, particularly that which is brought in favor of the accused." One who loves mercifully

---

134Ibid.
135"Sermon on the Mount," 22, B 1:497 – 98, J V:269, sec. 2.5.
136Ibid.; cf. John 4:14.
137"Sermon on the Mount," 22, B 1:498, J V:269, sec. 2.6; cf. Isa. 55:2.
138"Sermon on the Mount," 22, B 1:498, J V:269, sec. 2.6.
139Matt. 5:7 NIV.
140"Sermon on the Mount," 22, B 1:499, J V:269 – 70, sec. 3.1.
141Ibid.
142"Sermon on the Mount," 22, B 1:499, J V:270, sec. 3.2; cf. 1 Cor. 13:1 – 3.
1431 Cor. 13:4 – 5 NIV.

THE BELIEVER'S GUIDE TO THE GOOD LIFE

does not "see a little, presume a great deal, and so jump to the conclusion. No: He proceeds with wariness and circumspection."[144] Love is "not puffed up.... It destroys all high conceits, engendering pride; and makes us rejoice to be as nothing."[145]

"It is not rude, or willingly offensive to any." It renders to all their due with "courtesy, civility, humanity to all the world," honoring all persons in their various social roles, exhibiting a continual desire to "please all men for their good to edification."[146] It never deceives. It appears open in every act and conversation, without guile or prejudice.[147]

Love is not self-seeking. It does not seek its own interest. At times "he may almost seem, through an excess of love, to give up himself, both his soul and his body," like Moses who prayed to God for his people: "Please forgive their sin — but if not, then blot me out of the book you have written."[148] Such love is not easily angered. "It is not provoked to unkindness toward anyone. Occasions indeed will frequently occur; outward provocations of various kinds; but love does not yield to provocation; it triumphs over all."[149]

c. Loves Does Not Rejoice in Iniquity

Love "keeps no record of wrongs."[150] Love prevents a thousand provocations that would otherwise arise, because it thinks no evil. "Indeed the merciful man cannot avoid knowing many things that are evil," but he does not willingly dwell on them.[151] Love "casts out all jealousies, all evil surmisings, all readiness to believe evil. It is frank, open, unsuspicious; and, as it cannot design, so neither does it fear, evil."[152] "Love does not delight in evil but rejoices with the truth."[153]

This is especially hard for those who are "zealously attached to any party! How difficult is it for them not to be pleased with any fault which they discover in those of the opposite party — with any real or supposed blemish, either in their principles or practice!... Who does not rejoice when his adversary makes a false step, which he thinks will advantage his own cause? Only a man of love. He alone weeps over either the sin or folly of his enemy, takes no pleasure in hearing or in repeating it, but rather desires that it may be forgotten forever."[154]

Instead, love rejoices in the truth wherever it is found. The one who loves "rejoices to find that even those who oppose him, whether with regard to opinions, or some points of practice ... is glad to hear good of them, and to speak all he can consistently with truth and justice." Thinking on the good is his glory and joy. "As

[144]"Sermon on the Mount," 22, B 1:500 – 501, J V:271, sec. 3.6.
[145]1 Cor. 13:4; "Sermon on the Mount," 22, B 1:500 – 501, J V:271, sec. 3.6.
[146]"Sermon on the Mount," 22, B 1:501, J V:271 – 72, sec. 3.8; cf. Rom. 15:2.
[147]"Sermon on the Mount," 22, B 1:501, J V:271 – 72, sec. 3.8.
[148]"Sermon on the Mount," 22, B 1:502, J V:272, sec. 3.9; Ex. 32:32 NIV; cf. Rom. 9:3.
[149]"Sermon on the Mount," 22, B 1:502 – 3, J V:272 – 73, sec. 3.10.
[150]1 Cor. 13:5 NIV.
[151]"Sermon on the Mount," 22, B 1:503 – 4, J V:273, sec. 3.11.
[152]Ibid.
[153]1 Cor. 13:6 NIV; "Sermon on the Mount," 22, B 1:503 – 4, J V:273, sec. 3.11.
[154]"Sermon on the Mount," 22, B 1:504, J V:273 – 74, sec. 3.12.

a citizen of the world, he claims a share in the happiness of all the inhabitants of it. Because he is a man, he is not unconcerned in the welfare of any man but enjoys whatsoever brings glory to God, and promotes peace and goodwill among men."[155]

d. Love Always Protects, Always Trusts, Always Hopes, Always Perseveres

Whatever evil the merciful person sees, hears, or knows, there is not loose talk about it. If he sees anything of which he does not approve, "it goes not out of his lips, unless to the person concerned," in hopes he can help his brother. He hopes not to make himself a "partaker of other men's sins."[156] He does not make the faults of others a matter of conversation. He does not speak at all unless he can speak well or speak in the interest of the neighbor's good. He is not a talebearer, backbiter, or whisperer.

Wesley made only one exception: "Sometimes he is convinced that it is for the glory of God, or ... the good of his neighbor, that an evil should not be covered ... and that for the benefit of the innocent, he is constrained to declare the guilty."[157] Even in that case, Wesley set forth rigorous cautions on disclosure: not speaking at all "till love, superior love, constrains him," and not "unless he be fully convinced that this very means is necessary to that end; that the end cannot be answered, at least not so effectually, by any other way"; and that he does it with regret and with fear and trembling.[158]

e. Thinking the Best

Love "believeth all things," reads the KJV, while the NIV reads simply love "always trusts."[159] Wesley comments, "[Love] is always willing to think the best; to put the most favourable construction on everything. It is ever ready to believe whatever may tend to the advantage of anyone's character. It is easily convinced of (what it earnestly desires) the innocence or integrity of any man." If it is a question of "the sincerity of his repentance," love is prone "to condemn the offender as little as possible; and to make all the allowance for human weakness which can be done without betraying the truth of God."[160]

And when love "can no longer believe, then love hopes all things."[161] Was the action apparently undeniably evil? "Love hopes the intention was not so.... And even when it cannot be doubted, but all the actions, designs, and tempers are equally evil; still love hopes that God will at last make bare his arm, and get himself the victory." Then there shall be joy "in heaven over one sinner that repenteth, more than over ninety and nine just persons, which need no repentance."[162]

---

[155]"Sermon on the Mount," 22, B 1:504, J V:274, sec. 3.13.
[156]1 Tim. 5:22 NIV; "Sermon on the Mount," 22, B 1:505–6, J V:274–75, sec. 3.14.
[157]"Sermon on the Mount," 22, B 1:505–6, J V:274–75, sec. 3.14.
[158]Ibid.
[159]1 Cor. 13:7.
[160]"Sermon on the Mount," 22, B 1:506, J V:275, sec. 3.15.
[161]"Sermon on the Mount," 22, B 1:506, J V:275–76, sec. 3.16
[162]Ibid.; Luke 15:7.

The call to hope for all things and endure all things completes the character of him who is truly merciful. One who is truly merciful endures "not most, but absolutely all things. Whatever the injustice, the malice, the cruelty of men can inflict, he is able to suffer. He calls nothing intolerable. He is given grace to suffer all things through Christ who strengthens him.... And all he suffers does not destroy his love, nor impair it in the least."[163] Love never fails, because it is eternal.

f. The Consolation of the Merciful: They Will Receive Mercy

The truly merciful obtain mercy by receiving "the blessing of God upon all their ways." By their mercy, they are participating in God's mercy for themselves and for their fellow human beings. They receive "an exceeding and eternal weight of glory," in the coming kingdom.[164]

Those who have not the mind that was in Christ will be prone to cry out in despair over Christian armies that wage continual war, Christian nations that are divided into opposing camps, and Christian families who are torn apart by envy, jealousy, and anger. They will cry out: "O God! How long? Shall thy promise fail?"

The Lord will answer, "Fear it not, ye little flock! Against hope, believe in hope! It is your Father's good pleasure yet to renew the face of the earth.... Surely all these things shall come to an end, and the inhabitants of the earth shall learn righteousness."[165]

So "be a part of the firstfruits, if the harvest is not yet."[166] Let the Lord fill your heart with such love for every soul that you will be ready to lay down your life for his sake.

E. Purity of Heart

The text of Wesley's third discourse on the Sermon on the Mount consists of the last three beatitudes: "Blessed are the pure in heart: for they shall see God. Blessed are the peacemakers: for they shall be called the children of God. Blessed are they which are persecuted for righteousness' sake: for theirs is the kingdom of heaven. Blessed are ye, when men shall revile you, and persecute you, and shall say all manner of evil against you falsely, for my sake. Rejoice, and be exceeding glad: For great is your reward in heaven: for so persecuted they the prophets which were before you" [Matt. 5:8 – 12; Homily #23, "Upon Our Lord's Sermon on the Mount: Discourse 3," B 1:510 – 30, J V:278 – 93 (1748)].

The love of the neighbor springs from love of God who first loved us. According to Paul in 1 Corinthians 13, unless we love our neighbor, the next one we meet, all we do, all we suffer, all doctrines and works are worthless in the sight of God. Hence love is "the fulfilling of the law" and "the end of the commandment."[167] The

---

[163]"Sermon on the Mount," 22, B 1:507, J V:276, sec. 3.17.
[164]Ibid.
[165]"Sermon on the Mount," 22, B 1:507 – 9, J V:276 – 77, sec. 3.18.
[166]Ibid.
[167]Rom. 13:10; 1 Tim. 1:5; "Sermon on the Mount," 23, B 1:510, J V:278, sec. 1.1.

foundation of our love of our neighbor stands on "whether we do 'love him because he first loved us'; whether we are pure in heart: For this is the foundation which shall never be moved. 'Blessed are the pure in heart: For they shall see God.'"[168]

1. Blessed Are the Pure in Heart

a. The Faithful Are Made Pure in Heart Only by Grace

Who are "the pure in heart"? They are those whose hearts God has purified even as God is pure.[169] They are purified through faith in the cross of Christ "from every unholy affection," so that being cleansed from all sin they may be ready to receive God's love and pass it on to the next one they meet.[170] The work God the Spirit intends to do in them is to purify them from pride through their poverty of spirit and to penetrate anger through meekness.

Grace seeks to free them "from every desire but to please and enjoy God, to know and love him more and more, by that hunger and thirst after righteousness which now engrosses their whole soul." The Spirit is at work to enable them to "love the Lord their God with all their heart, and with all their soul, and mind, and strength."[171] In this summary of the previous beatitudes, Wesley acknowledges the delicate cohesion of the Lord's sermon. The order of the Beatitudes is not haphazard.

In the history of ethical reflection, too little attention has been paid to this purity of heart. Moralists have too often focused on impurities of outward action without dealing with inward corruptions; hence they "did not strike at the heart."[172]

Here Jesus provides a teaching graphic. Picture a teacher of the law saying, "You shall not commit adultery," yet at the same time the lawyer is looking at a woman lustfully. Jesus concludes, "I tell you that anyone who looks at a woman lustfully has already committed adultery with her in his heart."[173] The purity of heart that flows from the love of God deals with the inward motive first, allowing the inward redemption to redeem the outward behavior. For God requires truth in the inward parts, searching the heart, and testing the reins.[174]

If your eternal soul is at stake, how do you value your little finger or your eye compared to eternal life with God? Jesus presses the analogy: "If your right eye causes you to stumble" so as to offend God's holiness, "gouge it out and throw it away. It is better for you to lose one part of your body than for your whole body to be thrown into hell."[175] Anything that is an occasion for impure action must be resisted.[176] Cut the inward impurity off at a stroke. Give it up to God. Any temporal

---

[168]"Sermon on the Mount," 23, B 1:510, J V:278, sec. 1.1.
[169]"Sermon on the Mount," 23, B 1:510–11, J V:278–79, sec. 1.2.
[170]Ibid.
[171]Ibid.; cf. Mark 12:30.
[172]"Sermon on the Mount," 23, B 1:511, J V:279, sec. 1.3.
[173]Matt. 5:28 NIV.
[174]"Sermon on the Mount," 23, B 1:511, J V:279, sec. 1.3; cf. Ps. 51:6 (BCP).
[175]Matt. 5:29 NIV.
[176]"Sermon on the Mount," 23, B 1:511–12, J V:279–80, sec. 1.4.

loss is less than an eternal loss.[177] First examine your conscience. By fasting and prayer drive out the unclean spirit that becomes an occasion of evil.[178]

Sexual temptation makes this principle easy to understand. Jesus taught that marriage is holy and honorable. Sexuality is consecrated by marriage. But sexual desire cannot be "a pretense for giving a loose [a free leash] to our desires."[179] The Greek word *porneia* signifies "unchastity in general either in the married or unmarried state."[180] It is the inward impurity that elicits adultery.[181] The arguments against polygamy hinge on inward impurity.[182]

b. The Consolation: The Pure in Heart Will See God

Jesus' concentration is on inward motive in ethics, the condition of the heart. "Such is the purity of heart which God requires, and works in those who believe on the Son of his love. And 'blessed are' they who are thus 'pure in heart; for they shall see God.'" God will make himself known by blessing them "with the clearest communications of his Spirit, the most intimate fellowship with the Father and with the Son.... He will cause his presence to go continually before them and the light of his countenance to shine upon them."[183]

The pure in heart have prayed that God would show them his glory. "They now see him by faith (the veil of the flesh being made as [if] it were transparent) even in these his lowest works, in all that surrounds them, in all that God has created and made. They see him in the height above, and in the depth beneath; they see him filling all in all."[184]

The pure in heart see all things full of God. They recognize his providential action in their lives. "They see his hand ever over them for good, giving them all things in weight and measure, numbering the hairs of their head, making a hedge round about them and all that they have, and disposing all the circumstances of their life according to the depth both of his wisdom and mercy."[185]

The pure in heart feel God's presence especially in the Eucharist, where he shows forth his death until he comes. They hear him in the preaching of the Word. In common worship they pour out their souls before their Father. "They see him, as it were, face-to-face, and 'talk with him, as a man talking with his friend' — a fit preparation for those mansions above, wherein they shall see him as he is."[186]

c. The Pure of Heart Do Not Make Vows Thoughtlessly

We have been rightly taught by the law to "'fulfill to the Lord the vows you have

---

[177]Ibid.
[178]Ibid.
[179]"Sermon on the Mount," 23, B 1:512, J V:280, sec. 1.5.
[180]Ibid.
[181]Matt. 5:31 – 32.
[182]"Sermon on the Mount," 23, B 1:512, J V:280, sec. 1.5.
[183]"Sermon on the Mount," 23, B 1:513, J V:280 – 81, sec. 1.6.
[184]Ibid.
[185]"Sermon on the Mount," 23, B 1:514, J V:281, sec. 1.7.
[186]"Sermon on the Mount," 23, B 1:514, J V:281, sec. 1.8.

made.'" But on the Mount Jesus taught the deeper intention of vows, which the pure in heart grasp: "Do not swear an oath at all: either by heaven, for it is God's throne; or by the earth.... All you need to say is simply 'Yes' or 'No'; anything beyond this comes from the evil one."[187] The Lord did not forbid swearing when required by the justice system. Rather, he was reproving "false swearing and common swearing."[188]

The lesson concerning swearing is that "God is in all things, and that we are to see the Creator in the glass of every creature; that we should use and look upon nothing as separate from God."[189] All things are "contained by God in the hollow of his hand, who by his intimate presence holds them all in being, who pervades and actuates the whole created frame."[190]

2. Blessed Are the Peacemakers

a. Peace Is the Fruit of the Love and Favor of God

The religion of the pure heart shows "how inward holiness is to exert itself in our outward conversation,"[191] our interpersonal behavior. For example, in peacemaking: the word peacemakers in its Greek root refers to those who seek every kind of good for another, "every blessing that relates either to the soul or the body, to time or eternity."[192]

Peace is a "fruit of the free [and] undeserved love and favor of God," enabling the faithful to "enjoy all blessings, spiritual and temporal; all the good things which God hath prepared for them that love him."[193] Enjoyment. Happiness. Receiving what is good. That is the peaceful kingdom. It is a peace that lasts not for a day or a year but for eternity.

This peace does not refer to international relations alone, but to all relations touched by the grace of God. In its literal meaning, a peacemaker is one of those "lovers of God and man who utterly detest and abhor all strife and debate, all variance and contention, and accordingly labor with all their might, either to prevent this fire of hell from being kindled, or, when it is kindled, from breaking out, or, when it is broke out, from spreading any farther."[194] They seek to "calm the stormy spirits of men, to quiet their turbulent passions, to soften the minds of contending parties, and, if possible, reconcile them to each other. They use all innocent arts and employ all their strength, all the talents which God has given them, as well to preserve peace where it is, as to restore it where it is not."[195]

---

[187]Matt. 5:33–37 NIV.
[188]"Sermon on the Mount," 23, B 1:515–16, J V:282–83, sec. 1.10.
[189]"Sermon on the Mount," 23, B 1:516–17, J V:283, sec. 1.11.
[190]Ibid.
[191]"Sermon on the Mount," 23, B 1:517, J V:283, sec. 2.1.
[192]"Sermon on the Mount," 23, B 1:517, J V:283–84, sec. 2.2.
[193]Ibid.
[194]"Sermon on the Mount," 23, B 1:517–18, J V:284, sec. 2.3.
[195]Ibid.

The theological ground of peacemaking is the awareness that "they have all 'one Lord, one faith,' as they are all 'called in one hope of their calling,'"[196] so they may all "walk worthy of the vocation wherewith they are called; with all lowliness and meekness, with long-suffering." Out of this understanding they voluntarily forbear one another in love, "endeavoring to keep the unity of the Spirit in the bond of peace."[197]

b. The Peacemaker Does Good to All

A peacemaker is one who does good to all humanity. "Therefore, as we have opportunity, let us do good to all people, especially to those who belong to the family of believers."[198]

The peacemaker cannot confine peacemaking "to his own family, or friends, or acquaintance, or party, or to those of his own opinions — no, nor those who are partakers of like precious faith.... He steps over all these narrow bounds, that he may do good to every man, that he may, some way or other, manifest his love to neighbors and strangers, friends and enemies," as he has opportunity, "'redeeming the time' ... buying up every opportunity, improving every hour, losing no moment wherein he may profit another," employing all his talents, powers, and faculties of body and soul, "all his fortune, his interest, his reputation" to do good to all.[199] If they are hungry, he offers bread, if naked a garment. He welcomes a stranger. Those sick or in prison he visits, always remembering the one who said, "Inasmuch as ye have done it unto one of the least of these my brethren, ye have done it unto me."[200]

Whatever good is done by a human being is preceded by the good that God has done for all humanity and for that person. Whatever good may come from the heart for the soul of another, it is God who stirs the heart.[201] God gives each person freedom to serve the next one they meet (the neighbor) with his or her own hands.

It pleases God, who works all in all, to help one person chiefly by another, and to "convey his own power, and blessing, and love, through one [person] to another."[202] No one should conclude that since God is taking care of humanity, humans have nothing to do to help themselves and others. Do not stand idle in God's vineyard. You are "an instrument in God's hand, preparing the ground for his Master's use, or sowing the seed of the kingdom, or watering what is already sown."[203] According to the grace you have received, give all diligence "to give light to them that sit in darkness, lift up the fallen and bring healing to the lame."[204]

---

[196] Ibid.
[197] Ibid.
[198] Gal. 6:10 NIV.
[199] "Sermon on the Mount," 23, B 1:518, J V:284, sec. 2.4.
[200] Matt. 25:40; "Sermon on the Mount," 23, B 1:519, J V:285, sec. 2.5.
[201] "Sermon on the Mount," 23, B 1:519 – 20, J V:285, sec. 2.6.
[202] Ibid.
[203] Ibid.
[204] Ibid.

c. Those Who Bring Peace Will Be Called Children of God

Do good especially to the family of God.[205] Help those who know in whom they have believed. Stir up the gift of God in them.

The peacemaker is blessed by being a blessing to others. Those who bring blessings will be called God's own children. God will sustain them through the Spirit of adoption and pour his Spirit ever more abundantly into their hearts. "He shall bless them with all the blessings of his children," acknowledging them as sons and daughters, and if children then "heirs — heirs of God, and co-heirs with Christ."[206]

Finally, what is peace, in the biblical sense? Wesley answers, "What is this 'peace,' the peace of God, but that calm serenity of soul, that sweet repose in the blood of Jesus, which leaves no doubt of our acceptance in him; which excludes all fear, but the loving filial fear of offending our Father which is in heaven?"[207]

The peace of which the Bible speaks is an "inward kingdom [that] implies also 'joy in the Holy Ghost'; who seals upon our hearts 'the redemption which is in Jesus,' the righteousness of Christ imputed to us 'for the remission of the sins that are past.'" It is given in this life as a promise of our eternal inheritance.[208]

3. Persecution for Righteousness' Sake

a. Those Persecuted for Righteousness' Sake Are Being Blessed as Heirs of God's Kingdom

One would think that such a humble, merciful, peaceful person would be highly valued by the human community anywhere he or she went: full of gentleness and goodness. But our Lord was better acquainted with human nature. He warned that the blessed life when lived out will be so powerful as to become disruptive to the community bent on worldly values.

The faithful do well to expect this abuse in a fallen world. They will be persecuted precisely because of their hunger for righteousness. "All those who are meek and lowly in heart, that mourn for God, that hunger after his likeness; all that love God and their neighbor" should not be surprised at being persecuted precisely due to their pursuit of righteousness.[209] But even in being maligned, they are being blessed as recipients of the kingdom of heaven.[210]

We learn how the world of the flesh treats the world of the Spirit from the apostle John: "Do not be surprised, my brothers and sisters, if the world hates you. We know that we have passed from death to life, because we love each other. Anyone who does not love remains in death."[211] Jesus said, "If the world hates you, keep

---

[205]Gal. 6:10 NIV; "Sermon on the Mount," 23, B 1:519–20, J V:285, sec. 2.6.

[206]Rom. 8:17 NIV; "Sermon on the Mount," 23, B 1:520, J V:285–86, sec. 2.7.

[207]"Sermon on the Mount," 21, B 1:481, J V:256–57, sec. 1.11.

[208]Ibid.

[209]"Sermon on the Mount," 23, B 1:520–21, J V:286, sec. 3.2.

[210]"Sermon on the Mount," 23, B 1:520, J V:286, sec. 3.1.

[211]1 John 3:13–14 NIV.

in mind that it hated me first. If you belonged to the world, it would love you as its own. As it is, you do not belong to the world, but I have chosen you out of the world. That is why the world hates you.... If they persecuted me, they will persecute you also."[212] Similarly, Paul cautioned Timothy: "In fact, everyone who wants to live a godly life in Christ Jesus will be persecuted."[213]

b. Why the Righteous Are Persecuted

Why are the righteous persecuted? Precisely "for righteousness' sake." They are persecuted expressly because they are born after the Spirit, live lives hidden in Christ, and are not of the world. They are persecuted precisely because they are poor in spirit and because they mourn for God, are meek, merciful, pure in heart, and lovers of all. "This is the grand reason why they have been persecuted in all ages, and will be till the restitution of all things."[214] "Whatever may be pretended, this is the real cause."[215]

If the faithful would only keep their religion to themselves, they would be viewed as tolerable, but just by being in the world they seem to make mischief for the world.[216] Sadly, "the more the kingdom of God prevails, the more mischief is done, and the more outrage against them. The more the peacemakers are enabled to propagate lowliness, meekness, and all other divine tempers," the more do they challenge the prevailing order.[217]

Those born after the flesh "have not passed from death unto life."[218] The spirit that is in the world is directly opposite of the Spirit who is of God. The proud, because they are proud, cannot help but persecute the lowly.[219]

c. The Forms of Persecution

How will persecution happen to the faithful? "Just in that manner and measure which the wise Disposer of all sees will be most for his glory — will tend most to his children's growth in grace, and the enlargement of his own kingdom."[220] God's providence allows this struggle to strengthen our souls. "His eye is ever open, and his hand stretched out to direct even the minutest circumstance. When the storm shall begin, how high it shall rise, which way it shall point its course, when and how it shall end, are all determined by his unerring wisdom."[221]

Especially when Christianity was first planted, God permitted the storm to rise high. This happened in order "that their evidence might be the more

---

[212]John 15:18–20 NIV.
[213]2 Tim. 3:12 NIV; "Sermon on the Mount," 23, B 1:520–21, J V:286, sec. 3.2.
[214]"Sermon on the Mount," 23, B 1:521–22, J V:287, sec. 3.3.
[215]Ibid.
[216]Ibid.
[217]Ibid.
[218]"Sermon on the Mount," 23, B 1:522–23, J V:288, sec. 3.4; cf. 1 John 3:14.
[219]"Sermon on the Mount," 23, B 1:522–23, J V:288, sec. 3.4.
[220]"Sermon on the Mount," 23, B 1:523–25, J V:288–89, sec. 3.5.
[221]Ibid.

unexceptionable,"[222] that their struggle may point to God's glory, and because the mystery of iniquity is still so strongly at work.

Compare that to England, where God dealt very graciously with a particular people. Wesley acknowledged that chief among God's blessings was that he "caused the pure light of his gospel to arise and shine amongst us. But what return did he find? More evil." Then God sold his witnesses "into the hands of their persecutors, by a judgment mixed with mercy; an affliction to punish, and yet a medicine to heal the grievous backslidings of his people."[223] But the storm did not rise so high as torture or death. The most frequent form of suffering for his children was "the estrangement of kinsfolk — the loss of the friends that were as their own soul … [or] loss of business or employment."[224] Compared to the prophets and apostles, these were light forms of persecution.

The persecution that accompanies all the children of God is clearly indicated by Jesus: "Blessed are you when people insult you, persecute you and falsely say all kinds of evil against you because of me."[225] This is a badge of our discipleship, a seal of our calling. Without it we are like illegitimate children.

The way to the kingdom lies in going straight through these challenges, confident of their passing. "The meek, serious, humble, zealous lovers of God and man are of good report among their brethren; but of evil report with the world, who count and treat them 'as the filth and offscouring of all things.'"[226] This is to be expected for good people in a fallen world. There may be some exceptions during periods when Christians are highly esteemed, but even then "the scandal of the cross is not yet ceased."[227] Jesus' words in John's gospel are expressly clear: "If you belonged to the world, it would love you as its own. As it is, you do not belong to the world, but I have chosen you out of the world. That is why the world hates you."[228] On the whole, the meek and pure of heart are not welcome in the fallen world.

d. Do Not Seek Persecution

Believers "ought not knowingly or designedly to bring [persecution] upon themselves." We are not to seek, but to avoid persecution "as far as we can, without injuring our conscience."[229] For this reason our Lord expressly said: "When you are persecuted in one place, flee to another."[230] This flight is viewed in relation to the coming return of the Son of Man, who did not seek persecution but endured it.

But do not imagine you can always avoid persecution. Rather, "be as shrewd as

---

[222]Ibid.
[223]Ibid.
[224]"Sermon on the Mount," 23, B 1:525, J V:289, sec. 3.6.
[225]Matt. 5:11 NIV.
[226]"Sermon on the Mount," 23, B 1:525 – 26, J V:289 – 90, sec. 3.7; cf. 1 Cor. 4:13.
[227]"Sermon on the Mount," 23, B 1:526, J V:290, sec. 3.8.
[228]John 15:19 NIV; "Sermon on the Mount," 23, B 1:527, J V:291, sec. 3.10.
[229]"Sermon on the Mount," 23, B 1:527, J V:291, sec. 3.10.
[230]Matt. 10:23 NIV.

snakes and as innocent as doves."[231] If you try to escape persecution completely, "you are none of his. If you escape the persecution, you escape the blessing."[232] Better to believe with the Lord that "blessed are those who are persecuted because of righteousness, for theirs is the kingdom of heaven. Blessed are you when people insult you, persecute you and falsely say all kinds of evil against you because of me."[233]

e. Rejoice and Be Glad, for Great Is Your Reward in Heaven

How are the persecuted being blessed? Jesus answers: "Rejoice and be glad, because great is your reward in heaven, for in the same way they persecuted the prophets who were before you."[234]

When they persecute you by reviling you and by "falsely saying all kinds of evil against you," you are sharing in the lives of the prophets before you and in the life of the Lord.

Rejoice, because this is a sign that you know the one to whom you belong. " 'Be exceeding glad,' knowing that 'these light afflictions, which are but for a moment, work out for you a far more exceeding and eternal weight of glory.' "[235]

4. How to Treat the Enemy

a. Nonretaliation

"You have heard that it was said, 'Eye for eye, and tooth for tooth.' But I tell you, do not resist an evil person. If anyone slaps you on the right cheek, turn to them the other cheek also. And if anyone wants to sue you and take your shirt, hand over your coat as well. If anyone forces you to go one mile, go with them two miles."[236] Let your meekness be abundant.

"Give to the one who asks you, and do not turn away from the one who wants to borrow from you."[237] Cautions: Do not give away something that does not belong to you. Avoid debt. Provide for your own household since God requires this. Then "give or lend all that remains, from day to day, or from year to year."[238]

We are to show kindness to those who persecute us for righteousness' sake. Love your enemies. Bless those that curse you. "Say all the good you can, without violating the rules of truth and justice."[239] Return good for evil. Overcome evil with good. If you can do nothing more, at least "pray for them that despitefully use you

---

[231] Matt. 10:16 NIV.
[232] "Sermon on the Mount," 23, B 1:527, J V:291, sec. 3.11.
[233] Matt. 5:10–11 NIV.
[234] Matt. 5:12 NIV.
[235] "Sermon on the Mount," 23, B 1:527, J V:291, sec. 3.11; cf. 2 Cor. 4:17.
[236] Matt. 5:38–41 NIV.
[237] Matt. 5:42 NIV.
[238] "Sermon on the Mount," 23, B 1:528, J V:291–92, sec. 3.12.
[239] "Sermon on the Mount," 23, B 1:528–30, J V:292–93, sec. 3.13.

and persecute you."[240] Forgive them seventy times seven, whether they repent or not.[241]

b. The Unity of the Teaching on the Mount

When we listen to Jesus speaking on the Mount, we behold "Christianity in its native form as delivered by its great Author! This is the genuine religion of Jesus Christ!" Here we see "a picture of God, so far as he is imitable by man!"[242]

"What beauty appears in the whole! How just a symmetry! What exact proportion in every part! How desirable is the happiness here described! How venerable, how lovely the holiness!… These are indeed the fundamentals of Christianity."[243]

Be a doer and not a hearer only.[244] Look steadily into "this perfect law of liberty."[245] Do not rest until "every part of it shall appear in our soul, graven there by the finger of God," till we are holy as God is holy.[246]

---

[240]Ibid.
[241]Cf. Matt. 18:22.
[242]"Sermon on the Mount," 23, B 1:528–30, J V:292–93, sec. 3.13.
[243]Ibid.
[244]See James 1:22.
[245]"Sermon on the Mount," 23, B 1:528–30, J V:292–93, sec. 3.13; cf. James 1:25.
[246]"Sermon on the Mount," 23, B 1:528–30, J V:292–93, sec. 3.13; cf. 1 Peter 1:15.

CHAPTER 7

Salt and Light for the World

A. Succulence and Radiance in Human Relationships

As salt is to food, love is to the world. It enhances the taste of human relationships. Love is the world's preservative.

1. The Social Contagiousness of Holy Living

The influence of believers in the world is like light to darkness and salt to food.[1] The faithful are like the world's saltiness. They bring light and liveliness into the dark and despairing world.

The text of Wesley's fourth discourse on the Sermon on the Mount is Matthew 5:13–16 on holy living as salt and light: "You are the salt of the earth. But if the salt loses its saltiness, how can it be made salty again? It is no longer good for anything, except to be thrown out and trampled underfoot. You are the light of the world. A town built on a hill cannot be hidden. Neither do people light a lamp and put it under a bowl. Instead they put it on its stand, and it gives light to everyone in the house. In the same way, let your light shine before others, that they may see your good deeds and glorify your Father in heaven" [Matt. 5:13–16 NIV; Homily #24, "Upon Our Lord's Sermon on the Mount: Discourse 4," B 1:531–49, J V:294–310 (1748)].

2. Salt as a Preservative and Light as a Guide

The salt and light metaphors reveal how holy living is engaging and contagious to those who glimpse it. It is intrinsically beautiful and admirable. It is beautiful because it reflects the beauty of holiness. This theme of "the beauty of holiness" in Wesley's homilies became a central feature of the sanctification and holiness movements in the nineteenth century. This homily became a key text for holiness preaching. The beauty of holiness is seen in one whose inward heart is being renewed in accord with the image of God.[2] The ornaments of this beauty are meekness, humility, and love.

Wesley said, "From the hour men begin to emerge out of the darkness which covers the giddy, unthinking world, they cannot but perceive how desirable a thing it is

---

[1]Cf. Matt. 5:13–16.
[2]"Sermon on the Mount," 24, B 1:531, J V:294–95, proem, sec. 1.

to be thus transformed into the likeness of him that created us."[3] Unless the onlooker is irreversibly sunken in worldliness, it is easy to see something of the shape of God visibly impressed on such a soul. Few who see it can doubt its divine origin.

It was said of the Son of God that he manifested the "brightness of his glory, the express image of his person," beaming forth God's eternal beauty "yet so tempered and softened, that even the children of men may herein see God and live."[4] Having beheld the light of the coming of the Son, we can reflect that light proximately in our human interactions.

As Jesus' radiance went out into a dark world, so those who follow him in a holy life lived out in faith bear in their bodies "the character, the stamp, the living impression" of the divine image in his person, reflecting the glory of "the fountain of beauty and love, the original source of all excellency and perfection."[5] Where religion exhibits these qualities, few can reasonably object. But religion too often seems to be "clogged with other things."[6] All the more compelling are those few whose lives behaviorally attest it.

3. Flavoring Human Interactions

a. Why Christianity Is the Most Social of All Religions

Christianity is the most social of all religions because inward intent has outward consequences. It would be a mistake to imagine that Christianity is only an inward religion with no outward, visible expressions. Some have been tempted to view Christianity essentially as heavenly contemplation, communing only with God with no outward actions or social outcomes. Some think, *Why will it "not suffice to worship God, who is a Spirit, with the spirit of our minds," without visible fruits?*[7]

This view has had powerful advocates in Christian history, particularly in some forms of hermetic, monastic, and withdrawal movements. Some have advised us simply "to cease from all outward action ... to withdraw from the world; to leave the body behind us; to abstract ourselves from all sensible things; to have no concern at all about outward religion, but to work all virtues in the will; as the far more excellent way, more perfective of the soul, as well as more acceptable to God."[8] Taken too far toward individualist isolation, Wesley regarded this tendency as a temptation of the ancient enemy designed to "deceive, if it were possible, the very elect."[9]

But by viewing the Christian life as salt and light *in* the world, Jesus has guarded the faithful against this "pleasing delusion."[10] On the Mount, Jesus "defend[ed], in the clearest and strongest manner, the active, patient religion he had just described"[11]

---

[3]Ibid.
[4]Ibid.; cf. Heb. 1:3.
[5]"Sermon on the Mount," 24, B 1:531, J V:294–95, proem, sec. 1.
[6]"Sermon on the Mount," 24, B 1:532, J V:295, proem, sec. 2.
[7]Ibid.
[8]"Sermon on the Mount," 24, B 1:532, J V:295, proem, sec. 3.
[9]Ibid.
[10]"Sermon on the Mount," 24, B 1:533, J V:296, proem, sec. 5.
[11]See above, on the Beatitudes; "Sermon on the Mount," 24, B 1:533, J V:296, proem, sec. 5.

as meek, persecuted, poor in spirit, and thirsting for righteousness. It is both active and patient in perfect coordination according to the need at hand.

Faith is to the world as salt is to food. Christianity is to the city as light is to darkness. Faith active in love floods the city with light.

b. Savoring Human Relationships

Each genuine believer improves the taste of daily human interactions. Just as salt provides taste for food, the holy life of the believer mixes in with the habits and daily lives of others to flavor the fallen and mending family or the darkened world. It makes human behavior savorier in the presence of God and humanity. By this means every human interaction may lead in some measure to the person-by-person spread of the gospel of social holiness in the family and social order.[12]

Hence Christianity is essentially a social religion. To turn it into a solitary religion is to destroy it. It cannot subsist at all without "living and conversing" with others.[13] It is impossible to conceal its sociality, its love of others, and its engagement with the redemption of the fallen world.[14]

Wesley makes clear that he is not condemning the creative intermixing of solitude and society. Within bounds, retreat is an essential part of prayer. "It can hardly be that we should spend one entire day in a continued intercourse with men, without suffering loss in our soul, and in some measure grieving the Holy Spirit of God. We have need daily to retire from the world, at least morning and evening, to converse with God, to commune more freely with our Father which is in secret."[15]

Yet inward holiness cannot stand alone without human interaction. Meekness, for example, implies actions and outward expressions manifesting "mildness, gentleness, and long-suffering." These are not "solitary virtues," but those that express themselves in relationships.[16]

Peacemaking, which more broadly means doing good, does not call us to the wilderness but to the human community.[17]

c. Interacting with Sinners: The Satisfying Salt of Social Relationships

Without interacting with others, we cannot be Christians at all. "Some intercourse even with ungodly and unholy men is absolutely needful, in order to the full exertion of every temper which he has described as the way of the kingdom."[18] This interaction completes the exercise of poverty of spirit and meekness and "every other disposition which has a place here, in the genuine religion of Jesus Christ."[19]

Wesley had a providential view of interpersonal transactions. The faithful are

---

[12]"Sermon on the Mount," 24, B 1:536, J V:299, sec. 1.6.
[13]"Sermon on the Mount," 24, B 1:533–34, J V:296–97, sec. 1.1.
[14]"Sermon on the Mount," 24, B 1:533, J V:296, proem, sec. 5.
[15]"Sermon on the Mount," 24, B 1:533–34, J V:296–97, sec. 1.1.
[16]"Sermon on the Mount," 24, B 1:534, J V:297, sec. 1.3.
[17]"Sermon on the Mount," 24, B 1:534–35, J V:297–98, sec. 1.4.
[18]"Sermon on the Mount," 24, B 1:536, J V:299, sec. 1.6.
[19]Ibid.

supplied with grace to engage with others: "It is your very nature to season whatever is round about you. It is the nature of the divine savor which is in you, to spread to whatsoever you touch; to diffuse itself, on every side, to all those among whom you are. This is the great reason why the providence of God has so mingled you together with other men, that whatever grace you have received of God may through you be communicated to others."[20] Every believer has a part to play to check in some measure the corruption of the world.

Impart the grace you have received. Let others benefit from it. Do not hold it in your own heart exclusively. If you withhold these gifts, "the salt loses its saltiness." In order to season all relationships "with every holy and heavenly temper," you must engage, not withdraw.[21]

The maturing believer is not like flat and tasteless salt. The holy life is full of flavor, and the flavoring of human relationships should not be withheld.[22]

d. Tasting the Heavenly Gift

Wesley was weaving his way through a tapestry of related apostolic teachings that correlate with the tasty salt metaphor in the Sermon on the Mount,[23] for example, in the difficult passage in Hebrews 6, where the author was speaking to a maturing community of faith that had gotten beyond elementary teaching and was moving toward full responsiveness to grace. Those who once "tasted the heavenly gift, who have shared in the Holy Spirit," but later fell away must be brought back to repentance and faith, but this repentance is hard if not impossible without special grace.[24]

The tasting metaphor of Hebrews correlates with the salt metaphor of the Sermon on the Mount. The point: those who have tasted of the Spirit share by their behavior so that others will sense, even if faintly, the aroma of grace. "Taste and see that the LORD is good."[25]

The Lord's teaching in John 15 complements his instruction on the Mount. The Son is the true vine and his Father is the gardener. You are a branch of the vine. Its fruit is delicious. Every branch that bears no fruit is cut. Every branch that bears fruit will remain in this providential ordering of relationships. "No branch can bear fruit by itself; it must remain in the vine. Neither can you bear fruit unless you remain in me. I am the vine; you are the branches. If you remain in me and I in you, you will bear much fruit."[26] For those who have never tasted such wonderful fruit, the Lord provides the savory companionship of those living the holy life.

---

[20]"Sermon on the Mount," 24, B 1:536 – 37, J V:299, sec. 1.7.
[21]Ibid.
[22]"Sermon on the Mount," 24, B 1:537, J V:299 – 300, sec. 1.8.
[23]See Matt. 5:13 – 14.
[24]Heb. 6:4 NIV; cf. Matt. 5:13 – 14.
[25]Ps. 34:8 NIV.
[26]John 15:4 – 5 NIV.

e. A Caution against Keeping Aloof from the Ungodly

One caution: Paul rightly advised the Corinthians to be careful about keeping company with the sexually licentious, and this for a very good reason:[27] mingling with the sexually immoral would expose them unnecessarily to an "abundance of dangers and snares."[28] This did not mean that the merciful lover of God and neighbor forbids interactions with those who do not know God,[29] for that would imply abandoning the lost in a fallen world.

When Paul urged the Christians of the raucous city of Corinth not to become cozy with "a fornicator, or covetous, or an idolater, or a railer, or a drunkard, or an extortioner," he meant to avoid unseemly familiarities that might bring disrepute to the whole community of faith.[30]

Paul provided this important qualifier: do not count the sinner out or treat him as an enemy, but admonish him as a brother; do not "renounce all fellowship with him."[31] Do not separate from the ungodly altogether, but remain in appropriate contact to seek to make things better. One who falls may rise again. If we should fall, we have an Advocate who is "the propitiation for our sins,"[32] unless our hearts have become "hardened by sin's deceitfulness."[33]

4. A City Set on a Hill Cannot Be Hid

a. Grace Will Always Communicate Itself

To communicate active grace to another is to reveal God's glory through the most inconspicuous human behavior. Like salt it conveys its taste without outward fanfare.[34] So season others' lives with the grace that God has planted in your heart. To withhold this flavoring of holiness or conceal this light of holy living under a bushel is hardly commendable "since it is the nature of grace to become communicated to others, even if inconspicuously, quietly, or in secret."[35] As long as true religion "abides in our hearts, it is impossible to conceal it," for this is "absolutely contrary to the design of its great Author."[36] In fact, it cannot be concealed, because it is human nature to be social and interactive.[37]

Jesus made this plain by comparing holy living with light. He said Christians are "the light of the world. A town built on a hill cannot be hidden."[38] "You are lit from

---

[27]See 1 Cor. 5:9.
[28]"Sermon on the Mount," 24, B 1:535 – 36, J V:298, sec. 1.5.
[29]Ibid.
[30]Ibid.
[31]Ibid.; cf. 2 Thess. 3:15.
[32]1 John 2:1 – 2.
[33]Heb. 3:13 NIV.
[34]"Sermon on the Mount," 24, B 1:539, J V:301, sec. 2.1.
[35]"Sermon on the Mount," 24, B 1:539, J V:301 – 2, sec. 2.2.
[36]"Sermon on the Mount," 24, B 1:539, J V:301, sec. 2.1.
[37]"Sermon on the Mount," 24, B 1:539, J V:301 – 2, sec. 2.2.
[38]Matt. 5:14 NIV; "Sermon on the Mount," 24, B 1:539, J V:301 – 2, sec. 2.2.

within with regard both to your tempers and actions. Your holiness makes you as conspicuous as the sun in the midst of heaven."[39]

It is impossible for you to obscure your lowliness and meekness if it is from the heart. Dispositions that reveal the glory of God are always becoming quietly visible. "Love cannot be hid any more than light, and least of all, when it shines forth in action."[40] Your joy is not in visibility as such, but in the glory of God that it reveals.

b. Loving Darkness Rather Than Light

But within the history of sin, others will always "love darkness rather than light, because their deeds are evil."[41] So they will "take all possible pains to prove that the light which is in you is darkness."[42] They will say all manner of evil against you falsely. But "your patient continuance in well-doing, your meek suffering of all things for the Lord's sake, your calm, humble joy in the midst of persecution, your unwearied labor to overcome evil with good, will make you still more visible and conspicuous than you were before."[43] "Whatever religion can be concealed is not Christianity.... Never, therefore, let it enter into the heart of him whom God hath renewed in the spirit of his mind to hide that light, to keep his religion to himself."[44]

c. Who Would Hide a Candle under a Bowl?

Jesus makes this plain on the mount when he next teaches, "Neither do people light a lamp and put it under a bowl. Instead they put it on its stand, and it gives light to everyone in the house. In the same way, let your light shine before others, that they may see your good deeds and glorify your Father in heaven."[45]

Nobody lights a candle to conceal it, since its purpose is to reveal. God does not "enlighten any soul with his glorious knowledge and love, to have it covered or concealed, either by prudence, falsely so called, or shame, or voluntary humility.... It is the design of God that every Christian should be in an open point of view; that he may give light to all around, that he may visibly express the religion of Jesus Christ."[46]

God has in all ages spoken to the world, both by precept and personal embodiment, never leaving himself without witness in any human culture, whether by law or gospel. The inward moral law of conscience is there even before it is ripe for the good news of salvation to appear.

The law brings the call to repentance, but Christ brings full salvation. But while both Scripture and reason speak in all cultures, hearing is dull because of sin, and many are without eyes to see.[47]

---

[39]"Sermon on the Mount," 24, B 1:539, J V:301–2, sec. 2.2.
[40]Ibid.
[41]"Sermon on the Mount," 24, B 1:540, J V:302, sec. 2.3; cf. John 3:19.
[42]Ibid.
[43]Ibid.
[44]"Sermon on the Mount," 24, B 1:540, J V:302, sec. 2.4.
[45]Matt. 5:15–16 NIV.
[46]"Sermon on the Mount," 24, B 1:540, J V:302, sec. 2.5.
[47]"Sermon on the Mount," 24, B 1:541, J V:303, sec. 2.6.

d. From the Heart of Faith Springs the Outward Act of Love

"Bare outside religion, which has no root in the heart" is of little value.[48] Let your outward actions spring from the heart. Let the heart bear fruits in outward deeds. The outward act is the evidence of the change of heart that accompanies the new birth.

It is true that religion does not, strictly speaking, lie in outward things. It resides "in the heart, the inmost soul ... the union of the soul with God, the life of God in the soul of man.... But if this root be really in the heart, it cannot but put forth branches."[49] The Lord commends visible actions and outward fruit that "partakes of the same nature with the root."[50] God is pleased not only with the good root but also with the visible fruits of that root in "outward service which arises from the heart."[51] This is seen not only in common prayer, but in acts of mercy, and by "our bodies, which he peculiarly claims." The apostle calls us "'by the mercies of God, to present unto him a living sacrifice, holy, acceptable to God.'"[52]

Without that faith active in love, "whatever we do, whatever we suffer, profits us nothing."[53] This does not mean that love leaves faith behind. Love is the fulfilling of the law. It does not release us from the law but moves us to obey the will of God. "Whatever we do or suffer in love, even if only giving a cup of cold water in his name, will not go unnoticed by God."[54]

e. Glorify God with Your Body

We are called "to glorify [God] with our bodies, as well as with our spirits; to go through outward work with hearts lifted up to him; to make our daily employment a sacrifice to God; to buy and sell, to eat and drink, to his glory—this is worshiping God in spirit and in truth, as much as the praying to him in a wilderness."[55]

"If so, then contemplation is only one way of worshiping God in spirit and in truth." Equally important are those visible acts to which the providence of God has called us.[56] The believer "does it all as unto the Lord."[57] Whatever he does in word or deed, he does all in the name of the Lord. That does not diminish or encumber the contemplative life of secret prayer.

We may be tempted to help others by outward works merely as a means to an end, as if the neighbor were only a means to our righteous action. We would do better by "letting the abuse be taken away, and the use remain."[58] That is, use the means of grace to do good, but do not treat the resulting act as an end in itself.

---

[48] "Sermon on the Mount," 24, B 1:541 – 42, J V:303 – 4, sec. 3.1.
[49] Ibid.
[50] Ibid.
[51] Ibid.
[52] Ibid.; cf. Rom. 12:1.
[53] Cf. 1 Cor. 13.
[54] "Sermon on the Mount," 24, B 1:542, J V:304, sec. 3.2; cf. Mark 9:41.
[55] "Sermon on the Mount," 24, B 1:543 – 44, J V:305 – 6, sec. 3.4.
[56] "Sermon on the Mount," 24, B 1:544, J V:306, sec. 3.5.
[57] Ibid.
[58] "Sermon on the Mount," 24, B 1:545 – 46, J V:307, sec. 3.7.

So "use all outward things, but use them with a constant eye to the renewal of your soul in righteousness and true holiness."[59] Whether the beneficiary of love is worthy or not, you are nonetheless "expressly commanded to feed the hungry and clothe the naked."[60]

f. Providence Works Typically through Human Interactions

Only God can change the heart, but he generally does it through some human hands. Our part is to do all the good we can and leave the outcome to God.[61] God "builds up his children by each other in every good gift, nourishing and strengthening the whole body."[62]

Those who withdraw from interaction with the world are tempted to say, "I have tried to help others into a new life, but what did it avail? On many I could make no impression at all. Some were only changed for a little while, and soon their improvement was 'but as the morning dew, and they were soon as bad, nay, worse than ever.' So maybe I should have 'kept [my] religion to [myself].'"[63]

But Scripture teaches that we cannot keep our lives with God to ourselves.[64] They want to shine in the darkness. Jesus also strove "to save sinners, and they would not hear; or when they had followed him awhile, they turned back."[65] Do not fret over outcomes that are in God's hands. Do not desist from striving to do good, whatever your success be. It is your part to let your light shine.[66] The outcome is in God's hands. You are not accountable for what you cannot control. Leave it to God who orders all things well. "In the morning sow thy seed, and in the evening withhold not thine hand: for thou knowest not whether shall prosper either this or that, or whether they both shall be alike good."[67] So "cast your bread upon the waters, and you shall find it again after many days."[68]

g. Let Your Light Shine That They May See Your Good Works

So let it be your desire, not to conceal the light of God — "not to put the light under a bushel. Let it be your care to place it on a candlestick, that it may give light to all that are in the house." Only be careful not to seek your own praise. "Let it be your sole aim that all who see your good works may glorify your Father."[69]

Let your love be "without dissimulation: Why should you hide fair, disinterested love? Let there be no guile found in your mouth: Let your words be the genuine pic-

[59]"Sermon on the Mount," 24, B 1:545, J V:306–7, sec. 3.6.
[60]"Sermon on the Mount," 24, B 1:546, J V:308, sec. 3.7.
[61]Ibid.
[62]"Sermon on the Mount," 24, B 1:545–46, J V:307, sec. 3.7.
[63]Ibid.
[64]"Sermon on the Mount," 24, B 1:546, J V:308, sec. 3.8.
[65]"Sermon on the Mount," 24, B 1:547, J V:308, sec. 4.1.
[66]Ibid.
[67]Eccl. 11:6.
[68]"Sermon on the Mount," 24, B 1:546–47, J V:307–8, sec. 3.8; cf. Eccl. 11:1.
[69]"Sermon on the Mount," 24, B 1:548, J V:309, sec. 4.2.

ture of your heart. Let there be no darkness or reservedness in your conversation, no disguise in your behavior ... that all may see the grace of God which is in you."[70] Let the light that is in your heart shine in all good works.

B. How the Gospel Reframes the Law

1. Fulfilling the Law: The Righteousness of God through Faith Active in Love

a. Exceeding the Superficial Righteousness of Legalistic Religion

We enter God's kingdom by sharing in God's righteousness. That righteousness was declared and demonstrated on the cross. We share in it by faith. It exceeds the superficial righteousness of legalistic religion.

The law is fulfilled through seeing it in the light of the Son's complete obedience to it. The text of Wesley's fifth discourse on the Sermon on the Mount is from Matthew 5:17 – 20: "Do not think that I have come to abolish the Law or the Prophets; I have not come to abolish them but to fulfill them. For truly I tell you, until heaven and earth disappear, not the smallest letter, not the least stroke of a pen, will by any means disappear from the Law until everything is accomplished. Therefore anyone who sets aside one of the least of these commands and teaches others accordingly will be called least in the kingdom of heaven, but whoever practices and teaches these commands will be called great in the kingdom of heaven. For I tell you that unless your righteousness surpasses that of the Pharisees and the teachers of the law, you will certainly not enter the kingdom of heaven" (NIV) [Homily #25, "Upon Our Lord's Sermon on the Mount: Discourse 5," B 1:550 – 71, J V:310 – 27 (1748)].

In the Sermon on the Mount, Jesus vindicated the law under grace. He affirmed the continuing relevance of the eternal moral law within the coming reign of God. He explained the relation of the law to the Good News and the new relation of pardoned believers to the law.[71]

The Wesleyan homilies on the law and gospel stand in close relation with the work of the Creator and Redeemer discussed in volumes 1 and 2 of this series (*God and Providence* and *Christ and Salvation*). Wesley's ethics (this volume) brings to embodiment the theological grounding in the earlier volumes.

b. The Enduring Relevance of the Eternal Moral Law

Jesus did not come to destroy the eternal moral law written on human hearts. Jesus was criticized for being a teacher of novelties and introducing a new religion.[72] Some have imagined that he was abolishing the old religion and bringing another.[73] In the Sermon on the Mount, he clarified that the coming kingdom of God stands

---

[70]"Sermon on the Mount," 24, B 1:548, J V:309, sec. 4.3.
[71]Cf. Matt. 5:17 – 20.
[72]"Sermon on the Mount," 25, B 1:550, J V:310, proem, sec. 1.
[73]"Sermon on the Mount," 25, B 1:551, J V:311, proem, sec. 2.

in continuity with the history of the people of Israel and the giving of the Law to the covenant people. The law is not forgotten but is transformed in the light of grace.[74]

Neither the eternal moral law recognized by conscience nor the moral law contained in the Ten Commandments were swept away by the gospel. Rather, the work of the Son fulfilled the law in an incomparable way. Far from revoking the moral law, Jesus confirmed its authority as the faithful witness in heaven.

Therefore the moral life stands on a very different foundation than "the ceremonial or ritual law, which was designed for a temporary restraint upon a disobedient and stiff-necked people."[75] "The ritual or ceremonial law ... which related to the old sacrifices and service of the temple"[76] was transformed by the cross. Paul resisted those who taught the detailed observance of the yoke of the ritual law.[77] The apostles agreed that "'it seemed good to the Holy Ghost' and to them, to lay no such burden upon them,"[78] since their sins were pardoned on the cross.[79]

c. Jesus Came Not to Destroy but to Fulfill the Moral Law

The eternal moral law was "'written not on tables of stone,' but on the hearts of all the children of men," accessible through reason and conscience.[80] "Every part of this law must remain in force, upon all mankind, and in all ages, as not depending either on time or place, or any other circumstances liable to change, but on the nature of God and the nature of man, and their unchangeable relation to each other."[81] He did indeed come to fulfill the moral law by his "entire and perfect obedience to it."[82]

The moral law was "never so fully explained, nor so thoroughly understood till the great Author of it himself condescended" to become incarnate to show its continuing and eternal authority.[83] If so, God's purpose in the law was not fully understood until the Lord showed its relation to the coming reign of God.

Wesley's evangelical ethic stems from salvation history. It is grounded in God's pardon in the atonement made known on the cross.

Jesus came to establish the law in its fullness by fulfilling it, and in doing so clarifying whatever was dark and obscure in the law.[84] "I am come to declare the true and full import of every part of it; to show the length and breadth, the entire extent of every commandment contained therein, and the height and depth, the inconceivable purity and spirituality of it in all its branches."[85] All this is fulfilled in faith active in love, which reflects the love of God.

[74]Cf. Matt. 5:17.
[75]"Sermon on the Mount," 25, B 1:551–52, J V:311–12, sec. 1.2.
[76]"Sermon on the Mount," 25, B 1:551, J V:311, sec. 1.1.
[77]Acts 15:5.
[78]Acts 15:28; "Sermon on the Mount," 25, B 1:551, J V:311, sec. 1.1.
[79]"Sermon on the Mount," 25, B 1:551, J V:311, sec. 1.1.
[80]"Sermon on the Mount," 25, B 1:551–52, J V:311–12, sec. 1.2.
[81]Ibid.
[82]"Sermon on the Mount," 25, B 1:552, J V:312, sec. 1.3.
[83]"Sermon on the Mount," 25, B 1:552–53, J V:312, sec. 1.4.
[84]Matt. 5:17.
[85]"Sermon on the Mount," 25, B 1:552, J V:312, sec. 1.3.

Jesus himself clearly taught on the mount that none of the requirements of the moral law would disappear until the end time, "until everything is accomplished."[86] "One jot" literally means not a single vowel, and tittle not a single point of a consonant. Not one part of it, however seemingly insignificant, shall pass away.[87] It is all encompassed by the active and passive obedience of Christ on the cross, in which we participate by faith active in love.

d. Every Command Is a Covered Promise

The righteousness of the law is fulfilled in us "through faith which is in Christ Jesus."[88] Thus every command is "a covered promise."[89] The gospel covers all that the law promises. The law points toward the gospel. The gospel fulfills the law.

Those who have been saved by grace through faith stand in a different relation with the Lawgiver than they did before. Hence "there is no contrariety at all between the law and the gospel," Wesley argued. "Neither of them supersedes the other, but they agree perfectly well together.... Thus, 'Thou shalt love the Lord thy God with all thy heart,' when considered as a commandment, is a branch of the law; when regarded as a promise, is an essential part of the gospel."[90]

The law looks toward the promises of the gospel for its fulfillment. The previously discussed call to poverty in spirit and purity of heart, "and whatever else is enjoined in the holy law of God, are no other, when viewed in a gospel light, than so many great and precious promises."[91]

"We feel that we are not sufficient for these things," understandably, for "with man this is impossible." But in the gospel we have a promise from God that he will give us by grace "that love, and to make us humble, meek, and holy."[92]

2. The Peril of Teaching Others to Disobey the Law

a. Antinomian License

Antinomians are those who teach that the law is made void in every sense by the gospel. Wesley saw in the Sermon on the Mount a strong argument against both antinomianism and legalism. The antinomians are tempted to "change or supersede" the commands of God. Presumptuously they may think they are acting "by the peculiar direction of his Spirit." But according to Jesus, the moral law is designed "to endure till the consummation of all things."[93]

It is a serious offense to teach another to break the eternal moral law of God. When such talk pretends to be the gospel itself, it must be resisted.

---

[86]Matt. 5:18 NIV.

[87]"Sermon on the Mount," 25, B 1:553, J V:312–13, sec. 2.1.

[88]"Sermon on the Mount," 25, B 1:554–55, J V:313–14, sec. 2.3; cf. Rom. 8:4.

[89]"Sermon on the Mount," 25, B 1:554–55, J V:313–14, sec. 2.3.

[90]"Sermon on the Mount," 25, B 1:554, J V:313, sec. 2.2. Wesley was here resisting the antinomian temptations of a licentious interpretation of the gospel.

[91]"Sermon on the Mount," 25, B 1:554, J V:313, sec. 2.2.

[92]"Sermon on the Mount," 25, B 1:554–55, J V:313–14, sec. 2.3.

[93]"Sermon on the Mount," 25, B 1:555, J V:314, sec. 2.4.

No one ever preached the law more thoroughly than Jesus. "Who is he that shall instruct the Son of God how to preach? Who will teach him a better way of delivering the message which he hath received of the Father?"[94] Anyone who teaches another willfully to break one of these commandments, even the least one, is defying the Lord's explicit teaching.

The teaching office in Christianity includes teaching the law. To ignore the teaching of the law is to ignore the teaching of the gospel.[95]

b. The Least in the Kingdom of Heaven

The teaching given on the mount is quite specific about the moral hazard of teaching others to ignore the law. Those who mistake the gospel as an excuse to ignore or circumvent the law will have no place in the reign of God. "Trivialize even the smallest item in God's Law and you will only have trivialized yourself. But take it seriously, show the way for others, and you will find honor in the kingdom. Unless you do far better than the Pharisees in the matters of right living, you won't know the first thing about entering the kingdom."[96]

We teach others by our behavior more than our words: "Every open drunkard is a teacher of drunkenness; every sabbath-breaker is constantly teaching his neighbor to profane the day of the Lord."[97] Yet unhappily a "habitual breaker of the law is seldom content to stop here; he generally teaches other men to do so too.... He excuses the sin which he will not leave, and thus directly teaches every sin which he commits."[98]

Those who fail to teach the law shall have no part either in the kingdom or the glory to be revealed.[99] Those who pretending to bear "the character of Teachers sent from God, do nevertheless themselves break his commandments, yea, and openly teach others so to do [are] corrupt both in life and doctrine."[100] Some of these may live in willful, habitual sin; others may live a seemingly harmless life. Those who most seriously offend "are they who openly and explicitly 'judge the law' itself, and 'speak evil of the law.' "[101]

Many of these teachers have corrupted Protestantism by teaching that "all commands are unfit for our times."[102] Some think they "honor Christ by overthrowing his law."[103] Antinomians who teach in this way are deniers of the deepest teachings of the Reformation.

---

[94]"Sermon on the Mount," 25, B 1:555, J V:314–15, sec. 3.1.
[95]Ibid.
[96]Matt. 5:19–20 MSG.
[97]"Sermon on the Mount," 25, B 1:556–57, J V:315–16, sec. 3.3.
[98]Ibid.
[99]Ibid.
[100]"Sermon on the Mount," 25, B 1:557, J V:316, sec. 3.4.
[101]"Sermon on the Mount," 25, B 1:558–59, J V:317, sec. 3.7.
[102]Ibid.
[103]"Sermon on the Mount," 25, B 1:559, J V:317, sec. 3.8.

3. Fulfilling the Law through Unmerited Grace Active in Love

a. Practicing and Teaching Gospel and Law

The faith of God's people over the centuries is clear: "By grace are ye saved through faith ... not of works, lest any man should boast."[104] Both Paul and James make it clear that faith works by active love.[105] We do not "step from sin to heaven without any holiness coming between."[106] Faith is not a substitute for holiness, nor is holiness a substitute for faith. Rather, grace makes holiness possible.[107]

In faith active in love we find "peace and power together," the peace that comes from pardon, which enables the power to overcome sin.[108]

"Whoever practices and teaches these commands" on the right relation between gospel and law "will be called great in the kingdom of heaven."[109] Those who practice and teach cheap grace, or gospel without law, or law without gospel, miss the joys of faith active in the works of love.[110]

b. What the Legalistic Righteousness of the Scribes and Pharisees Missed about the Law

Faith that works without love and without serious behavioral response to grace will not bring peace to the soul. Grace-enabled holy living will bring peace to the soul.

This was made clear on the mount when Jesus said, "For I tell you that unless your righteousness surpasses that of the Pharisees and the teachers of the law, you will certainly not enter the kingdom of heaven."[111]

The scribes and lawyers who most vehemently opposed Jesus studied the law constantly. "It was their proper and peculiar business to read and expound the Law and the Prophets, particularly in the synagogues. They were the ordinary, stated preachers among the Jews.... For these were the men who made divinity their profession: and they were generally (as their name literally imports) men of letters, men of the greatest account for learning that were then in the Jewish nation."[112]

The apostle Paul knew what legalism was because he himself had lived it. Many of the scribes were of the sect of the Pharisees, as was Paul. The root word of Pharisee means to divide or be separate in the sense of being distinguished from others "by greater strictness of life, by more exactness of conversation. For they were zealous of the law in the minutest points, paying tithes of mint, anise, and cumin: and hence they were held in honor of all the people and generally esteemed the holiest of

---

[104]Eph. 2:8 – 9; "Sermon on the Mount," 25, B 1:559 – 60, J V:318, sec. 3.9.
[105]Cf. Gal. 5:6.
[106]"Sermon on the Mount," 25, B 1:559 – 60, J V:318, sec. 3.9.
[107]Ibid.
[108]Ibid.
[109]Matt. 5:19 NIV.
[110]"Sermon on the Mount," 25, B 1:559 – 60, J V:318, sec. 3.9.
[111]Matt. 5:20 NIV.
[112]"Sermon on the Mount," 25, B 1:560 – 61, J V:318 – 19, sec. 4.1.

men."[113] Paul was first educated as a Pharisee in Tarsus and then in Jerusalem at the feet of Gamaliel. He described himself as "a Pharisee, the son of a Pharisee,"[114] who "conformed to the strictest sect of our religion."[115] The Pharisees were viewed not only as the most eminent professors of religion, but also as the holiest of the faithful.[116] "The righteousness of the scribes and Pharisees" was portrayed by Jesus in his parable of the Pharisee and the tax collector. The Pharisee went up to the temple to pray. But he did not pray at all. He only told God how wise and good he was: "God, I thank you that I am not like other people — robbers, evildoers, adulterers — or even like this tax collector. I fast twice a week and give a tenth of all I get."[117]

c. Embodying a Righteousness in Christ That Exceeds That of the Pharisees and the Teachers of the Law

The righteousness of the scribes and Pharisees was a righteousness that in many respects attempted to go far beyond the letter of the law, even attending to every vowel and consonant of every word of the law. Wesley noted, "These are they whom our Lord so severely condemns, so sharply reproves, on many occasions."[118] The distinguishing mark of their sect was that they "trusted in themselves that they were righteous and despised others."[119] The scribe or Pharisee who was commending himself to God in the parable unquestionably thought himself righteous.

Those who live in Christ by faith active in love have received a righteousness of faith in Christ that exceeds the righteousness of the Pharisees.[120] Ask yourself soberly: Are you sure that you do no harm, and do nothing for which your own heart condemns you? Do you pay tithes and fast? You must go beyond this to enter the kingdom.[121] In what way does the righteousness of a Christian exceed that of a scribe or Pharisee? The Pharisees "endeavored to keep all the commandments.... But still the righteousness of a Christian exceeds all this righteousness of a scribe or Pharisee." How? "By fulfilling the spirit as well as the letter of the law; by inward as well as outward obedience."[122]

Legalistic righteousness is not from the heart. It is "external only: Christian righteousness is in the inner man.... The Pharisee labored to present God with a good life; the Christian ... with a holy heart ... not being content with the outward form of godliness ... unless the life, the Spirit, the power of God unto salvation, be felt in the inmost soul."[123] God's pardon of sinners on the cross ignites the passion for holy living.

---

[113]"Sermon on the Mount," 25, B 1:561, J V:319, sec. 4.2.
[114]Acts 23:6.
[115]Acts 26:5 NIV.
[116]"Sermon on the Mount," 25, B 1:561, J V:319, sec. 4.2.
[117]Luke 18:11 – 12 NIV; "Sermon on the Mount," 25, B 1:562, J V:319, sec. 4.3.
[118]"Sermon on the Mount," 25, B 1:564 – 65, J V:321 – 22, sec. 4.5 – 6.
[119]Ibid.
[120]See Matt. 5:20.
[121]"Sermon on the Mount," 25, B 1:565, J V:322 – 23, sec. 4.7.
[122]"Sermon on the Mount," 25, B 1:567 – 68, J V:324 – 25, sec. 4.11.
[123]Ibid.

"To do no harm, to do good, to attend the ordinances of God (the righteousness of a Pharisee) are all external; whereas, on the contrary, poverty of spirit, mourning, meekness, hunger and thirst after righteousness, the love of our neighbor, and purity of heart (the righteousness of a Christian) are all internal."[124] Only when they become internalized can faith become active in love. God judges the heart above the outward act. Jesus was especially interested in the change of the heart from the inside out to reach every external or visible behavior. God estimates the outward actions "only by the tempers from which they spring,"[125] such as humility and gentleness.

d. Let Your Righteousness Exceed That of the Pharisees

If you bear the name of Christian, see to it that your righteousness does not fall short of the righteousness of the Pharisees. Do not fall short of a Pharisee in doing good. "Give alms of all thou dost possess. Is any hungry? Feed him. Is he athirst? Give him drink. Naked? Cover him with a garment."[126]

Let your righteousness exceed the righteousness of the scribes. You can "do all things through Christ" who strengthens you. "Without him you can do nothing."[127] Let the whole stream of your "thoughts, words, and works be such as flows from the deepest conviction that you stand on the edge of the great gulf, you and all the children of men, just ready to drop in," either into everlasting glory or everlasting death.[128] Let your soul be filled with mildness, gentleness, and patience toward all humanity.

---

[124]Ibid.
[125]Ibid.
[126]"Sermon on the Mount," 25, B 1:568 – 70, J V:325 – 26, sec. 4.12.
[127]"Sermon on the Mount," 25, B 1:570 – 71, J V:326 – 27, sec. 4.13.
[128]Ibid. Wesley does not cover all points of theology in every homily. How could he? In my view, what is not expressed in Wesley's view of the rigor of the law is supplied elsewhere, especially in Wesley's first nine homilies on salvation by grace through faith. See *JWT*, vol. 2, *Christ and Salvation*. The reader of the first nine homilies of the Standard Sermons, all written between 1738 and 1746, would readily know that this rigorous homily of 1748 cannot be split apart from those major grounding homilies on salvation by faith, justification, and the righteousness of faith. If this volume is read without the implicit background of those grounding homilies on salvation by grace, the whole premise of Wesley's ethic could easily be misread. Here Wesley was resisting the antinomian temptations of some radical Protestant misreadings of the gospel. The purpose of this four-volume work is to set forth the whole range of Wesley's teaching. Each part is seen in relation to the whole.

CHAPTER 8

Nurturing Pure Intentions for Good Works

A. Purity of Intent for Works of Mercy

1. The Blessed Dispositions Shape the Life of Love and Prayer

Previously in the Sermon on the Mount the Lord had been teaching us of "those dispositions of soul which constitute real Christianity; the inward tempers contained in that 'holiness, without which no man shall see the Lord.'" The previous focus was inward, upon "the affections, which when flowing from their proper fountain, from a living faith in God through Christ Jesus, are intrinsically and essentially good, and acceptable to God."[1]

Then beginning in Matthew 6, he is showing us how all our actions and works of mercy are to be consecrated to God, so as to be made holy "by a pure and holy intention."[2] In this way, our Lord shows that our giving and our praying are rightly grounded in the very purity of intention that we have already seen in the Beatitudes.

a. Jesus' Guide to Giving and Praying

The weighty text of Wesley's sixth discourse on the Sermon on the Mount is a large section of Matthew 6:6–13 on giving and praying, including Wesley's guide to interpretation of the Lord's Prayer [Matt. 6:6–13; Homily #26, "Upon Our Lord's Sermon on the Mount: Discourse 6," B 1:572–91, J V:328–43 (1748)].

Here is a contemporary rendering of this extended text:

"Be careful not to practice your righteousness in front of others to be seen by them. If you do, you will have no reward from your Father in heaven.

"So when you give to the needy, do not announce it with trumpets, as the hypocrites do in the synagogues and on the streets, to be honored by others. Truly I tell you, they have received their reward in full. But when you give to the needy, do not let your left hand know what your right hand is doing, so that your giving may be in secret. Then your Father, who sees what is done in secret, will reward you.

"And when you pray, do not be like the hypocrites, for they love to pray standing in the synagogues and on the street corners to be seen by others. Truly

---

[1]"Sermon on the Mount," 26, B 1:572–73, J V:328, proem, sec. 1; cf. Heb. 12:14.
[2]Ibid.

I tell you, they have received their reward in full. But when you pray, go into your room, close the door and pray to your Father, who is unseen. Then your Father, who sees what is done in secret, will reward you. And when you pray, do not keep on babbling like pagans, for they think they will be heard because of their many words. Do not be like them, for your Father knows what you need before you ask him.

"This, then, is how you should pray:

"'Our Father in heaven,
hallowed be your name,
your kingdom come,
your will be done,
      on earth as it is in heaven.
Give us today our daily bread.
And forgive us our debts,
      as we also have forgiven our debtors.
And lead us not into temptation,
      but deliver us from the evil one.'"[3]

b. The Right Intention Is to Act Mercifully, Not Be Seen

The next subject is giving in secret.[4] How is this consistent with letting your light shine? In letting God's light shine, do not give and pray with the purpose of being seen.

The intent of a merciful act is not to be seen as an end in itself, but to convey the mercy of God to humanity. On the Mount, Jesus compared the believing community to light in a dark world. Your love is to shine in the world like a light in darkness. The pride of being seen is not the goal. The witness to God's mercy is the goal.

If so, how can Jesus at the same time call you to "let your light shine before others, that they may see your good deeds and glorify your Father in heaven"?[5] How can you be light without making it your objective to be seen?

In order that your light may shine through your behavior, your actions must be transparent, so that "they may glorify our Father which is in heaven" — not for the purpose of others seeing your righteousness. In true giving do nothing with a view toward your own glory. "A regard to the praise of men [has] no place at all in your works of mercy."[6] If you seek your glory, you have your own reward but not God's blessing.

2. Giving

a. Give Alms Quietly

"Take heed that ye do not your alms before men, to be seen of them: otherwise ye have no reward of your Father which is in heaven."[7] This is more easily rendered

---

[3]Matt. 6:1 – 13 NIV.
[4]Matt. 6:3 – 4.
[5]Matt. 5:16 NIV.
[6]"Sermon on the Mount," 26, B 1:574, J V:329, sec. 1.2.
[7]Matt. 6:1.

in the NIV: "Be careful not to practice your righteousness in front of others to be seen by them. If you do, you will have no reward from your Father in heaven."

Alms here refer to all works of charity, not just to the pious act of giving alms. Alms pertain to "everything which we give, or speak, or do, whereby our neighbor may be profited." These acts of mercy include "the feeding the hungry, the clothing the naked, the entertaining or assisting the stranger, the visiting those that are sick or in prison, the comforting the afflicted, the instructing the ignorant, the reproving the wicked, the exhorting and encouraging the well-doer."[8]

Acts of mercy are not done to be seen but to be helpful. What is forbidden here is an intent to be seen, to be regarded as righteous more than to be compassionate to the needy one.

b. Give without Hypocrisy

The hypocrites give in a public way in the synagogues and on the streets and in the markets in order to be honored by others.[9] "When you give to the needy, do not announce it with trumpets, as the hypocrites do."[10] The Pharisees had a public practice of announcing their gifts conspicuously with a trumpet. "The pretended reason for this was to call the poor together to receive it; but the real design, that they might have praise of men." Those who seek the praise of men have their reward but not God's blessing.[11] Rather, "when you give to the needy, do not let your left hand know what your right hand is doing, so that your giving may be in secret. Then your Father, who sees what is done in secret, will reward you."[12] Do not let your consciousness be filled with the thought of reward while you are engaged in an act of mercy. Focus on the act.

Do what must not be left undone. Do it whether secretly or openly as the situation requires, but without attention to your own righteousness. Wesley's rule of thumb: "When you are fully persuaded in your own mind, that by your not concealing the good which is done, either you will yourself be enabled, or others excited, to do the more good, then you may not conceal it: Then let your light appear, and 'shine to all that are in the house' … [but] act in as private and unobserved a manner as the nature of the thing will admit."[13]

c. Pray without Hypocrisy: Close the Door When You Pray

Wesley distinguished between works of mercy, a major concern of Matthew 5, and works of piety, a major concern of Matthew 6.

Do not pray as the hypocrites pray. "Prayer is the lifting up of the heart to God: All words of prayer, without this, are mere hypocrisy."[14] Rather, make your single

---

[8]"Sermon on the Mount," 26, B 1:573, J V:329, sec. 1.1.
[9]"Sermon on the Mount," 26, B 1:574, J V:329, sec. 1.2.
[10]Matt. 6:2 NIV.
[11]"Sermon on the Mount," 26, B 1:574–75, J V:329–30, sec. 1.3.
[12]Matt. 6:3–4 NIV.
[13]"Sermon on the Mount," 26, B 1:575, J V:330, sec. 1.4.
[14]"Sermon on the Mount," 26, B 1:575–76, J V:330–31, sec. 2.1.

purpose "to commune with God, to lift up thy heart to him, to pour out thy soul before him." Do not pray to be "seen of men." Those who pray to be seen have their pathetic reward.[15]

Purity of intention is tainted by seeking "any temporal reward whatever.... Any design but that of promoting the glory of God, and the happiness of men for God's sake, makes every action, however fair it may appear to men, an abomination unto the Lord."[16] "When you pray, go into your room, close the door and pray to your Father, who is unseen. Then your Father, who sees what is done in secret, will reward you."[17]

There are times to glorify God in public, in the great congregation. But when you desire to pour out your heart to God who is unseen, close the door.[18] When you pray, "do not use abundance of words without any meaning. Say not the same thing over and over again; think not the fruit of your prayers depends on the length of them."[19]

"Your Father knows what you need before you ask him."[20] The purpose of your praying is "not to inform God, as though he knew not your wants already; but rather to inform yourselves; to fix the sense of those wants more deeply in your hearts, and the sense of your continual dependence on Him who only is able to supply all your wants. It is not so much to move God, who is always more ready to give than you to ask, as to move yourselves, that you may be willing and ready to receive the good things he has prepared for you."[21] Following is Wesley's advice on how to pray.

B. Praying for God's Guidance

1. The Lord's Prayer

Having taught the true nature and ends of prayer, our Lord provides a guide to prayer, which has over centuries become the pattern of all our prayers. The Lord's Prayer "contains all we can reasonably or innocently pray for. There is nothing which we have need to ask of God, nothing which we can ask without offending him, which is not included, either directly or indirectly.... It contains all our duty to God and man; whatsoever things are pure and holy, whatsoever God requires of the children of men, whatsoever is acceptable in his sight, whatsoever it is whereby we may profit our neighbor, being expressed or implied therein."[22] It also points out to us all those temperaments fitting to approach God "if we desire either our prayers or our lives should find acceptance with him."[23]

---

[15]Ibid.
[16]"Sermon on the Mount," 26, B 1:576, J V:331, sec. 2.2.
[17]Matt. 6:6 NIV.
[18]"Sermon on the Mount," 26, B 1:576, J V:331, sec. 2.3; Matt. 6:6 NIV.
[19]"Sermon on the Mount," 26, B 1:576–77, J V:331–32, sec. 2.4.
[20]Matt. 6:8 NIV.
[21]"Sermon on the Mount," 26, B 1:577, J V:332, sec. 2.5.
[22]"Sermon on the Mount," 26, B 1:577–78, J V:332–33, sec. 3.2.
[23]"Sermon on the Mount," 26, B 1:578, J V:333, sec. 3.3.

The Lord's Prayer "consists of three parts — the preface, the petitions, and the doxology, or conclusion. The preface, 'Our Father which art in heaven,' lays a general foundation for prayer; comprising what we must first know of God before we can pray in confidence of being heard."[24]

a. Our Father

"This, then, is how you should pray." When you pray, do not hesitate to call the holy God your own heavenly Father, since you have become his child by faith. "If he is a Father, then he is good, then he is loving, to his children."[25]

" 'Our Father,' not mine only who now cry unto him; but ours in the most extensive sense."[26] Because he is our Father who loves us as his own, "God is willing to bless" his beloved children, so "let us ask for a blessing.... If he made us, let us ask, and he will not withhold any good thing from the work of his own hands."[27]

Like an earthly father, he preserves us day by day, sustaining the life he has given us. So we are invited to come and ask for his mercy, especially in time of need. If you are a father of your own children, you know that you would want to listen to your own child's needs. If so, would not God even more do so when you need his help?[28]

But God is our Father in a much more profound sense. He is "above all, the Father of our Lord Jesus Christ, and of all that believe in him, who justifies us 'freely by his grace, through the redemption that is in Jesus.' "[29] Through the prayers of his own eternal Son, the heavenly Father has "blotted out all our sins, and healed all our infirmities," and has "received us for his own children, by adoption and grace."[30]

Because we are sons and daughters through Christ, the Father has " 'sent forth the Spirit of his Son into' our 'hearts, crying, Abba, Father' who 'hath begotten us again of incorruptible seed,' and 'created us anew in Christ Jesus.' "[31] It is as if our human child voices are included in the voice of his own eternal Son on our behalf. Therefore we pray to him knowing he will hear us.

We pray not only as an individual son or daughter but as a worshiping community, a family of faith. Together we meet to say, "Our Father." We pray with one voice as children of the family of God. We pray together to the Father of "all the families both in heaven and earth."[32] Since God loves all that he has made, he hears the prayers of all humanity, both those fallen and those redeemed. "His tender mercies are over all his works."[33]

---

[24]Ibid.

[25]Matt. 6:9 NIV.

[26]"Sermon on the Mount," 26, B 1:579, J V:333 – 34, sec. 3.5.

[27]"Sermon on the Mount," 26, B 1:578 – 79, J V:333, sec. 3.4.

[28]Ibid.

[29]Ibid.

[30]Ibid.; cf. Ps. 51:9; 103:3.

[31]"Sermon on the Mount," 26, B 1:578 – 79, J V:333, sec. 3.4; Gal. 4:6; cf. Eph. 2:10; 1 Peter 1:23.

[32]"Sermon on the Mount," 26, B 1:579, J V:333 – 34, sec. 3.5.

[33]Ps. 145:9.

b. The Lord of Heaven

Heaven is the place where the glory of God dwells. God is incomparably present there. Heaven is full of the glory of God.[34] Heaven means "high and lifted up." Hence God is "over all, blessed for ever: Who, sitting on the circle of the heavens, beholdeth all things both in heaven and earth."[35]

Wesley painted a moving picture of the heavenly Father: His "eye pervades the whole sphere of created being."[36] God beholds the inner thoughts and outward works of every creature, not only now but from the beginning of the world, from all eternity, inspiring awe.[37]

The Lord and Ruler of all superintends and disposes all things, the Almighty whom the faithful serve "with fear, and rejoice unto him with reverence. Therefore should we think, speak, and act, as continually under the eye, in the immediate presence, of the Lord, the King."[38]

c. Hallowed Be Thy Name

Being who he is as incomparably powerful and just, his name is holy. "Hallowed be thy name."[39] The Lord's Prayer is composed of six petitions. Hallowed be thy name; thy kingdom come; thy will be done; give us this day our daily bread; forgive us our trespasses; and lead us not into temptation, but deliver us from evil. It concludes with a doxology.

"The name of God is God himself, the nature of God, so far as it can be discovered to man."[40] The name points to God's necessary existence and to all of God's attributes or perfections.

The divine attributes show the character of the one God to whom we pray:

- his eternity, particularly signified by his great and incommunicable name, Yahweh, "the Alpha and Omega, the beginning and the end; he which is, and which was, and which is to come"[41]
- his fullness of being, or aseity, "denoted by his other great name, I AM THAT I AM!"[42]
- his omnipresence
- his omnipotence, by which all matter is moved by the finger of God
- his wisdom, "clearly deduced from the things that are seen, from the goodly order of the universe"
- his trinity in unity and unity in trinity
- his essential purity and holiness
- his love, "which is the very brightness of his glory"[43]

---

[34]"Sermon on the Mount," 26, B 1:579–80, J V:334, sec. 3.6; cf. 1 Tim. 6:16.
[35]"Sermon on the Mount," 26, B 1:579–80, J V:334, sec. 3.6; cf. Wisd. Sol. 13:2.
[36]"Sermon on the Mount," 26, B 1:579–80, J V:334, sec. 3.6.
[37]Ibid.
[38]Ibid.
[39]"Sermon on the Mount," 26, B 1:580–81, J V:334–35, sec. 3.7; Matt. 6:9.
[40]"The Sermon on the Mount," 26, B 1:581, J V:334, sec. 3.7; cf. Rev. 1:8.
[41]"Sermon on the Mount," 26, B 1:581, J V:334–35, sec. 3.7.
[42]Ibid; cf. Ex. 3:14.
[43]Ibid.

The attributes of God reveal the character of God. When we call upon his name, we know whom we are addressing. He is the Holy One who encompasses all the goodness we can conceive. It is he who enables us to conceive his goodness to the extent of our finite abilities.

In praying that God's name may be hallowed and glorified, "we pray that he may be known, such as he is, by all that are capable thereof, by all intelligent beings, and with affections suitable to that knowledge; that he may be duly honored, and feared, and loved, by all in heaven above and in the earth beneath; by all angels and men, whom for that end he has made capable of knowing and loving him to eternity."[44]

d. Your Kingdom Come

"In order that the name of God might be hallowed, we pray that his kingdom, the kingdom of Christ, may come."[45] The kingdom comes to you when you repent and believe.[46] This kingdom is eternal life. It is "the kingdom of God begun below, set up in the believer's heart" where God reigns now and eternally.[47]

Through the power of the Spirit, God's reigning power may come into our hearts, "conquering and to conquer, till he hath put all things under his feet, till 'every thought is brought into captivity to the obedience of Christ.'"[48] In due time, all kingdoms to the uttermost parts of the earth will be received into God's inheritance.[49] Hence the worshiping community prays that God will hasten that time, so that all humanity "may be filled with righteousness, and peace, and joy, with holiness and happiness — till they are removed hence into his heavenly kingdom, there to reign with him for ever and ever."[50]

Jesus taught us to pray: "Thy kingdom come." This prayer is constantly "offered up for the whole intelligent creation, who are all interested in this grand event, the final renovation of all things, by God's putting an end to misery and sin, to infirmity and death, taking all things into his own hands, and setting up the kingdom which endureth throughout all ages."[51] At death we pray that "we, with all those that are departed in the true faith of thy holy name, may have our perfect consummation and bliss, both in body and soul, in thy eternal and everlasting glory."[52]

e. Your Will Be Done on Earth as It Is in Heaven

This is the petition that follows immediately after "Thy kingdom come." The primary sense of this petition is not for resignation, but a prayer for our voluntary, "active, conformity to the will of God."[53] Angels and humans pray that God's will

---

[44]"Sermon on the Mount," 26, B 1:580–81, J V:334–35, sec. 3.7.
[45]"Sermon on the Mount," 26, B 1:581–82, J V:335–36, sec. 3.8; cf. Matt. 6:10.
[46]Cf. Mark 1:15.
[47]"Sermon on the Mount," 26, B 1:581–82, J V:335–36, sec. 3.8.
[48]Ibid.; cf. 2 Cor. 10:5.
[49]"Sermon on the Mount," 26, B 1:581–82, J V:335–36, sec. 3.8; cf. Ps. 2:8.
[50]"Sermon on the Mount," 26, B 1:581–82, J V:335–36, sec. 3.8.
[51]Ibid.
[52]Ibid.; *Book of Common Prayer* (New York: Seabury, 1953), 334.
[53]"Sermon on the Mount," 26, B 1:583–84, J V:336–37, sec. 3.9; cf. Matt. 6:10.

be done. The angels who circle God's throne eagerly will that God's will be done in heaven and on earth as it is in heaven. "It is their meat and drink to do his will; it is their highest glory and joy. They do it continually; there is no interruption in their willing service.... And they do it perfectly."[54] "They do nothing else, nothing but what they are absolutely assured is his will. Again they do all the will of God as he willeth; in the manner which pleases him."[55]

When we pray that God's will may be done "on earth as it is in heaven," the specific meaning is "that all the inhabitants of the earth, even the whole race of mankind, may do the will of their Father which is in heaven, as willingly as the holy angels," continually and completely.[56] The whole church of all times prays that "the God of peace, who through the blood of the eternal covenant brought back from the dead our Lord Jesus, that great Shepherd of the sheep, [may] equip you with everything good for doing his will, and may he work in us what is pleasing to him, through Jesus Christ, to whom be glory for ever and ever."[57] The specific intent of this oft-prayed phrase is that we pray for all humanity to do the whole will of God in all things and that all may also do it willingly.[58]

f. Our Daily Bread

As we are invited to pray for all humanity, we are also invited to pray for ourselves. God has given us this privilege. In praying for "our daily bread," we are praying for "all things needful, whether for our souls or bodies."[59] By this prayer, we are praising God that "his divine power has given us everything we need for a godly life through our knowledge of him who called us by his own glory and goodness."[60]

Our daily bread does indeed refer to physical bread that spoils, but much more to "the spiritual bread, the grace of God, the food that endures to eternal life, which the Son of Man will give you. For on him God the Father has placed his seal of approval."[61]

We are not here praying for a whole store of bread, only for "what is sufficient for this day; and so for each day as it succeeds."[62]

g. Give Us What We Truly Need to Live

We do not pray for our daily bread as if it were a natural right or a moral merit, "but only of free mercy. We deserve not the air we breathe, the earth that bears [us], or the sun that shines upon us."[63] Nothing we ever could have done would have merited God giving us life. Before our birth, we were unable to ask. Yet we are

[54]"Sermon on the Mount," 26, B 1:583–84, J V:336–37, sec. 3.9.
[55]Ibid.
[56]"Sermon on the Mount," 26, B 1:584, J V:337–38, sec. 3.10.
[57]Heb. 13:20–21 NIV.
[58]"Sermon on the Mount," 26, B 1:584, J V:337–38, sec. 3.10.
[59]"Sermon on the Mount," 26, B 1:584–85, J V:338, sec. 3.11.
[60]2 Peter 1:3 NIV.
[61]"Sermon on the Mount," 26, B 1:584–85, J V:338, sec. 3.11; cf. John 6:27.
[62]"Sermon on the Mount," 26, B 1:584–85, J V:338, sec. 3.11.
[63]"Sermon on the Mount," 26, B 1:585, J V:338–39, sec. 3.12.

confident in asking freely because "God loves us freely."[64] We stand before him as his own dear children.

Meanwhile the fact that God gives us the provisions of reason and imagination and bodily strength is no cause for us to stand idle. "It is his will that we should use all diligence in all things, that we should employ our utmost endeavors, as much as if our success were the natural effect of our own wisdom and strength. And then, as though we had done nothing, we are to depend on him, the giver of every good and perfect gift."[65]

We pray only for "this day," taking no thought of tomorrow, since we trust God's provision and mercy. It is a useful discipline for us to pray only for this day, in order "that we might look on every day as a fresh gift of God."[66]

In the paraphrased hymn for daily bread that concludes this homily, the Wesleys celebrated the Giver of daily bread:

> Father, 'tis thine each day to yield
> Thy children's wants a fresh supply:
> Thou cloth'st the lilies of the field,
> And hearest the young ravens cry.
> On thee we cast our care; we live
> Through thee, who know'st our every need;
> O feed us with thy grace, and give
> Our souls this day the living bread![67]

h. Forgive Us as We Forgive Our Debtors

In this model prayer, Jesus teaches us to pray for God to "forgive us our trespasses, as we forgive those who trespass against us."[68] Nothing but sin can hinder the bounty of God from flowing forth upon every creature. To remove all hindrance to receiving God's good gifts, we pray that we may forgive the offenses of others toward us just as God forgives our trespasses.

Every sin puts us "under a fresh debt to God, to whom we already owe, as it were, ten thousand talents. What then can we answer when he shall say, 'Pay me what you owe.'[69] In our sin before the incomparably holy God, "we are utterly insolvent; we have nothing to pay; we have wasted all our substance. Indeed we are already bound hand and foot by the chains of our own sins."[70]

To forgive implies "either to forgive a debt or to unloose a chain."[71] When we receive complete forgiveness from God, we find that "sin has lost its power; it has no dominion over those who 'are under grace,' that is, in favor with God. As 'there is now no condemnation for them that are in Christ Jesus,' so they are freed from

[64]Ibid.
[65]Ibid.
[66]Ibid.
[67]"Sermon on the Mount," 26, B 1:588–91, J V:341–43, sec. 3.16.
[68]Cf. Matt. 6:12.
[69]"Sermon on the Mount," 26, B 1:585–86, J V:339–40, sec. 3.13; cf. Matt. 18:28.
[70]"Sermon on the Mount," 26, B 1:585–86, J V:339–40, sec. 3.13.
[71]Ibid.

sin as well as from guilt."[72] In offering forgiveness, God declares the condition for receiving it — repentance. "All our trespasses and sins are forgiven us if we forgive, and as we forgive, others."[73]

i. Lead Us Not into Temptation

The apostle James uses the word *temptation* in two senses, both as an enticement to sin and a moral trial to test faith.[74] We pray to God that we not be led into temptation.

Human freedom is forever subject to temptation. Otherwise we would be machines. We cannot control the conditions that lead to temptation, but we are accountable for our own responses to temptation. "When tempted, no one should say, 'God is tempting me.' For God cannot be tempted by evil, nor does he tempt anyone; but each person is tempted when they are dragged away by their own evil desire and enticed."[75]

j. Deliver Us from the Evil One

The evil one refers to the incomparably corrupted and corrupting demonic power who has fallen from heavenly favor to appear as "the prince and god of this world, who works with mighty power in the children of disobedience. But all those who are the children of God by faith are delivered out of his hands."[76] Expect this adversary to fight against us. But he cannot conquer us unless we voluntarily "betray our own souls. He may torment the people of God for a time, but he cannot destroy, for God is on their side, who will not fail, in the end."[77]

God has promised not to allow us to be tempted beyond our powers: "No temptation has overtaken you except what is common to mankind. And God is faithful; he will not let you be tempted beyond what you can bear. But when you are tempted, he will also provide a way out so that you can endure it."[78]

k. Fulfill in Us Your Kingdom, Your Power, and Your Glory

Having instructed the multitudes on the mount on how to give to the needy and pray to God, Jesus concluded his pattern of prayer with a doxology, "a solemn thanksgiving," which constitutes "a compendious acknowledgment of the attributes and works of God," which begins with the ascription: "For thine is the kingdom."[79]

This prayer ascribes to God "the sovereign right of all things that are or ever were created." "The power" refers to the executive authority by which God governs all things eternally. "And the glory" refers to "the praise due from every creature."

---

[72]Ibid.
[73]"Sermon on the Mount," 26, B 1:587, J V:340, sec. 3.14.
[74]James 1:12 – 13.
[75]James 1:13 – 14 NIV. See Wesley's sermon "On Temptation."
[76]"Sermon on the Mount," 26, B 1:578 – 88, J V:341, sec. 3.15; cf. John 12:31.
[77]"Sermon on the Mount," 26, B 1:578 – 88, J V:341, sec. 3.15.
[78]1 Cor. 10:13 NIV.
[79]"Sermon on the Mount," 26, B 1:588 – 91, J V:341 – 43, sec. 3.16.

Amen means "So be it!"[80] To this Wesley subjoins a hymnic "paraphrase of the Lord's Prayer."[81]

C. Purity of Intent

The text of Wesley's seventh discourse on the Sermon on the Mount is Matthew 6:16 – 18 on fasting in a way honoring to God: "When you fast, do not look somber as the hypocrites do, for they disfigure their faces to show others they are fasting. Truly I tell you, they have received their reward in full. But when you fast, put oil on your head and wash your face, so that it will not be obvious to others that you are fasting, but only to your Father, who is unseen; and your Father, who sees what is done in secret, will reward you" [Matt. 6:16 – 18 NIV; Homily #27, "Upon Our Lord's Sermon on the Mount: Discourse 7," B 1:592 – 611, J V:344 – 60 (1748)].

1. Purity of Intent Motivating Outward Acts

Jesus held closely together inward purity of intent with outward acts of mercy. The demonic powers have from the beginning of the fallen world sought to "put asunder what God hath joined together; to separate inward from outward religion; to set one of these at variance with the other."[82] Fasting has been too often separated from its profound inward motivation.

Those who have unwisely attached greatest importance to "the performance of outward duties" have been trapped in pursuing the "righteousness of the law … regardless of inward righteousness."[83] They may have "a zeal for God but not according to knowledge"[84] — the knowledge of grace. Separating outward acts of piety from inner intent produces a life entirely different from those who hold inward intent and outward performance tightly together. Those who seek "the righteousness which is of God by faith" know the intrinsic connection of inward motive to outward act.[85]

Outward religion without purity of intent is familiar to all. It is seen in those who have "seemed to place all religion in attending the Prayers of the Church, in receiving the Lord's Supper, in hearing sermons, and reading books of piety; neglecting, meantime, the end of all these, the love of God and their neighbor."[86] The disconnect has weakened the power of the good news of free grace.[87]

The antinomians have run the disconnect in "the opposite extreme, disregarding all outward duties, perhaps even speaking evil of the law, and judging the law,"

---

[80]Ibid.

[81]See *HSP* (1742), 275 – 77. See above.

[82]"Sermon on the Mount," 27, B 1:592, J V:344, proem, sec. 1; cf. 2 Cor. 2:11.

[83]"Sermon on the Mount," 27, B 1:592, J V:344, proem, sec. 1; cf. Rom. 8:4.

[84]"Sermon on the Mount," 27, B 1:592, J V:344, proem, sec. 1; cf. Rom. 10:2.

[85]Phil. 3:9; "Sermon on the Mount," 27, B 1:592, J V:344, proem, sec. 1.

[86]"Sermon on the Mount," 27, B 1:593, J V:345, proem, sec. 3.

[87]Ibid.

especially when the law requires real performance on their part.[88] They have been tempted to magnify "faith to the utter exclusion of good works."[89]

Meanwhile others, eager to avoid this mistake, have run as much too far in the opposite direction by maintaining that good works are the cause of justification.[90] The result in both the cases of legalism and antinomianism are formally the same: ends and means have been "set at variance with each other."[91]

a. Fasting as a Means of Grace

Fasting "is not the end, but it is a precious means ... which God himself has ordained."[92] It will bless those who rightly understand and employ it.

Jesus called for prayer and fasting. Fasting is a means of grace. But its practice has run into such extremes that its meaning has been obscured. Some have treated fasting only outwardly as an act of bodily discipline. Others "utterly have disregarded it."[93] Over time it has become either undervalued or overvalued.

Ask freshly: What is fasting, and what are the reasons, grounds, and ends of it? If Jesus himself commends its proper use, what can we learn from fasting?

To fast in its literal sense is quite simply "not to eat, to abstain from food" for a specific time.[94] It is a discipline practiced by David; God's people as recorded in the books of Nehemiah, Isaiah, and the Prophets; the Son of God; his apostles; and "the Christians of the purer ages."[95] The biblical examples of fasting did not "beat or tear their own flesh," as did the worshipers of Baal, but they did at times accompany fasting with symbols of grief over sin, such as ashes and mourning clothes.[96]

Fasting appears throughout the Bible. Moses, Elijah, and Jesus fasted for forty days. The book of Leviticus prescribes fasting on the Day of Atonement, the tenth day of the seventh month.[97] "But the time of fasting more frequently mentioned in Scripture is one day, from morning till evening."[98] It was a discipline "commonly observed among the ancient Christians."[99] Fasting called for abstinence — abstaining from certain foods or habits.[100] The most common fast in the ancient church was the period preceding Easter — the forty days of Lent, with special emphasis on Holy Week.

Among other common fasts in Wesley's church tradition were "the Ember days at the four seasons, the Rogation days, and the Vigils or Eves of several solemn

---

[88]"Sermon on the Mount," 27, B 1:592, J V:344, proem, sec. 1.
[89]"Sermon on the Mount," 27, B 1:592–93, J V:344–45, proem, sec. 2.
[90]Ibid.
[91]Ibid.
[92]"Sermon on the Mount," 27, B 1:593–94, J V:345, proem, sec. 4.
[93]Ibid.
[94]"Sermon on the Mount," 27, B 1:594, J V:345, sec. 1.1.
[95]"Sermon on the Mount," 27, B 1:594, J V:345, sec. 1.2.
[96]Ibid.
[97]See Lev. 23:27.
[98]"Sermon on the Mount," 27, B 1:595, J V:345, sec. 1.3.
[99]Ibid.
[100]"Sermon on the Mount," 27, B 1:595, J V:346, sec. 1.4.

festivals," and Fridays "in recollection of Good Friday."[101] Others in the Protestant traditions who "desire to walk humbly and closely with God," were more likely to have found "frequent occasion for private seasons" of repentance.[102]

2. Reasons for Fasting

a. Fasting in Times of Crisis

During times when persons are facing crisis, anxiety, grief, despair, or depression, their bodies naturally may be less interested in food. "David, and all the men that were with him, when they heard that the people were fled from the battle, and that many of the people were fallen and dead, and Saul and Jonathan his son were dead also, 'mourned, and wept, and fasted until even[ing], for Saul and Jonathan, and for the house of Israel.'"[103] Fasting also appeared fitting in the case of Paul on the ship amid a heavy storm when "all hope that they should be saved was taken away."[104] The passengers "continued fasting, having taken nothing."[105]

This is "the natural ground of fasting. One who is under deep affliction, overwhelmed with sorrow for sin and a strong apprehension of the wrath of God, would, without any rule, without knowing or considering whether it were a command of God or not, 'forget to eat his bread.'"[106] Paul "who, after he was led into Damascus, 'was three days without sight ... neither did eat nor drink.'"[107]

The prophetic call to fasting was passionately expressed by the prophet Joel when the army of locusts swept into Israel:

"Even now," declares the LORD,
　"return to me with all your heart,
　　with fasting and weeping and mourning."
Rend your heart
　and not your garments.
Return to the LORD your God,
　for he is gracious and compassionate,
slow to anger and abounding in love,
　and he relents from sending calamity.
Who knows? He may turn and relent
　and leave behind a blessing —
grain offerings and drink offerings
　for the LORD your God."[108]

---

[101]"Sermon on the Mount," 27, B 1:596–97, J V:347–48, sec. 1.6.
[102]Ibid.
[103]Cf. 2 Sam. 1:12.
[104]"Sermon on the Mount," 27, B 1:597–98, J V:348–49, sec. 2.1; cf. Acts 27:20.
[105]Acts 27:33.
[106]"Sermon on the Mount," 27, B 1:598–99, J V:349, sec. 2.2; cf. Ps. 102:4.
[107]Acts 9:9; "Sermon on the Mount," 27, B 1:598–99, J V:349, sec. 2.2.
[108]Joel 2:12–14 NIV; "Sermon on the Mount," 27, B 1:603, J V:353–54, sec. 2.11.

b. Withdrawing the Incentives of Foolish Desires

The prayer book of Wesley's Church of England had a prescribed order for fasting with this instruction: "When men feel in themselves the heavy burden of sin, see damnation to be the reward of it, and behold, with the eye of their mind, the horror of hell, they tremble, they quake, and are inwardly touched with sorrowfulness of heart, and cannot but accuse themselves, and open their grief unto Almighty God, and call unto him for mercy."[109]

The felt need for crisis fasting is common to human experience. "Many of those who now fear God are deeply sensible how often they have sinned against him, by the abuse of these lawful things. They know how much they have sinned by excess of food; how long they have transgressed the holy law of God, with regard to temperance, if not sobriety too; how they have indulged their sensual appetites."[110]

This is what we find among wise persons in all cultures: weaning themselves "from all those indulgences of the inferior appetites, which naturally tend to chain it down to earth, and to pollute as well as debase it," and to "withdraw the incentives of foolish and hurtful desires."[111] They keep at a distance from all excess. This may also apply to the intense awareness of "foolish and unholy desires ... and vile affections."[112]

Fasting may prepare the soul for deeper prayer and timely repentance. "Then especially it is that God is often pleased to lift up the souls of his servants above all the things of earth, and sometimes to [rapture] them up, as it were, into the third heaven." It may become a means of engendering virtue, increasing "tenderness of conscience ... and every holy and heavenly affection."[113]

c. Turning Away God's Anger

There is no predictable or necessary connection between fasting and obtaining God's blessing. For God "will have mercy as he will have mercy."[114] So there is no certainty of outcome. Yet in all ages God has appointed fasting as an appropriate means for seeking the grace of repentance, with the hope of averting God's displeasure and of "obtaining whatever blessings we, from time to time, stand in need of."[115]

Wesley provided examples of the ancient practice of fasting. Daniel sought God "with fasting, and sackcloth, and ashes" to turn away God's anger.[116] Ezra "proclaimed a fast there, at the river Ahava, that we might afflict ourselves before our God, to seek of him a right way for us, and for our little ones."[117] Nehemiah "fasted, and prayed before the God of heaven, and said, ... Prosper, I pray thee, thy servant

---

[109]"Sermon on the Mount," 27, B 1:598 – 99, J V:349, sec. 2.2.
[110]"Sermon on the Mount," 27, B 1:599, J V:349 – 50, sec. 2.3.
[111]"Sermon on the Mount," 27, B 1:599 – 600, J V:350, sec. 2.4.
[112]Ibid.
[113]"Sermon on the Mount," 27, B 1:600, J V:351, sec. 2.6.
[114]Cf. Rom. 9:18.
[115]"Sermon on the Mount," 27, B 1:600 – 601, J V:351, sec. 2.7.
[116]Ibid.; Dan. 9:3 – 19; cf. Jonah 3:5.
[117]Ezra 8:21; cf. Judg. 20:26; 1 Sam. 7:6.

this day, and grant him mercy in the sight of this man." And God granted him mercy.[118]

d. Prayer and Fasting

Not only in the Old Testament but also in the New, the apostles "always joined fasting with prayer when they desired the blessing of God on any important undertaking."[119] In Acts we read: "While they were worshiping the Lord and fasting, the Holy Spirit said, 'Set apart for me Barnabas and Saul for the work to which I have called them.' So after they had fasted and prayed, they placed their hands on them and sent them off."[120] "These were the appointed means: For it was not merely by the light of reason, or of natural conscience, as it is called, that the people of God have been, in all ages, directed to use fasting as a means to these ends; but they have been, from time to time, taught it of God himself, by clear and open revelations of his will."[121]

The gospel promise is anticipated in Joel's prophecy: "I will pour out my spirit upon all flesh; and your sons and your daughters shall prophesy, your old men shall dream dreams, and your young men shall see visions: and also upon the servants and upon the handmaids in those days will I pour out my spirit."[122] Those who give, pray, and fast in quiet trust in the Lord will be rewarded openly. "Your Father, who sees what is done in secret, will reward you."[123]

e. Answering Objections: Abstaining from Food and Abstaining from Sin

Some might argue in this way: "Let a Christian fast from sin, and not from food,"[124] thus presumably making fasting as a temporary cessation from food irrelevant.

A Christian fast from sin is always fitting. But penitents are also invited to receive the means of grace provided by fasting in the proper spirit, as commended by the Lord on the mount. It is a leap in logic to argue, "If a Christian ought to abstain from sin, then he ought not to abstain from food.... Let him, by the grace of God, always abstain from sin; and let him often abstain from food, for such reasons and ends as experience and Scripture plainly show to be answered thereby."[125]

The grace of God is "conveyed into our souls through this outward means, in conjunction with all the other channels of his grace which he hath appointed [that] we may be enabled to abstain from every passion and temper which is not pleasing in his sight."[126] These little instances of self-denial are the ways God has chosen to bestow his great salvation.

---

[118]Neh. 1:4–5, 11.
[119]"Sermon on the Mount," 27, B 1:602–3, J V:352–53, sec. 2.10.
[120]Acts 13:2–3 NIV.
[121]"Sermon on the Mount," 27, B 1:603, J V:353–54, sec. 2.11.
[122]Joel 2:28–29.
[123]Matt. 6:18 NIV; "Sermon on the Mount," 27, B 1:604, J V:354, sec. 2.12.
[124]"Sermon on the Mount," 27, B 1:604–5, J V:354–55, sec. 3.1.
[125]Ibid.
[126]"Sermon on the Mount," 27, B 1:605, J V:355, sec. 3.2.

We may hear others argue, "We have fasted much and often; but what did it avail? We were not a whit better; we found no blessing therein. Nay, we have found it a hindrance rather than a help. Instead of preventing anger, for instance, or fretfulness, it has been a means of increasing them to such a height that we could neither bear others nor ourselves."[127]

If you fast unworthily, you may make your life less happy and holy than before, but the purpose of Jesus' teaching on the mount is to commend fasting in an effective way. "Do what God commands as he commands it; and then, doubtless, his promise shall not fail."[128]

The discipline of rightly motivated fasting is so universally commended in Scripture that it cannot be said that God regards it a little thing. After they were "filled with the Holy Ghost, and with wisdom," the apostles fasted.[129] It was after they had received the "'unction of the Holy One, teaching them all things,'" that they engaged in fasting to pray for God's continual approval of their ministries. In the Acts, the apostles would hardly do anything about which the glory of God was concerned without fasting. They would not send "forth laborers into the harvest, without solemn fasting as well as prayer."[130] If you had been with the apostles in Antioch "at the time when they fasted and prayed, before the sending forth of Barnabas and Saul, can you possibly imagine that your temperance or abstinence would have been a sufficient cause for not joining" in the fast?[131]

Some have gone overboard with fasting by arguing that we should "keep a continual fast to use as much abstinence, at all times, as our bodily strength will bear."[132] Scriptural fasting is for a time, not for all times. Wesley urged, "Practice it by all means; but not so as thereby to set aside a command of God."[133] Routinized fasting may lead to bodily harm. Excessive fasting might not enable you to "endure even to take such supplies as were needful for the body."[134]

f. Do Not Fast as the Hypocrites Do

Having dealt with the common objections to fasting, we now ask how Jesus calls us to fast with a right spirit. "When you fast, do not look somber as the hypocrites do, for they disfigure their faces to show others they are fasting."[135]

Fasting is a way that God has ordained by which we wait for his unmerited mercy, and, without any merit of ours, he has promised freely to give us his blessing.[136] "First, let it be done unto the Lord, with our eye singly fixed on Him. Let our intention herein be this, and this alone, to glorify our Father which is in heaven; to

[127]"Sermon on the Mount," 27, B 1:605, J V:355, sec. 3.3.
[128]Ibid.
[129]"Sermon on the Mount," 27, B 1:606, J V:355–56, sec. 3.4.
[130]Ibid.
[131]"Sermon on the Mount," 27, B 1:607–8, J V:357, sec. 3.7.
[132]"Sermon on the Mount," 27, B 1:606, J V:356, sec. 3.5.
[133]Ibid.
[134]"Sermon on the Mount," 27, B 1:607, J V:356–57, sec. 3.6.
[135]Matt. 6:16 NIV.
[136]"Sermon on the Mount," 27, B 1:608–9, J V:358, sec. 4.2.

express our sorrow and shame for our manifold transgressions of his holy law; to wait for an increase of purifying grace, drawing our affections to things above; to add seriousness and earnestness to our prayers; to avert the wrath of God, and to obtain all the great and precious promises which he hath made to us in Jesus Christ."[137]

"Beware of mocking God, of turning our fast, as well as our prayers, into an abomination unto the Lord … by seeking the praise of men."[138] In particular, Jesus warned: "When you fast, do not look somber as the hypocrites do."[139] Too many among the people of God come to fasting with "'a sad countenance,' sour, affectedly sad, putting their looks into a peculiar form. 'For they disfigure their faces,' not only by unnatural distortions, but also by covering them with dust and ashes 'that they may appear unto men to fast.' This is their chief, if not only design."[140] Such was the fasting of the hypocrites. Jesus said, "Truly I tell you, they have received their reward in full."[141] Their reward is nothing more than the admiration and praise of men.

g. Fasting as an Act of Repentance

Fasting according to the Lord's instruction is different: "But when you fast, put oil on your head and wash your face, so that it will not be obvious to others that you are fasting."[142] The anointing of the head with oil is a symbol of inward penitence with a humble heart. Washing the face signifies you come having no intent of appearing to others as seeking their approval, with no pretenses toward corrupt intentions.[143] "Let this be no part of thy intention." Let the focus be not on human observers but wholly on the sole divine observer. He will see you in secret and deal justly with your repentance: "Your Father, who sees what is done in secret, will reward you."[144]

"Beware of fancying we merit anything of God by our fasting."[145] Since the desire to establish our own righteousness is so deeply rooted in all our hearts, we cannot be too often warned of this. The bare outward act receives no blessing from God. Would you call this a fast, an act acceptable to the Lord? "If it be a mere external service, it is all but lost labor. Such a performance may possibly afflict the body; but as to the soul, it profits nothing."[146]

h. Godly Sorrow Leads to Repentance

Rather, "Let every season, either of public or private fasting, be a season of exercising all those holy affections which are implied in a broken and contrite heart. Let it be a season of devout mourning, of godly sorrow for sin."[147]

---

[137] "Sermon on the Mount," 27, B 1:608, J V:358–59, sec. 4.1.
[138] Ibid.
[139] Matt. 6:16 NIV.
[140] "Sermon on the Mount," 27, B 1:608, J V:358–59, sec. 4.1.
[141] Matt. 6:16 NIV.
[142] Matt. 6:17–18 NIV; "Sermon on the Mount," 27, B 1:608, J V:358–59, sec. 4.1.
[143] "Sermon on the Mount," 27, B 1:608, J V:358–59, sec. 4.1.
[144] Matt. 6:18 NIV.
[145] "Sermon on the Mount," 27, B 1:608–9, J V:358, sec. 4.2.
[146] "Sermon on the Mount," 27, B 1:609, J V:358, sec. 4.3.
[147] "Sermon on the Mount," 27, B 1:609–10, J V:359–60, sec. 4.5.

Paul wrote poignantly to the Corinthians on the reasons why he was glad that through sorrow they were led to repentance:

> Even if I caused you sorrow by my letter, I do not regret it. Though I did regret it — I see that my letter hurt you, but only for a little while — yet now I am happy, not because you were made sorry, but because your sorrow led you to repentance. For you became sorrowful as God intended and so were not harmed in any way by us. Godly sorrow brings repentance that leads to salvation and leaves no regret, but worldly sorrow brings death. See what this godly sorrow has produced in you: what earnestness, what eagerness to clear yourselves, what indignation, what alarm, what longing, what concern, what readiness to see justice done. At every point you have proved yourselves to be innocent in this matter.[148]

Godly sorrow is "a precious gift of his Spirit, lifting the soul to God from whom it flows." Let it "work in us the same inward and outward repentance; the same entire change of heart, renewed after the image of God, in righteousness and true holiness; and the same change of life, till we are holy as he is holy, in all manner of conversation."[149]

"With fasting let us always join fervent prayer, pouring out our whole souls before God, confessing our sins with all their aggravations, humbling ourselves under his mighty hand, laying open before him all our wants, all our guiltiness and helplessness."[150]

i. Fasting as an Act of the Worshiping Community

Fasting is "a season for enlarging our prayers, both in behalf of ourselves and of our brethren. Let us now bewail the sins of our people; and cry aloud for the city of our God, that the Lord may build up Zion, and cause his face to shine on her desolations."[151] Fasting calls for change both in ourselves and in our community life. By fasting in a way acceptable to the Lord, we add to our works of mercy.[152]

The crucial biblical teaching of the social and national meaning of fasting is in Isaiah 58. Wesley ends his teaching on Jesus' view of right fasting by quoting it extensively:

The people were asking:

> "'Why have we fasted,' they say,
>   'and you have not seen it?
> Why have we humbled ourselves,
>   and you have not noticed?'
>
> "Yet on the day of your fasting, you do as you please
>   and exploit all your workers.

---

[148]2 Cor. 7:8–11 NIV; "Sermon on the Mount," 27, B 1:609–10, J V:359–60, sec. 4.5.
[149]"Sermon on the Mount," 27, B 1:609–10, J V:359–60, sec. 4.5.
[150]Ibid.
[151]"Sermon on the Mount," 27, B 1:610, J V:360, sec. 4.6.
[152]"Sermon on the Mount," 27, B 1:610–11, J V:360, sec. 4.7.

Your fasting ends in quarreling and strife,
    and in striking each other with wicked fists.
You cannot fast as you do today
    and expect your voice to be heard on high.
Is this the kind of fast I have chosen,
    only a day for people to humble themselves?
Is it only for bowing one's head like a reed
    and for lying in sackcloth and ashes?
Is that what you call a fast,
    a day acceptable to the LORD?

"Is not this the kind of fasting I have chosen:
to loose the chains of injustice
    and untie the cords of the yoke,
to set the oppressed free
    and break every yoke?
Is it not to share your food with the hungry
    and to provide the poor wanderer with shelter —
when you see the naked, to clothe them,
    and not to turn away from your own flesh and blood?
Then your light will break forth like the dawn,
    and your healing will quickly appear;
then your righteousness will go before you,
    and the glory of the LORD will be your rear guard.
Then you will call, and the LORD will answer;
    you will cry for help, and he will say: Here am I.

"If you do away with the yoke of oppression,
    with the pointing finger and malicious talk,
and if you spend yourselves in behalf of the hungry
    and satisfy the needs of the oppressed,
then your light will rise in the darkness,
    and your night will become like the noonday."[153]

D. Enlightening the Eyes

1. Seeing the Light

The text of Wesley's eighth discourse on the Sermon on the Mount is Matthew 6:19 – 23 on treasures in heaven:

"Do not store up for yourselves treasures on earth, where moths and vermin destroy, and where thieves break in and steal. But store up for yourselves treasures in heaven, where moths and vermin do not destroy, and where thieves do not break in and steal. For where your treasure is, there your heart will be also.

"The eye is the lamp of the body. If your eyes are healthy, your whole body

---

[153]Isa. 58:3 – 10 NIV; "Sermon on the Mount," 27, B 1:610 – 11, J V:360, sec. 4.7.

will be full of light. But if your eyes are unhealthy, your whole body will be full of darkness. If then the light within you is darkness, how great is that darkness!" [Matt. 6:19–23 NIV, Homily #28, "Upon Our Lord's Sermon on the Mount: Discourse 8," B 1:611–32, J V:361–77 (1748)]

a. The Light of the Body Is the Eye

Jesus chose a simple metaphor to instruct the multitude on the relation of a pure intention and a fitting action. It is the relation of the eye to light. The text: "The eye is the lamp of the body."[154] By this means the Lord explained and enlarged upon the relation of inward intention and outward action. Our alms and devotions are an acceptable service when they proceed from a pure intention.[155]

Pure religion springs from a pure and holy intent that produces outward actions fitting to life with God.[156] The same purity of intention that makes our alms and devotions acceptable applies also to our employment and use of our income and resources. "If a man pursues his business that he may raise himself to a state of honor and riches in the world, he is no longer serving God in his employment, and has no more title to a reward from God than he who gives alms that he may be seen, or prays that he may be heard of men."[157]

b. The Healthy Eye Receives the Light

An eye is healthy if it is able to see light. Jesus taught: "If your eyes are healthy, your whole body will be full of light."[158] The version Wesley used in worship says, "If therefore thine eye be single, thy whole body shall be full of light."[159] "Single" here means whole, or healthy.

The key premise: "The eye is the intention: what the eye is to the body, the intention is to the soul." The bodily eye guides the body. The eye of the soul guides the soul.[160] "This eye of the soul is then said to be single when it looks at one thing only." This is purity of heart, to will one thing. When we have no other design but to "know God, and Jesus Christ whom he hath sent," we have a single eye toward the good with no blurred vision.[161] We have a healthy eye when we "know him with suitable affections, loving him as he hath loved us; to please God in all things; to serve God (as we love him) with all our heart and mind and soul and strength; and to enjoy God in all and above all things, in time and in eternity."[162]

"If your eyes are unhealthy, your whole body will be full of darkness."[163] With

---

154 Matt. 6:22 NIV.
155 "Sermon on the Mount," 28, B 1:612–13, J V:361–62, sec. 1.
156 Ibid.
157 Ibid.
158 Matt. 6:22; "Sermon on the Mount," 28, B 1:613, J V:362, sec. 2.
159 Matt. 6:22.
160 "Sermon on the Mount," 28, B 1:613, J V:362, sec. 2.
161 Ibid.
162 Ibid.
163 Matt. 6:23 NIV.

healthy eyes of the soul, everything you are and all you do, your desires, tempers, affections, thoughts, words, and actions will be full of light, illumined by right recognition of reality.

c. Enlightening the Eyes of Understanding Regarding the Deep Things of God

Our eyes see in the light of the Giver of light. "He which of old commanded light to shine out of darkness, shall shine in thy heart."[164] So shall he "enlighten the eyes of thy understanding with the knowledge of the glory of God."[165] It is God's Spirit who reveals to you "the deep things of God."[166]

The psalmist sang of God: "For with you is the fountain of life; in your light we see light."[167] The light enables us to see. If we lose track of this light shining in our hearts, we are soon "tossed to and fro, and know not what to do, or which is the path wherein we should go. But when we desire and seek nothing but God, clouds and doubts vanish away."[168] We who were once in darkness have seen a great light, making plain the way.[169]

d. The Surpassing Pleasure of Walking in the Holy Light

The light is holy and pleasurable to see. The light of God's holy love makes us holier and more loving. We are pleased to behold God's light shining through us.

When the "fountain of all holiness" is "continually filling us with his own likeness, with justice, mercy, and truth," then our moral life is made beautiful. Our souls are being "renewed day by day after the image of him that created [us]."[170] This is confirmed daily by the experience of those saved by grace through faith. "It is by faith that the eye of the mind is opened to see the light of the glorious love of God. And as long as it is steadily fixed thereon, on God in Christ, reconciling the world unto himself, we are more and more filled with the love of God and man, with meekness, gentleness, long-suffering; with all the fruits of holiness."[171] Those saved by grace "walk in the light as God is in the light, rejoicing evermore, praying without ceasing, and in everything giving thanks."[172]

Seeing all things in this light gives pleasure to the eye. When the eye is healthy, "Light is sweet, and it pleases the eyes to see" whatever is reflected by the sun.[173] Then the whole body is filled with light.[174]

---

[164]Cf. 2 Cor. 4:6.
[165]"Sermon on the Mount," 28, B 1:613–14, J V:362–63, sec. 3.
[166]Ibid.
[167]Ps. 36:9 NIV.
[168]"Sermon on the Mount," 28, B 1:613–14, J V:362–63, sec. 3.
[169]Ibid.
[170]"Sermon on the Mount," 28, B 1:614, J V:363, sec. 4.
[171]Ibid.
[172]"Sermon on the Mount," 28, B 1:615, J V:363, sec. 5.
[173]Eccl. 11:7 NIV.
[174]See Matt. 6:22 NIV.

e. If the Light within You Is Darkness

But if the eye is unhealthy, the whole body is full of darkness.[175] The opposite is blindness. Either the eye is able to see or not able to see. If unable to see, what good is the eye? "If the eye be not single, then it is evil. If the intention in whatever we do be not singly to God, if we seek anything else,"[176] then we walk in darkness, since the veil still remains in our hearts.[177] To be pure in heart is to seek nothing else in seeking God.

"If then the light within you is darkness, how great is that darkness!"[178] If the eye of understanding has been corrupted, then your desires, tempers, and affections will all be unserviceable. The behavioral outcome is being "idle, unprofitable, corrupt, grievous to the Holy Spirit of God."[179] "There is no peace, no settled, solid peace, for them that know not God."[180]

If the intention that ought to enlighten the whole soul and fill it with knowledge, and love, and peace is faulty, it may "cover the soul with darkness instead of light, with ignorance and error, with sin and misery." So "O how great is that darkness!... It is the essential night which reigns in the lowest deep, in the land of the shadow of death!"[181]

E. Treasures on Earth and in Heaven

1. Storing Up Treasures on Earth

a. Comparing Native American Indian and European Models of Storing Up Treasures on Earth

Wesley's text comes straight from the Sermon on the Mount. It is clear, "Do not store up for yourselves treasures on earth."[182] Do not lay up for yourselves passing, temporal, material goods in a place "where moth and rust doth corrupt, and where thieves break through and steal."[183] If you do, it is plain that your eye is not healthy and not singly fixed on God.

Wesley here inserts a surprising comparison. The Native American Indian population to whom Wesley had been sent to Georgia in 1736 to serve, mostly, Chickasaw, Choctaw, Creek, and Yamacraw Indians, became for Wesley a model for living humbly. They did not seek anything "more than plain food to eat and plain raiment to put on. And he seeks this only from day to day. He reserves, he lays up nothing, unless it be as much corn at one season of the year as he will need before that season returns."[184] They do not lay up for themselves treasures on earth, "no

---

175Cf. Matt. 6:23.
176"Sermon on the Mount," 28, B 1:615, J V:364, sec. 6.
177"Sermon on the Mount," 28, B 1:615–16, J V:364, sec. 7.
178Matt. 6:23 NIV.
179"Sermon on the Mount," 28, B 1:615–16, J V:364, sec. 7.
180"Sermon on the Mount," 28, B 1:616, J V:364–65, sec. 8.
181Ibid.
182Matt. 6:19 NIV.
183"Sermon on the Mount," 28, B 1:616–18, J V:365–66, sec. 9; Matt. 6:19.
184"Sermon on the Mount," 28, B 1:616–18, J V:365–66, sec. 9.

stores of purple or fine linen, of gold or silver."[185] When it comes to having a single eye toward the Spirit, "the heathens of Africa or America" are commendable when compared to many who are called "Christians."[186]

On the other hand, Europeans "do not scruple the 'laying up treasures upon earth,' but the laying them up by dishonesty. From their youth up it never entered into their thoughts," to not store up treasures on earth. "They were bred up by their Christian parents, masters, and friends, without any instruction at all concerning it; unless it were this — to break [the command to not store up treasures on earth] as soon and as much as they could, and to continue breaking it to their lives' end."[187] "They have read or heard these words a hundred times, and yet never suspect that they are themselves condemned thereby, any more than by those which forbid parents to offer up their sons or daughters unto Moloch."[188]

"It is not easy to say, when we compare the bulk of the nations in Europe with those in America, whether the superiority lies on the one side or the other. At least the American has not much the advantage." Yet "in what Christian city do you find one man of five hundred who makes the least scruple of laying up just as much treasure as he can?"[189]

b. Permitted Forms of Saving and Providing

What does the maxim on storing up treasures reasonably permit? We are not absolutely forbidden to store up anything at all. To store up treasures on earth does not imply that there is no place for savings or planning for a family's future. To interpret what the command means, it is necessary to show what it does not mean.

First, we are not forbidden altogether to save for the future. Wesley, in "The Use of Money," calls us to "save all we can." We must therefore explore what it means justly or unjustly to save for future contingencies.[190]

Second, we are taught of God to "owe no man any thing."[191] If so, we must be prepared to pay debts. "We ought therefore to use all diligence in our calling, in order to owe no man anything, this being no other than a plain law of common justice."[192]

Third, we are not forbidden to provide "for ourselves such things as are needful for the body; a sufficiency of plain, wholesome food to eat, and clean raiment to put on. Yea, it is our duty, so far as God puts it into our power, to provide these things" in order to "eat our own bread," and not be burdensome to anyone.[193]

Fourth, we are not forbidden to provide for our children and for those of our own household. Every man ought to provide the plain necessaries of life both for

---

[185]Ibid.
[186]Ibid.
[187]Ibid.
[188]"Sermon on the Mount," 28, B 1:618, J V:366, sec. 10.
[189]"Sermon on the Mount," 28, B 1:616–18, J V:365–66, sec. 9.
[190]"Sermon on the Mount," 28, B 1:618–19, J V:366–67, sec. 11.
[191]Rom. 13:8.
[192]"Sermon on the Mount," 28, B 1:618–19, J V:366–67, sec. 11.
[193]Ibid.

his own wife and children, and to lift them "into a capacity of providing these for themselves when he is gone hence and is no more seen."[194] If we become slothful dependents willing to take but not to give, we do an injustice both to our own free self-esteem and our neighbor upon whose charity we depend. If any man does not provide for his own children, as well as for the widows of his own house, Paul says he has "denied the faith, and is worse than an infidel."[195] To provide another with a means of idleness is no help to his soul.

Fifth, we are not forbidden to lay up from time to time what is needful for the carrying on of our worldly business in such a measure as to owe no man anything and to procure for ourselves the necessaries of life, and to furnish those of our own house with the means of procuring necessities when we are gone to God.[196] This applies to plain necessaries, "not delicacies, not superfluities."[197]

c. What the Maxim Forbids

Having considered what we are reasonably permitted to do in laying aside worldly resources, according to Scripture, we now consider what we are indeed forbidden to do by Jesus' teaching on the mount.

This much is clear: We are forbidden to procure more of this world's goods than will answer to just purposes and the keeping of our hearts pure from corruption. We live in "open habitual denial" of accountability to the Lord, who gives us sufficient resources if we seek "a still larger portion on earth."[198]

How did Wesley define *sufficient*? If you are not indebted to any man, and have food and raiment for yourself and your household, together with a sufficiency to carry on your worldly business so far as answers these reasonable purposes, you may in good conscience put in store worldly goods, but only within these parameters.[199]

2. Storing Treasure in Heaven

How long will you keep loading yourself up with heavy burdens of worldly goods? When will you wake up and become "persuaded to choose the better part — that which cannot be taken away from you"?[200] When will you seek only to "lay up … treasures in heaven"?[201] Do not lose all your time and spend all your strength for that which is passing. Do not try to gain all while you lose your own soul. "You are a living man but a dead Christian."[202] "For where your treasure is, there your heart will be also."[203]

---

[194]Ibid.
[195]1 Tim. 5:8; "Sermon on the Mount," 28, B 1:618 – 19, J V:366 – 67, sec. 11.
[196]"Sermon on the Mount," 28, B 1:618 – 19, J V:366 – 67, sec. 11.
[197]Ibid.
[198]"Sermon on the Mount," 28, B 1:619 – 20, J V:367 – 68, sec. 12.
[199]Ibid.
[200]"Sermon on the Mount," 28, B 1:620, J V:368, sec. 13.
[201]Matt. 6:20.
[202]"Sermon on the Mount," 28, B 1:620, J V:368, sec. 13.
[203]Matt. 6:21 NIV.

When your heart is sunk into the dust, your soul cleaves to the ground. "Your affections are set, not on things above, but on things of the earth; on poor husks that may poison, but cannot satisfy an everlasting spirit made for God.... You have thrown away the treasure in heaven."[204]

a. Remember How Hard It Is to Enter Heaven with Riches

Jesus said, "How hardly shall they that have riches enter into the kingdom of God!"[205] When questioned, Jesus stated in stronger terms: "It is easier for a camel to go through the eye of a needle, than for a rich man to enter into the kingdom of God."[206] "How hard for them not to think themselves better than the poor, base, uneducated herd of men! How hard not to seek happiness in their riches, or in things dependent upon them; in gratifying the desire of the flesh, the desire of the eye, or the pride of life!"[207]

Only on the assumption that "with God all things are possible" can we imagine how the rich can gain heaven! The rich fall more easily into a trap of "many foolish and hurtful lusts."[208] "Riches, dangerous as they are, do not always 'drown men in destruction and perdition,' but the desire of riches does.... These are they that sell him who bought them with his blood."[209]

Who but Christians saved by faith are prepared to confront the rich man? The rich will not be confronted by those who court their favor. But if they meet someone who has "overcome the world, who desires nothing but God, and fears none but him that is able to destroy both body and soul in hell," that man is able to speak candidly and spare nothing of the truth.[210]

b. What Excess Wealth Requires of the Soul

Jesus said to the rich young ruler, "Sell all that thou hast."[211] Note that Jesus was not thereby laying down a general rule for every man; this drastic measure was necessary for one so preoccupied with riches. It was needful in this case because the rich man had asked, "What must I do to be saved." Where the idolatry of wealth prevails, so must the radical claim of God prevail more.[212]

Weigh yourselves on a different scale. Estimate yourself only by the measures of faith and love that God has given you. The lowest beggar laid at the gate full of sores may be better off than a rich man in God's eyes.[213] Do not trust in riches either for help or happiness. They can all be swept away in this life. They will get

---

[204]"Sermon on the Mount," 28, B 1:620, J V:368, sec. 13.
[205]Mark 10:23.
[206]Mark 10:25.
[207]"Sermon on the Mount," 28, B 1:620–21, J V:368–69, sec. 14.
[208]"Sermon on the Mount," 28, B 1:621, J V:369, sec. 15.
[209]Ibid.
[210]"Sermon on the Mount," 28, B 1:622, J V:369–70, sec. 16.
[211]Luke 18:22.
[212]Ibid.
[213]"Sermon on the Mount," 28, B 1:622–23, J V:370, sec. 17.

you nowhere in eternity.[214] In grave illness they are of no avail.[215] With God wealth is "as dung and dross."[216]

Perhaps your day is far spent, when "the noon of life is past and the evening shadows begin to rest upon you. You feel in yourself sure approaching decay."[217] What help is there in riches? It was to a rich man with full barns that these words were spoken: "This night thy soul shall be required of thee."[218] "Naked came you into this world; naked must you return."[219] "No man that is to die could possibly trust for help in uncertain riches."[220] Only in trusting the living God will you "be safe under the shadow of the Almighty."[221]

The Lord has taught the faithful to say:

For the perishable must clothe itself with the imperishable, and the mortal with immortality. When the perishable has been clothed with the imperishable, and the mortal with immortality, then the saying that is written will come true: "Death has been swallowed up in victory."

"Where, O death, is your victory?
Where, O death, is your sting?"

The sting of death is sin, and the power of sin is the law. But thanks be to God! He gives us the victory through our Lord Jesus Christ.[222]

So "do not store up for yourselves treasures on earth."[223]

c. The Lord's Charge to Those with Excess Riches

If someone should choose to amuse himself with hoarding up riches rather than "entitle himself to an eternal reward by giving them to those that wanted eyes and hands, might we not justly reckon him mad.... Now money has very much the nature of eyes and feet. If therefore we lock it up in chests, while the poor and distressed want it for their necessary uses," we are undeniably cruel.[224] In "the general tenor of their lives, they are not only robbing God continually, embezzling and wasting their Lord's goods, and by that very means corrupting their own souls; but also robbing the poor, the hungry, the naked, wronging the widow and the fatherless, and making themselves accountable for all the want, affliction, and distress which they may but do not remove."[225]

[214]"Sermon on the Mount," 28, B 1:623, J V:370–71, sec. 18.
[215]Ibid.
[216]"Sermon on the Mount," 28, B 1:622–23, J V:370, sec. 17.
[217]"Sermon on the Mount," 28, B 1:624, J V:371, sec. 19.
[218]Luke 12:20.
[219]"Sermon on the Mount," 28, B 1:624, J V:371, sec. 19; cf. Job 1:21.
[220]"Sermon on the Mount," 28, B 1:624, J V:371, sec. 19.
[221]"Sermon on the Mount," 28, B 1:625–26, J V:372–73, sec. 21.
[222]1 Cor. 15:53–57 NIV; "Sermon on the Mount," 28, B 1:625–26, J V:372–73, sec. 21.
[223]Matt. 6:19 NIV. At this point, Wesley inserted an extensive quote from William Law, *A Serious Call to the Devout and Holy Life* (1729), *Works* 4:50–51, www.ccel.org/ccel/law/serious, which is best read in connection with two other Wesley homilies: "The Use of Money" and "On Riches."
[224]"Sermon on the Mount," 28, B 1:628, J V:375, sec. 24.
[225]"Sermon on the Mount," 28, B 1:628–29, J V:375, sec. 25.

Empty your pockets of whatever you can spare "upon better security than this world can afford." "Whoever is kind to the poor lends to the LORD, and he will reward them for what they have done."[226] Give to the poor with a single eye, with an upright heart, and write, "So much given to God."[227] Jesus said, for "inasmuch as ye have done it unto one of the least of these my brethren, ye have done it unto me."[228] The "faithful and wise steward" employed what he was given "wholly to those wise and reasonable purposes for which his Lord has lodged it in his hands."[229]

The Lord charges you to " 'be rich in good works.'... 'Freely ye have received; freely give' so as to lay up no treasure but in heaven."[230] "Disperse abroad, give to the poor: deal your bread to the hungry. Cover the naked with a garment, entertain the stranger, carry or send relief to them that are in prison. Heal the sick; not by miracle, but through the blessing of God upon your seasonable [timely] support. Let the blessing of him that was ready to perish through pining want come upon thee.... Defend the oppressed, plead the cause of the fatherless, and make the widow's heart sing for joy."[231]

F. The Futile Attempt to Serve Both God and Mammon

1. Guidance for Those Torn by Conflicting Idolatries

The text of Wesley's ninth discourse on the Sermon on the Mount is Matthew 6:24–34 on God, mammon, and anxiety. Ponder this text carefully to grasp Wesley's purpose:

"No one can serve two masters. Either you will hate the one and love the other, or you will be devoted to the one and despise the other. You cannot serve both God and money.

"Therefore I tell you, do not worry about your life, what you will eat or drink; or about your body, what you will wear. Is not life more than food, and the body more than clothes? Look at the birds of the air; they do not sow or reap or store away in barns, and yet your heavenly Father feeds them. Are you not much more valuable than they? Can any one of you by worrying add a single hour to your life?

"And why do you worry about clothes? See how the flowers of the field grow. They do not labor or spin. Yet I tell you that not even Solomon in all his splendor was dressed like one of these. If that is how God clothes the grass of the field, which is here today and tomorrow is thrown into the fire, will he not much more clothe you — you of little faith? So do not worry, saying, 'What shall we eat?' or 'What shall we drink?' or 'What shall we wear?' For the pagans run after all these things, and your heavenly Father knows that you need them. But seek first his

---

[226]Prov. 19:17 NIV; "Sermon on the Mount," 28, B 1:629, J V:375–76, sec. 26.
[227]"Sermon on the Mount," 28, B 1:629, J V:375–76, sec. 26.
[228]Matt. 25:40.
[229]"Sermon on the Mount," 28, B 1:629, J V:375–76, sec. 26.
[230]"Sermon on the Mount," 28, B 1:630, J V:376–77, sec. 27.
[231]Ibid.

kingdom and his righteousness, and all these things will be given to you as well. Therefore do not worry about tomorrow, for tomorrow will worry about itself. Each day has enough trouble of its own." [Matt. 6:24 – 34 NIV; Homily #29, "Upon Our Lord's Sermon on the Mount: Discourse 9," B 1:632 – 49, J V:379 – 93 (1748)]

a. Why the Attempt to Worship Both the One God and the Many Idols Won't Work

The practice of most modern Christians resembles that of the ancient Israelites in one respect: "They perform an outward service to God, but also 'serve their own gods.'"[232] "They worshiped the LORD, but they also served their own gods in accordance with the customs of the nations from which they had been brought."[233] "They bowed down to all the starry hosts, and they worshiped Baal. They sacrificed their sons and daughters in the fire. They practiced divination and sought omens and sold themselves to do evil in the eyes of the LORD, arousing his anger."[234] Meanwhile they had not "laid aside the outward form of worshipping [the Lord].... This is the manner both of 'their children and their children's children; as did their fathers, so do they unto this day.'"[235]

Such people both in ancient and modern times try to serve two masters. The command of the Lord of Israel was "Thou shalt have no other gods before me."[236] They were trying vainly to have it both ways — to worship God and mammon.[237]

b. The Forced Choice between Money and God

The attempt to love two masters is foolish and vain. You may try it but without durable satisfaction. The double-minded may waver for a while between love and hate: "He will naturally hold to him whom he loves. He will so cleave to him, as to perform to him a willing, faithful, and diligent service. And, in the meantime, he will so far at least despise the master he hates as to have little regard to his commands, and to obey them, if at all, in a slight and careless manner."[238] No matter what advocates of moral laxity might surmise, this double-mindedness does not lead to a happy life. It inevitably creates a divided self.

"Ye cannot serve God and mammon."[239] "No one can serve two masters. Either you will hate the one and love the other, or you will be devoted to the one and despise the other."[240] Mammon was the name of one of the heathen gods, who was presumed to preside over riches. The clear meaning is: "You cannot serve both God and money."[241]

---

[232]"Sermon on the Mount," 29, B 1:633, J V:379, sec. 1; cf. 2 Kings 17:27 – 41.
[233]2 Kings 17:33 NIV.
[234]2 Kings 17:16 – 17 NIV; "Sermon on the Mount," 29, B 1:633, J V:379, sec. 1.
[235]"Sermon on the Mount," 29, B 1:633, J V:379, sec. 1.
[236]Ex. 20:3.
[237]"Sermon on the Mount," 29, B 1:633 – 34, J V:379 – 80, sec. 2.
[238]"Sermon on the Mount," 29, B 1:634, J V:380, sec. 3.
[239]Matt. 6:24.
[240]Matt. 6:24 NIV.
[241]Ibid.

2. Serving God

a. Serving God as Believing, Imitating, Loving, and Obeying God Alone

What does it mean to believe? "To believe in God implies to trust in him as our strength, without whom we can do nothing, who every moment endues us with power from on high, without which it is impossible to please him. It implies to trust in God as our happiness; as the center of spirits; the only rest of our souls; the only good who is adequate to all our capacities and sufficient to satisfy all the desires he hath given us."[242]

The reason why it is futile to try to serve both God and mammon is that "we cannot serve God unless we believe in him. This is the only true foundation of serving him." The most basic affirmation of Christianity is that we can believe and trust in God and therefore serve him since we know that God has "reconciled the world to himself through Christ Jesus."[243] To believe is "the first thing we are to understand by serving God."[244]

The second thing we are to understand by serving God is to love him. Believing and loving God are intrinsically interconnected. To love God is "to desire God alone for his own sake; and nothing else, but with reference to him."[245]

"A third thing we are to understand by serving God is to resemble or imitate him."[246] The best service of God is to become as much like God as is possible. "We here speak of imitating or resembling him in the spirit of our minds.... 'God is a Spirit,' and they that imitate or resemble him must do it 'in spirit and in truth.' "[247] If God is love, then "they who resemble him in the spirit of their minds are transformed into the same image. They are merciful even as he is merciful. Their soul is all love."[248]

By serving God, if we know who he truly is, we obey his commands, as a child to a father. We do what he asks and avoid what he forbids.[249] Only by obedience in love do we resemble him and serve him. The choice is between worshiping God and worshiping creatures.

b. Serving Mammon Implies Believing, Imitating, Loving, and Obeying That Which Is Passing Away

To serve mammon implies, first, "trusting in riches, in money," or the things it can purchase, "by which we look to be comforted in or delivered out of trouble."[250]

More commonly it implies "trusting in the world for happiness" and supposing

---

[242]"Sermon on the Mount," 29, B 1:634–35, J V:380–81, sec. 4.

[243]Ibid.; cf. 2 Cor. 5:19.

[244]"Sermon on the Mount," 29, B 1:635, J V:381, sec. 5.

[245]Ibid.

[246]"Sermon on the Mount," 29, B 1:635–36, J V:381, sec. 6.

[247]Ibid.

[248]Ibid.

[249]"Sermon on the Mount," 29, B 1:636, J V:381–82, sec. 7.

[250]"Sermon on the Mount," 29, B 1:636–37, J V:382, sec. 8.

that comfort consists in the abundance of things possessed.[251] It means "gaining a larger measure of temporal things without any reference to things eternal."[252] That is the service of mammon.

Further, to serve mammon is to love creatures above the Creator. Serving mammon implies "loving the world; desiring it for its own sake; the placing our joy in the things thereof, and setting our hearts upon them."[253] It means to rest "with the whole weight of our souls upon the staff of this broken reed, although daily experience shows it cannot support but will only 'enter into our hand and pierce it.' "[254]

Third, to serve mammon means "to resemble, to be conformed to the world ... to have desires, tempers, affections, suitable to those of the world ... to be self-willed, inordinate lovers of ourselves."[255]

Finally, those who trust in mammon and love and resemble mammon are in service to mammon. To serve mammon means "to obey the world by outwardly conforming to its maxims and customs; to walk as other men walk, in the common road, in the broad, smooth, beaten path; to be in the fashion; to follow a multitude; to do like the rest of our neighbors ... to aim at our own ease and pleasure."[256]

c. Why You Cannot Serve Both God and Mammon

A sure way to unhappiness is to try to serve both God and mammon. It is clear that if we serve mammon, we cannot be serving God. "To trim [navigate] between God and the world is the sure way to be disappointed in both."[257] There is no rest in either when one tries to serve both.[258]

One who tries to serve two gods "has religion enough to make him miserable but not enough to make him happy." His religion will not let him enjoy the world, and the world will not let him enjoy God.[259] By vacillating between both, he has peace neither with God or the world.

He is always going "one step forward and another backward. He is continually building up with one hand and pulling down with the other. He loves sin, and he hates it: He is always seeking, and yet always fleeing from, God. He would, and he would not. He is not the same man for one day; no, not for an hour together. He is a motley mixture of all sorts of contrarieties, a heap of contradictions jumbled in one." Be consistent with yourself. Never think of serving either at all, unless it be with your whole heart.[260] Whenever you serve the one, "you necessarily renounce the other."[261]

---

[251]Ibid.
[252]Ibid.
[253]"Sermon on the Mount," 29, B 1:637, J V:382, sec. 9.
[254]Ibid.
[255]"Sermon on the Mount," 29, B 1:637, J V:382, sec. 10.
[256]"Sermon on the Mount," 29, B 1:637, J V:382–83, sec. 11.
[257]"Sermon on the Mount," 29, B 1:637, J V:383, sec. 12.
[258]Ibid.
[259]Ibid.
[260]"Sermon on the Mount," 29, B 1:638, J V:383, sec. 13.
[261]"Sermon on the Mount," 29, B 1:638–39, J V:383–84, sec. 14.

d. A Quiet Self-Examination on Serving God or Mammon

Wesley calls for a realistic self-examination in which each one asks about trusting, loving, emulating, and obeying.

First ask: In whom do you trust — God or mammon? Do you trust in God as your strength, your help, your shield, and your happiness? If so, you cannot trust in riches.[262]

Then ask yourself: Whom do you love? "Do you love God? Do you seek and find happiness in him? Then you cannot love the world, neither the things of the world. You are crucified to the world, and the world crucified to you."[263]

Third, ask yourself honestly: "Are you being transformed by the renewal of your mind into the image of him that created you? Then you cannot be conformed to the present world. Have you renounced all its affections?"[264] "Do you resemble God? Are you merciful as your Father is merciful?" Or "Are you conformed to the world?... Then you are not renewed in the spirit of your mind."[265]

Finally ask: "Do you obey God? Are you zealous to do his will?... Then it is impossible you should obey mammon.... Do you please yourself? Then you cannot be a servant of God."[266]

By asking yourself these questions truthfully, it is evident whether you are serving God or mammon. Therefore, "thou shalt worship the Lord thy God, and him only shalt thou serve."[267]

G. Do Not Worry

1. Proper and Balanced Caring

What follows from this, for those who trust and love and emulate God and share in God's life, is freedom from worry. It is to care appropriately and proportionally for the world's goods in relation to the Creator of the world.

Jesus said, "Therefore I tell you, do not worry about your life, what you will eat or drink; or about your body, what you will wear. Is not life more than food, and the body more than clothes?" The King James Version has, "Take no thought for your life, what ye shall eat, or what ye shall drink; nor yet for your body, what ye shall put on."[268]

Jesus is not advising us here to care nothing about temporal values at all, but to treat them in relation to the eternal. The faithful are still called to take care of others for whom we are responsible. He is not encouraging us to be idle, slothful, or dilatory. That would be contrary to the whole spirit and genius of his religion.[269]

---

[262]Ibid.
[263]Ibid.
[264]Ibid.
[265]Ibid.
[266]Ibid.
[267]Luke 4:8.
[268]Matt. 6:25.
[269]"Sermon on the Mount," 29, B 1:639 – 40, J V:385, sec. 16.

The believing community knows "that there is one kind of thought and care with which God is well pleased,"[270] as distinguished from another kind of anxious care for the world.

Taking thought for what you eat, drink, and wear is not negligible to the Christian life when properly placed within the realm of trusting, loving, following, and obeying God. For "it is the will of God that every man should labor to eat his own bread; yea, and that every man should provide for his own, for them of his own household," and that we should "owe no man anything, but provide things honest in the sight of all men."[271] Caring for a family takes forethought, planning, and imagination, and often hard work for the good of the family. Obviously, "this care, to provide for ourselves and our household, this thought how to render to all their dues, our blessed Lord does not condemn."[272]

It is good and acceptable to God that we should take care for whatever it is that we are responsible, planning for its accomplishment, and executing plans. We should prepare all things in advance for effectively carrying out these responsibilities.[273] Wesley distinguishes this sort of reasonable planning from the anxious life.

2. Anxious Care Distinguished from Balanced and Proportional Care

What Jesus warns against is "the anxious, uneasy care; the care that hath torment; all such care as does hurt, either to the soul or body." It drinks up our energy. It "anticipates all the misery it fears and comes to torment us before the time." It is an anxiety that "poisons the blessings of today, by fear of what may be tomorrow." Such anticipation of potential discomfort can become an obsession, "which cannot enjoy the present plenty through apprehensions of future want."[274] Wesley presented this description of habituated anxiety long before modern psychology described it.

Obsessive anxiety, this persistent anxious form of care "is not only a sore disease, a grievous sickness of soul, but also a heinous offense against God, a sin of the deepest dye,"[275] because it despairs over whether God has rightly ordered the world. It has a theological basis in idolatry. It is deficient in trusting providence. It implies that God is lacking "either in wisdom, if he does not know what things we stand in need of; or in goodness, if he does not provide those things for all who put their trust in him."[276]

"This is a plain, sure rule: uneasy care is unlawful care. With a single eye to God,

[270]Ibid.
[271]Ibid.
[272]Ibid.
[273]Ibid.
[274]"Sermon on the Mount," 29, B 1:640–41, J V:385–86, sec. 17.
[275]Ibid.
[276]Ibid.

do all that in you lies to provide things honest in the sight of all men. And then give up all into better hands; leave the whole event to God."[277]

3. Keeping the Value of Food and Clothing in Due Proportion

Jesus says to the faithful: "'Take no thought' of this kind, no uneasy thought, no undue care over what you will eat or drink or wear." Life is more than food and clothing. If God gave you a body, doesn't it make sense that he would give you the means of clothing yourself, the ability to put a shirt on your back? Why make so much out of being slightly or partially deprived of worldly goods?[278]

"Look at the birds of the air; they do not sow or reap or store away in barns."[279] They lack nothing because your heavenly Father feeds them. "Are you not much more valuable than they?"[280] Surely God has made you capable of caring for yourself if you are capable of having a life with God. If God finds a way to care for the birds, wouldn't he find a way to care for you by making you capable of caring for yourself and others?

"Can any one of you by worrying add a single hour to your life?"[281] How does it make it better if you relate to your future with crippling anxiety, trying to anticipate every contingency instead of just receiving what God gives now?[282]

4. Avoid Excessive Anxiety about Covering the Body

The covering we worry over includes clothing and housing. Both are encompassed in the idea of covering. "And why do you worry about clothes?"[283] Have you not yet seen a daily demonstration wherever you turn your eyes, the lives of plants are being cared for, within the limits of their finitude? Does the fact that finite creatures die negate the good that they receive while alive?

"Consider the lilies of the field, how they grow; they toil not, neither do they spin. And yet I say unto you, that even Solomon in all his glory was not arrayed like one of these."[284] The plants just take what God gives every day from sun and rain. They do not fret about what might happen tomorrow. They draw in the heat of the sun and the moisture of the rain into their systems without thought of the morrow. The plants were made to endure for a short time in finite space. You are different. You were made to endure for eternity. Where did you get the idea that you are of less value than grass?[285]

"If God so clothe the grass of the field, which to day is, and to morrow is cast

---

[277]Ibid.
[278]"Sermon on the Mount," 29, B 1:641, J V:386 – 87, sec. 18.
[279]Matt. 6:26 NIV.
[280]Ibid.
[281]Matt. 6:27 NIV.
[282]"Sermon on the Mount," 29, B 1:641, J V:386 – 87, sec. 18.
[283]Matt. 6:28 NIV.
[284]Matt. 6:28 – 29.
[285]"Sermon on the Mount," 29, B 1:641, J V:386 – 87, sec. 18.

into the oven [is cut down, burned up, and seen no more] shall he not much more clothe you, O ye of little faith?"[286] Compare your eternal value with the value of finite plants, as wonderful as they are. You have been created with a soul "to endure for ever and ever, to be pictures of his own eternity! Ye are indeed of little faith; otherwise ye could not doubt of his love and care; no, not for a moment."[287]

Yet in our fallen condition we become intensely fixated on securing food, clothing, and shelter. This is the kind of anxiety that those without a relationship with the eternally merciful God have. The world runs after these things. Sure you have need of food and clothing, but already "your heavenly Father knows that you need them."[288] The plants do not have imagination and reason, but you are created to have rational sense to care for you and yours. God has already provided you with the means of having or creating what you need. Don't conform to the world's anxiety and despair. You are God's own.[289]

[286] Matt. 6:30.
[287] "Sermon on the Mount," 29, B 1:641, J V:386–87, sec. 18.
[288] Matt. 6:32 NIV.
[289] "Sermon on the Mount," 29, B 1:642, J V:387, sec. 19.

CHAPTER 9

Entering the Kingdom

A. Seek First His Kingdom

"Seek first his kingdom and his righteousness, and all these things will be given to you as well."[1] This is the sure and only way to be "constantly supplied."[2]

Seeking God first means that "before ye give place to any other thought or care, let it be your concern that the God and Father of our Lord Jesus Christ (who 'gave his only begotten Son,' to the end that, believing in him, 'ye might not perish, but have everlasting life') may reign in your heart, may manifest himself in your soul, and dwell and rule there; that he may 'cast down every high thing which exalteth itself against the knowledge of God, and bring into captivity every thought to the obedience of Christ.'"[3]

Before you seek any worldly value, seek the one who created all worldly values. He redeemed you in order that you might be free to believe and trust and love him as who he is. "Let him reign without a rival. Let him possess all your heart, and rule alone. Let him be your one desire, your joy, your love."[4] With eternity secure, everything in time and space will fall into its proper place.

1. Seek the Realm of God's Righteousness First

"Righteousness is the fruit of God's reigning in the heart. And what is righteousness, but love — the love of God and of all mankind, flowing from faith in Jesus Christ, and producing humbleness of mind, meekness, gentleness, longsuffering, patience, deadness to the world; and every right disposition of heart, toward God and toward man."[5] The righteousness you are seeking is God's "own free gift to us, for the sake of Jesus Christ the righteous, through whom alone it is purchased for us. And it is his work; it is he alone that worketh it in us, by the inspiration of the Holy Spirit."[6] In doing so you are not seeking a righteousness gained by your own

[1] Matt. 6:33 NIV.
[2] "Sermon on the Mount," 29, B 1:642, J V:387, sec. 19.
[3] "Sermon on the Mount," 29, B 1:642–43, J V:387, sec. 20; cf. John 3:16.
[4] Ibid.
[5] Ibid.
[6] Ibid.

merit under the law.[7] The righteousness you seek is already given in the good news of Jesus, as preached by Paul, who was praying for Israel as he wrote: "Brothers and sisters, my heart's desire and prayer to God for the Israelites is that they may be saved. For I can testify about them that they are zealous for God, but their zeal is not based on knowledge. Since they did not know the righteousness of God and sought to establish their own, they did not submit to God's righteousness. Christ is the culmination of the law so that there may be righteousness for everyone who believes."[8]

The righteousness of Christ you seek is already given to all who have ears to hear. It is "imputed to every believer, whereby all his sins are blotted out, and he is reconciled to the favor of God."[9] This righteousness is "that inward righteousness of that holiness of heart, which is with the utmost propriety termed God's righteousness, as being both his own free gift through Christ, and his own work by his almighty Spirit."[10]

Those who remain willfully ignorant of this gift continue to go "about to establish their own righteousness."[11] They worked hard to establish an "outside righteousness which might very properly be termed their own," instead of receiving the gift "wrought by the Spirit of God."[12] Trusting only in their own strength, they refused to receive the righteousness freely given by God, which is available for all who believe.[13]

2. All These Things Will Be Added

"All these things [the food, clothing, and necessities mentioned in Matt. 6:25 – 32] will be given to you as well" if you seek first his kingdom and his righteousness.[14] Simply receive "the gift and work of God, the image of God renewed in your souls, 'and all these things shall be added unto you'; all things needful for the body."[15]

Seek the peace and love of God, and you will find more — "the kingdom that cannot be moved; but also what you seek not" — all these things, in relation to this first thing sought.[16]

You will find on your way to the eternal kingdom "all outward things, so far as they are expedient for you." Cast you all your care upon him who knows your wants and needs.[17]

---

[7]"Sermon on the Mount," 29, B 1:643 – 44, J V:388, sec. 21.
[8]Rom. 10:1 – 4 NIV.
[9]"Sermon on the Mount," 29, B 1:643 – 44, J V:388, sec. 21.
[10]Ibid.
[11]Cf. Rom. 10:3.
[12]"Sermon on the Mount," 29, B 1:643 – 44, J V:388, sec. 21.
[13]Ibid.
[14]Matt. 6:33 NIV.
[15]"Sermon on the Mount," 29, B 1:643 – 44, J V:388, sec. 22.
[16]"Sermon on the Mount," 29, B 1:644, J V:389, sec. 23.
[17]Ibid.

3. Tomorrow and Today

a. So Take No Thought for the Morrow

Therefore, within the frame of trusting first in God's righteousness, "take no thought for the morrow."[18] "Do not worry about tomorrow, for tomorrow will worry about itself. Each day has enough trouble of its own."[19] "Take ... no thought of how to lay up treasures on earth, how to increase in worldly substance ... or more money than is required from day to day for the plain, reasonable purposes of life.... Do not trouble yourself now, with thinking what you shall do at a season which is yet afar off.... Why should you perplex yourself without need?"[20]

Breadwinners are called especially to note: "God provides for you today what is needful to sustain the life which he hath given you."[21] Do not make anxious care for future things "a pretense for neglecting present duty" to family and society.[22] Those who "forsake God for the world, lose what they sought, as well as what they sought not."[23] There is "a visible blast on all their undertakings," and whatever they do does not prosper.[24]

Some in despair are tempted to say, "O how I will praise God when the light of his countenance shall be again lifted up upon my soul! How will I exhort others to praise him, when his love is again shed abroad in my heart! Then I will do thus and thus."[25] Wesley cautioned that you will not do it then if you will not do it now. In his own words, Jesus said: "Whoever has will be given more, and they will have an abundance. Whoever does not have, even what they have will be taken from them."[26] To not have is to reject God's pardoning gift of righteousness. "He that is faithful in that which is least," however little, whether of worldly substance or spiritual value, "will be faithful in that which is much."[27] If you will hide one talent, you will hide five.[28]

b. Let Tomorrow Worry about Itself—Live Today

Jesus on the mount taught how to live today. "Tomorrow will worry about itself."[29] When temptation comes, grace will come. "In greater trials you will have greater strength. When sufferings abound, the consolations of God will, in the same proportion, abound also. So that, in every situation, the grace of God will be sufficient for you."[30]

---

[18]Matt. 6:34.
[19]Ibid. NIV.
[20]"Sermon on the Mount," 29, B 1:645, J V:389, sec. 24.
[21]Ibid.
[22]"Sermon on the Mount," 29, B 1:645–46, J V:390, sec. 25.
[23]Ibid.
[24]Ibid.
[25]"Sermon on the Mount," 29, B 1:646–47, J V:390–91, sec. 26.
[26]Matt. 13:12 NIV; "Sermon on the Mount," 29, B 1:646–47, J V:390–91, sec. 26.
[27]Cf. Luke 16:10.
[28]"Sermon on the Mount," 29, B 1:646–47, J V:390–91, sec. 26.
[29]Matt. 6:34 NIV.
[30]"Sermon on the Mount," 29, B 1:647, J V:391, sec. 27.

When tomorrow comes, then think of its possibilities. Live today. "Improve the present hour. This is your own; and it is your all. The past is as nothing, as though it had never been. The future is nothing to you. It is not yours; perhaps it never will be. There is no depending on what is yet to come; for you 'know not what a day may bring forth.'"[31]

"Each day has enough trouble of its own."[32] Gladly endure whatever God permits today to come upon you. "But look not at the sufferings of tomorrow."[33] "Sufficient unto the day is the evil thereof."[34] It is viewed as "evil" from worldly assumptions, "but in the language of God, all is blessing."[35]

B. Hindrances to Living Well and Doing Good

1. As You Judge Others, You Will Be Judged

a. How Purity of Heart Transforms Conflicted Relationships

Those who enter the kingdom in faith with purity of heart will find that their relationships are being transformed. They are living a different life than before. They do not judge uncharitably. They are not intemperately zealous. They do not neglect charity. They are not hypocrites. They treat others as they themselves would want to be treated.

The text of Wesley's tenth discourse on the Sermon on the Mount is about intemperate judging, hypocrisy, and the neglect of prayer and love — all hindrances to life with God [Matt. 7:1 – 12; Homily #30, "Upon Our Lord's Sermon on the Mount: Discourse 10," B 1:650 – 62, J V:393 – 404 (1750)].

"Do not judge, or you too will be judged. For in the same way you judge others, you will be judged, and with the measure you use, it will be measured to you.

"Why do you look at the speck of sawdust in your brother's eye and pay no attention to the plank in your own eye? How can you say to your brother, 'Let me take the speck out of your eye,' when all the time there is a plank in your own eye? You hypocrite, first take the plank out of your own eye, and then you will see clearly to remove the speck from your brother's eye.

"Do not give dogs what is sacred; do not throw your pearls to pigs. If you do, they may trample them under their feet, and turn and tear you to pieces.

"Ask and it will be given to you; seek and you will find; knock and the door will be opened to you. For everyone who asks receives; the one who seeks finds; and to the one who knocks, the door will be opened.

"Which of you, if your son asks for bread, will give him a stone? Or if he asks for a fish, will give him a snake? If you, then, though you are evil, know how to

---

[31]"Sermon on the Mount," 29, B 1:647 – 48, J V:391 – 92, sec. 28; cf. Prov. 27:1.
[32]Matt. 6:34 NIV.
[33]"Sermon on the Mount," 29, B 1:648 – 49, J V:392 – 93, sec. 29.
[34]Matt. 6:34.
[35]"Sermon on the Mount," 29, B 1:648 – 49, J V:392 – 93, sec. 29.

give good gifts to your children, how much more will your Father in heaven give good gifts to those who ask him!

"So in everything, do to others what you would have them do to you, for this sums up the Law and the Prophets."[36]

b. Good Acts Come Out of Intentions Purified by Grace

Wesley begins this tenth discourse by reviewing the overall pattern of Jesus' moral teachings:

On the mount, Jesus set forth those dispositions of soul that constitute real Christianity. These are the tempers of the happy and holy life. They embody that "holiness, without which no man shall see the Lord."[37]

The temperate dispositions that flow from a living faith in God begin with humility, poverty of spirit, mercy, and love. These affections flow from the fountain of God's love made known in Jesus Christ.

In the first nine of Wesley's discourses on the Sermon on the Mount, he has firmly established the correspondence between inner intent and outer act as the key to Jesus' ethic. The remainder of the discourses, 10 through 13, deal with crucial moral questions that confront the life of faith active in love. The themes of these discourses include not judging uncharitably, the Father's invitations to ask in prayer, the golden rule of the Christian life, not casting pearls to swine, the many who go the easy way of death and the few who go the difficult way of life, entering the kingdom by the narrow gate, resisting false prophets, and building the house of responsible behavior on rock instead of sand.

The remaining passages of Jesus' teaching on the mount complete the summary of everything that is crucial to the Christian life. Together they spell out the core of Christian ethics as that life that emerges out of life in Christ. Throughout the Lord's instructions, a right intention is the beginning of outward acts pleasing to God.[38] Good actions acceptable to God come out of a "pure and holy intention."[39]

Wesley's Homily 30, his tenth discourse on the Sermon on the Mount, deals with hindrances to holiness: intemperate judging of others, excessive zealousness, and neglect of prayer and charity. These hindrances prevent believers from securing "that prize of our high calling."[40]

2. Unfairly Judging Others

a. You Will Be Judged Eternally as You Judge Others in Time

The first hindrance Jesus cautions us against is unfair judging. "Judge not, that ye be not judged."[41] Do not judge the neighbor at all unfairly in this world, for you

---

[36]Matt. 7:1–12 NIV.
[37]Heb. 12:14; "Sermon on the Mount," 30, B 1:651, J V:394, sec. 2.
[38]"Sermon on the Mount," 30, B 1:650, J V:394, sec. 1.
[39]"Sermon on the Mount," 30, B 1:651, J V:394, sec. 2.
[40]"Sermon on the Mount," 30, B 1:651, J V:394, sec. 3.
[41]Matt. 7:1.

will ultimately be judged entirely fairly by the eternal Lord. So "do not judge, or you too will be judged."[42] "For in the same way you judge others, you will be judged, and with the measure you use, it will be measured to you."[43]

This is "a plain and equitable rule," by which "God permits you to determine for yourselves in what manner he shall deal with you in the judgment of the great day."[44] God offers you freedom to settle your own destiny.

This warning applies to all stations of life, all times, all cultures. All are endowed with some measure of reason and conscience. Those deficient in some measure of reason or conscience must be judged fairly according to the deficiency.

Every day we have plenty of opportunities to make judgments about each other. Each brings temptations to exaggerate. We fall into the sin of judging unfairly "before we suspect any danger. And unspeakable are the mischiefs produced."[45] Many may be harmed when this "root of bitterness springs up."[46]

b. Let the Fairness Ethic of the Community of Faith Be Openly Seen

The community of faith is like a city set upon a hill. The interpersonal behaviors of the Christians are open for the world to see. The world can see the struggle going on in the Christian life. Many will see that Christians seek "to be humble, serious, gentle, merciful, and pure in heart." If so, they are likely to earnestly desire "these holy tempers as they have not yet attained, and wait for them in doing all good to all men, and patiently suffering evil."[47]

But if that fairness is not really there to be plausibly taken into account by the world, then Christians are easily dismissed as hypocritical and insincere. Unfairness within the believing community provides the world with an excuse for condemning those whom they might otherwise do well to imitate,[48] for example, when Christians "spend their time in finding out their neighbor's faults instead of amending their own." In that case, Christians may appear to "never go beyond a poor dead form of godliness without the power."[49]

3. Focusing on the Mote in Another's Eye

Jesus asked why we see so clearly the speck in another's eye yet "pay no attention to the plank in [our] own eye."[50] Why inspect "the infirmities, the mistakes, the imprudence, the weakness" of others without considering your own self-will and the idolatrous love of the world? "With what supine carelessness and indifference art thou dancing over the mouth of hell!"[51]

---

[42]Matt. 7:1 NIV.
[43]Matt. 7:2 NIV.
[44]"Sermon on the Mount," 30, B 1:651, J V:394, sec. 4.
[45]"Sermon on the Mount," 30, B 1:651–52, J V:395, sec. 5.
[46]Cf. Heb. 12:15.
[47]"Sermon on the Mount," 30, B 1:652, J V:395, sec. 6.
[48]Ibid.
[49]Ibid.
[50]Matt. 7:3 NIV.
[51]"Sermon on the Mount," 30, B 1:652–54, J V:395–97, sec. 7.

"How can you say to your brother, 'Let me take the speck out of your eye,' when all the time there is a plank in your own eye?" Jesus asked.[52] Suppose you as a Christian become caught up in "the excess of zeal for God, the extreme of self-denial, the too great disengagement from worldly cares and employments, the desire to be day and night in prayer, or hearing the words of eternal life." You set yourself up for criticism unless you act accordingly. If you judge your neighbor harshly or tell him you would like to help him with the mote in his eye, that only rankles him.[53]

a. First Cast Out the Beam from Your Own Eye

You will be more able to remove the speck from another's eye if you first take the plank out of your own.[54] This is a reasonable moral requirement for anyone offering criticism: the willingness first to critique oneself. The most ancient rule of moral knowledge since Socrates has been: "Know thyself!" Since you know your own inadequacies, do not forget them in criticizing others. Be honest about the incongruities in your own life. "Cast out the beam of self-will!"[55]

Before judging others, the believer does well to ponder the meaning of Jesus' imperative: "If any man will come after me, let him renounce himself."[56] Deny yourself. Take up your cross daily. "Cast out the beam of love of the world! Love not the world, neither the things of the world. Be thou crucified unto the world, and the world crucified unto thee."[57] You are free to make use of the world as long as your use corresponds with the will of the Giver of the world. "Only use the world, but enjoy God." Remember the "one thing needful,"[58] that your eternal happiness is at stake in your temporal decisions. Then you will be able to see more clearly how to help remove the speck from your brother's eye.[59]

C. Forms of Thinking or Speaking Evil of Another

1. Thinking Evil of Another

You can judge another unfairly in your heart without speaking anything at all, and whether the other is absent or present.[60]

The kind of unfair judging that is here condemned is primarily "the thinking of another in a manner that is contrary to love."[61] This may occur when we blame another when he is not to blame. Or we may judge another "by words which he has never spoke, or the actions which he has never done."[62] Or we may think evil

---

[52]Matt. 7:4 NIV; "Sermon on the Mount," 30, B 1:652–54, J V:395–97, sec. 7.
[53]"Sermon on the Mount," 30, B 1:652–54, J V:395–97, sec. 7.
[54]Cf. Matt. 7:5.
[55]"Sermon on the Mount," 30, B 1:652–54, J V:395–97, sec. 7; cf. Luke 9:23.
[56]"Sermon on the Mount," 30, B 1:652–54, J V:395–97, sec. 7.
[57]Ibid.
[58]See Wesley's homily "The One Thing Needful" in *JWT*, vol. 3.
[59]"Sermon on the Mount," 30, B 1:652–54, J V:395–97, sec. 7.
[60]"Sermon on the Mount," 30, B 1:654, J V:397, sec. 8.
[61]"Sermon on the Mount," 30, B 1:654, J V:397, sec. 9.
[62]Ibid.

of another by "condemning him to a higher degree than he deserves." This is an "offense against justice as well as mercy."[63] Or we may "suppose one who is acknowledged to be in fault to be more in fault than he really is." Or we may "undervalue whatever good is found in him."[64] Yet worse, we may even assume that there is no good in him at all, especially when we do not see clearly with our own eyes.

2. Speaking Evil of One Who Is Absent

Speaking evil of another ordinarily implies a judgmental form of speech not directly to the person present but about one who is absent. Here an injustice is being done that is incommensurable with God's justice.

The ethic of not speaking evil is rooted in love as described by Paul in this way: Love "does not dishonor others, it is not self-seeking, it is not easily angered, it keeps no record of wrongs. Love does not delight in evil but rejoices with the truth. It always protects, always trusts, always hopes, always perseveres."[65]

Wesley commented on Paul's intriguing phrase "Love does not delight in evil": "Love will not infer from a person's falling once into an act of open sin that he is accustomed so to do.... And if he was habitually guilty once, love does not conclude he is so still, much less, that if he is now guilty of this, therefore he is guilty of other sins also. These evil reasonings all pertain to that sinful judging which our Lord here guards us against."[66]

A similar type of unfair judging is to condemn someone where there is not sufficient evidence. The facts "ought not to have been supposed, but proved" before judgment is formed.[67] Nor should we "pass a full sentence before the accused has spoken for himself."[68]

The remedy for correcting unfair judging is candid, straightforward admonition. In reconciling with another, follow Jesus' instruction on dealing with accusations in the church: "If your brother or sister sins, go and point out their fault, just between the two of you. If they listen to you, you have won them over. But if they will not listen, take one or two others along, so that 'every matter may be established by the testimony of two or three witnesses.' If they still refuse to listen, tell it to the church."[69] If you take all these steps, you have done your part. Don't dwell on it. Commend the neighbor to God in prayer.[70]

---

[63]"Sermon on the Mount," 30, B 1:654–55, J V:397, sec. 10.
[64]Ibid.
[65]1 Cor. 13:5–7 NIV.
[66]"Sermon on the Mount," 30, B 1:655, J V:397–98, sec. 11.
[67]"Sermon on the Mount," 30, B 1:655, J V:398, sec. 12.
[68]Ibid.
[69]Matt. 18:15–17 NIV.
[70]"Sermon on the Mount," 30, B 1:656, J V:399, sec. 14.

3. Do Not Give Dogs What Is Sacred

a. Do Not Obsess on Exhorting the Petulant

"Do not give dogs what is sacred; do not throw your pearls to pigs. If you do, they may trample them under their feet."[71] Our Lord gives us this needful caution in order to prevent our "spending our strength in vain."[72] This caution pertains especially to those young in faith and without realistic experience of the persistence of sin in human history. When we are young in faith, we may naively hope to persuade the incorrigible, "whether they will or no. And by the ill success of this intemperate zeal, we often suffer in our own souls."[73] You yourself can be harmed by attempting to do something good for an irrational being.

Suppose you have made every effort at reconciliation, including by grace casting out the beam in your own eye. In an effort to correct another's behavior, beware that you do not hurt yourself inordinately in the attempt to help another.[74] Do not give that which is holy to dogs.[75]

"When it is clearly and indisputably proved that they are unholy and wicked men, not only strangers to, but enemies to God, to all righteousness and true holiness," do not give them holy things to trample.[76] Those who contradict and blaspheme or seek to prostitute these holy things must not be encouraged. "Lead them as they are able to bear."[77]

b. Do Not Cast Pearls before Swine

If the swine insist on "glorying in their shame, making no pretense to purity either of heart or life, but working all uncleanness with greediness; then do not cast your pearls before them."[78]

Do not talk with the hopelessly immoral about "the mysteries of the kingdom; of the things which eye hath not seen, nor ear heard," which it is impossible for them to hear. Since they have no spiritual senses, "it cannot enter into their hearts to conceive.... What conception can they have of being made partakers of the divine nature" if they are "immersed in the mire of this world, in worldly pleasures, desires, and cares."[79]

Do not cast pearls before hardened cynics. They will "despise what they cannot understand, and speak evil of the things which they know not."[80] Do not give to them a gratuitous opportunity to "return you evil for good, cursing for blessing, and hatred for your goodwill."[81]

---

[71]Matt. 7:6 NIV.
[72]"Sermon on the Mount," 30, B 1:656–57, J V:399, sec. 15.
[73]Ibid.
[74]"Sermon on the Mount," 30, B 1:656, J V:399, sec. 14.
[75]"Sermon on the Mount," 30, B 1:656–57, J V:399, sec. 15.
[76]"Sermon on the Mount," 30, B 1:657, J V:399–400, sec. 16.
[77]Ibid.
[78]"Sermon on the Mount," 30, B 1:658, J V:400–401, sec. 17.
[79]Ibid.
[80]Ibid.
[81]Ibid.

4. The Father's Invitation: Ask in Prayer for What You Need

a. Ask, Seek, Knock

After removing the hindrances just mentioned — intemperate judging and excessive zeal — Jesus warned about a third "grand hindrance of holiness," the neglect of prayer. Prayer is "frequently found effectual when no other method avails."[82] If all your attempts fail, turn it over to God in prayer. *Ask* in prayer for guidance. "Ask and it will be given to you."[83]

Many of us do not have the vigor of full participation in God's life because we have not really asked for it. "O how meek and gentle, how lowly in heart, how full of love both to God and men, might ye have been at this day, if you had only asked."[84] Just ask God. After all, he is your Father. Ask that you might "thoroughly experience and perfectly practice the whole of that religion which our Lord has here so beautifully described. It shall then be given you, to be holy as he is holy, both in heart and in all manner of conversation."[85]

Having asked, you are then called to actively *seek* that for which you have asked. Actively search for what you asked God for. Seek by using the means of grace God has already provided: searching Scripture, hearing God's Word, and partaking of the Supper of the Lord. These are the ordered and provided means of grace. The promise: seek and you will find.[86]

After you ask and seek diligently for the way to the kingdom, go ahead and *knock* on the door. Expect to be welcomed by the Father. He has invited you to ask, seek, and knock. The promise of the Father is that the door will be opened to those who ask and seek.[87]

Jesus knows the hardness of our hearts and how unready we are "to believe the goodness of God."[88] But God has provided gracious remedies even for our resistances to God. He assures us that "everyone who asks receives; the one who seeks finds; and to the one who knocks, the door will be opened."[89] The blessed life will be given to those who ask. The way will be found by those who diligently seek. The gate of righteousness will be opened to those who earnestly knock.[90]

b. The Father Wants to Be Trusted by His Children

God wants to cut off every one of our temptations to give up. He cuts off "every pretense for unbelief" or discouragement. He conveys this by a powerful metaphor: "Which of you, if your son asks for bread, will give him a stone?"[91] What father out

---

[82]"Sermon on the Mount," 30, B 1:659, J V:401, sec. 18.
[83]Matt. 7:7 NIV.
[84]"Sermon on the Mount," 30, B 1:659, J V:401, sec. 18.
[85]Ibid.
[86]Ibid.
[87]Ibid.
[88]"Sermon on the Mount," 30, B 1:659, J V:402, sec. 19.
[89]Matt. 7:8 NIV.
[90]"Sermon on the Mount," 30, B 1:659, J V:402, sec. 19.
[91]Matt. 7:9 NIV.

of natural affection would "refuse the reasonable request of one he loved? What decent father would answer a request with an intentionally hurtful response? If asked by his own son for a bite of fish, what father would 'give him a snake'?"[92] No father would do that. So would the Father in heaven not respond to his child's request by giving him "hurtful instead of profitable things"?[93]

By this stunning analogy, the Lord was teaching believers to have full confidence in God's promise.[94] "If you, then, though you are evil, know how to give good gifts to your children, how much more will your Father in heaven give good gifts to those who ask him!"[95] The heavenly Father is "pure, unmixed, essential goodness," who gives "good things to them that ask him." So ask God for what you truly need and want.[96]

5. The Golden Rule

Wesley's homily ends with a celebration of "that royal law, the golden rule of mercy as justice."[97] Jesus' golden rule of his Sermon on the Mount is easy to state: "In everything, do to others what you would have them do to you, for this sums up the Law and the Prophets."[98] It is so reasonable that it "commends itself, as soon as heard, to every man's conscience and understanding.... No man can knowingly offend against it without carrying his condemnation in his own breast."[99] It is "a rule which many believe to be naturally engraved on the mind of everyone that comes into the world."[100]

The history of salvation teaches us to do to others as you would wish they would do to you. Wesley commented on the claim that the Golden Rule "sums up the Law and the Prophets." Both salvation history and conscience attest what is written on our hearts and in our rational self-awareness.

The rule can be stated negatively or positively. The negative meaning of the rule is powerful: whatever you would not want anyone to do to you, don't ever do that to anyone! It is "a plain rule, always ready at hand, always easy to be applied." In every interaction with another, "make his case your own."[101]

The Golden Rule is based on empathy — the ability to enter into the consciousness of the other and ask how that person feels. Would he not want this to happen to him? Then you will know how to avoid making that person unhappy, by knowing exactly how you would want to be treated in that instance.

The positive meaning of the rule is, suppose you are in the spot your neighbor

---

[92]Matt. 7:10 NIV.
[93]"Sermon on the Mount," 30, B 1:660, J V:402, sec. 20.
[94]Ibid.
[95]Matt. 7:11 NIV.
[96]"Sermon on the Mount," 30, B 1:660, J V:402, sec. 20.
[97]"Sermon on the Mount," 30, B 1:660–61, J V:403, sec. 22.
[98]Matt. 7:12 NIV.
[99]"Sermon on the Mount," 30, B 1:660–61, J V:403, sec. 22.
[100]Ibid.
[101]Ibid.

is in — what would you like to happen? You know clearly since you know your own feelings. Think: What would you like that person to do for your happiness? Do positively for the other what you would have him do for you. Take whatever step you would for him that you would like him to do to increase your happiness. Whatever you could "reasonably desire of him, supposing yourself to be in his circumstances, that do, to the uttermost of your power, to every child of man."[102]

"It is clear to every man's own conscience" that no one would wish another to judge him unfairly or dismiss him as valueless or "causelessly or lightly think evil of us." If you know you do not want people to judge you harshly, then apply this rule to your own behavior: do not speak harshly of him in an unfair way. "Never mention even the real fault of an absent person, unless so far as you are convinced it is absolutely needful for the good of other souls."[103]

a. Superfluities, Conveniencies, and Necessities

Wouldn't we like for the other person's superficial desires to yield to our necessities? We can all understand that. If so for others, we should reasonably walk by the same rule: "Let us do unto all as we would they should do to us. Let us love and honor all men. Let justice, mercy, and truth govern all our minds and actions. Let our superfluities give way to our neighbor's conveniencies ... our conveniencies to our neighbor's necessities; our necessities to his extremities."[104]

Since this rule is accessible to all human moral awareness of any culture, it does not, strictly speaking, depend on the history of revelation, but its meaning is made more powerful by seeing it in relation to the empathy of God for fallen humanity.[105] "This is pure and genuine morality.... But then be it observed, none can walk by this rule (nor ever did from the beginning of the world), none can love his neighbor as himself, unless he first love God. And none can love God unless he believe in Christ,"[106] according to classic Christian teaching, due to the distortions of the history of sin. But believe in him and your faith will work by love. You will love the Lord because he has loved you in his incarnate life. You will love your neighbor as yourself. "And then it will be thy glory and joy to exert and increase this love ... by showing all that kindness" to everyone you would want to show it to you.[107]

---

[102]"Sermon on the Mount," 30, B 1:661, J V:403, sec. 24.

[103]"Sermon on the Mount," 30, B 1:661, J V:403, sec. 25.

[104]"Sermon on the Mount," 30, B 1:662, J V:404, sec. 26. This is a brilliant statement of the rational idea that would later become the center of Kant's "categorical imperative," only a few years before it appeared in Kant as a postulate of practical reason. In my view, this is a sentence that deserves historic recognition as an anticipation of Kant. It is clearer and better than Kant's subsequent rendering of the same idea. Why is Wesley not recognized as an ethicist who preceded Kant in this formulation? Largely because Kant had not read Wesley, and contemporary ethicists have not read Wesley. They have thereby missed a lot.

[105]"Sermon on the Mount," 30, B 1:661, J V:403, sec. 25.

[106]"Sermon on the Mount," 30, B 1:662–63, J V:404, sec. 27.

[107]Ibid.

D. The Way of Life

1. Enter the Kingdom

a. The Narrow and Wide Gates Compared

The text of Wesley's eleventh discourse on the Sermon on the Mount is Matthew 7:13 – 14 on the narrow gate that leads to life: "Enter through the narrow gate. For wide is the gate and broad is the road that leads to destruction, and many enter through it. But small is the gate and narrow the road that leads to life, and only a few find it" [Matt. 7:13 – 14 NIV; Homily #31, "Upon Our Lord's Sermon on the Mount: Discourse 11," B 1:664 – 74, J V:405 – 13 (1750)].

Those who believe and follow the way to life with God face many dangers, hindrances, and challenges. Many come from their own hearts. Some come from poor guidance.[108] Jesus offers the most reliable guidance. Many who once experienced saving grace have by their own neglect forgotten or denied it. They may have started but did not press on to the goal.[109] The high calling is: "Enter through the narrow gate."

For the multitudes, Jesus broke it down simply: there are two ways ahead for every soul. The two ways are built oppositely: one is wide, one narrow. Wide and narrow are the two basic characteristics of the two ways. One leads to destruction, the other to salvation. You cannot separate the intrinsic property of wideness from the gate to destruction. You cannot separate the intrinsic property of narrowness from the gate to eternal happiness.[110]

The wide gate opens to a broad highway. The majority prefer this road. "Wide indeed is the gate, and broad the way, that leadeth to destruction! For sin is the gate of hell.... And how wide a gate is that of sin! How broad is the way of wickedness!"[111]

Ponder the characteristics of the two ways. Each has a gate, a way, an end, and a choice. The gate may be wide or tight. The way may be broad or narrow. The end of one is destruction, the other is happiness. Most choose the wide gate. Only a few choose the narrow gate.

b. How Parent-Sins Shape the Wide Way to Destruction

One of Wesley's terms for original sin was "parent-sins." Since everyone has parents, everyone must deal with parent-sins.

Sin did not begin with each one of us individually, but with parents and our parents' parents, and all acts of parenting back to the first parents in primal human history. That is called "original sin," which we discussed in depth in volumes 1 and 2 of this series. This history includes a flood of individual decisions that swept

---

[108]"Sermon on the Mount," 31, B 1:664, J V:405, proem, sec. 1.
[109]Ibid.
[110]"Sermon on the Mount," 31, B 1:664 – 65, J V:406, proem, sec. 3.
[111]"Sermon on the Mount," 31, B 1:665, J V:406, sec. 1.2.

humanity along before we arrived. We cannot change that past, but we are given an opportunity to respond to the unique way God has changed it.

We have inherited a history of a huge accumulation of decision making that went wrong. Is this unfair to us? It is the price of freedom, since all free acts have good or bad consequences. All humanity shares in this history of freedom and its abuse.

This piled-up flood is what Christian teaching calls the "carnal mind which is enmity against God, pride of heart, self-will, and love of the world!"[112] "Can we fix any bounds to them? Do they not diffuse themselves through all our thoughts, and mingle with all our tempers!" They seep into "the whole mass of our affections.... How innumerable an offspring do they bring forth, in every age and nation!"[113]

What God requires of us extends "not only to all our actions," indeed to every word we speak and "every thought that rises in our heart."[114] There are many ways to miss the mark of our human purpose. These ways are staggeringly varied. We can sin in our thoughts in hundreds of ways each day. Sin is a thousand times wider and seemingly easier than following the simple divine command. "There are a thousand ways of breaking every commandment; so that this gate is wide indeed."[115] There is only one way to keep the divine commandment: simple repentance and faith in grace revealed and embraced in our hearts as the single ground of all our acts and thoughts.

c. The Breadth of the Way That Leads to Destruction

This historical burden of universal sin is shared by agnostics, Muslims, and Christians alike. "Survey any one kingdom, any single country, or city, or town; and how plenteous is this harvest! And let it not be one of those which are still over-spread with Mahometan or pagan darkness; but of those which name the name of Christ, which profess to see the light of his glorious gospel."[116]

Even among so-called Christian cultures, "the generality of every age and sex, of every profession and employment, of every rank and degree, high and low, rich and poor, are walking in the way of destruction. The far greater part of the inhabitants of this city, to this day, live in sin; in some palpable, habitual, known transgression of the law they profess to observe."[117] Protestantism claims to "carry on the reformation of our opinions into our hearts and lives."[118] But even there, wide is the gate and broad is the way that leads to destruction. Many who have had fair opportunities for hearing the Good News remain entirely " 'ignorant of God's righteousness ... seeking to establish their own righteousness' as the ground of their reconciliation to God

---

[112]"Sermon on the Mount," 31, B 1:665, J V:406, sec. 1.3.
[113]Ibid.
[114]"Sermon on the Mount," 31, B 1:665, J V:406, sec. 1.2.
[115]Ibid.
[116]Ibid.
[117]"Sermon on the Mount," 31, B 1:665, J V:406, sec. 1.5.
[118]"Sermon on the Mount," 31, B 1:666, J V:406–7, sec. 1.4.

and acceptance with him." Protestants have failed to proclaim "'the righteousness which is of God' by faith."[119]

The history of sin refers not only to "the vulgar herd — the poor, base, stupid part of mankind."[120] It was recognized even by the saints and martyrs who knew their sins better than their persecutors did. Most are ready to fight to remain on this broad thoroughfare that leads to destruction.[121] Many persons of eminence are found on this wide road. "The higher they are raised in fortune and power, the deeper do they sink into wickedness. The more blessings they have received from God, the more sins do they commit; using their honor or riches, their learning or wisdom, not as means of working out their salvation, but rather of excelling in vice, and so insuring their own destruction!"[122] They despise the narrow way. They adore the broad way. "The thoroughfare has to be broad to be able to accommodate so many."[123]

2. Few Find the Narrow Way That Leads to Life

"Small is the gate and narrow the road that leads to life, and only a few find it."[124] The decisive description of the way to heaven is that it is narrow. Few have chosen this way. Why? Because "nothing unclean, nothing unholy, can enter.... No sinner can pass through that gate until he is saved from all his sins. Not only from his outward sins," but from his bosom sins.[125] He must be liberated not only from "all sinful actions, and from all evil and useless discourse; but inwardly changed, thoroughly renewed in the spirit of his mind: Otherwise he cannot pass through the gate of life, he cannot enter into glory."[126] This is why the way is so narrow that leads to life. "Narrow indeed is the way of poverty of spirit; the way of holy mourning; the way of meekness; and that of hungering and thirsting after righteousness. Narrow is the way of mercifulness; of love unfeigned; the way of purity of heart; of doing good unto all men; and of gladly suffering evil, all manner of evil, for righteousness' sake."[127]

What a small proportion who, having their hearts right before God, are "truly meek and gentle," who are seldom overcome by evil, but "overcome evil with good," who continually seek to be renewed in God's likeness.[128] "How few are there that do nothing to another which they would not another should do unto them!"[129] "How thinly are they scattered over the earth, whose souls are enlarged in love to

[119]"Sermon on the Mount," 31, B 1:665, J V:406, sec. 1.5.
[120]"Sermon on the Mount," 31, B 1:667 – 68, J V:408, sec. 1.6.
[121]Ibid.
[122]Ibid.
[123]"Sermon on the Mount," 31, B 1:668, J V:408, sec. 2.1.
[124]Matt. 7:14 NIV.
[125]"Sermon on the Mount," 31, B 1:668, J V:408, sec. 2.2.
[126]Ibid.
[127]"Sermon on the Mount," 31, B 1:668, J V:408 – 9, sec. 2.3.
[128]"Sermon on the Mount," 31, B 1:669, J V:409, sec. 2.4.
[129]Ibid.

all mankind.... How few are those lovers of God and man that spend their whole strength in doing good unto all men; and are ready to suffer all things, yea, death itself, to save one soul from eternal death!"[130]

a. The Weak Are Swept Away by the Torrent of the Examples of the Many

Every human act serves as an example to others, whether for good or ill. This produces a torrent of demoralizing examples from human history. All are in danger of being swept away.[131] "Even a single example, if it be always in our sight, is apt to make much impression upon us; especially when it has nature on its side, when it falls in with our own inclinations. How great then must be the force of so numerous examples, continually before our eyes."[132]

It is not the rude or brutish parts of humanity who are alone on this broad way. Among those on the broad way are the powerful and the rich. They "set us the example, who throng the downward way." They are often "the well-bred, the genteel, the wise, the men who understand the world, the men of knowledge, of deep and various learning, the rational, the eloquent!"[133] They have learned the arts of persuasion and reasoning, so it seems easy for them "to prove that the way is right because it is broad; that he who follows a multitude cannot do evil, but only he who will not follow them; that your way must be wrong, because it is narrow, and because there are so few that find it." They go to great lengths to demonstrate that "evil is good, and good is evil; that the way of holiness is the way of destruction, and the way of the world the only way to heaven," or if not heaven, at least it is normative for the world.[134]

Besides the genteel and well-bred, there are many more who are "mighty, and noble, and powerful" on the broad way to destruction.[135] They appeal not to reason or understanding but to power and fear. The power they have causes the weak to fear them.[136]

Then there are the rich. They love the broad way. Their lifestyle appeals to all our "foolish desires as strongly and effectually as the mighty and noble" to our fears.[137] In the midst of all this flood of advocates, the weak are left "almost unable to propose an argument to any advantage." They do not know how to defend "what they profess to believe; or to explain even what they say they experience."[138] Thus few even find their way to the straight gate. Even fewer walk on the narrow highway. Meanwhile "all your natural passions continually incline you to return into

---

[130]Ibid.
[131]Ibid.
[132]"Sermon on the Mount," 31, B 1:669–70, J V:409, sec. 2.5.
[133]"Sermon on the Mount," 31, B 1:670, J V:409–10, sec. 2.6.
[134]Ibid.
[135]"Sermon on the Mount," 31, B 1:670, J V:410, sec. 2.7.
[136]Ibid.
[137]"Sermon on the Mount," 31, B 1:671, J V:410, sec. 2.8.
[138]"Sermon on the Mount," 31, B 1:671, J V:410–11, sec. 2.9.

the broad way." This is not new or a special feature of any particular culture. It is endemic to humanity and the perennial human predicament.[139]

Is this an indication that Wesley had a dismal estimate of human nature? Rather, he was more typically viewed as an optimist on the power of grace to fully redeem humanity. As discussed above in his teaching about man as created and man as fallen, it is clear that Wesley had a high view of human nature as created but a dismal view of human nature as fallen. Wesley did not invent these ideas of human sinfulness. It was Jesus, not Wesley, who preached the Sermon on the Mount about the narrowness of the way.

b. The Narrow Door

Luke 13:22 – 24 is a similar passage that deals with the narrow door. It shows that those who strive halfheartedly will not make it through the narrow entryway. Their outcome is dismal.

> Then Jesus went through the towns and villages, teaching as he made his way to Jerusalem. Someone asked him, "Lord, are only a few people going to be saved?"
>
> He said to them, "Make every effort to enter through the narrow door, because many, I tell you, will try to enter and will not be able to. Once the owner of the house gets up and closes the door, you will stand outside knocking and pleading, 'Sir, open the door for us.'
>
> "But he will answer, 'I don't know you or where you come from.'
>
> "Then you will say, 'We ate and drank with you, and you taught in our streets.'
>
> "But he will reply, 'I don't know you or where you come from. Away from me, all you evildoers!'" (NIV)

Delaying the invitation to repent is dangerous. At a certain point, repenting may become impossible.[140] Jesus spoke of those who "did seek before the door was shut, but that did not suffice; and they did strive after the door was shut, but then it was too late."[141] The time to decide is now. Another opportunity may not come. If you delay, you may have "many wise, many rich, many mighty, or noble" accompanying you on the way to destruction.[142]

Entering the narrow gate makes you countercultural from the first step. "If you move but one step toward God, you are not as other men are.... It is far better to stand alone than to fall into the pit." Run, then, with patience the race that is set before you, though your companions are but few. The race is only for a short time from the viewpoint of the eternal. "Yet a little while, and thou wilt 'come to an innumerable company of angels, to the general assembly and church of the firstborn, and to the spirits of just men made perfect.'"[143]

---

[139]"Sermon on the Mount," 31, B 1:671, J V:411, sec. 2.10.
[140]"Sermon on the Mount," 31, B 1:672, J V:411, sec. 3.2.
[141]"Sermon on the Mount," 31, B 1:672, J V:411, sec. 3.3.
[142]"Sermon on the Mount," 31, B 1:672 – 73, J V:412, sec. 3.4.
[143]"Sermon on the Mount," 31, B 1:674, J V:412, sec. 3.6.

E. True and False Disciples

1. Beware of False Prophets

The text of Wesley's twelfth discourse on the Sermon on the Mount is Matthew 7:15 – 20 on false prophets:

> "Watch out for false prophets. They come to you in sheep's clothing, but inwardly they are ferocious wolves. By their fruit you will recognize them. Do people pick grapes from thornbushes, or figs from thistles? Likewise, every good tree bears good fruit, but a bad tree bears bad fruit. A good tree cannot bear bad fruit, and a bad tree cannot bear good fruit. Every tree that does not bear good fruit is cut down and thrown into the fire. Thus, by their fruit you will recognize them." [NIV; Homily #32, "Upon Our Lord's Sermon on the Mount: Discourse 12," B 1:675 – 86, J V:413 – 22 (1750)]

There are compelling reasons why Jesus so solemnly cautioned us in the Sermon on the Mount to discern false prophecy.[144] Countless souls run toward destruction because they follow evil teachers who refuse to walk in the narrow way even when they are aware of the hazards of destruction.[145] They have so many companions on this broad way that they are mesmerized by its popularity. "Such is the amazing influence of example over the weak."[146]

To guard as many as possible against this contagion, God has called forth watchmen to cry out, to show multitudes the danger they are in. Throughout the generations, God has sent prophets "to point out the narrow path, and exhort all men not to be conformed to this world."[147]

But what happens "if the watchmen themselves fall into the snare against which they should warn others"?[148] What if they deceive the people to fall into the errors of the watchmen?[149] We find such deceivers in every age and nation.

Wesley asks who are these false prophets, what is their typical disguise, and by what means can the faithful discover who they are and discern their reliability?

a. Outwardly They Appear in Sheep's Clothing

Ravenous wolves can appear in innocent sheep's clothing.[150] Wesley found it necessary to speak out in "rough, plain truths, such as none can deny."[151] They "teach a false way to heaven."[152] They pretend to "speak in the name of God," professing "to be sent of God, to teach others the way to heaven."[153] They have taken

---

[144]Cf. Matt. 7:15.
[145]"Sermon on the Mount," 32, B 1:675, J V:413 – 14, proem, sec. 1.
[146]Ibid.
[147]"Sermon on the Mount," 32, B 1:675 – 76, J V:414, proem, sec. 2.
[148]Ibid.
[149]Ibid.
[150]"Sermon on the Mount," 32, B 1:676, J V:414, proem, sec. 3.
[151]"Sermon on the Mount," 32, B 1:677, J V:415, sec. 1.2.
[152]Ibid.
[153]Ibid.

Holy Scripture and grossly distorted it. They appear to clarify God's Word while undermining it. They distort the truthful stability of apostolic teaching. Their teaching causes the destruction of others. "Since you have been forewarned, be on your guard so that you may not be carried away by the error of the lawless."[154]

As Jesus had established in the previous verses: "Every broad way is infallibly a false one." Jesus' "plain, sure rule" is this: "Those who teach others to walk in a broad way are false prophets."[155] The true way to heaven by Jesus' definition is always a narrow way. Narrowness is intrinsic to the definition of the way of life. "They are false prophets who do not teach men to walk in this way."[156] The way to participate in life in Christ has already been made clear. It is "lowliness, mourning, meekness, and holy desire, love of God and of our neighbor, doing good, and suffering evil for Christ's sake."[157] It matters less what you call this way than that you follow it.[158]

They are false prophets "who teach the directly opposite way, the way of pride … of worldly desires, of loving pleasure more than God, of unkindness to our neighbor, of unconcern for good works."[159] They may appear at first to be "wise and honorable." Meanwhile they teach others to imagine they are on the way to heaven while stumbling in the opposite direction.[160] They are "traitors both to God and man," because their teaching ends in destroying the souls of others.

b. They Appear Harmless, Useful, Religious, and Loving

The false prophets come in disguise, "with an appearance of harmlessness. They come in the most mild, inoffensive manner, without any mark or token of enmity. Who can imagine that these quiet creatures would do any hurt to anyone?"[161]

They come with "an appearance of usefulness," with the pretense that they were "set apart for this very thing … particularly commissioned to watch over your soul" and teach you about "healing those that are oppressed."[162] And they come "with an appearance of religion," as if "all they do is for conscience' sake!" While they appear to be zealous for God, "they are making God a liar."[163] They may even have a stamp of approval or degree certifying their religious qualifications.

Finally, they come "with an appearance of love," making conspicuous "professions of their goodwill, and of their concern."[164]

2. Know Them by Their Fruits

How do we recognize false teachers? How do we find out what they are really up

---

[154]2 Peter 3:17 NIV.
[155]"Sermon on the Mount," 32, B 1:677, J V:415, sec. 1.2.
[156]"Sermon on the Mount," 32, B 1:677, J V:415, sec. 1.4.
[157]Ibid.
[158]"Sermon on the Mount," 32, B 1:677, J V:415, sec. 1.5.
[159]"Sermon on the Mount," 32, B 1:677, J V:416, sec. 1.6.
[160]"Sermon on the Mount," 32, B 1:678, J V:416, sec. 1.7.
[161]"Sermon on the Mount," 32, B 1:679, J V:416, sec. 2.2.
[162]"Sermon on the Mount," 32, B 1:679, J V:416, sec. 2.3.
[163]"Sermon on the Mount," 32, B 1:679, J V:417, sec. 2.4.
[164]"Sermon on the Mount," 32, B 1:679, J V:417, sec. 2.5.

to? By their fruit we will recognize them.[165] Our Lord was not a master of disguise; he was a master of removing disguises. He did not propose a long, complicated series of arguments by which one might analyze deception, but rather "a short and plain rule, easy to be understood" by anyone on any occasion: "You shall know them by their fruits."[166]

To discover their fruitfulness, ask first, "What effect does their teaching have on their own behavior? Does their temperament show a picture of that mind in them which is in Christ Jesus? Are they in practice 'meek, lowly, patient, lovers of God and man, and zealous of good works'?"[167] Then ask, "What are the fruits of their teaching?" Look at those who are following them: Do they walk as Christ walked? If not, then you know that God has not sent them.[168]

a. Analogies for Determining Authenticity of Witnesses

Our Lord has provided several clear and convincing analogies for discernment. Jesus asked the multitude on the mount to consider: "Do people pick grapes from thornbushes, or figs from thistles?"[169] "Do you expect that these evil men should bring forth good fruit? As well might you expect that thorns should bring forth grapes, or that figs should grow upon thistles!"[170] A true prophet sent by God will bear the fruits of holy living. A false prophet, a teacher not sent by God, will bring forth corruption. A true prophet or teacher "does not bring forth evil fruit accidentally or sometimes only, but always, and of necessity."[171] Test them by their fruits in engendering the holy life.[172]

"Every tree that does not bear good fruit is cut down and thrown into the fire."[173] The outcome of the teaching of false prophets will always be destructiveness lacking saving grace.

b. They Come to Destroy

Their purpose is to destroy the worshiping community. "They only destroy and devour the flock. They tear them in pieces.... O beware they do not turn you out of the way."[174] "They come to you in sheep's clothing, but inwardly they are ferocious wolves."[175]

If this is what Jesus taught, should believers even listen to the ordained ministers who evidence false teaching? Surprisingly, Wesley turned to the unique wisdom of the Lord in Matthew 23:2–4: "The teachers of the law and the Pharisees sit in

---

[165]Cf. Matt. 7:16.
[166]"Sermon on the Mount," 32, B 1:680, J V:417, sec. 3.1.
[167]"Sermon on the Mount," 32, B 1:680, J V:417, sec. 3.2.
[168]"Sermon on the Mount," 32, B 1:680, J V:418, sec. 3.3.
[169]Matt. 7:16 NIV.
[170]"Sermon on the Mount," 32, B 1:680–81, J V:418–19, sec. 3.4.
[171]Ibid.
[172]Ibid.
[173]Matt. 7:19 NIV.
[174]"Sermon on the Mount," 32, B 1:681, J V:419, sec. 3.5.
[175]Matt. 7:15 NIV.

Moses' seat. So you must be careful to do everything they tell you. But do not do what they do, for they do not practice what they preach. They tie up heavy, cumbersome loads and put them on other people's shoulders, but they themselves are not willing to lift a finger to move them."[176] Do what Jesus did. Jesus himself listened to them but judged them by their fruits. To the people he gave the warning: It is not forbidden that you listen even to false prophets, but attend to the quality of lives they lead and elicit in others.[177]

In listening to and discerning false and true prophets, do not cut the people of God off from the ordinances of God. "The validity of the ordinance doth not depend on the goodness of him that administers [it], but on the faithfulness of him that ordained it. Do not neglect the sacraments just because they are offered by those who teach inappropriately.... Even by these who are under a curse themselves, God can and doth give us his blessing. For the bread which they break, we have experimentally known to be 'the communion of the body of Christ,' and the cup which God blessed, even by their unhallowed lips, was to us the communion of the blood of Christ."[178]

Do not let the false teachers prevent you from hearing the Word and receiving the sacrament. "Wait upon God by humble and earnest prayer, and then act according to the best light you have. Act according to what you are persuaded, upon the whole, will be most for your spiritual advantage. Take great care that you do not judge rashly; that you do not lightly think any to be false prophets: and when you have full proof, see that no anger or contempt have any place in your heart."[179]

After you have listened to and received their ministries, determine for yourself in the presence and in the fear of God what you should do. God will guide you. "If by experience you find that the hearing them hurts your soul, then hear them not; then quietly refrain, and hear those that profit you. If, on the other hand, you find it does not hurt your soul, you then may hear them still. Only 'take heed how you hear.'... Hear with fear and trembling, lest you should be deceived. Receive nothing untried, nothing till it is weighed in the balance of the sanctuary" and confirmed by Holy Writ.[180]

c. Woe: A Word to False Prophets

Jesus pronounced woe upon the blind leaders of the blind who shut the kingdom of heaven against men and women.[181] Similarly Paul in Paphos, "filled with the Holy Spirit," excoriated the sorcerer Elymas: "You are a child of the devil and an enemy of everything that is right! You are full of all kinds of deceit and trickery. Will you never stop perverting the right ways of the Lord? Now the hand of the Lord is against you.

---

[176]Matt. 23:2–4 NIV; "Sermon on the Mount," 32, B 1:681–82, J V:419, sec. 3.6.
[177]"Sermon on the Mount," 32, B 1:681–82, J V:419, sec. 3.6.
[178]"Sermon on the Mount," 32, B 1:682–83, J V:420, sec. 3.8.
[179]"Sermon on the Mount," 32, B 1:683–84, J V:420–21, sec. 3.9.
[180]Ibid.
[181]Cf. Matt. 15:14.

You are going to be blind for a time, not even able to see the light of the sun."[182] False disciples are responsible for their false teachings.

Ezekiel's warning is pertinent to false prophets of all times: "When I say to the wicked, 'You wicked person, you will surely die,' and you do not speak out to dissuade them from their ways, that wicked person will die for their sin, and I will hold you accountable for their blood."[183]

To the false teachers in Wesley's day, he said similarly, "Thus you cause them to stumble at the very threshold; yea, to fall and rise no more.... How long will ye pervert the right ways of the Lord, putting darkness for light, and light for darkness? How long will ye teach the way of death, and call it the way of life?"[184]

The annoying presence of false teachers does not cause the faithful to harden their hearts. Rather, it prompts them to open their eyes. "Eternity is at stake."[185] Ask God first to quicken your own soul, giving you the faith that works by love. In this way, the Spirit of glory and of Christ shall rest upon you. God will make it known whom he has and has not sent. So shall the word of God in your mouth be "like a hammer that breaks a rock in pieces."[186] So shall the teachers both true and false be known by their fruits.[187]

F. The Wise and Foolish Builders

No one can fake faith in the presence of God. Verbal affirmations are no substitute for the faith that elicits holy living. Being a religious professional will not help.

The text of Wesley's thirteenth discourse on the Sermon on the Mount is Matthew 7:21 – 29 on Jesus' parable of the wise and foolish builders:

"Not everyone who says to me, 'Lord, Lord,' will enter the kingdom of heaven, but only the one who does the will of my Father who is in heaven. Many will say to me on that day, 'Lord, Lord, did we not prophesy in your name and in your name drive out demons and in your name perform many miracles?' Then I will tell them plainly, 'I never knew you. Away from me, you evildoers!'

"Therefore everyone who hears these words of mine and puts them into practice is like a wise man who built his house on the rock. The rain came down, the streams rose, and the winds blew and beat against that house; yet it did not fall, because it had its foundation on the rock. But everyone who hears these words of mine and does not put them into practice is like a foolish man who built his house on sand. The rain came down, the streams rose, and the winds blew and beat against that house, and it fell with a great crash."

When Jesus had finished saying these things, the crowds were amazed at his

---

[182]Acts 13:10 – 11 NIV; "Sermon on the Mount," 32, B 1:684, J V:421, sec. 3.10.
[183]Ezek. 33:8 NIV.
[184]"Sermon on the Mount," 32, B 1:684, J V:421, sec. 3.11.
[185]"Sermon on the Mount," 32, B 1:685 – 86, J V:422, sec. 3.14.
[186]Jer. 23:29 NIV.
[187]"Sermon on the Mount," 32, B 1:685 – 86, J V:422, sec. 3.14.

teaching, because he taught as one who had authority, and not as their teachers of the law. [NIV; Homily #33, "Upon Our Lord's Sermon on the Mount: Discourse 13," B 1:686 – 98, J V:423 – 33 (1750)]

On the Mount our Lord declared the whole counsel of God with regard to the way of salvation and the chief hindrances to it. He closed the sermon with this weighty warning: "Not everyone who says to me, 'Lord, Lord,' will enter the kingdom of heaven, but only the one who does the will of my Father who is in heaven.... Therefore everyone who hears these words of mine and puts them into practice is like a wise man who built his house on the rock."[188]

1. Saying and Doing the Will of the Father

a. Not Everyone Who Says "Lord" Will Enter the Kingdom

What does it mean to say, "Lord, Lord"? The contrast is between saying and doing. Jesus is here referring to anyone who talks "Lord, Lord" but acts as if the Lord were not the Lord. It implies all who use "all good words, all verbal religion," creeds, prayers, talk of God and salvation, yet in practice go the other way.[189]

Those who say, "Lord, Lord," may include those who speak passionately about the power of God to save from sin. "And yet it is very possible, all this may be no more than saying, 'Lord, Lord,'" without doing the Lord's will.[190]

b. Only One Who Does the Will of the Father

These people may appear to be "doing no harm," abstaining from all outward misdoings. They may be outwardly "clear of all uncleanness, ungodliness, and unrighteousness" yet without doing what is necessary to enter the kingdom: the will of God.[191]

They may even engage in "many of what are usually styled good works" — feeding, visiting, clothing, and even giving all their goods to feed the poor, yet without doing "all this with a desire to please God.... Still [they] may have no part in the glory which shall be revealed."[192]

All talk falls short of living out the teaching. The talkers may remain strangers "to the whole religion of Jesus Christ," which is incomparably set forth in sum in Jesus' Sermon on the Mount. "For how far short is all this of that righteousness and true holiness" proclaimed in Jesus' teachings; how distant from "that inward kingdom of heaven which is now opened in the believing soul — which is first sown in the heart as a grain of mustard seed but afterwards putteth forth great branches, on which grow all the fruits of righteousness, every good temper, and word, and work."[193]

---

[188]Matt. 7:21, 24 NIV; "Sermon on the Mount," 33, B 1:687 – 88, J V:423, proem, secs. 1 – 3.
[189]"Sermon on the Mount," 33, B 1:688 – 89, J V:424 – 25, sec. 1.1.
[190]Ibid.
[191]"Sermon on the Mount," 33, B 1:689, J V:425, sec. 1.2.
[192]"Sermon on the Mount," 33, B 1:689, J V:425, sec. 1.3.
[193]"Sermon on the Mount," 33, B 1:690, J V:425, sec. 1.4.

c. Depart from Me

Our natural desire is to come into God's presence with claims of our goodness, with evidences like our prayers, praise, refraining from evil, doing good, and even in some cases prophesying in God's name and casting out demons.[194]

It is just to this self-assertiveness and lack of humility that the Lord responds, "I never knew you." "When you were 'casting out devils in my name,' even then I did not know you as my own; for your heart was not right toward God."[195] You were not yourselves meek and lowly, not lovers of all humanity in God, not "renewed in the image of God," not "holy as I am holy. 'Depart from me,' ye who, notwithstanding all this, are … transgressors of my law, my law of holy and perfect love."[196]

2. The Parable of the Houses Built on Sand and Rock

a. Building on Sand

The Lord put the matter of readiness for the kingdom beyond all possibility of ambiguity by making this comparison: "Everyone who hears these words of mine and does not put them into practice is like a foolish man who built his house on sand. The rain came down, the streams rose, and the winds blew and beat against that house, and it fell with a great crash."[197]

When the floods come you will find out about the durability of the house. The floods of affliction, temptation, pride, and desire will wash it away. "Such must be the portion of all who rest in anything short" of true religion. "And the greater will their fall be, because they 'heard those sayings,' and yet 'did them not.' "[198]

b. When the Rains Come

He builds on rock who does the will of the Father, because his "righteousness exceeds the righteousness of the scribes and Pharisees."[199] You can see it in what he does: "He is poor in spirit; knowing himself even as also he is known. He sees and feels all his sin, and all his guilt, till it is washed away by the atoning blood. He is conscious of his lost estate, of the wrath of God abiding on him, and of his utter inability to help himself, till he is filled with peace and joy in the Holy Ghost."[200]

These are the inward character traits already set forth on the mount: the one who follows and obeys Christ is meek, gentle, patient, and athirst for the living God, overcoming evil with good, "ready to lay down his life for his enemies. He loves the Lord his God with all his heart, and with all his mind, and soul, and strength. He alone shall enter into the kingdom of heaven, who, in this spirit, doeth good unto all men; and who, being for this cause despised and rejected of men, being hated,

---

[194]"Sermon on the Mount," 33, B 1:690, J V:426, sec. 1.5.
[195]Ibid.
[196]Ibid.
[197]Matt. 7:26–27 NIV.
[198]"Sermon on the Mount," 33, B 1:691, J V:426–27, sec. 1.6.
[199]Cf. Matt. 5:20.
[200]"Sermon on the Mount," 33, B 1:691–92, J V:427, sec. 2.1.

reproached, and persecuted, rejoices and is 'exceeding glad,' knowing in whom he hath believed, and being assured these light, momentary afflictions will 'work out for him an eternal weight of glory.' "[201]

c. Because He Is Wise, He Builds on the Rock

The truly wise person in Jesus' parable knows his own life as having been given him by God to inhabit a house of clay, "not to do his own will, but the will of him that sent him." He recognizes the temporal world as a place of time and space that he inhabits for a short time between birth and death "as a stranger and sojourner, in his way to the everlasting habitations."[202] "Time is short. From now on those who have wives should live as if they do not; those who mourn, as if they did not; those who are happy, as if they were not; those who buy something, as if it were not theirs to keep; those who use the things of the world, as if not engrossed in them. For this world in its present form is passing away."[203]

He is wise because he knows God as "his Father and his Friend, the parent of all good, the center of the spirits of all flesh, the sole happiness of all intelligent beings. He sees, clearer than the light of the noonday sun, that this is the end of man, to glorify him who made him for himself, and to love and enjoy him forever."[204]

He is wise because he builds on "the Rock of Ages, the everlasting Rock, the Lord Jesus Christ," who does not change, who is "the same yesterday and today and forever."[205] Abraham is the model of the wise man who "when called to go to a place he would later receive as his inheritance, obeyed and went, even though he did not know where he was going. By faith he made his home in the promised land like a stranger in a foreign country; he lived in tents, as did Isaac and Jacob, who were heirs with him of the same promise. For he was looking forward to the city with foundations, whose architect and builder is God."[206] "On this cornerstone [the wise man] fixes his faith, and rests the whole weight of his soul upon it."[207]

The wise man is able to say with complete trust in his heart, "I have been crucified with Christ and I no longer live, but Christ lives in me. The life I now live in the body, I live by faith in the Son of God, who loved me and gave himself for me."[208] He is wise because, having been raised with Christ, he has set his mind "on things above, not on earthly things. For you died, and your life is now hidden with Christ in God. When Christ, who is your life, appears, then you also will appear with him in glory."[209]

Yet he is not so unrealistic as to "think that he shall not see war anymore; that

[201]Ibid.

[202]"Sermon on the Mount," 33, B 1:692, J V:427, sec. 2.2.

[203]1 Cor. 7:29 – 31 NIV; "Sermon on the Mount," 33, B 1:692, J V:427, sec. 2.2.

[204]"Sermon on the Mount," 33, B 1:692, J V:427, sec. 2.2.

[205]Heb. 13:8 NIV; "Sermon on the Mount," 33, B 1:692 – 93, J V:428, sec. 2.3.

[206]Heb. 11:8 – 10 NIV; "Sermon on the Mount," 33, B 1:692 – 93, J V:428, sec. 2.3.

[207]"Sermon on the Mount," 33, B 1:692 – 93, J V:428, sec. 2.3.

[208]Gal. 2:20 NIV.

[209]Col. 3:2 – 4 NIV; "Sermon on the Mount," 33, B 1:692 – 93, J V:428, sec. 2.3.

he is now out of the reach of temptation." For the grace he has been given must be "tried as gold in the fire. He shall be tempted not less than they who know not God: Perhaps abundantly more."[210]

The rain will come in unexpected times, and the floods "will lift up their waves and rage horribly."[211] He will not be cast down, because he is wise. He will "not fear, though the earth give way and the mountains fall into the heart of the sea."[212]

3. Build on Truth, Not Falsehood

a. Self-Examination

Everyone must diligently examine his own conscience "on what foundation he builds, whether on a rock or on the sand!"[213] Do not build on the sand of "right opinions, which, by a gross abuse of words, I have called faith."[214] Do not build on the sand of belonging to a particular church that might provide "helps to holiness; but they are not holiness itself."[215]

Do not build on the thin basis of "doing no harm," or being "a downright honest man," or giving every man his due, or good works, or attending services of worship as such. Although these are laudable virtues, they are not the way to heaven. That requires simply doing God's will.[216]

Then go and learn for yourselves what you have been so often taught by others: "'By grace ye are saved through faith.' 'Not by works of righteousness which we have done, but of his own mercy he saves us.'"[217] The faith that does not work through love is of no avail. Faith that does not elicit the holy life is not Christian faith. Faith nurtures "both inward and outward holiness. It stamps the whole image of God on the heart, and purifies us as he is pure."[218]

b. Final Appeals from the Sermon on the Mount

Wesley ends this grand thirteen-part series on basic evangelical ethics by summarizing the narrow way of holiness and the life built on a rock. He reviews the major teachings of the Sermon on the Mount: knowing yourself as sinner and weeping for your sins, hungering for righteousness, being merciful, seeking a pure heart.

"By the grace of God, know thyself," that you are a sinner redeemed by the Son and purified by his Spirit, knowing your "utter inability to all good unless he 'water thee every moment.'"[219] Pray that God may turn your heaviness into joy. "Weep with them that weep; and for them that weep not for themselves. Mourn for the sins

[210]"Sermon on the Mount," 33, B 1:692–93, J V:428, sec. 2.3.
[211]"Sermon on the Mount," 33, B 1:693, J V:428–29, sec. 2.4.
[212]Ps. 46:2 NIV; "Sermon on the Mount," 33, B 1:693, J V:428–29, sec. 2.4.
[213]"Sermon on the Mount," 33, B 1:694, J V:429, sec. 3.1.
[214]Ibid.
[215]Ibid.
[216]"Sermon on the Mount," 33, B 1:694, J V:429–30, sec. 3.2.
[217]"Sermon on the Mount," 33, B 1:695, J V:430, sec. 3.4; cf. Eph. 2:8–9.
[218]"Sermon on the Mount," 33, B 1:695–96, J V:430–31, sec. 3.5.
[219]"Sermon on the Mount," 33, B 1:696, J V:431, sec. 3.6; cf. Isa. 27:3.

and miseries of mankind; and see, but just before your eyes, the immense ocean of eternity, without a bottom or a shore."[220]

"Hold an even scale as to all your passions, but in particular, as to anger, sorrow, and fear.... Learn in every state wherein you are, therewith to be content."[221] Be merciful as God is merciful. "Love thy neighbor as thyself!"[222] Rejoice in truth wherever it is found. "Enjoy whatever brings glory to God, and promotes peace and goodwill among men."[223] Be "pure in heart; purified through faith from every unholy affection."[224] "Let your religion be the religion of the heart. Let it lie deep in your inmost soul.... Let the whole stream of your thoughts, words, and actions flow from the deepest conviction that you stand on the edge of the great gulf" between everlasting glory or everlasting destruction.[225]

c. The Effect of the Sermon on the Mount

"When Jesus had finished saying these things, the crowds were amazed at his teaching, because he taught as one who had authority, and not as their teachers of the law."[226] Its authenticity was instantly recognizable.

---

[220]"Sermon on the Mount," 33, B 1:696, J V:431, sec. 3.7.
[221]"Sermon on the Mount," 33, B 1:696–97, J V:431, sec. 3.8.
[222]"Sermon on the Mount," 33, B 1:697–98, J V:432, sec. 3.10.
[223]Ibid.
[224]"Sermon on the Mount," 33, B 1:698, J V:432, sec. 3.11.
[225]"Sermon on the Mount," 33, B 1:698, J V:432–33, sec. 3.12.
[226]Matt. 7:28–29 NIV.

CHAPTER 10

How the Gospel Redefines the Law

A. The Origin, Nature, and Uses of the Law

1. The Original, Nature, Property, and Use of the Law

After writing his thirteen discourses on the Sermon on the Mount, which he called a summary of Christian ethics, Wesley wrote more deliberately on the central theme of evangelical ethics: how the gospel fulfills and establishes the law. He covered this theme in three closely argued essays: "The Original, Nature, Property, and Use of the Law," "The Law Established through Faith, Discourse 1," and "The Law Established through Faith, Discourse 2."

The relation of the gospel to the law is the pivotal doctrine of evangelical ethics. Wesley was scrupulous in following the core consensus of Augustine, Luther, Calvin, and the Anglican divines. He was closer to Calvin on the third use of the law but held closely to Luther on justification by grace alone through faith alone. He clearly affirmed salvation by grace without human merit of any kind. He was resistant to antinomian temptations whenever they appeared. He was not concerned in these essays with arguing doctrinal opinions but with teaching his connection of spiritual formation about how the law is established through grace alone by faith alone, which is the root of works of love.

The theme of gospel and law is one of only a few that Wesley worked out systematically and deliberately in the form of scholarly instructional homilies. The four other doctrines he similarly explored at much greater length were original sin, predestination, assurance of salvation, and the completing work of grace.

Wesley focused closely on Paul's understanding of the relation of the gospel to the law. The first pivotal verse was Romans 7:12: "So then, the law is holy, and the commandment is holy, righteous and good" [NIV; Homily #34, "The Original, Nature, Property, and Use of the Law," B 2:4 – 19, J V:433 – 46 (1750)].

There are two dismissive ideas that do not plumb the depths of this passage: first, that the law refers only to the old Jewish religious law, and second, that the law refers to the old Roman civil law. Both premises are flawed.[1]

---

[1] "The Original, Nature, Property, and Use of the Law," B 2:4, J V:433, proem, sec. 1.

Paul is probing something much deeper when, despite his firm rejection of self-justifying temptations of the law, he states that the law is and remains "holy, and the commandment is holy, righteous and good." In this discourse, Wesley carefully tracks Paul's intention and explicit language. "All who attentively consider the tenor of his discourse" will understand the origin of the law in creation by grace and the continuing validity of the eternal moral law.[2]

Both legalism and antinomianism are wholly inconsistent with the Pauline view of the law. Paul did not offer the reader any easy excuses to completely dismiss the law as if ignorable due to the gospel. From Moses through the Prophets and Psalms to John the Baptist, the law impinges on the moral life.

a. Reading Romans 7

To understand what Wesley meant by law requires reviewing the meaning of Paul's letter to the Romans, especially chapter 7. Paul began his decisive discussion of gospel and law with a brilliant comparison that may at first seem confusing but upon reflection has great profundity. The comparison is between a widow's responsibility to her former husband and the Christian believer's responsibility to the eternal moral law. The moral law guides human behavior as long as one lives. But the gospel changes the way the newly born Christian sees the law. The law is both fulfilled and established in Christ.

As long as you are alive, you are constrained by the eternal moral law laid bare in conscience and in a more evident way in the history of salvation. The law that has eternal authority is not limited to either the Jewish ceremonial law or the Roman civil law. It is the moral law embedded in the very conscience of all humanity. No one can avoid this law because no one can avoid evaluating his own behavior.

b. The Gospel Premises of the Law as Holy, Just, and Good

Romans 7 was one of the most hotly debated passages in the New Testament in the eighteenth century and remains so today. However disputed, Wesley had a clear position within this debate: The law is fulfilled in Christ's active obedience in his life and passive obedience in his death on the cross. The atoning deed both fulfills the law and establishes the law in a new and gracious frame of reference.

The analogy: Those who know Jewish marriage law understand that it pertains only to a man and a woman who are living. Under the law, a wife, for example, is legally bound to her husband while he lives. But if the husband dies, the wife is not bound to one who is dead; she is free to remarry.[3] This is analogous to the situation of Christian believers in relation to Jewish law. On the cross, Christ buried that entire legalistic way of life of the pharisaic opponents of Jesus. That makes the faithful dead to the claims of the law as a means to righteousness. In this sense, penitent believers are released from the bondage of the law, though not from the

---

[2]Ibid.
[3]Cf. Rom. 7:2.

requirements of the eternal moral law. By sharing in the death of Christ, they have become, so to speak, dead to the panoply of specific Jewish law codes but not to the law written on the heart and discernible by conscience.

Paul stated the analogy carefully: "You also died to the law [of Moses] through the body of Christ, that you might belong to another," the law of Christ, "to him who was raised from the dead, in order that we might bear fruit for God."[4] The fruits of faith are the works of love that arise out of gratitude for the mercy of God given freely apart from all self-justifying works of the law.

Now the penitent faithful are free to enter into a new covenant relationship with the God of unmerited grace and pardon. As long as they were living the old way of life, the old law was at work to intensify their bondage to sin. Sin was in charge. The law increased the offense. Then they were hemmed in by the law, increasing their despair and frustration.[5] Sin found a way to pervert the command into a temptation toward self-righteousness, making it like a forbidden fruit. Instead of being a useful guide, the law became an occasion of seduction to pride in the religious life.

c. A New Dispensation

In Christ we are in a new dispensation. We were previously under the power of a corrupted nature. It dominated our actions. But now we can know experientially the power of Christ's resurrection. Sin remains but does not reign.[6]

The guilt of the law had been inflamed by pride spawned by the Mosaic law, producing death. But now we are delivered from the law as a means of righteousness, in order that we might participate in the life of the risen Lord who died for us and rose again in newness of spirit.[7]

The eternal moral law never passes away, because it is eternally embedded in human consciousness. There is no human consciousness that can act without being aware of its actions. Yet even the moral law now stands on a different foundation than before the light of the gospel.

Does this make the law in itself sinful? No. But we would not even have known what sin was had it not been for the law. We would not have known what an offense to God coveting really was if God had not commanded: "You shall not covet."[8] "But sin, seizing the opportunity afforded by the commandment, produced in me every kind of coveting. For apart from the law, sin was dead."[9] "Sin sprang to life and I died. I found that the very commandment that was intended to bring life actually brought death. For sin, seizing the opportunity afforded by the commandment, deceived me, and through the commandment put me to death."[10]

---

[4]"The Original, Nature, Property, and Use of the Law," B 2:5, J V:434, proem, sec. 2; cf. Rom. 7:4.
[5]Ibid.
[6]See *JWT* 2:266 – 80.
[7]"The Original, Nature, Property, and Use of the Law," B 2:5, J V:434, proem, sec. 2; cf. Rom. 7:1 – 6.
[8]Rom. 7:7 NIV.
[9]Rom. 7:8 NIV.
[10]Rom. 7:9 – 11 NIV.

d. The Law Is Holy, Righteous, and Good

Now that we have been raised from the dead from the old type of legal relation to God, we have a new relation with God. This bears fruit in our new life.

Now the claims of the old law are dissolved, since the previous legal relation has been buried in Jesus' death. "But now, by dying to what once bound us, we have been released from the law so that we serve in the new way of the Spirit, and not in the old way of the written code."[11]

With these premises, Paul then comes to our sermon text: "So then, the law is holy, and the commandment is holy, righteous and good."[12] How can it be that if the law is dead, it continues to be holy, just, and good in the Christian life? In the remainder of this homily, Wesley explained the origin of the law, the nature of the law, the properties of the law (holiness, justice, and goodness), and the uses of the law.[13]

2. The Origin of the Law

a. The Reception of Moral Law in Angelic Creation

The eternal moral law existed before the law of Moses, as is clear from the biblical narratives of Noah and Enoch. Scripture makes it clear that the law existed before the foundation of the world, "when 'the morning stars' first 'sang together.'"[14]

The awareness of the law is an intrinsic aspect of angelic creation, angelic freedom, and angelic consciousness. God made intelligent, noncorporeal spiritual beings, the angels, "that they might know him that created them," enduing them "with understanding, to discern truth from falsehood, good from evil; and, as a necessary result of this, with liberty — a capacity of choosing the one and refusing the other. By this they were, likewise, enabled to offer him a free and willing service; a service rewardable in itself, as well as most acceptable to their gracious Master."[15]

The faculties of understanding and liberty were given by God to intelligent spiritual creatures. The eternal moral law, accessible to rational conscience, is "a complete model of all truth, so far as is intelligible to a finite being, and of all good, so far as angelic minds were capable of embracing it. It was also the design of their beneficent Governor herein to make way for a continual increase of their happiness; seeing every instance of obedience to that law would ... add to the perfection of their nature."[16] The angels were given not only the capacity to understand the truth, but to continually increase in happiness. Every moment of obedience to the eternal law adds to the perfection of their nature.[17]

---

[11]Rom. 7:6 NIV.
[12]Rom. 7:12 NIV.
[13]"The Original, Nature, Property, and Use of the Law," B 2:6, J V:435, proem, sec. 4.
[14]Job 38:7; "The Original, Nature, Property, and Use of the Law," B 2:6, J V:435, sec. 1.1.
[15]Ibid.
[16]"The Original, Nature, Property, and Use of the Law," B 2:6, J V:436, sec. 1.2.
[17]Ibid.

b. The Law in Human History — Fallen and Redeemed

On the sixth day of creation, God created man from the dust of the earth, and "breathed into him the breath of life," and caused him to become a living soul. Adam is distinguished from angels by having flesh, but similar to angels by having reason, freedom, and moral awareness. Man is similarly "endued with power to choose good or evil." The law was "engraven on his heart by the finger of God; wrote in the inmost spirit both of men and of angels; to the intent it might never be far off, never hard to be understood, but always at hand, and always shining with clear light, even as the sun in the midst of heaven."[18]

This eternal moral law is what Wesley called "the original of the law of God," embedded first in angelic creation and then human nature. "But it was not long before man rebelled against God, and by breaking this glorious law, well nigh effaced it out of his heart." The eyes of his understanding were darkened. His soul was "alienated from the life of God."[19]

God did not give up on humanity, but redeemed him through his Son, wherein God "in some measure, reinscribed the law on the heart of his dark, sinful creature." By this God once again showed man what is good. All creatures with reason can grasp the good: "to do justly, and to love mercy, and to walk humbly with thy God."[20]

c. The Law in the History of Sin

The capacity for moral awareness was given not only to our first parents but to all their posterity. The original law of God became "that true Light which enlightens every man that cometh into the world."[21] But the whole of Adam and Eve's progeny followed them in sin.[22]

At length God "chose out of mankind a peculiar people, to whom he gave a more perfect knowledge of his law." Because through the history of sin they had become slow of understanding, God "wrote on two tables of stone, which he commanded the fathers to teach their children, through all succeeding generations."[23]

Thus, through a tangled history, the original law of God was further clarified and expressed through the written law of Moses. But due to persistent sin, this still did not suffice for reconciling the holy God with wayward creatures. "They cannot, by this means, comprehend the height, and depth, and length, and breadth thereof."[24] God alone can reveal this by his Spirit. Without God's own Spirit, the law could not be appropriated, no matter how clearly it was given. The reception of the eternal law has a history darkened by sin.

The promise of a new covenant was required to reconcile God's holiness and

---

[18]"The Original, Nature, Property, and Use of the Law," B 2:7, J V:436, sec. 1.3.
[19]"The Original, Nature, Property, and Use of the Law," B 2:7, J V:436, sec. 1.4.
[20]Ibid.; Mic. 6:8.
[21]"The Original, Nature, Property, and Use of the Law," B 2:7, J V:436, sec. 1.5; cf. John 1:9.
[22]*LJW* 4:155; 6:240.
[23]"The Original, Nature, Property, and Use of the Law," B 2:8, J V:437, sec. 1.5.
[24]Ibid.

human sin. "And so he does to all that truly believe, in consequence of that gracious promise made to all the Israel of God." God promises to "make a new covenant with the house of Israel.... I will put my law in their inward parts, and write it in their hearts; and will be their God, and they shall be my people."[25]

Having discussed the origin of the law, we turn to the nature of the law. How do we define the law?

3. The Nature of the Law

What is the nature of this law? "It is the heart of God disclosed to man ... the express image of his person."[26] The law gives us "a picture of the Eternal One ... the face of God unveiled; God manifested to his creatures as they are able to bear it."[27] "The law of God is all virtues in one," in a shape to be beheld by all whose eyes God has enlightened. "What is it but the original ideas of truth and good, which were lodged in the uncreated mind from eternity, now drawn forth and clothed with such a vehicle as to appear even to human understanding?"[28] The eternal law is "unchangeable reason; it is unalterable rectitude, it is the everlasting fitness of all things."[29]

Now we know only in part. While we are in this house of clay, while we are speaking as a child would speak, we hope for that time when we can put away childish things, "when that which is perfect is come, then that which is in part shall be done away."[30] Scripture teaches that "the law of God (speaking after the manner of men) is a copy of the eternal mind, a transcript of the divine nature."[31]

A property of the law is that which belongs to it, that which uniquely characterizes and defines it. The properties of the law are holiness, justice, and goodness.[32]

a. The Law Is Holy

The holiness of the law means that this image of the heart of God is pure, chaste, spotless, undefiled, unpolluted,[33] "pure from all sin, clean and unspotted from any touch of evil."[34] "As sin is, in its very nature, enmity to God, so his law is enmity to sin."[35]

The law of God is neither sin itself, nor the cause of sin. "God forbid that we should suppose it is the cause of sin, because it is the discoverer of it; because it

---

[25]Jer. 31:31 – 33; "The Original, Nature, Property, and Use of the Law," B 2:8, J V:437, sec. 1.6.

[26]"The Original, Nature, Property, and Use of the Law," B 2:9, J V:438, sec. 2.3.

[27]Ibid.; cf. Heb. 1:3.

[28]"The Original, Nature, Property, and Use of the Law," B 2:9, J V:438, sec. 2.4.

[29]"The Original, Nature, Property, and Use of the Law," B 2:10, J V:438, sec. 2.5.

[30]1 Cor. 13:10 – 11; "The Original, Nature, Property, and Use of the Law," B 2:10, J V:438, sec. 2.5.

[31]"The Original, Nature, Property, and Use of the Law," B 2:10, J V:438, sec. 2.6; cf. Col. 1:15 – 19.

[32]"The Original, Nature, Property, and Use of the Law," B 2:10, J V:439, sec. 3.1.

[33]"The Original, Nature, Property, and Use of the Law," B 2:10 – 11, J V:439, sec. 3.2; cf. James 1:27; 3:17.

[34]"The Original, Nature, Property, and Use of the Law," B 2:11, J V:439, sec. 3.3.

[35]"The Original, Nature, Property, and Use of the Law," B 2:11, J V:439, sec. 3.4.

detects the hidden things of darkness and drags them out into open day."[36] Even if it is by the law that sin appears, that does not mean the law is sin.[37]

All of sin's disguises are torn away by the law. Sin "loses its excuse, as well as disguise" under the divine command. "When it is dragged out to light, it rages the more."[38]

b. The Law Is Just

A defining property of the law of God is that it is just. It belongs to the law to be just. What is unjust cannot be according to the eternal moral law. "It renders to all their due. It prescribes exactly what is right, precisely what ought to be done, said, or thought."[39] Our human justice is an inexact reflection of the eternal law in the mind of God.

Nothing in the law of God is arbitrary. The law's command is adapted to the nature of each thing, to the whole, and to every part, "suited to all the circumstances of each, and to all their mutual relations.... It is exactly agreeable to the fitnesses of things."[40] In every command the law says, "Thy will be done."[41]

"Is a thing therefore right, because God wills it, or does he will it because it is right?" Wesley viewed this conundrum as an absentminded question because it presumed that God's will is distinct from God.[42] The question is "more curious than useful."[43]

Finite creatures stand in awe of the mystery of the relation of God's being to God's willing. Judging only from within finite creation, humans are in an insufficient position to fully grasp the Infinite One who justly provides a created order. Creatures do not call the Creator to accountability, although their finite minds strive to grasp how they have been created by an eternal justice not their own. "By his will, 'for his pleasure' alone, they all 'are and were created.'"[44] In every particular case, God wills this or that "because it is right, agreeable to the fitness of things, to the relation wherein they stand."[45]

c. The Law Is Good

The third property of the law is that it is good. It is good because God is good.[46]

"To what else can we impute his bestowing upon man the same transcript of his own nature?... This law, which the goodness of God gave at first, and has preserved through all ages, is, like the fountain from whence it springs, full of goodness and

---

[36]Ibid.
[37]Cf. Rom. 7:13.
[38]"The Original, Nature, Property, and Use of the Law," B 2:11, J V:439, sec. 3.4.
[39]"The Original, Nature, Property, and Use of the Law," B 2:12, J V:440, sec. 3.5.
[40]Ibid.
[41]Ibid.
[42]"The Original, Nature, Property, and Use of the Law," B 2:13, J V:441, sec. 3.7.
[43]"The Original, Nature, Property, and Use of the Law," B 2:12–13, J V:440–41, sec. 3.6.
[44]"The Original, Nature, Property, and Use of the Law," B 2:13, J V:441, sec. 3.8.
[45]"The Original, Nature, Property, and Use of the Law," B 2:13, J V:441, sec. 3.9.
[46]"The Original, Nature, Property, and Use of the Law," B 2:13, J V:441, sec. 3.10.

benignity; it is mild and kind; it is, as the psalmist expresses it, 'sweeter than honey and the honeycomb.'"[47]

The law of God "is good in its effects, as well as in its nature. As the tree is, so are its fruits. The fruits of the law of God written in the heart are 'righteousness, and peace, and assurance for ever.'"[48]

Having now set forth the origin, nature, and properties of the law, we turn to the uses and benefits of the law. The law has three uses according to a balanced reading of Scripture. How does the law work to our benefit?

4. The Uses of the Law

a. The First Use of the Law: To Convict of Sin

The first benefit of the law is to convict the world of sin. This is a peculiar work of the Holy Spirit, who can use any means or work without any means at all to convict the conscience.

The Spirit may work to break old molds to create a new life. There are those "whose hearts have been broken in pieces in a moment, either in sickness or in health, without any visible cause."

Repentance precedes faith. The law elicits humility and penitence. This is the ordinary method of the Spirit of God: "to convict sinners by the law."[49] The law provides the service of bringing conscience to humbling recognitions.

This work is often "quick and powerful ... and sharper than any two edged sword." The hand of God and those he sends "pierces through all the folds of a deceitful heart, and 'divides asunder even the soul and the spirit'" even to the very "joints and marrow. By this is the sinner discovered to himself. All his fig leaves are torn away, and he sees that he is 'wretched, and poor, and miserable, and blind, and naked.' The law flashes conviction on every side. He feels himself a mere sinner. He has nothing to pay. His 'mouth is stopped,' and he stands 'guilty before God.'"[50] The Spirit works graciously to "slay the sinner ... to destroy the life [idolatrous] and strength wherein he trusts."[51]

b. The Second Use of the Law: To Bring the Sinner to Life by Grace through Faith

When the sinner learns that Christ has fulfilled the law for him, he is ready to receive grace by faith. In this way, the law plays a role beyond eliciting repentance to eliciting readiness for faith.

The law is not a means of procuring our justification. There is no need for that because it is already accomplished by grace through faith. "We have done with the moral law as a means of procuring our justification; for we are 'justified freely by his

---

[47]"The Original, Nature, Property, and Use of the Law," B 2:14, J V:441, sec. 3.11.
[48]"The Original, Nature, Property, and Use of the Law," B 2:15, J V:442, sec. 3.12.
[49]"The Original, Nature, Property, and Use of the Law," B 2:15, J V:442, sec. 4.1.
[50]Ibid.
[51]"The Original, Nature, Property, and Use of the Law," B 2:16, J V:443, sec. 4.2.

grace, through the redemption that is in Jesus'; yet, in another sense, we have not done with this law: for it is still of unspeakable use." For the law continues to convict the faithful of "the sin that yet remains both in our hearts and lives."[52]

The law is like a tough, loving schoolmaster. The performance of the law does not justify but leads us to justification. "It drives us by force, rather than draws us by love. And yet love is the spring of all. It is the spirit of love, which, by this painful means, tears away our confidence in the flesh, which leaves us no broken reed whereon to trust, and so constrains the sinner, stripped of all, to cry out in the bitterness of his soul, or groan in the depth of his heart."[53]

c. The Third Use of the Law: To Keep Us Close to Christ

"The grand means whereby the blessed Spirit prepares the believer for larger communications of the life of God" is to keep faith alive.[54]

In what sense is "Christ ... the end of the law for righteousness to every one that believeth"?[55] Christ brings to an end our self-justifying pretenses. The law justifies no one, since the righteousness of God has acted justly to pardon the faithful. The law has a role in this history: it draws humanity close to Christ who is "the end or scope of the law — the point at which it continually aims."[56] The law not only guides us toward repentance that welcomes Christ but also keeps us closely bonded with Christ.

Further, the Spirit empowers the believer to do what the law commands, "deriving strength from our Head into his living members," and "in confirming our hope of whatsoever it commands and we have not yet attained — of receiving grace upon grace, till we are in actual possession of the fulness of his promises."[57]

The believer continues to study the law and be guided by it. He cries out, "Oh, how I love your law! I meditate on it all day long."[58] The law teaches the faithful that every temptation to backslide into sin is an opportunity to return to the unmerited grace and favor of God. We need the law to keep us close to Christ by leading us to daily repentance.

"Indeed each is continually sending me to the other — the law to Christ, and Christ to the law."[59] "Keep close to the law, if thou wilt keep close to Christ; hold it fast; let it not go," till all the "righteousness of the law is fulfilled in thee," and you are "filled with all the fullness of God."[60]

If the Lord has already written his law in your heart, then "'stand fast in the liberty wherewith Christ hath made thee free.' Thou art not only made free from

---

[52]"The Original, Nature, Property, and Use of the Law," B 2:17, J V:444, sec. 4.4.
[53]"The Original, Nature, Property, and Use of the Law," B 2:15, J V:442, sec. 4.2.
[54]Ibid.
[55]Rom. 10:4.
[56]"The Original, Nature, Property, and Use of the Law," B 2:16, J V:443 – 44, sec. 4.3.
[57]"The Original, Nature, Property, and Use of the Law," B 2:17, J V:444, sec. 6.
[58]Ps. 119:97 NIV.
[59]"The Original, Nature, Property, and Use of the Law," B 2:18, J V:445, sec. 4.7.
[60]"The Original, Nature, Property, and Use of the Law," B 2:18 – 19, J V:446, sec. 4.9.

Jewish ceremonies, from the guilt of sin, and the fear of hell … but, what is infinitely more, from the power of sin … from offending God. O stand fast in this liberty.… This is perfect freedom; thus to keep his law, and to walk in all his commandments blameless."[61]

B. The Law Established through Faith

1. Does the Gospel Totally Nullify the Law?

a. The Law Established through Faith: Discourse 1

Homilies 30 and 31 have the same generic title: "The Law Established through Faith." Together they constitute Wesley's most sustained argument of the theological grounding of Christian ethics. Here he makes clear that the gospel does not nullify the law. Rather, the gospel establishes the law under the new conditions of unmerited grace.

Wesley took as his text for both discourses this crucial passage from Paul's letter to the Romans: "Do we then make void the law through faith? God forbid: yea, we establish the law" [Rom. 3:31; Homily #30, J #35, "The Law Established through Faith: Discourse 1," B 2:22 – 32, J V:447 – 57 (1750)].

Those who wish to grasp the relation of law and gospel in Wesley's view must study carefully these two homilies. The insights they yield are well worth the effort.

b. The Status of the Law after Christ's Coming

The question of the status of the law after the coming of Christ is answered in Romans 3:31. The gospel does not nullify the law but rather establishes the law. This is Paul's conclusion to all that has been previously stated in his introduction to the letter from Romans 1:1 to Romans 3:30.[62]

Paul laid down his general proposition for the letter in Romans 1:16: "For I am not ashamed of the gospel, because it is the power of God that brings salvation to everyone who believes" (NIV). God has offered a way of pardon to all who have ears to hear.[63]

There is no other way humanity can be saved but by the way God has provided.[64] That way is the good news of God's saving action in Jesus Christ. No one under the law can plead that he or she has no sin whatsoever. All stand in need of salvation from the guilt of sin. All humanity stands in need of God's pardoning action. To rightly view the law under faith, "every mouth must be 'stopped' from excusing or justifying himself, 'and all the world become guilty before God.' "[65] Paul

---

[61]"The Original, Nature, Property, and Use of the Law," B 2:19, J V:445, sec. 4.10.

[62]The premise for Romans 3:31 is carefully laid out in Paul's introduction to the letter, Romans 1:1 – 3:20. Without this premise, our text is taken out of context.

[63]"The Law Established through Faith," 1, B 2:20 – 21, J V:447 – 48, proem, sec. 1.

[64]Cf. Acts 4:12.

[65]Ibid. "Now we know that whatever the law says, it says to those who are under the law, so that every mouth may be silenced and the whole world held accountable to God" (Rom. 3:19 NIV).

"speaks particularly of salvation from the guilt of sin, which he commonly terms justification."[66]

c. Righteousness of God Given Apart from the Law

The good news is not about our righteousness under the law, but God's righteousness received through faith: "Now apart from the law the righteousness of God has been made known, to which the Law and the Prophets testify. This righteousness is given through faith in Jesus Christ to all who believe."[67] It is given both to Jews and Gentiles.

"All have sinned and fall short of the glory of God, and all are justified freely by his grace through the redemption that came by Christ Jesus."[68]

We were all created in the glorious image of God. We are "justified freely by his grace through the redemption that is in Christ Jesus: whom God hath set forth to be a propitiation through faith in his blood, to declare his righteousness for the remission of sins."[69]

The justice of God is not diminished by the mercy of God: "Without any impeachment to his justice," God shows humanity "mercy for the sake of that propitiation."[70] God is righteous in showing this mercy through the atoning work of his Son. "Therefore we conclude ... that a man is justified by faith, without the works of the law."[71]

d. Paul's Answer to Those Who Would Use the Gospel to Invite License

There is a perennial objection to this Good News: the fear of antinomian license that to some it seems to extend. If a blanket permission is being issued by God, doesn't it invite illegal acts? This question has been asked from New Testament times by critics from Celsus to the opponents of Luther. It is even raised by Paul himself. "Shall we continue in sin, that grace may abound?"[72] It seems to some that Paul's proclamation of freedom from the law and Christ as the end of the law stands without any qualification. If so, it would seem to mean that for Christians there is no law.

Here comparing Scripture with Scripture is necessary to keep the whole of apostolic testimony in balance. Though Paul may appear to argue in highly select texts that the law in every sense has been abolished, his own text here shows that is not his intent, as we will see by attending to the apostolic consensus.

No apostolic writer or classic Christian teacher ever taught lawlessness or the end of the law without careful qualification. For two millennia it has been called "antinomianism." Paul's purpose in Romans 3:31 is to answer this objection

---

[66]"The Law Established through Faith," 1, B 2:20, J V:447, proem, sec. 1.
[67]Rom. 3:21–22 NIV.
[68]Rom. 3:23–24 NIV. "The Law Established through Faith," 1, B 2:20, J V:447, proem, sec. 1.
[69]Rom. 3:24–25.
[70]"The Law Established through Faith," 1, B 2:20–21, J V:447–48, proem, sec. 1.
[71]"The Law Established through Faith," 1, B 2:20, J V:447, proem, sec. 1; cf. Rom. 3:28.
[72]Rom. 6:1.

definitively. Rather, by this gracious act of forgiveness "we establish the law."[73] According to Wesley, God did transcend that law through faith. Paul openly avowed his doing so, but with this crucial qualification: the moral law given in creation is eternal and hence not transcended. Instead, it is through God's pardon that the law is established on new ground: gratitude for God's mercy. Hence "we do not make void, but establish this through faith."[74] This qualification saves Christianity from being wrongly viewed as opposed to the moral law given from the foundation of the world. That could never be God's intention in saving humanity by grace alone through faith alone.

The use of the law has been a point of contention in Christian history over centuries. Many have wrongly contended that "'the faith once delivered to the saints' was designed to make void the whole law," including both the eternal moral law and the Mosaic ceremonial law. "They would no more spare the moral than the ceremonial law." The antinomians have said generation after generation, "If you establish any law, Christ shall profit you nothing."[75]

They miss Paul's insistence that the law is established through faith. They are recklessly ready to claim that the gospel destroys both the ceremonial and moral law. They forget that to abolish the moral law is to undermine faith itself.[76] All who desire to walk with Christ must resist this exaggeration by heeding Romans 3:31.[77]

There are three ways of illegitimately "making void the law": (1) not preaching the law at all, (2) preaching the law so as to excuse the believer from requiring any response to grace, and (3) simply by treating the law practically as if faith was designed to excuse those justified from holy living.[78]

e. Making Void the Law by Not Teaching It at All

The first way is not to teach the law at all — ignore the law altogether. The most common way to make void the law through faith is seen in the teacher who makes it void in a single stroke by avoiding teaching it. This is tantamount to blotting the relevance of the law totally out of scriptural teaching. This undermines both the gospel and the law "under the color of preaching Christ."[79]

This is all the more absurd "when it is done with design; when it is made a rule, not to preach the law; and the very phrase 'a Preacher of the law' is used as a term of reproach, as though it meant little less than 'an enemy of the gospel.'"[80]

Antinomian license "proceeds from the deepest ignorance of the nature, properties, and use of the law" among those "unskilled in the word of righteousness." By

---

[73]"The Law Established through Faith," 1, B 2:21, J V:448, proem, sec. 1.

[74]"The Law Established through Faith," 1, B 2:21, J V:448, proem, sec. 3.

[75]"The Law Established through Faith," 1, B 2:21, J V:448, proem, sec. 4. Wesley's highly respected Moravian friends were saying just that to him in his trip to Moravia.

[76]"The Law Established through Faith," 1, B 2:22, J V:448, proem, sec. 5.

[77]"The Law Established through Faith," 1, B 2:22, J V:448, proem, sec. 6.

[78]Ibid.

[79]"The Law Established through Faith," 1, B 2:22, J V:449, sec. 1.1.

[80]Ibid.

doing so they show that they are "utter strangers to living faith," and "but babes in Christ."[81]

f. Preach Christ without Making Void the Law

Wesley followed Augustine and the core classic Reformation teaching of Luther, Calvin, and the Anglican divines in affirming the first use of the law. According to this wide consensus, the first purpose of the law is the convicting of sin — "awakening those who are still asleep"[82] by preaching repentance and faith. The law is intended to convince the sinner of his sin and let the mercy of God be its only remedy. "It is absurd, therefore, to offer a physician to them that are whole, or that at least imagine themselves so to be."[83] It is like casting pearls before swine to offer sinners the gospel without allowing the law to do its proper work of conviction and repentance. Only then can the pearls be offered to those who are prepared to receive them.[84]

Wesley asked, "Who preached the law more than St. Paul?" On this premise we preach "not ourselves, but Christ Jesus the Lord."[85] The apostle "first reminds them, that they could not be justified by the law of Moses, but only by faith in Christ," and then immediately calls the law "holy, just, and good."[86]

Where there is no teaching of the law, there can be no teaching of Christ: "To preach Christ is to preach all things that Christ hath spoken; all his promises, all his threatenings and commands, all that is written in his book, and then you will know how to preach Christ, without making void the law."[87] To preach Christ without preaching the law, and hence without letting the law call us to repentance, is "to make void the gospel as well as the law."[88]

g. Making Void the Law by Teaching That Faith Supersedes the Call to Holiness

The second way of making void the law is to preach the law in a way that excuses the believer from requiring any serious response to grace. Suppose the law is taught only superficially so as to leave the impression that faith supersedes the imperative of holiness. That is the subtler way to make void the law, against Paul's clear teaching.

The idea that faith circumvents the call to holiness leads into a thousand ill-advised outcomes.[89] This error comes in three common forms: (1) people suppose that holiness is less necessary now than it was before Christ came, or (2) that a lesser

[81]"The Law Established through Faith," 1, B 2:22, J V:449, sec. 1.2.
[82]"The Law Established through Faith," 1, B 2:22, J V:449, sec. 1.3.
[83]Ibid.
[84]Ibid.
[85]"The Law Established through Faith," 1, B 2:23, J V:450, sec. 1.5; cf. 2 Cor. 4:5.
[86]"The Law Established through Faith," 1, B 2:23–24, J V:449, sec. 1.6; cf. Acts 13:39.
[87]"The Law Established through Faith," 1, B 2:25, J V:452, sec. 1.11.
[88]"The Law Established through Faith," 1, B 2:25, J V:452, sec. 1.12.
[89]"The Law Established through Faith," 1, B 2:26, J V:452, sec. 2.1.

degree of it is necessary, or (3) that it is less necessary to believers than to others.[90] In each case, they use the term *liberty* in a way that becomes liberty from obedience and liberty for license.[91]

Adam and Eve before the fall were under that original covenant that required perfect obedience as the one condition of acceptance. They disobeyed. All their subsequent offspring have been under the law, but in history they are given merciful time for repentance. The death of sinners, which is the just price of sin, is delayed mercifully, calling for repentance and faith through unmerited grace. "The manner of their acceptance is this: the free grace of God, through the merits of Christ, gives pardon to them that believe; that believe with such a faith as, working by love, produces all obedience and holiness."[92]

What about those like Abraham who lived according to faith in the promise before Christ's coming? They were given the sufficient grace of hoping in the promise of his coming, as did Isaiah and Joel. Along with Abraham, the prophetic teachers were justified by their faith in what was to come in Christ, even without knowing of the unseen future in which their hope would be fulfilled.[93] "The covenant of grace gives you no ground, no encouragement at all, to set aside any insistence or degree of obedience, any part or measure of holiness."[94]

h. Both Legalism and License Deny Grace

Legalism follows the letter of the law instead of its spirit. The hyper-legalistic Pharisees ran in such an extremely literalistic and meticulous direction contrary to grace that they serve as the "occasion [for] others to run" away from religion altogether.[95] Those immature Christians are like Pharisees who seek to be justified by works. The overreaction of antinomianism occurs when faith seeks to be justified without fruits of faith, hope, and love.

The truth of the good news of salvation lies neither in legalism nor in antinomian license. Wesley followed in the steps of Paul, Augustine, Luther, Calvin, and the Anglican and Puritan divines in teaching, "We are, doubtless, justified by faith. This is the cornerstone of the whole Christian building. We are justified without the works of the law, as any previous condition of justification." But good works are "an immediate fruit of that faith whereby we are justified,"[96] since faith is always active in good works.[97]

Faith in God's unmerited grace has consequences for responsive behavior: "So that if good works do not follow our faith, even all inward and outward holiness,

[90]"The Law Established through Faith," 1, B 2:26, J V:452, sec. 2.2.
[91]Ibid.
[92]"The Law Established through Faith," 1, B 2:26, J V:452, sec. 2.4.
[93]"The Law Established through Faith," 1, B 2:26, J V:452, sec. 2.3.
[94]"The Law Established through Faith," 1, B 2:26, J V:452, sec. 2.4.
[95]"The Law Established through Faith," 1, B 2:26, J V:452, sec. 2.5.
[96]"The Law Established through Faith," 1, B 2:26, J V:452, sec. 2.6.
[97]For a fuller understanding of antinomianism, see *JWT* 2:64–66, 81–82, 259–60.

it is plain our faith is worth nothing; we are yet in our sins." Hence justification by grace alone is "no ground for making void the law through faith."[98]

i. Why Holiness Cannot Precede Justification

So, if justification by grace alone is no ground for making void the law through faith, how does Wesley understand Romans 4:5 (NIV): "However, to the one who does not work but trusts God who justifies the ungodly, their faith is credited as righteousness"? This does not mean that faith is a substitute for a righteous and good life of faith, hope, and love. The misunderstanding of this passage, read alone without comparing Scripture with Scripture, is "the main pillar of Antinomianism."[99]

In what sense does God "justify the ungodly"? Wesley's answer has three parts:

1. "God justifies the ungodly; him that, till that hour, is totally ungodly — full of all evil, void of all good."[100]
2. God "justifies the ungodly" who up to the moment of receiving saving grace have offered their good works to God in a way unpleasing to God, namely, without trust in God's righteousness alone, since "an evil tree cannot bring forth good fruit."[101]
3. God "justifies him by faith alone, without any goodness or righteousness preceding."[102] Therefore faith is counted for righteousness due to God's righteousness communicated. God's preceding righteousness antecedes faith's subsequent righteousness. In this sense, "faith is then counted to him for righteousness; namely, for preceding righteousness; that is, God, through the merits of Christ, accepts him that believes as if he had already fulfilled all righteousness."[103]

Mark well: If God has "already fulfilled all righteousness" in his gift of grace in the risen Lord, that is merit sufficient. Good works that flow naturally from this grace are without merit toward justification. But "the apostle does not say, either here or elsewhere, that this faith is counted to him for subsequent righteousness. He does teach that there is no righteousness before faith; but where does he teach that there is none after it? He does assert, holiness cannot precede justification, but not that it need not follow it."[104] Paul also warns about making void the law by appealing to grace.[105]

j. Making Void the Law by Living as If Faith Were Designed to Excuse Us from Holiness

The third way of making void the law is the most common. It makes void the law

---

[98]"The Law Established through Faith," 1, B 2:26, J V:452, sec. 2.6.
[99]"The Law Established through Faith," 1, B 2:26, J V:452, sec. 2.7.
[100]Ibid.
[101]Ibid.; cf. Matt. 7:18.
[102]"The Law Established through Faith," 1, B 2:26, J V:452, sec. 2.7.
[103]"The Law Established through Faith," 1, B 2:26, J V:452, sec. 3.2.
[104]Ibid.
[105]"The Law Established through Faith," 1, B 2:31, J V:452, sec. 3.2.

in practice, "though not in principle; the living or acting as if faith were designed to excuse us from holiness."[106] This is the most common way of dismissing the relevance of the law. This evasion says, in principle we may be under the law, but in practice we are excused from accountability. It is not the intention of the gospel to offer that excuse.

Rather, the apostle cautions the faithful specifically against this evasion with the well-known words: "What then? shall we sin, because we are not under the law, but under grace? God forbid."[107] From the moment of believing and trusting in God's righteousness revealed, the faithful are not "under the law," viewed as the ceremonial law of the whole Mosaic institution. Rather, they are "'under grace,' under a more benign, gracious dispensation."[108]

Grace frees us from living "under a sense of guilt and condemnation, full of horror and slavish fear."[109] The believer is "not without law to God, but under the law to Christ."[110] He is no longer under the ceremonial law or the Mosaic institution. However much the believer may be exempt from the Jewish ceremonial law of animal sacrifice, he is not exempt from the eternal moral law of God. Even reason and conscience teach us that. But that law is more clearly manifested in the history of salvation in a special way in the Mosaic and prophetic Scriptures.

Living "under the law to Christ" means living a grateful, pardoned life. The believer is delivered from all sense of guilt and condemnation. "He now performs (which while 'under the law' he could not do) a willing and universal obedience. He obeys not from the motive of slavish fear, but on a nobler principle; namely, the grace of God ruling in his heart, and causing all his works to be wrought in love."[111] When grace rules the heart, the inward intent is manifested in behavior. We act responsibly out of grace not law, out of filial law not servile fear.[112]

k. Self-Examination

Wesley concluded his first discourse on this text with a serious call to self-examination. Examine yourself honestly and closely. Beware lest you sin under the promise that you are "not under the law but under grace."[113] "God forbid you should any longer continue thus to 'turn the grace of God into lasciviousness!'"[114] Remember how strong a conviction you once had when you first heard the gospel. "Let not the mercy of God weigh less with you now, than his fiery indignation did before. Is love a less powerful motive than fear?" Let gracious love be your invariable rule.[115]

---

[106]"The Law Established through Faith," 1, B 2:31, J V:452, sec. 3.1.
[107]"The Law Established through Faith," 1, B 2:31, J V:454–55, sec. 3.1; Rom. 6:15.
[108]"The Law Established through Faith," 1, B 2:29, J V:455, sec. 3.3.
[109]"The Law Established through Faith," 1, B 2:29, J V:455, sec. 3.2.
[110]"The Law Established through Faith," 1, B 2:29, J V:455, sec. 3.3.
[111]Ibid.
[112]"The Law Established through Faith," 1, B 2:30, J V:455, sec. 3.4.
[113]"The Law Established through Faith," 1, B 2:30, J V:455, sec. 3.3.
[114]"The Law Established through Faith," 1, B 2:31, J V:457, sec. 3.7.
[115]Ibid.

C. The Law Not Nullified but Fulfilled

1. The Scriptural Remedy for Those Who Imagine Themselves Free from the Law

In Wesley's second discourse on "The Law Established through Faith" (Homily 31), he further pursued reasons why the gospel does not nullify the law but rather establishes the law on a new ground — namely, the basis of the gospel.

Wesley's text remains the same: "Do we then make void the law through faith? God forbid: yea, we establish the law" [Rom. 3:31; Homily #31, J #36, "The Law Established through Faith: Discourse 1," B 2:33 – 43, J V:458 – 66 (1750)].

The gospel does not seek to reestablish the old ceremonial and sacrificial Jewish laws of the old dead life of self-justifying claims. They are abolished forever. Much less do we reestablish the whole Mosaic dispensation. "This we know our Lord has nailed to his cross."[116]

Nor do we teach the moral law as if it justified, pardoned, or poured out grace upon us. No sinner can be justified simply by keeping the moral law. But aside from pretending that the moral law justifies, it is nonetheless established by faith by being understood from the viewpoint of the gospel.[117]

In what sense, then, do we establish the law? By our doctrine and by our preaching as confirmed by the redeemed condition of our hearts.

2. The Law Established through Faith by Biblical Teaching

a. Teaching the Wholeness of Faith

How do we make sure the law is being properly established in our doctrinal teaching? By teaching the wholeness of the faith once delivered to the saints. Our doctrinal task is "to preach it in its whole extent, to explain ... every part of it, in the same manner as our great Teacher did while upon earth."[118] We keep back nothing from our hearers "by declaring to them, without any limitation or reserve, the whole counsel of God."[119] Teaching on this subject calls for "great plainness of speech."[120] We do not corrupt the Word of God. We do not "mix, adulterate, or soften it to make it suit the taste of the hearers."[121]

We speak plainly because "we have renounced secret and shameful ways; we do not use deception, nor do we distort the word of God. On the contrary, by setting forth the truth plainly we commend ourselves to everyone's conscience in the sight of God."[122] We are not preaching ourselves but Christ, to let "his light shine in our

---

[116]"The Law Established through Faith," 2, B 2:73, J V:458 – 59, proem, sec. 2.
[117]Ibid.
[118]"The Law Established through Faith," 2, B 2:73, J V:459, sec. 1.1.
[119]Ibid.
[120]Ibid.
[121]Ibid.
[122]2 Cor. 4:2 NIV.

hearts to give us the light of the knowledge of God's glory displayed in the face of Christ."[123]

b. The Purpose of the Law: To Engender Purity of Heart That Bears Outward Fruit

Fragments of the law and fragments of the gospel are all distortable and potentially demeaning without the whole interface between law and gospel. Promise and fulfillment are intrinsically connected in the history of salvation. It is this wholeness of classic apostolic Christianity that is expressed in the doctrine of the gospel reframing the meaning of the law. "We then, by our doctrine, establish the law when we thus openly declare it to all men; and that in the fullness wherein it is delivered by our blessed Lord and his apostles; when we publish it in the height, and depth, and length, and breadth" of it.[124]

The ancient covenant community sang, "Blessed is man who delights in the law of the Lord."[125] Christians equally with Jews delight in the law of the Lord. It leads to happiness — genuine blessedness extending to the whole of life. The prophets were already standing in expectation of the fulfillment of the law according to God's promises for the future. We then "establish the law" when we explain and confirm the whole of it understood within the gospel frame of reference, "every part of it, every commandment contained therein, not only in its full, literal sense, but likewise in its spiritual meaning; not only with regard to the outward actions, which it either forbids or enjoins, but also with respect to the inward principle, to the thoughts, desires, and intents of the heart."[126] "All that is written in the book of God we are to declare, not as pleasing men, but the Lord."[127]

The purpose of the law is to make fair and just "the dispositions and tempers of the heart" in preparation for the good news of God's saving work.[128] "When taken in its full spiritual meaning, [the law] is 'a mystery which was hid from ages and generations since the world began.'"[129] That hiddenness was fully revealed in the cross and resurrection.

c. Teaching the Law

The law is not about cleaning the outside of a cup, but about the holiness of inward intentions. The inclination of the heart is the basis of outward actions. The purpose of the law is the purity of the heart it seeks to awaken. This is expressed in Psalm 66:18: "If I had cherished sin in my heart, the Lord would not have listened" (NIV).[130]

---

[123] 2 Cor. 4:6 NIV.
[124] "The Law Established through Faith," 2, B 2:74, J V:459, sec. 1.2.
[125] Cf. Ps. 1:2.
[126] "The Law Established through Faith," 2, B 2:74–75, J V:459–60, sec. 1.3.
[127] "The Law Established through Faith," 2, B 2:75–76, J V:460–61, sec. 1.5.
[128] "The Law Established through Faith," 2, B 2:74–75, J V:459–60, sec. 1.3.
[129] Cf. Col. 1:26.
[130] "The Law Established through Faith," 2, B 2:74–75, J V:459–60, sec. 1.3.

This fuller meaning of the law was "almost equally hid, as to its spiritual meaning, from the bulk of the Jewish nation," as is evident from "our Lord's continual reproof of the wisest among them for their gross misinterpretations of it."[131] Much of the Christian world has also tragically missed the deeper intention of the law.[132]

Those "who have the form but not the power of religion, and who are generally wise in their own eyes, and righteous in their own conceits" are deeply offended when evangelical faith speaks of the uses of the law bearing upon "the religion of the heart."[133]

Evangelical faith openly declares not only all the promises "all the blessings and privileges which God hath prepared for his children, [but] we are likewise to 'teach all the things whatsoever he hath commanded.'"[134] What God commands is sufficiently known in Scripture. "All Scripture is God-breathed and is useful for teaching, rebuking, correcting and training in righteousness, so that the servant of God may be thoroughly equipped for every good work."[135] This is why the Law and Prophets are included in the sacred text of Christianity and not Judaism alone.

There is a proper time to "dwell upon [Christ's] praise, as 'bearing the iniquities of us all, as wounded for our transgressions, and bruised for our iniquities, that by his stripes we might be healed.'" But we are not fully preaching Christ if we do not "proclaim him in all his offices," as Priest, Prophet, and King, "who, by his word and his Spirit, is with us always, 'guiding us into all truth,'" as one who is "giving laws to all whom he has bought with his blood; as restoring those to the image of God, whom he had first reinstated in his favor; as reigning in all believing hearts until he has 'subdued all things to himself' — until he hath utterly cast out all sin, and brought in everlasting righteousness."[136]

3. Establishing the Integrity of Law and Gospel through Preaching

In addition to establishing the law doctrinally, we also "establish the law, secondly, when we so preach faith in Christ as not to supersede, but produce holiness; to produce all manner of holiness, negative and positive, of the heart and of the life."[137] The gospel proclaims that wholesome faith that leads to full responsiveness to grace in the life of love.

Those who try to preach the gospel without preaching the law preach an unfinished gospel. The gospel does not demolish the law but establishes it in the context of revealed grace. Evangelical preaching establishes the law by showing the gathered community through Scripture the wholeness of the faith once delivered to the saints.

---

[131] Ibid. Excepting those who, like Abraham and Isaiah, look to the fulfillment of its promise in the Messiah.

[132] "The Law Established through Faith," 2, B 2:75, J V:460, sec. 1.4.

[133] "The Law Established through Faith," 2, B 2:75–76, J V:460–61, sec. 1.5.

[134] Ibid.

[135] 2 Tim. 3:16–17 NIV; "The Law Established through Faith," 2, B 2:75–76, J V:460–61, sec. 1.5.

[136] "The Law Established through Faith," 2, B 2:76, J V:461–62, sec. 1.6; cf. Isa. 53:5; John 16:13; Phil. 3:21.

[137] "The Law Established through Faith," 2, B 2:77, J V:462, sec. 2.1. "Negative" refers to negations of holiness.

a. Whether Faith Surpasses Love

"Love is the end of all the commandments of God. Love is the end, the sole end, of every dispensation of God, from the beginning of the world to the consummation of all things. And it will endure when heaven and earth flee away." For only love alone never fails. All else will "be swallowed up in sight, in the everlasting vision of God."[138] So do not exalt faith over love. Trusting in God's pardon looks toward the nurture of incarnate love.

"Faith itself, even Christian faith, the faith of God's elect, the faith of the operation of God, still is only the handmaid of love," as Paul declared in 1 Corinthians 13. "As glorious and honorable as [faith] is, it is not the end of the commandment. God hath given this honor to love alone."[139] "And now these three remain: faith, hope and love. But the greatest of these is love."[140] Love diffuses good endlessly, and love will receive endless praise.[141]

Paul proclaimed the excellence of faith: "Thanks be to God for his indescribable gift!"[142] But he placed faith in relation to love: "Yet still it [faith] loses all its excellence when brought into a comparison with love."[143]

In 2 Corinthians 3 Paul compared the ministry of the law under Moses with the ministry grace under the gospel: If the ministry of the law "that brought condemnation was glorious, how much more glorious is the ministry [of grace] that brings righteousness! For what was glorious has no glory now in comparison with the surpassing glory."[144] The law is "the great temporary means which God has ordained to promote that eternal end" of love of the neighbor.[145]

The antinomians are tempted to "magnify faith beyond all proportion, so as to swallow up" everything else, including love. They misapprehend the nature of faith by imagining that it stands as a substitute for love.

b. How Love Is Eternal in a Way That Faith Is Not

In resisting the antinomian tendency to exalt faith over love, Paul showed that while love necessarily existed before the fall, faith is not necessary until after the fall. To make this argument, Wesley relied on Genesis 1–3 and 1 Corinthians 13: "As love will exist after faith, so it did exist long before it. The angels who, from the moment of their creation, beheld the face of their Father that is in heaven, had no occasion for faith, in its general notion, as it is the evidence of things not seen," but "love existed from eternity, in God, the great ocean of love. Love had a place in all the children of God, from the moment of their creation. They received at once from their gracious Creator to exist, and to love."[146]

---

[138]Ibid.
[139]Ibid.
[140]1 Cor. 13:13 NIV.
[141]"The Law Established through Faith," 2, B 2:77, J V:462, sec. 2.1.
[142]2 Cor. 9:15 NIV; "The Law Established through Faith," 2, B 2:78, J V:462, sec. 2.2.
[143]"The Law Established through Faith," 2, B 2:78, J V:462, sec. 2.2.
[144]2 Cor. 3:9–10 NIV.
[145]"The Law Established through Faith," 2, B 2:78, J V:462, sec. 2.2.
[146]Ibid.

Since God is love, love is eternal in a way that faith is not eternal. Those who speak of faith in isolation as if it could be without love have forgotten that faith becomes active in love.[147] "Adam, before he rebelled against God, walked with him by sight and not by faith ... able to talk with him face to face, whose face we cannot now see and live; and consequently had no need of that faith whose office it is to supply the want of sight."[148] Since Adam was not created in sin and knew no sin until he freely disobeyed God, there was no need for pardon before the fall.

Thus in Adam's original and created state, "love even then filled his heart; it reigned in him without rival; and it was only when love was lost by sin that faith was added, not for its own sake, nor with any design that it should exist any longer than until it had answered the end for which it was ordained — namely, to restore man to the love from which he was fallen. At the fall, therefore, was added this evidence of things unseen, which before was utterly needless, this confidence in redeeming love, which could not possibly have any place till the promise was made."[149] The point: love is eternal. Faith is consequent to the fall. Thus Wesley cautioned antinomians not to exalt faith over love. "Faith, then, was originally designed of God to reestablish the law of love. Therefore, in speaking thus, we are not undervaluing it, or robbing it of its due praise; but on the contrary showing its real worth, exalting it in its just proportion, and giving it that very place which the wisdom of God assigned it from the beginning. It is the grand means of restoring that holy love wherein man was originally created."[150]

Nurturing faith as such without love is not the purpose of the gospel. Rather, faith leads to "the establishing anew the law of love in our hearts." On that account, faith is "an unspeakable blessing to man, and of unspeakable value before God."[151]

4. Establishing the Law in Our Hearts

a. Faith Elicits the Life of Love

Suppose we preached the law of love in its whole extent and established it firmly as a reliable doctrinal truth of Scripture but did not practice it. Suppose we expounded it "in its most spiritual meaning." Suppose we preached "Christ in all his offices, and faith in Christ as opening all the treasures of his love; and yet, all this time, if the law we preached were not established in our hearts, we should be of no more account before God than 'sounding brass, or tinkling cymbals.'"[152]

We now may "establish the law in our own hearts so that it may have its full influence on our lives. And this can only be done by faith."[153] "Let but the eye of the soul be constantly fixed, not on the things which are temporal, but on those

[147]"The Law Established through Faith," 2, B 2:78, J V:463 – 64, sec. 2.3.
[148]"The Law Established through Faith," 2, B 2:79, J V:463, sec. 2.4.
[149]"The Law Established through Faith," 2, B 2:79, J V:463 – 64, sec. 2.5.
[150]"The Law Established through Faith," 2, B 2:80, J V:464, sec. 2.6.
[151]Ibid.
[152]"The Law Established through Faith," 2, B 2:80, J V:464, sec. 3.1; cf. 1 Cor. 13:1.
[153]"The Law Established through Faith," 2, B 2:80 – 81, J V:464 – 65, sec. 3.2.

which are eternal, and our affections are more and more loosened from earth and fixed on things above."[154] Faith, therefore, is "the most direct and effectual means of promoting all righteousness and true holiness."[155] Nothing of the teaching of the law established through faith would avail for our salvation if the hearer did not take it to heart.[156]

b. Why Love Is the Fulfilling of the Law

Faith alone can lead to "a confidence in a pardoning God" who enables the penitent faithful to "establish his law in our own hearts in a still more effectual manner. For there is no motive which so powerfully inclines us to love God, as the sense of the love of God in Christ. And from this principle of grateful love to God arises love to our brother also."[157] This is why love is the fulfilling of the law.

"Whoever loves others has fulfilled the law."[158] Love "continually incites us to do good, as we have time and opportunity; to do good, in every possible kind, and in every possible degree, to all men."[159]

Faith "works inwardly by love, to the purifying of the heart ... cleansing it from all vile affections."[160] "Dear friends, now we are children of God, and what we will be has not yet been made known. But we know that when Christ appears, we shall be like him, for we shall see him as he is. All who have this hope in him purify themselves, just as he is pure."[161]

If we let love "have its perfect work," it fills us "with all goodness, righteousness, and truth. It brings all heaven into [our] soul[s]; and causes [us] to walk in the light, even as God is in the light."[162]

"Walking now with joy, and not with fear, in a clear, steady sight of things eternal, we shall look on pleasure, wealth, praise — all the things of earth — as on bubbles upon the water; counting nothing important, nothing desirable, nothing worth a deliberate thought, but only what is 'within the veil.'"[163] "You see the motes which you could not see before, when the sun shines into a dark place. In like manner you see the sins which you could not see before, now the Sun of Righteousness shines in your heart. Now, then, do all diligence to walk, in every respect, according to the light you have received! ... So shall you continually go on from faith to faith; so shall you daily increase in holy love, till faith is swallowed up in sight, and the law of love established to all eternity!"[164]

---

[154]Ibid.
[155]Ibid.
[156]"The Law Established through Faith," 2, B 2:80, J V:464, sec. 3.1.
[157]"The Law Established through Faith," 2, B 2:81, J V:465, sec. 3.3.
[158]Rom. 13:8 NIV.
[159]"The Law Established through Faith," 2, B 2:81, J V:465, sec. 3.3.
[160]"The Law Established through Faith," 2, B 2:81 – 82, J V:465, sec. 3.4.
[161]1 John 3:2 – 3 NIV.
[162]"The Law Established through Faith," 2, B 2:81 – 82, J V:465, sec. 3.4.
[163]"The Law Established through Faith," 2, B 2:82, J V:465 – 66, sec. 3.5; cf. Heb. 6:19.
[164]"The Law Established through Faith," 2, B 2:82 – 83, J V:466, sec. 3.6.

Further Reading on Theological Ethics

Abraham, William J. *Waking from Doctrinal Amnesia: The Healing of Doctrine in the United Methodist Church.* Nashville: Abingdon, 1995.

Allen, Ted. "John Wesley on the Mission of Church." In *The Mission of the Church in Methodist Perspective.* Edited by Alan Padgett, 45–62. Lewiston, NY: Edwin Mellen, 1992.

Anderson, Neil D. *A Definitive Study of Evidence Concerning John Wesley's Appropriation of the Thought of Clement of Alexandria.* Lewiston, NY: Edwin Mellen, 2004.

Arnett, William M. "A Study in John Wesley's Explanatory Notes upon the Old Testament." *WTJ* 8 (1973): 14–32.

Burwash, Nathaniel. *Wesley's Doctrinal Standard.* Introduction. 1881. Repr., Salem, OH: Schmul, 1967.

Callen, Barry L. *God as Loving Grace.* Nappanee, IN: Evangel, 1996.

Callen, Barry L., and William C. Kostlevy, eds. *Heart of the Heritage: Core Themes of the Wesleyan/Holiness Tradition.* Salem, OH: Schmul, 2001.

Cannon, W. R. *The Theology of John Wesley: With Special Reference to the Doctrine of Justification.* New York: Abingdon, 1946.

Clapper, Gregory S. *The Renewal of the Heart Is the Mission of the Church: Wesley's Heart Religion in the Twenty-First Century.* Eugene, OR: Cascade, 2010.

Collins, Kenneth J. "The Doctrine of Justification: Historic Wesleyan and Contemporary Understandings." In *Justification: What's at Stake in the Current Debate.* Edited by Mark Husbands and Daniel J. Treier, 177–204. Downers Grove, IL: InterVarsity, 2004.

———. *A Real Christian: The Life of John Wesley.* Nashville: Abingdon, 1999.

———. *The Scripture Way of Salvation: The Heart of John Wesley's Theology.* Nashville: Abingdon, 1997.

Cushman, R. E. *Faith Seeking Understanding.* Durham, NC: Duke Univ. Press, 1981.

Deschner, John. *Wesley's Christology.* Dallas: Southern Methodist Univ. Press, 1960. Repr., Grand Rapids: Zondervan, 1988.

Dunnam, Maxie D. *The Christian Way: A Wesleyan View of Spiritual Journey.* Grand Rapids: Zondervan, 1984.

Dunning, H. Ray. *Grace, Faith and Holiness.* Kansas City: Beacon Hill, 1988.

———. *Reflecting the Divine Image: Christian Ethics in Wesleyan Perspective.* Downers Grove, IL: InterVarsity, 1998.

Edwards, Maldwyn. *Family Circle: A Study of the Epworth Household in Relation to John and Charles Wesley.* London: Epworth, 1961.

Gambold, John. "The Character of Mr. John Wesley." *MM* 21, 1798.

Gunter, W. Stephen. *The Limits of "Love Divine": John Wesley's Response to Antinomianism and Enthusiasm.* Nashville: Kingswood, 1989.

Hildebrandt, Franz, *Christianity according to the Wesleys.* London: Epworth, 1956.

Hulley, Leonard D. *To Be and to Do: Exploring Wesley's Thought on Ethical Behavior.* Pretoria: Univ. of South Africa, 1988.

Hynson, Leon O. *Through Faith to Understanding: Wesleyan Essays on Vital Christianity*. Lexington, KY: Emeth, 2005.

Jones, Howard Watkins. *The Holy Spirit from Arminius to Wesley*. London: Epworth, 1929.

Jones, Ivor H., and Kenneth B. Wilson, eds. *Freedom and Grace*. London: Epworth, 1988.

Lerch, David. *Heil und Heiligung bei John Wesley*. Zürich: Christliche Vereinsbuch-handlung, 1941.

Marquardt, Manfred. "John Wesley's 'Synergismus.'" In *Die Einheit der Kirche: Dimensionen ihrer Heiligkeit Katholizitat und Apostolizitat: Festgabe Peter Hein*, 96–102. Weisbaden: Steiner Verlag, 1977.

McDonald, Frederick W. "Bishop Butler and John Wesley." *Methodist Recorder* (1896): 142, 156, 172.

Meeks, Merrill D. "The Future of the Methodist Theological Traditions." In *The Future of the Methodist Theological Traditions*. Edited by Merrill D. Meeks, 13–33. Nashville: Abingdon, 1985.

Miley, John. *Systematic Theology*. New York: Hunt and Eaton, 1892–94. Vol. 2, chap. 8, on sanctification.

Nicholson, Roy S. "John Wesley on Prevenient Grace." *Wesleyan Advocate* (1976): 5, 6.

Nilson, E. A. "Prevenient Grace." *LQHR* 184 (1959): 188–94.

Noll, Mark. "John Wesley and the Doctrine of Assurance." *Bibliotheca Sacra* 132 (1974): 195–223.

Page, Isaac E., and John Brash. *Scriptural Holiness: As Taught by John Wesley*. London: C. H. Kelly, 1891.

Pask, A. H. "The Influence of Arminius on John Wesley." *LQHR* 185 (1960): 258–63.

Runyan, Theodore, ed. *Sanctification and Liberation*. Nashville: Abingdon, 1981.

Sangster, W. E. *The Path of Perfection*. London: Hodder and Stoughton, 1943.

Smith, J. Weldon, III. "Some Notes on Wesley's Doctrine of Prevenient Grace." *RL* 34 (1964): 68–80.

Tillett, Wilbur. *Personal Salvation*. Nashville: Barbee and Smith, 1902.

Wood, A. Skevington. "The Contribution of John Wesley to the Theology of Grace." In *Grace Unlimited*. Edited by Clark Pinnock, 209–22. Minneapolis: Bethany Fellowship, 1975.

A Critical Method
for Studying Wesley

My sole purpose in these four volumes has been to make Wesley's thought accessible to nonprofessional readers today. His audience was not primarily an academic audience but common folk who spoke in ordinary language.

The method I have used in examining Wesley is argument analysis — analysis of his reasoning and argumentation on a text-by-text basis. This method asks, "What reasons does Wesley give for drawing his conclusions? Show me the text where these reasons are stated."

The reasons given by Wesley are not limited to those of natural reason and conscience but also depend heavily on reasoning out of the consensual Christian memory of sacred Scripture. For each homily or essay, I have sought to show why Wesley drew inferences from the sacred text about the topic at hand. Any who wish to know Wesley's mode of reasoning must take seriously his consistent affirmation of Scripture, classically understood, as a check to natural reasoning alone. Natural reasoning alone is tempted to rule out the evidences of the experiences of a community of faith stretching over many generations and cultures. No attempt to analyze evangelical ethics can rule out the history of salvation on which an understanding of the good life depends.

Having unpacked Wesley texts homily by homily and essay by essay, it is now time to set forth some tendencies in Wesley's argument, taken as a whole, about which I have some respectful reservations, although I am profoundly grateful for Wesley's basic lines of argument. I will be brief, because the subject of this series is not my opinions but Wesley's.

1. Wesley seems occasionally to have attributed to events an oversimplified view of special providence in which it appears that God is unilaterally decreeing events as if apart from human freedom. Elsewhere he makes clear that God exercises his almighty power by freely creating humans with their own freedom. The abuses that ensue from human freedom require further providential and redemptive actions to enable its redemption.[1] Hence Wesley's exaggerations of special providence need to be viewed in relation to his explicit teachings on providence. In most cases, the

---

[1]See *JWT*, vol. 1, chap. 6, C, "Providence."

critique of Wesley in specific passages was already made by Wesley himself else-where in his body of literature.

2. Wesley's method of comparing Scripture with Scripture does not require con-textualization of each text quoted, a process favored by modern biblical scholarship. Hence it appears that he took biblical texts out of their historical contexts. The context in which Wesley was seeing each text was the gist of the whole of Scripture as divine revelation, not merely the historical events pertinent to that text.

3. There are major differences between the historical situation Wesley faced and that which we face today. His country had a king; ours functions with elected rep-resentatives led by an elected executive who under the Constitution carries out the laws written by Congress. It is not an error of Wesley's that he was born British in the eighteenth century. It is an error of modern judgment to presume that modern reasoning is superior to all previous ages of reasoning or that our culture is intrinsi-cally and self-evidently superior to premodern cultures. The cultural differences account for most of the problems modern readers have with reading Wesley. It is difficult for us to listen fairly to an argument that assumes conditions that prevailed in the eighteenth century.

4. It is jarring for the modern reader to hear from Wesley what moderns con-sider harsh declarations about final judgment and hell and the devil. In the chapter on hell in volume 2 of this series, I attempted to express Wesley's intention on the radical anger of God toward sin and the justice of God's correctives for sin. Again, this illustrates a clash of cultures: modern versus classic evangelical. Wesley was not harsher than Jesus on the subject of hell.

5. Much that Wesley taught about the power of the Holy Spirit to transform human freedom may sound to modern ears utopian or exceedingly optimistic. But the man who wrote a treatise on the doctrine of original sin surely cannot be viewed as optimistic. If he was pessimistic about the human condition apart from grace, he was confident in the grace that transforms the human condition.

These are only a few of the neuralgic points in Wesley for many modern readers. None of these plausible criticisms is sufficient to dismiss Wesley. Rather, they invite further investigation of the clash of worldviews between modern consciousness and the classic historical roots of evangelical faith.

Alphabetical Correlation of the Sermons in the Jackson and Bicentennial Editions

The Bicentennial edition is represented by B. The Jackson edition is represented by J. Sermon numbers are preceded by the pound sign (#). An asterisk (*) indicates that the homily was wrongly attributed to Mr. Wesley in at least one of its early editions, with the correct author supplied, or has varying titles or numbers in different editions.

The Almost Christian (#2, B 1:131–41 = #2, J V:17–25) — Acts 26:28

Awake, Thou That Sleepest (#3, B 1:142–58 = #3, J V:25–36) — Ephesians 5:14

A Call to Backsliders (#86, B 3:201–26 = #86, J VI:514–27) — Psalm 77:7–8

The Case of Reason Impartially Considered (#70, B 2:587–600 = #70, J VI:350–60) — 1 Corinthians 14:20

The Catholic Spirit (#39, B 2:79–96 = #39, J V:492–504) — 2 Kings 10:15

*The Cause and Cure of Earthquakes (by Charles Wesley — #129, Jackson ed. only, VII:386–99) — Psalm 46:8

The Causes of the Inefficiency of Christianity (#122, B 4:85–96 = #122, J VII:281–90) — Jeremiah 8:22

A Caution against Bigotry (#38, B 2:61–78 = #38, J V:479–92) — Mark 9:38–39

Christian Perfection (#40, B 2:97–124 = #40, J VI:1–22) — Philippians 3:12

The Circumcision of the Heart (#17, B 1:398–414 = #17, J V:202–12) — Romans 2:29

The Cure of Evil Speaking (#49, B 2:251–62 = #49, J VI:114–24) — Matthew 18:15–17

The Danger of Increasing Riches (#131, B 4:177–86 = #131, J VII:355–62) — Psalm 62:10

The Danger of Riches (#87, B 3:227–46 = #87, J VII:1–15) — 1 Timothy 6:9

Death and Deliverance (#133, B 4:204–14; not in Jackson) — Psalm 37:37

Dives and Lazarus (#115, B 4:4–18 = The Rich Man and Lazarus, #112, J VII:244–55) — Luke 16:31

The Duty of Constant Communion (#101, B 3:427–39 = #101, J VII:147–57) — Luke 22:19

The Duty of Reproving Our Neighbor (#65, B 2:511–20 = #65, J VI:296–304) — Leviticus 19:17

The End of Christ's Coming (#62,

Of the Church (#74, B 3:45 – 57 = #74,
J VI:392 – 401) — Ephesians 4:1 – 6

Of Evil Angels (#72, B 3:16 – 29 = #72,
J VI:370 – 80) — Ephesians 6:12

Of Former Times (#102, B 3:440 – 53 =
#102, J VII:157 – 66) — Ecclesiastes 7:10

Of Good Angels (#71, B 3:3 – 15 = #71,
J VI:361 – 70) — Hebrews 1:14

On Attending the Church Service (#104,
B 3:464 – 78 = #104, J VII:174 – 85)
— 1 Samuel 2:17

On Charity (#91, B 3:290 – 307 = #91,
J VII:45 – 57) — 1 Corinthians 13:1 – 3

On Conscience (#105, B 3:478 – 90
= #105, J VII:186 – 94) — 2 Corinthians
1:12

On Corrupting the Word of God (#137,
B 4:244 – 51 = #137, J VII:468 – 73)
— 2 Corinthians 2:17

On the Death of Mr. Whitefield (#53,
B 2:325 – 48 = #53, J VI:167 – 82)
— Numbers 20:10

On the Death of the Rev. Mr. John
Fletcher (#133, B 3:610 – 29; #133
J VII:431 – 52, 1785) — Psalm 37:37

On the Deceitfulness of the Human
Heart (#128, B 4:149 – 60 = #128,
J VII:335 – 43) — Jeremiah 17:9

On the Discoveries of Faith (#117,
B 4:28 – 38 = #117, J VII:231 – 38)
— Hebrews 11:1

On Dissipation (#79, B 3:115 – 25 = #79,
J VI:444 – 52) — 1 Corinthians 7:35

On Divine Providence (#67, B 2:534 – 50
= #67, J VI:313 – 25) — Luke 12:7

On Dress (#88, B 3:247 – 61 = #88,
J VII:15 – 26) — 1 Peter 3:3 – 4

On the Education of Children (#95,
B 3:347 – 60 = #95, J VII:86 – 98)
— Proverbs 22:6

On Eternity (#54, B 2:358 – 72 = #54,
J VI:189 – 98) — Psalm 90:2

On Faith (#106, B 3:491 – 501 = #106,
J VII:195 – 202) — Hebrews 11:6

On Faith (#132, B 4:187 – 200 = #132,
J VII:326 – 35) — Hebrews 11:1

On the Fall of Man (#57, B 2:400 – 412
= #57, J VI:215 – 24) — Genesis 3:19

On Family Religion (#94, B 3:333 – 46
= #94, J VII:76 – 86) — Joshua 24:15

On Friendship with the World (#80,
B 3:126 – 40 = #80, J VI:452 – 63)
— James 4:4

On God's Vineyard (#107, B 3:502 – 17
= #107, J VII:203 – 13) — Isaiah 5:4

*On Grieving the Holy Spirit (by William
Tilly — #137, Jackson ed. only,
J VII:485 – 92) — Ephesians 4:30

*On the Holy Spirit (by John Gambold —
#141, Jackson ed. only, VII:508 – 20)
— 2 Corinthians 3:17

On Knowing Christ after the Flesh (#123,
B 4:97 – 106 = #123, J VII:291 – 96)
— 2 Corinthians 5:16

On Laying the Foundation of the New
Chapel (#112, B 3:577 – 93 = #112,
J VII:419 – 30) — Numbers 23:23

On Living without God (#130,
B 4:168 – 76 = #130, J VII:349 – 54)
— Ephesians 2:12

On Love (#149, B 4:378 – 88 = #149,
J VII:492 – 99) — 1 Corinthians 13:3

On Mourning for the Dead (#136,
B 4:236 – 43 = #136, J VII:463 – 68)
— 2 Samuel 12:23

On Obedience to Parents (#96,
B 3:361 – 72 = #96, J VII:98 – 108)
— Colossians 3:20

On Obedience to Pastors (#97,
B 3:373 – 83 = #97, J VII:108 – 16)
— Hebrews 13:17

On the Omnipresence of God (#118,
B 4:39 – 47 = #118, J VII:238 – 44)
— Jeremiah 23:24

Sermon on the Mount, 3 (#23,
B 1:510 – 30 = #23, J V:278 – 94
— Matthew 5:8 – 12

Sermon on the Mount, 4 (#24,
B 1:531 – 49 = #24, J V:294 – 310)
— Matthew 5:13 – 16

Sermon on the Mount, 5 (#25,
B 1:550 – 71 = #25, J V:310 – 27)
— Matthew 5:17 – 20

Sermon on the Mount, 6 (#26,
B 1:572 – 91 = #26 J V:327 – 43)
— Matthew 6:1 – 15

Sermon on the Mount, 7 (#27,
B 1:591 – 611= #27, J V:344 – 60)
— Matthew 6:16 – 18

Sermon on the Mount, 8 (#28,
B 1:612 – 31 = #28, J V:361 – 77)
— Matthew 6:19 – 23

Sermon on the Mount, 9 (#29,
B 1:632 – 49 = #29, J V:378 – 93)
— Matthew 6:24 – 34

Sermon on the Mount, 10 (#30,
B 1:650 – 63 = #30, J V:393 – 404)
— Matthew 7:1 – 12

Sermon on the Mount, 11 (#31,
B 1:664 – 74 = #31, J V:405 – 13)
— Matthew 7:13 – 14

Sermon on the Mount, 12 (#32,
B 1:675 – 686 = #32, J V:414 – 22)
— Matthew 7:15 – 20

Sermon on the Mount, 13 (#33,
B 1:687 – 98 = #33, J V:423 – 33)
— Matthew 7:21 – 27

The Signs of the Times (#66, B 2:521 – 33
= #66, J VI:304 – 13) — Matthew 16:3

Some Account of the Late Work of God
in North America (#113, B 3:594 – 608
= #131, J VII:409 – 29) — Ezekiel 1:16

The Spirit of Bondage and of Adoption
(#9, B 1:248 – 66 = #9, J V:98 – 111) —
Romans 8:15

Spiritual Idolatry (#78, B 3:103 – 14 = #78,
J VI:435 – 44) — 1 John 5:21

Spiritual Worship (#77, B 3:88 – 102
= #77, J VI:424 – 35) — 1 John 5:20

The Trouble and Rest of Good Men
(#109, B 3:531 – 41= #109,
J VII:365 – 372) — Job 3:17

True Christianity Defended (#134,
Jackson ed. only, VII:452 – 62) —
Isaiah 1:21

The Unity of the Divine Being (#120,
B 4:61 – 71 = #114, J VII:264 – 73)
— Mark 12:32

The Use of Money (#50, B 2:263 – 80
= #50, J VI:124 – 36) — Luke 16:9

Walking by Sight and Walking by Faith
(#119, B 4:48 – 59 = #113,
J VII:256 – 64) — 2 Corinthians 5:7

Wandering Thoughts (#41, B 2:125 – 37 =
#41, J VI:23 – 32) — 2 Corinthians 10:5

The Way to the Kingdom (#7,
B 1:217 – 32 = #7, J V:76 – 86)
— Mark 1:15

What Is Man? (#103, B 3:454 – 63 = #103,
J VII:167 – 74) — Psalm 8:4

Wilderness State (#46, B 2:202 – 21 = #46,
J VI:77 – 91) — John 16:22

The Wisdom of God's Counsels (#68,
B 3:551 – 66 = #68, J VI:325 – 33) —
Romans 11:33

The Wisdom of Winning Souls (#142,
in Bicentennial ed. only, B
4:305 – 17) — 2 Corinthians 1:12

The Witness of the Spirit, 1 (#10,
B 1:267 – 84 = #10, J V:111 – 23)
— Romans 8:16

The Witness of the Spirit, 2 (#11,
B 1:285 – 98 = #11, J V:123 – 34)
— 2 Corinthians 1:12

Bicentennial Volume Titles Published to Date

Note: Volume 1 was published in 1984. Subsequently, ten more volumes have been published. As of this date of publication, nineteen Bicentennial volumes remain to be published. They are marked with an asterisk (*). Here we have used the Jackson, Sugden, Telford, Curnock, and other editions to supplement the preferred Bicentennial edition.

1. Sermons 1–33
2. Sermons 34–70
3. Sermons 71–114
4. Sermons 115–51
*5. Explanatory Notes upon the New Testament I
*6. Explanatory Notes upon the New Testament II
7. A Collection of Hymns for the Use of the People Called Methodist
*8. Forms of Worship and Prayer
9. The Methodist Societies, History, Nature, and Design
*10. The Methodist Societies: The Conference
11. Appeals to Men of Reason and Religion and Certain Related Open Letters
*12. Doctrinal Writings: Theological Treatises
*13. Doctrinal Writings: The Defense of Christianity
*14. Pastoral and Instructional Writings I

*15. Pastoral and Instructional Writings II
*16. Editorial Work
*17. Natural Philosophy and Medicine
18. Journals and Diaries I
19. Journals and Diaries II
20. Journals and Diaries III
21. Journals and Diaries IV
22. Journals and Diaries V
23. Journals and Diaries VI
24. Journals and Diaries VII
25. Letters I
*26. Letters II
*27. Letters IIIa
*28. Letters IIIb
*29. Letters IV
*30. Letters V
*31. Letters VI
*32. Letters VII
*33. Bibliography of the Publications of John and Charles Wesley Letters VIII
*34. Miscellanea and General Index

Subject Index

A

accountability
  money and, 61–62
  moral accountability,
    28–29, 45
  personal accountability, 15
  in societies, 28–29
Adanson, Monsignor, 163
adornment, 82–87. *See also*
  clothing
alms, giving, 226–227
American Revolution
  address to British,
    145–150
  address to colonies,
    138–145
  consequences of, 129–140,
    144–145
  costs of, 134
  results of, 148–150
  taxation and, 139–143
anger
  purity of heart and,
    136–137
  restraining, 192–194
  turning away, 238–239
antinomianism
  elitism and, 83
  fear of, 297–300
  legalism and, 219–220,
    235–236, 288
  overreaction of, 300–301
  self-denial and, 89
  temptations and, 287–288
apostolic testimony, 297–302
Aquinas, Thomas, 16
Augustine, 287, 300

B

band of believers, 29–31
band societies
  accountability in, 28–29
  admission to, 31–33
  directions given to, 27,
    50–51
  rules of, 27–34, 45–51
  self-examination for, 33
Baxter, Richard, 16, 95, 104
beatitudes, 180–183, 187,
  191–200
Benson, Joseph, 18
Berkeley, George, 27
betting games, 114–115,
  121–123
Bicentennial edition of
  sermons, 17, 313–317
Bicentennial volume titles,
  318
Blackstone, William, 168
blessed life. *See also* good life;
  happy life
  beatitudes of, 180–183,
    187, 191–200
  features of, 36–39
  knowing, 37–38
  living, 34–39
  of meek, 191–194
  of merciful, 196–201
  model of, 35–36
  of peacemakers, 199,
    202–205
blessed soul, 34–36
Boardman, Richard, 154
British, addressing, 145–150.
  See also American
  Revolution
Brue, Monsignor, 164
Butler, Joseph, 27, 28

C

Calvin, John, 287, 300
care and proper caring,
  255–257
Christ. *See also* Sermon on
  the Mount
  coming of, 62, 296–297,
    300
  death of, 62, 87
  merits of, 40–42,
    300–301
  radiance of, 209–210
  resurrection of, 62, 87, 179,
    190, 194, 289, 304
  teachings of, 179–184,
    233, 240, 248, 263,
    281, 298–299
Christian life, 35–36, 44. *See
  also* blessed life
civil discourse, 119–121
civil obedience, 149–150
Clarke, Samuel, 27
Clement of Alexandria,
  35–36, 51–52
clothing, 71, 82–87, 105,
  257–258
colonial crisis, 132–133
colonialism, 135–136
colonies, addressing,
  138–145. *See also*
  American Revolution
comfort of God, 187–191.
  See also God
commands of God, 29, 185,
  219–220, 237–240,
  306. *See also* God
community of faith
  fairness ethic of, 264
  grace and, 109–111
  nurturing, 27–52, 59
conflict
  facing, 113–114
  with idols, 251–255
  transforming, 262–263
consent
  individual consent,
    142–143
  on laws, 141–142

O

obedience, 149–150

O'Brien, Glen, 139

opportunities, missing, 121

oppression, 166–167. *See also* slavery

original sin, 142, 145, 172, 271–272, 287. *See also* sins

ornamentation, 82–87. *See also* clothing

Outler, Albert C., 18

P

parent-sins, 271–272

partisan fervor, 132–133

peace, God and, 202–204

peace, seeking, 109, 127, 129–130, 137–139

peacemakers, 199, 202–205

peacemaking, 115–116, 137–139, 202–205, 211

pearls, casting, 267–268

perfection, sinless, 39, 43–45

persecution, 204–207

personal accountability, 15

personal time, redeeming, 96–98

Pillmoor, Joseph, 154

political calamity, 132–133

political ethics. *See also* ethics
basics of, 15
evangelical political ethics, 107–109
partisan fervor, 132–133

politics of envy, 143, 155–156

politics of slavery, 15, 113, 134, 157, 161–173. *See also* slavery

poor
giving to, 78–81
ignoring, 85–86
relief for, 47–48
in spirit, 187

praying

for deliverance, 173–174

fasting and, 239

giving and, 225–226

for guidance, 228–235, 268

love and, 225–226

for needs, 268–269

without cease, 37

without hypocrisy, 227–228

Price, Richard, 27, 28

pride
of life, 73–75
ornamentation and, 82–87
temptation to, 83–87

Providence, wheels of, 151–160

provisions
from God, 256–261, 268–269
for household, 67, 72, 78
value of, 256–258

public diversions, 121–127

public order offenses, 112–113

pure intentions
fasting and, 235–243
for good works, 225–258, 263
mercy and, 225–228, 235–237

purity of heart
anger and, 136–137
clothing and, 82–83
evangelical ethics, 104
in faithful, 199–201, 219, 244
fruit from, 304
love and, 223, 273
transforming relationships, 262–263

R

Reformation
of manners, 109–112
of morals, 109–113
objections to, 116–117

reform plan, 115–116

Reid, Thomas, 27

relapse, 91–92

relationships
enhancing, 209–217
holy living and, 209
radiance in, 209–217
salt and light metaphors, 209–210
savoring, 211
social interactions, 209–216
transforming, 262–263

religion
Great Awakening of, 152–153
hindrances to progress of, 154–155
religious revival, 150–160
true religion, 180–183, 187, 194–195, 213, 282

repentance
evidence of, 48–49
fasting and, 241
sorrow, 241–242

resentment, 143, 155–156

resurrection, 62, 87, 179, 190, 194, 289, 304. *See also* Christ

revival of religion
Great Awakening, 152–153
hindrances to progress, 154–155
in North America, 150–160

Revolutionary War
address to British, 145–150
address to colonies, 138–145
consequences of, 129–140, 144–145
costs of, 134
results of, 148–150
taxation and, 139–143

riches. *See also* money
danger of, 70–71, 78–81
desire for, 71–72, 79–81
excess riches, 249–251

Scripture Index

John Wesley's Teachings, Volume 1

God and Providence

Thomas C. Oden

John Wesley's Teachings is the first systematic exposition of John Wesley's theology that encompasses all of his writings. Wesley was a prolific writer and commentator on Scripture — his collected works fill eighteen volumes — and yet it is commonly held that he was not systematic or consistent in his theology and teachings. On the contrary, Thomas C. Oden demonstrates that Wesley displayed a remarkable degree of internal consistency over sixty years of preaching and ministry. This series of 4 volumes is a text-by-text guide to John Wesley's teaching. It introduces Wesley's thought on the basic tenets of Christian teaching: God, providence, and man (volume 1), Christ and salvation (volume 2), the practice of pastoral care (volume 3), and issues of ethics and society (volume 4). In everyday modern English, Oden clarifies Wesley's explicit intent and communicates his meaning clearly to a contemporary audience. Both lay and professional readers will find this series useful for devotional reading, moral reflection, sermon preparation, and for referencing Wesley's opinions on a broad range of pressing issues of contemporary society.

Available in stores and online!

ZONDERVAN®
.com

John Wesley's Teachings, Volume 2

Christ and Salvation

Thomas C. Oden

John Wesley's Teachings is the first systematic exposition of John Wesley's theology that encompasses all of his writings. Wesley was a prolific writer and commentator on Scripture — his collected works fill eighteen volumes — and yet it is commonly held that he was not systematic or consistent in his theology and teachings. On the contrary, Thomas C. Oden demonstrates that Wesley displayed a remarkable degree of internal consistency over sixty years of preaching and ministry. This series of 4 volumes is a text-by-text guide to John Wesley's teaching. It introduces Wesley's thought on the basic tenets of Christian teaching: God, providence, and man (volume 1), Christ and salvation (volume 2), the practice of pastoral care (volume 3), and issues of ethics and society (volume 4). In everyday modern English, Oden clarifies Wesley's explicit intent and communicates his meaning clearly to a contemporary audience. Both lay and professional readers will find this series useful for devotional reading, moral reflection, sermon preparation, and for referencing Wesley's opinions on a broad range of pressing issues of contemporary society.

John Wesley's Teachings, Volume 3

Pastoral Theology

Thomas C. Oden

John Wesley's Teachings is the first systematic exposition of John Wesley's theology that encompasses all of his writings. Wesley was a prolific writer and commentator on Scripture — his collected works fill eighteen volumes — and yet it is commonly held that he was not systematic or consistent in his theology and teachings. On the contrary, Thomas C. Oden demonstrates that Wesley displayed a remarkable degree of internal consistency over sixty years of preaching and ministry. This series of 4 volumes is a text-by-text guide to John Wesley's teaching. It introduces Wesley's thought on the basic tenets of Christian teaching: God, providence, and man (volume 1), Christ and salvation (volume 2), the practice of pastoral care (volume 3), and issues of ethics and society (volume 4). In everyday modern English, Oden clarifies Wesley's explicit intent and communicates his meaning clearly to a contemporary audience. Both lay and professional readers will find this series useful for devotional reading, moral reflection, sermon preparation, and for referencing Wesley's opinions on a broad range of pressing issues of contemporary society.

Available in stores and online!

John Wesley's Teachings — Complete Set

Volumes 1–4

Thomas C. Oden

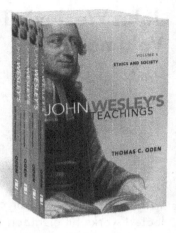

Now available as a complete set, *John Wesley's Teachings* is the first systematic exposition of John Wesley's theology that encompasses all of his writings. Wesley was a prolific writer and commentator on Scripture — his collected works fill eighteen volumes — and yet it is commonly held that he was not systematic or consistent in his theology and teachings. On the contrary, Thomas C. Oden demonstrates that Wesley displayed a remarkable degree of internal consistency over sixty years of preaching and ministry. This series of 4 volumes is a text-by-text guide to John Wesley's teaching. It introduces Wesley's thought on the basic tenets of Christian teaching: God, providence, and man (volume 1), Christ and salvation (volume 2), the practice of pastoral care (volume 3), and issues of ethics and society (volume 4). In everyday modern English, Oden clarifies Wesley's explicit intent and communicates his meaning clearly to a contemporary audience. Both lay and professional readers will find this series useful for devotional reading, moral reflection, sermon preparation, and for referencing Wesley's opinions on a broad range of pressing issues of contemporary society.

Share Your Thoughts

With the Author: Your comments will be forwarded to
the author when you send them to *zauthor@zondervan.com*.

With Zondervan: Submit your review of this book
by writing to *zreview@zondervan.com*.

Free Online Resources at
www.zondervan.com

Daily Bible Verses and Devotions: Enrich your life with daily
Bible verses or devotions that help you start every morning
focused on God. Visit www.zondervan.com/newsletters.

Free Email Publications: Sign up for newsletters on Christian
living, academic resources, church ministry, fiction, children's
resources, and more. Visit www.zondervan.com/newsletters.

Zondervan Bible Search: Find and compare Bible passages in
a variety of translations at www.zondervanbiblesearch.com.

Other Benefits: Register to receive online benefits like
coupons and special offers, or to participate in research.